Shojo Beat

VAMPIRE KNIGHT

Story & Art by
**Matsuri
Hino** **Vol. 5**

VAMPIRE KNIGHT

Contents

Twentieth Night: Game Over..........................5

Twenty-First Night: Guilty.........................57

Twenty-Second Night: Things That Changed,
Things That Did Not Change..................88

Twenty-Third Night: Lost Lambs.................120

Twenty-Fourth Night: A Small Incident.......151

Vampires Covered in Blood Are Prohibited
from Entering This Page!!.........................184

Editor's Notes...189

The Story of VAMPIRE KNIGHT

1 Cross Academy, a private boarding school, is where the Day Class and the Night Class coexist. The Night Class—a group of beautiful elite students—are all vampires!

2 Four years ago, the pureblood Shizuka Hio bit Zero and robbed him of his family. Zero turned into a vampire, and Yuki decided to protect him. But then Maria Kurenai, a mysterious transfer student, appeared. She was actually Shizuka Hio!

3 Zero will eventually become a Level E vampire unless he drinks Shizuka's blood. Yuki offered herself to Shizuka, and Zero attacked Shizuka to protect Yuki. However, the one who saved Shizuka was Ichiru, Zero's younger twin brother who betrayed Zero four years ago. Now Kaname has attacked Shizuka—and his hand has pierced Shizuka's chest!!

NIGHT CLASS
DAY CLASS
♡
?
?
CLASSMATE
FOSTER FATHER
KANAME KURAN
Night Class President and pureblood vampire. Yuki adores him.
YUKI CROSS
The heroine. The adopted daughter of the Headmaster, and a Guardian who protects Cross Academy.
ZERO KIRYU
Yuki's childhood friend, and a Guardian. His family was killed by a vampire a very long time ago.
HEADMASTER CROSS
NIGHT CLASS STUDENTS
COUSINS
HANABUSA AIDO
Nickname: Idol
AKATSUKI KAIN
Nickname: Wild
ICHIRU
Zero's younger twin brother. He double-crossed his family four years ago and serves Shizuka.
SHIZUKA HIO
The pureblood who robbed Zero of his family.
※Purebloods are vampires who do not have a single drop of human blood in their lineage. They are very powerful, and they can turn humans into vampires by drinking their blood.

I'M JUST LIKE YOU. I'LL DO ANYTHING...
...FOR THE SAKE OF THE ONE I LOVE...

Kaname delivers the final blow to Shizuka?!

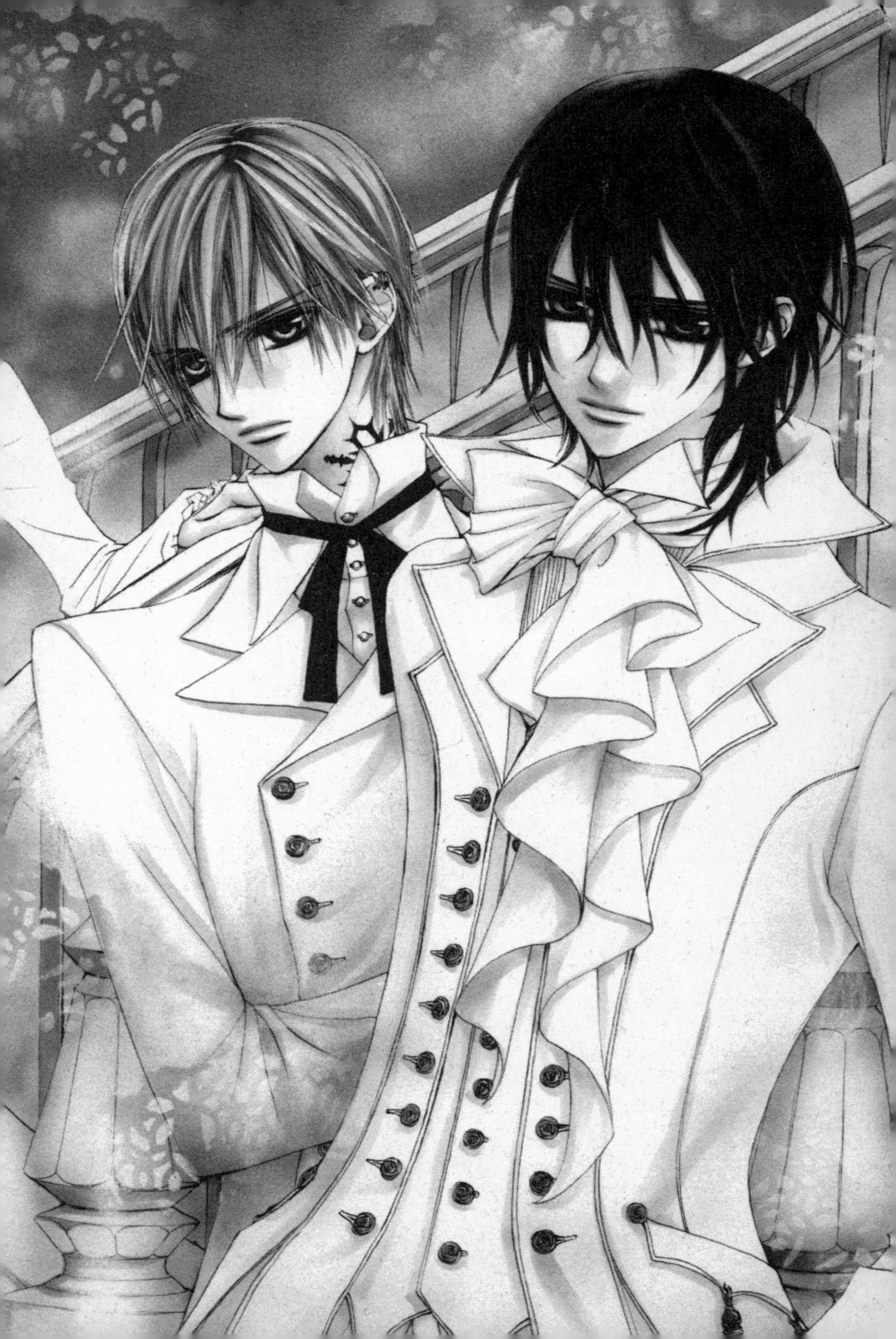

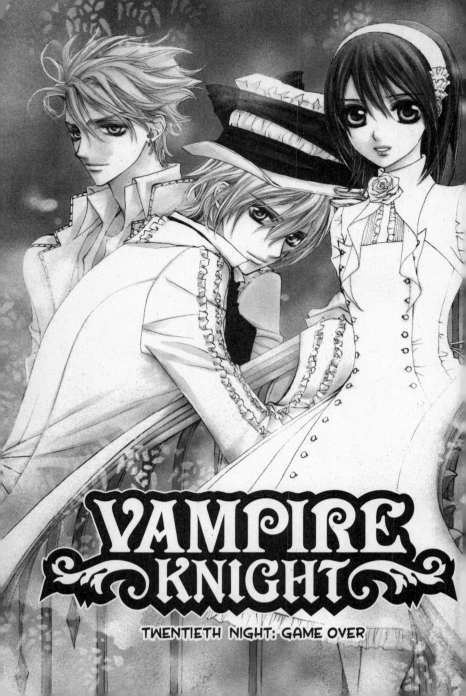

VAMPIRE KNIGHT

TWENTIETH NIGHT: GAME OVER

Results of the Character Popularity Poll

Numbers 1 through 5 are as shown in the chapter title illustration, from right to left

#6 Senri Shiki
#7 Hanabusa Aido
#8 Headmaster Cross
#9 Ichiru Kiryu
#10 Rima Toya
#11 Ruka Souen
#12 Toga Yagari, Shizuka Hio

Thank you, everybody!!

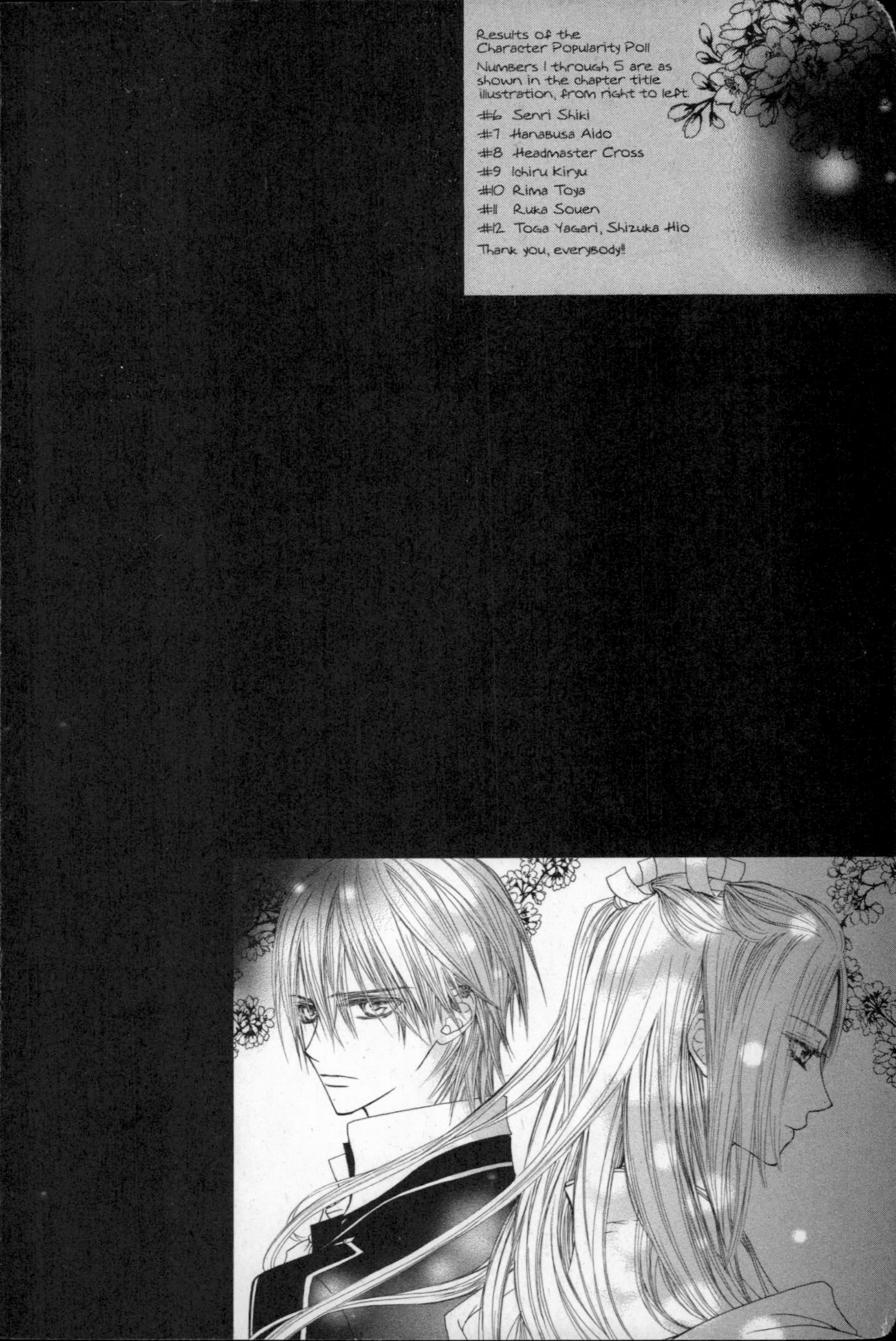

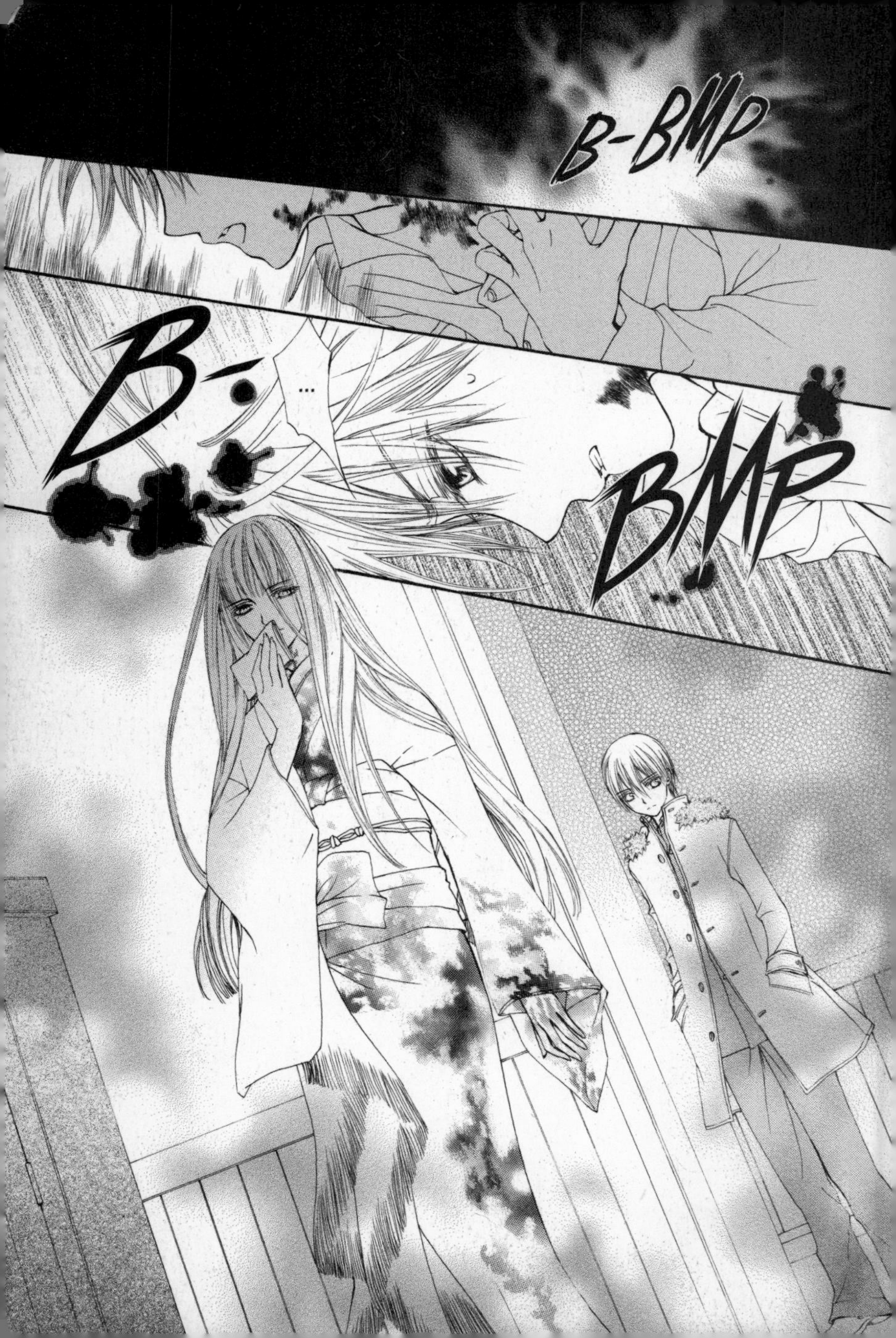
B-BMP
B-BMP
...

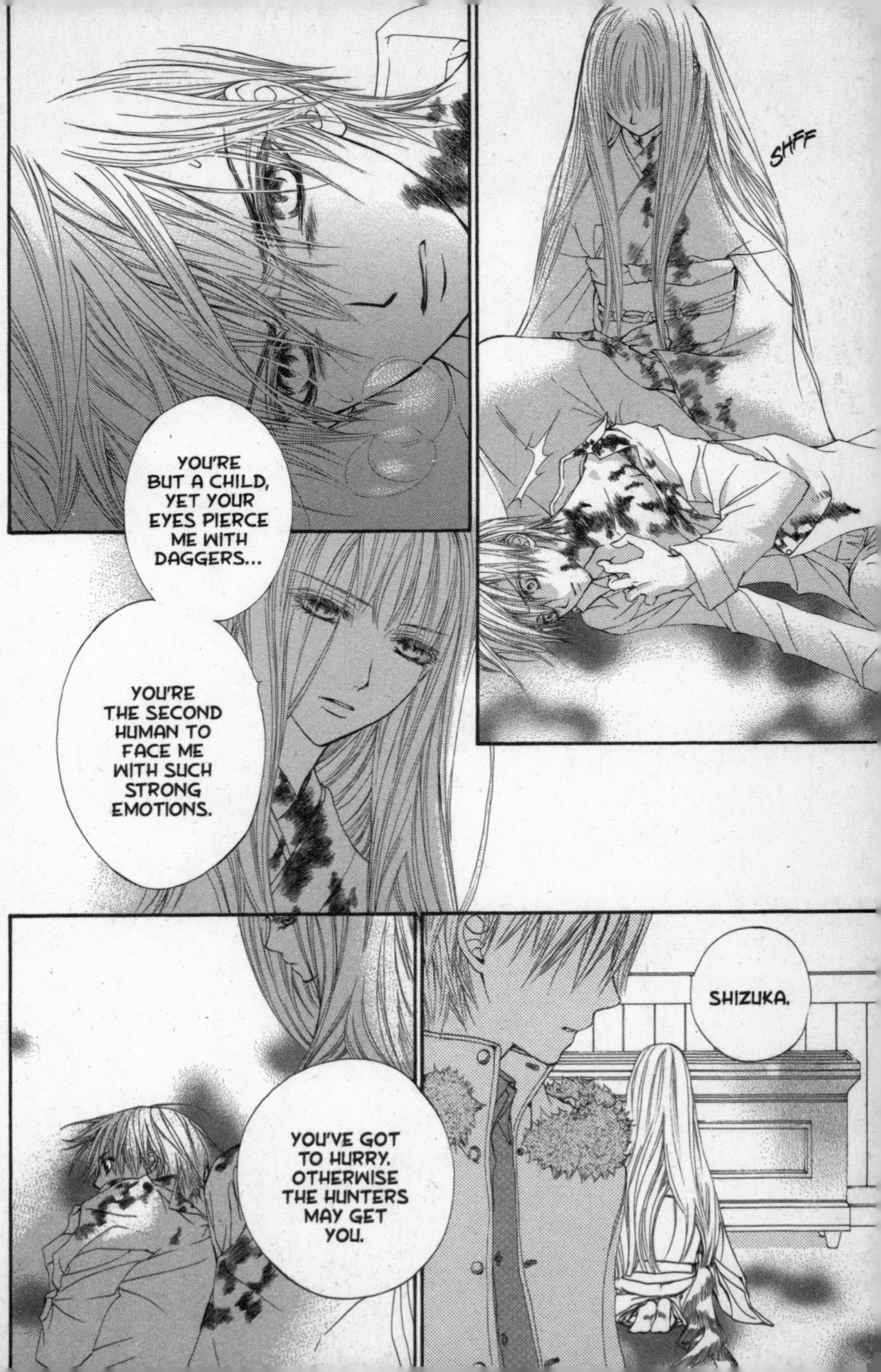
SHFF
YOU'RE BUT A CHILD, YET YOUR EYES PIERCE ME WITH DAGGERS...
YOU'RE THE SECOND HUMAN TO FACE ME WITH SUCH STRONG EMOTIONS.
SHIZUKA.
YOU'VE GOT TO HURRY. OTHERWISE THE HUNTERS MAY GET YOU.

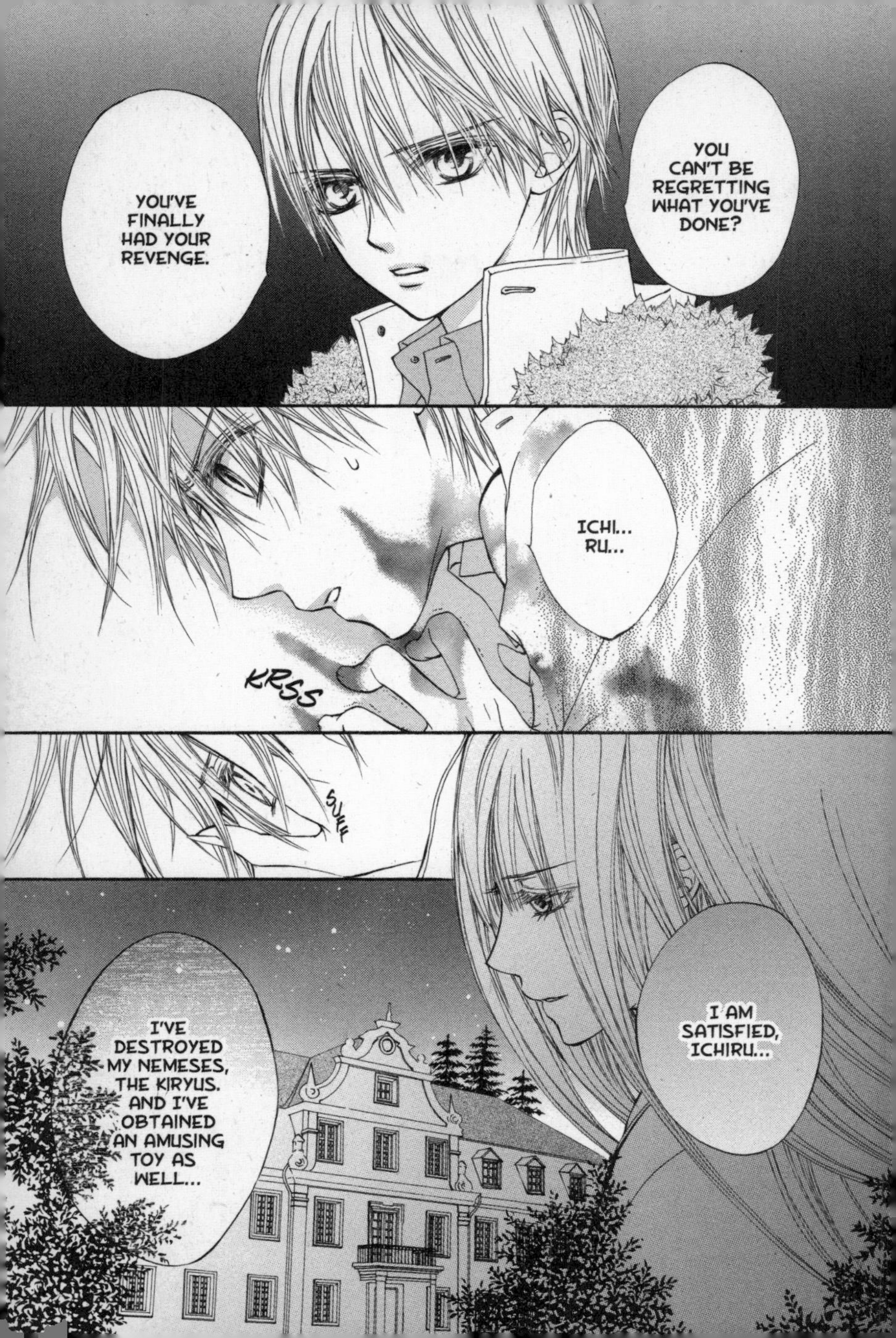
YOU CAN'T BE REGRETTING WHAT YOU'VE DONE?
YOU'VE FINALLY HAD YOUR REVENGE.
ICHI... RU...
KRSS
I AM SATISFIED, ICHIRU...
I'VE DESTROYED MY NEMESES, THE KIRYUS. AND I'VE OBTAINED AN AMUSING TOY AS WELL...

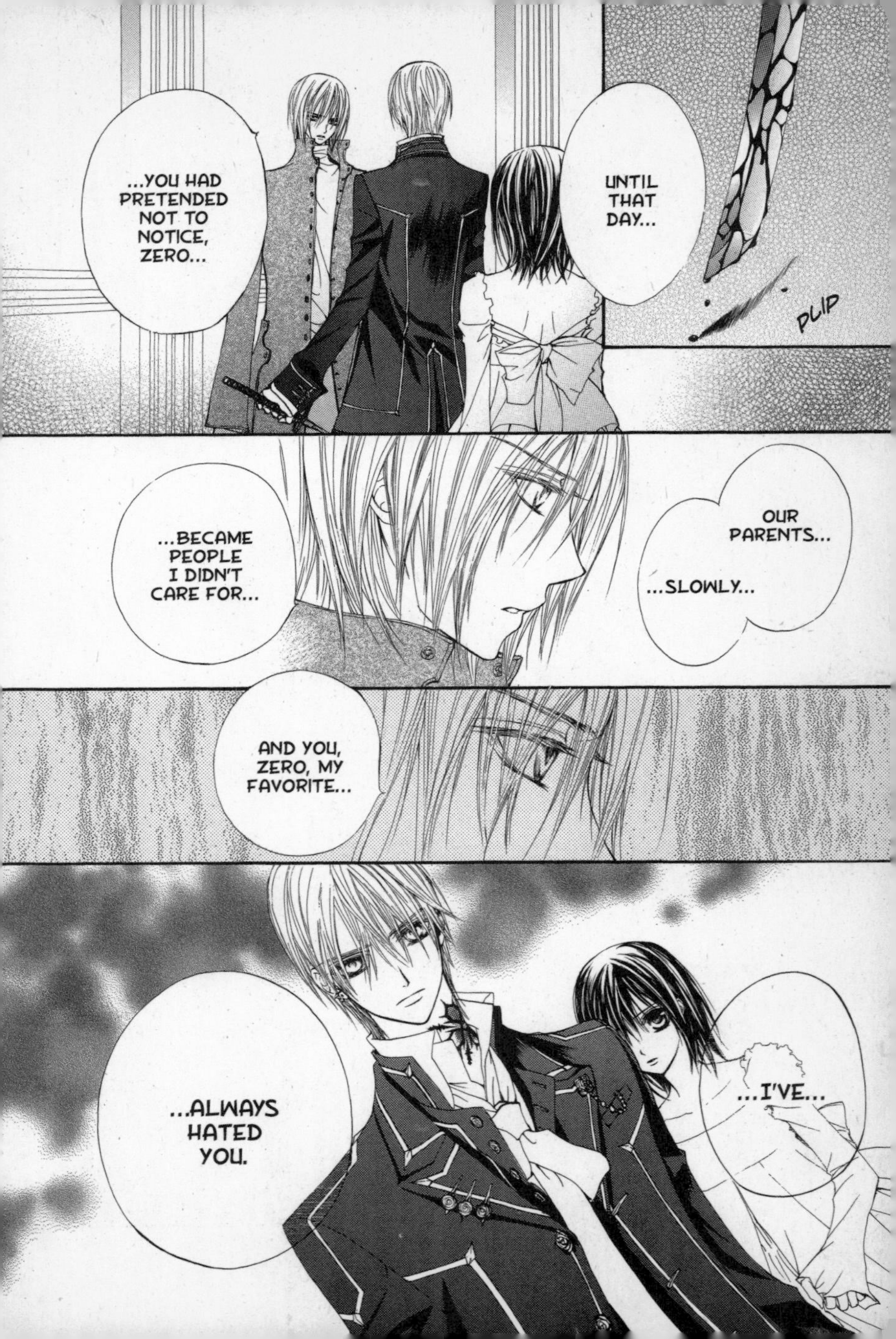
UNTIL THAT DAY...
PLIP
...YOU HAD PRETENDED NOT TO NOTICE, ZERO...
OUR PARENTS...
...SLOWLY...
...BECAME PEOPLE I DIDN'T CARE FOR...
AND YOU, ZERO, MY FAVORITE...
...I'VE...
...ALWAYS HATED YOU.

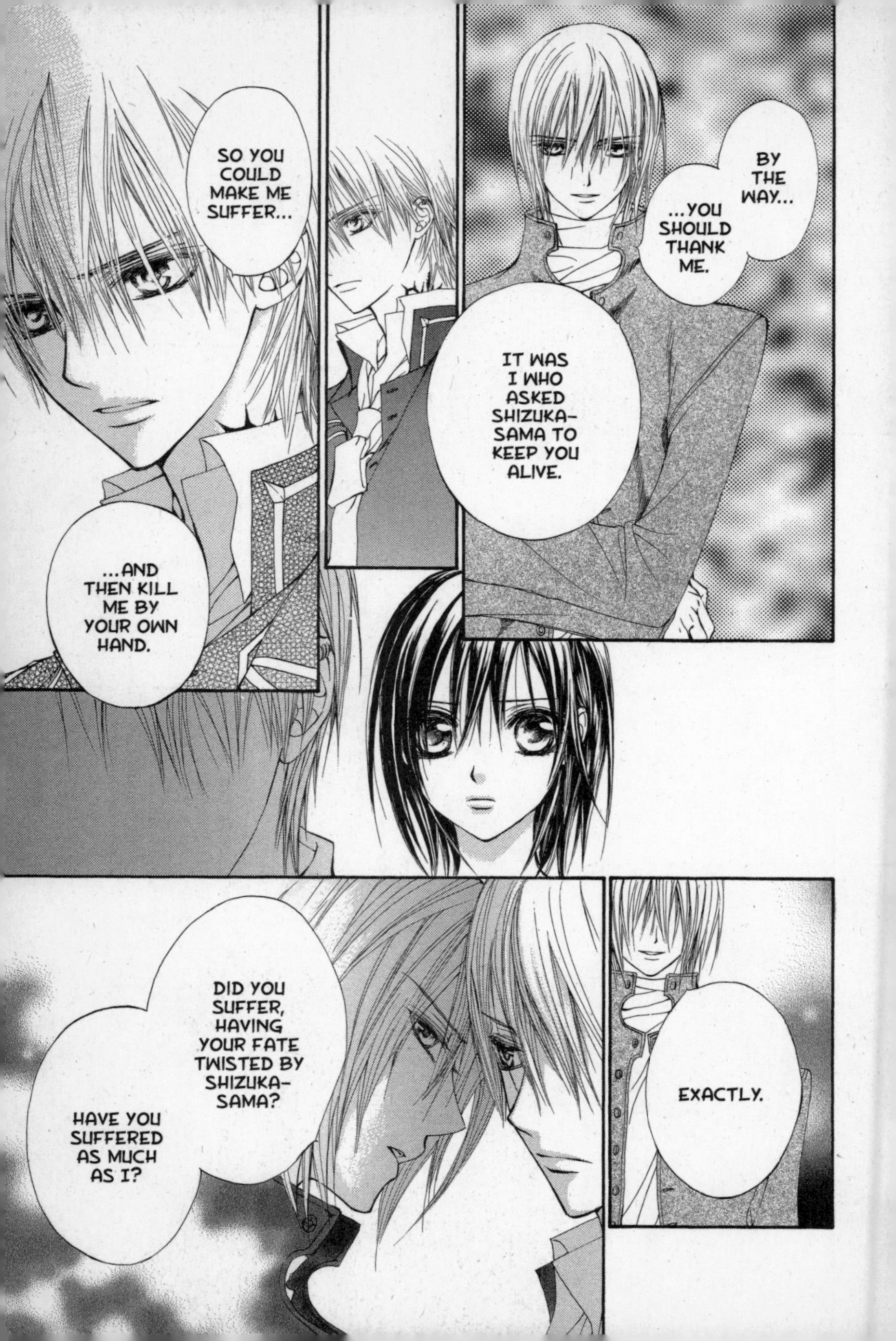
BY THE WAY...
...YOU SHOULD THANK ME.
IT WAS I WHO ASKED SHIZUKA-SAMA TO KEEP YOU ALIVE.
SO YOU COULD MAKE ME SUFFER...
...AND THEN KILL ME BY YOUR OWN HAND.
EXACTLY.
DID YOU SUFFER, HAVING YOUR FATE TWISTED BY SHIZUKA-SAMA?
HAVE YOU SUFFERED AS MUCH AS I?

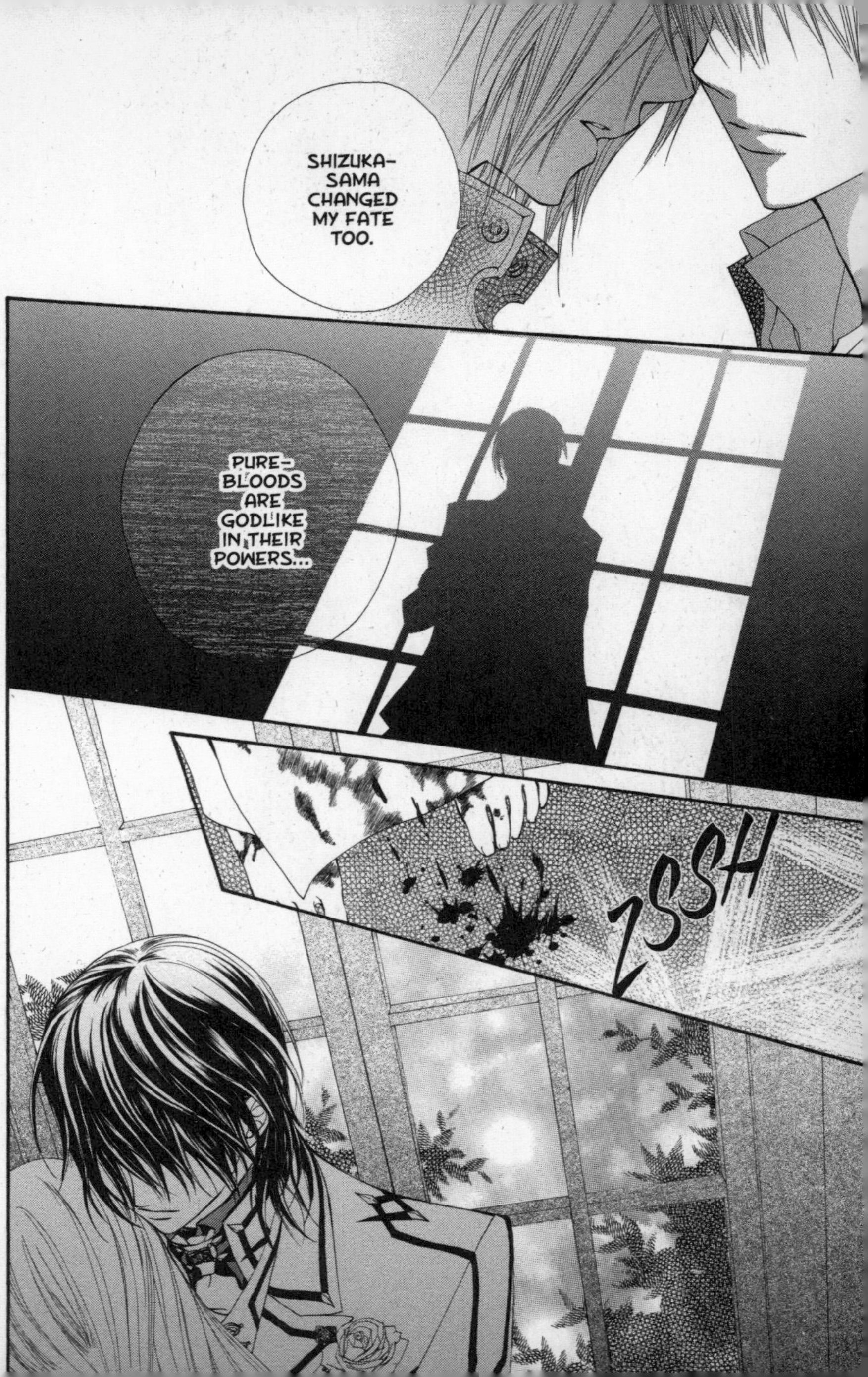
SHIZUKA-SAMA CHANGED MY FATE TOO.
PURE-BLOODS ARE GODLIKE IN THEIR POWERS...
ZSSH

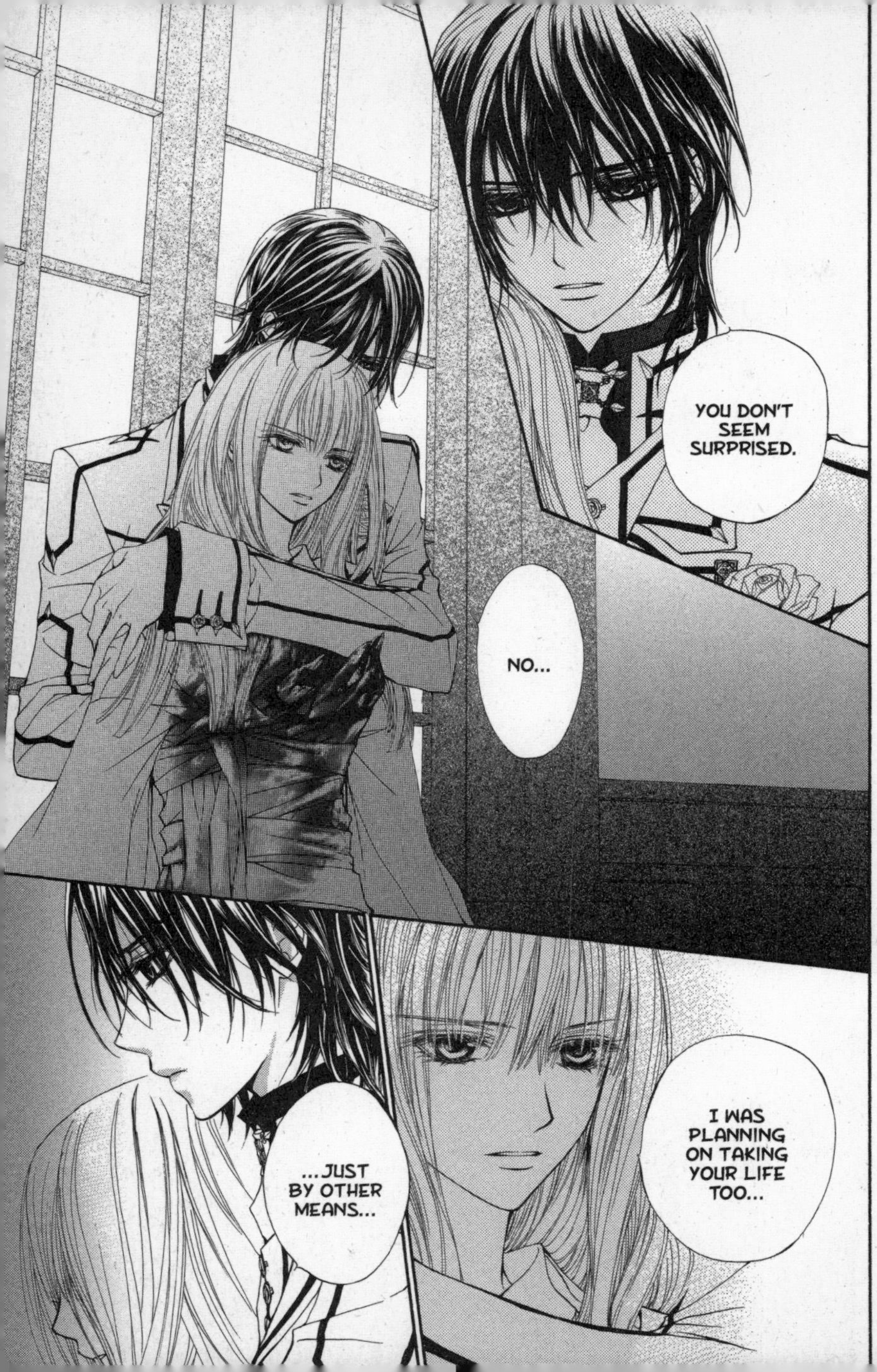
YOU DON'T SEEM SURPRISED.
NO...
I WAS PLANNING ON TAKING YOUR LIFE TOO...
...JUST BY OTHER MEANS...

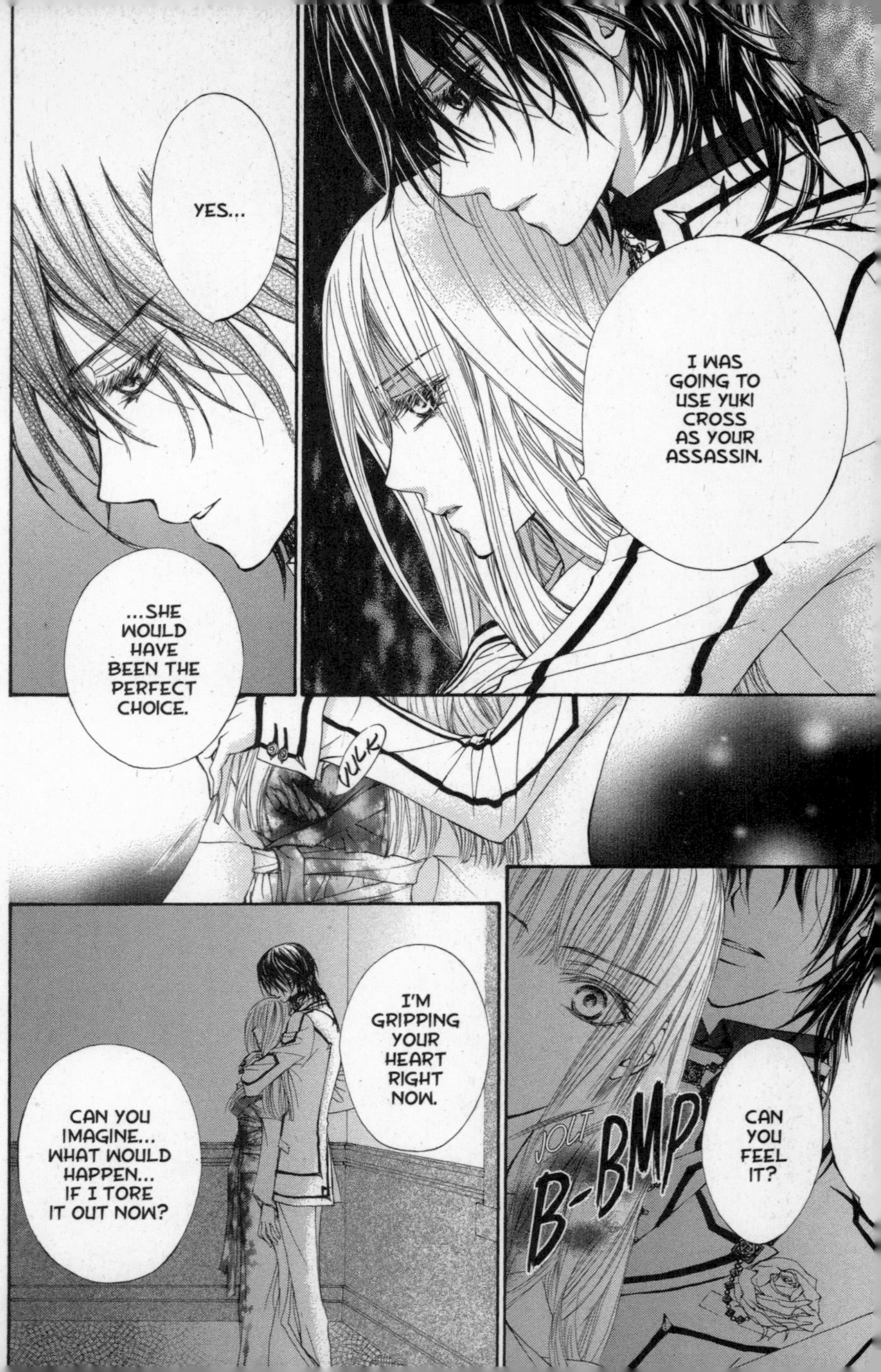
I WAS GOING TO USE YUKI CROSS AS YOUR ASSASSIN.
YES...
...SHE WOULD HAVE BEEN THE PERFECT CHOICE.
VULK
CAN YOU FEEL IT?
JOLT
B-BMP
I'M GRIPPING YOUR HEART RIGHT NOW.
CAN YOU IMAGINE... WHAT WOULD HAPPEN... IF I TORE IT OUT NOW?

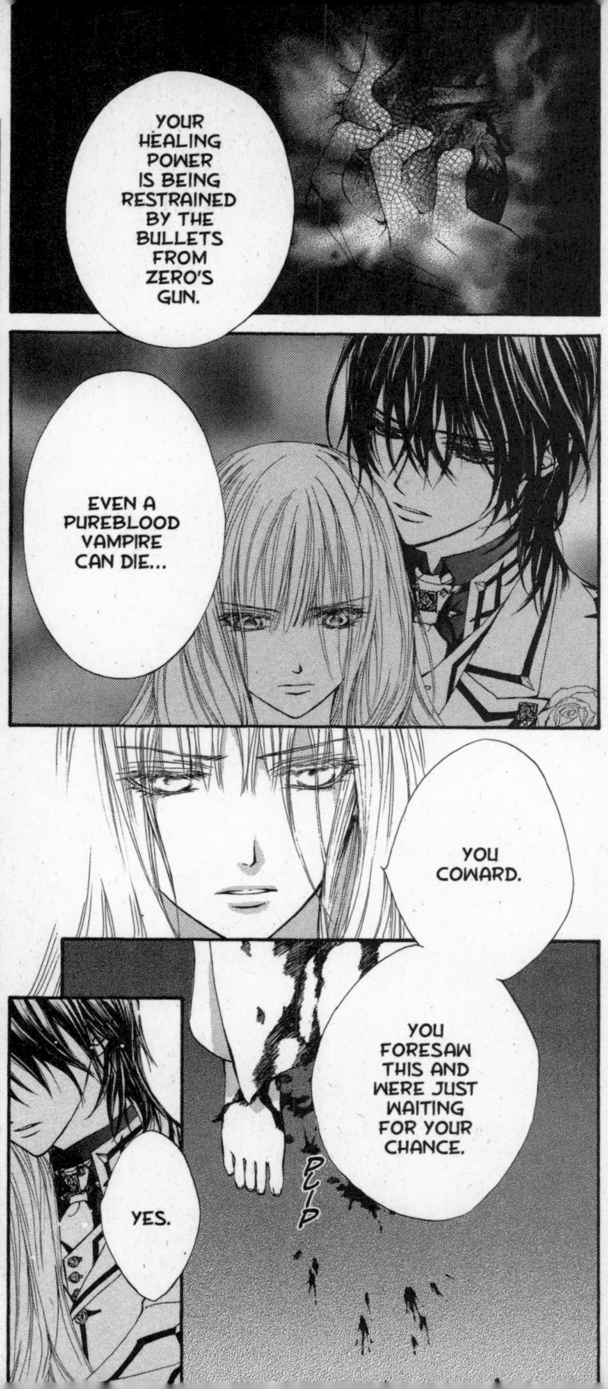
YOUR HEALING POWER IS BEING RESTRAINED BY THE BULLETS FROM ZERO'S GUN.
EVEN A PUREBLOOD VAMPIRE CAN DIE...
YOU COWARD.
YOU FORESAW THIS AND WERE JUST WAITING FOR YOUR CHANCE.
PLIP
YES.

1

Thank you for reading this book!

This is Matsuri Hino, whose favorite phrase has become "Kaname will curse me..."

Before I knew it, we're already at volume 5! This series will be the longest one I've drawn so far... I'm feeling something strange that I can't explain. But it's thanks to everyone that I can continue on! Thank you!!

By the way, I say that Kaname will curse me because I'm strangely nervous only when I'm drawing Kaname. For some reason... (faraway look)

This character to whom I gave birth is quite seriously making me feel that if I don't draw him properly, I'll pay for it.

Pity me...

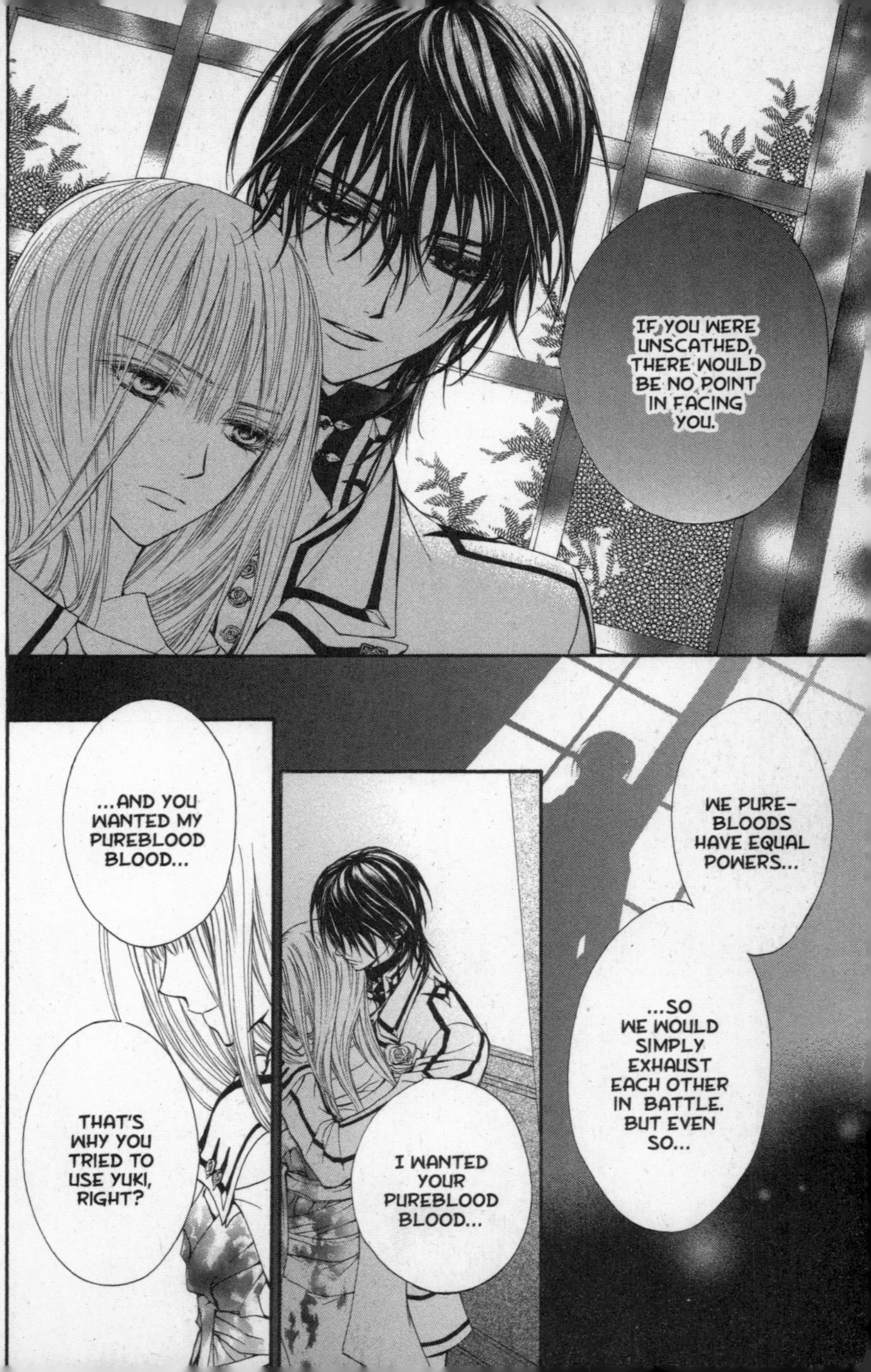
IF YOU WERE UNSCATHED, THERE WOULD BE NO POINT IN FACING YOU.
WE PURE-BLOODS HAVE EQUAL POWERS...
...SO WE WOULD SIMPLY EXHAUST EACH OTHER IN BATTLE. BUT EVEN SO...
I WANTED YOUR PUREBLOOD BLOOD...
...AND YOU WANTED MY PUREBLOOD BLOOD...
THAT'S WHY YOU TRIED TO USE YUKI, RIGHT?

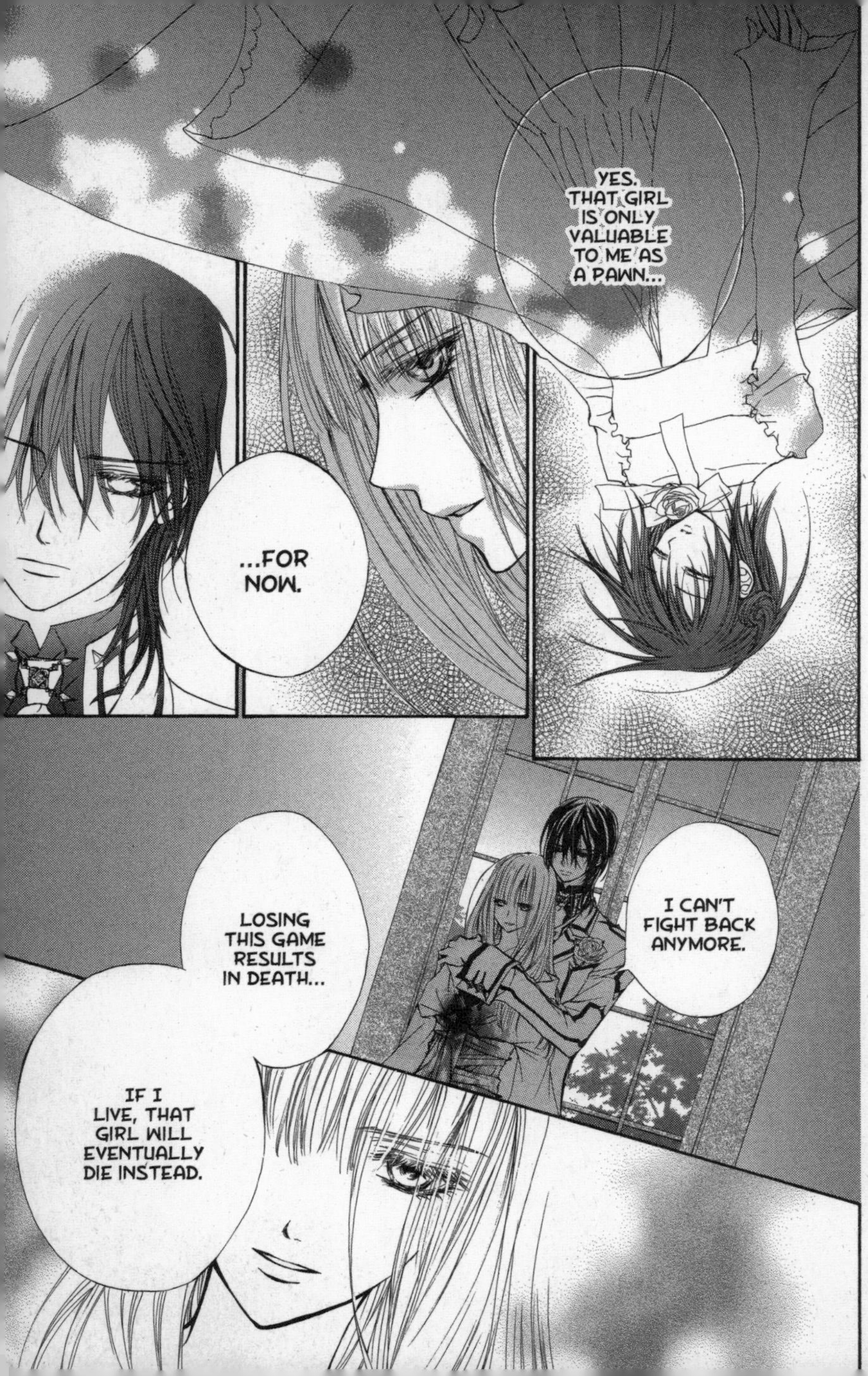
YES. THAT GIRL IS ONLY VALUABLE TO ME AS A PAWN...
...FOR NOW.
I CAN'T FIGHT BACK ANYMORE.
LOSING THIS GAME RESULTS IN DEATH...
IF I LIVE, THAT GIRL WILL EVENTUALLY DIE INSTEAD.

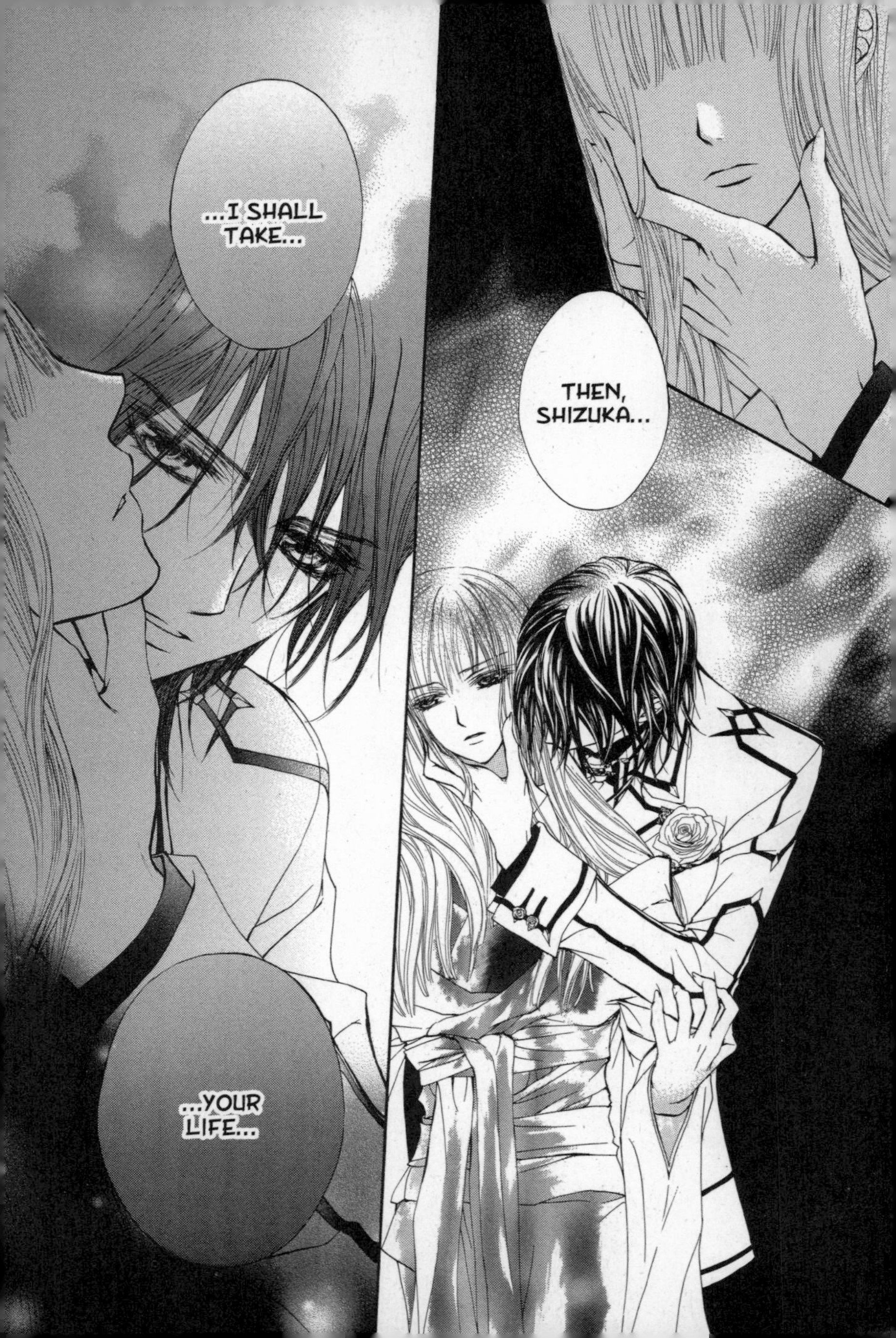
THEN, SHIZUKA...
...I SHALL TAKE...
...YOUR LIFE...

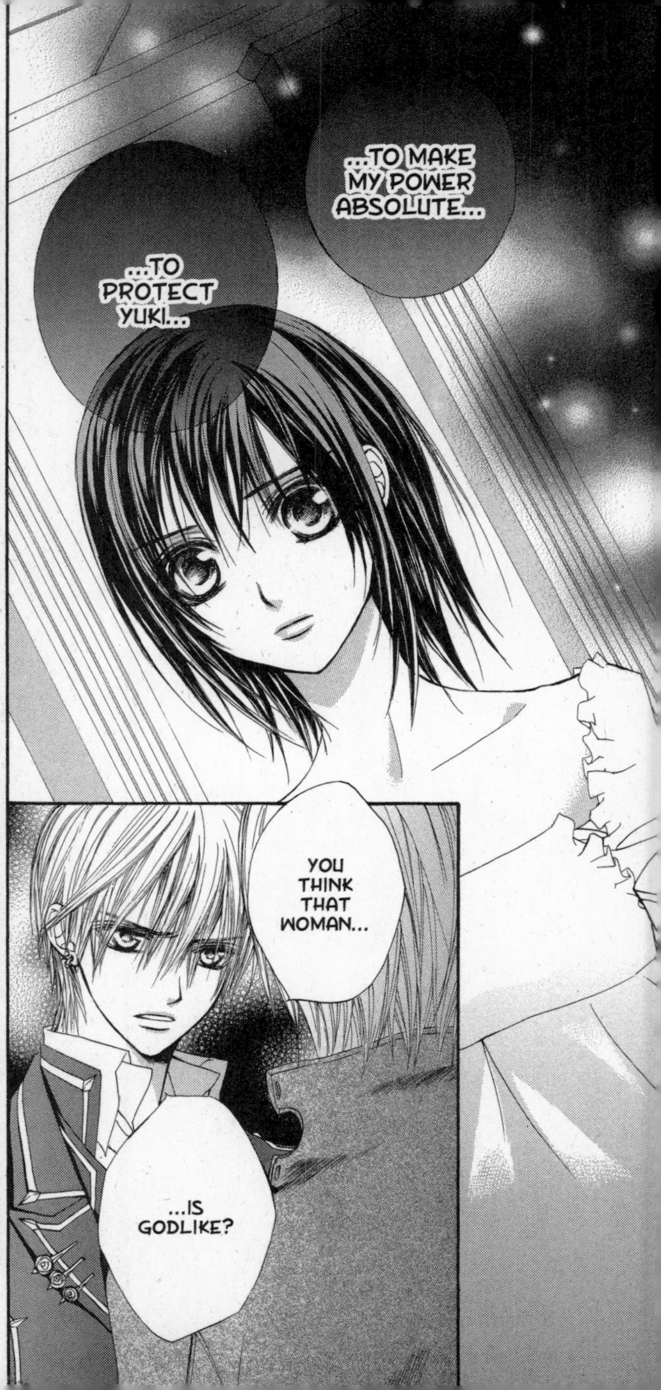
...TO MAKE MY POWER ABSOLUTE...
...TO PROTECT YUKI...
YOU THINK THAT WOMAN...
...IS GODLIKE?

II

The illustration of Zero and Kaname on the back cover was used for the July 2006 cover of *LaLa*. The one on the back cover of volume 4 was used for the March 2006 cover of *LaLa*. The illustration on volume 3's back cover was used for the October 2005 *LaLa* cover... The plan is to use the March 2007 *LaLa* cover for the back cover of volume 6...

I think people have already noticed, but the standard instructions for the magazine covers are "in black" and "you don't have to make the characters smile." But it's stamped on my brain that *LaLa* covers are drawn so that they're "brightly colored and show characters with cheerful expressions." So even now, I'm drawing with my heart in my mouth...

As for the chapter title pages in color, I'm agonizing over developing "vampireness" without using black. Maybe I should do that with the composition rather than color... I will try my best!!

↓(continues)

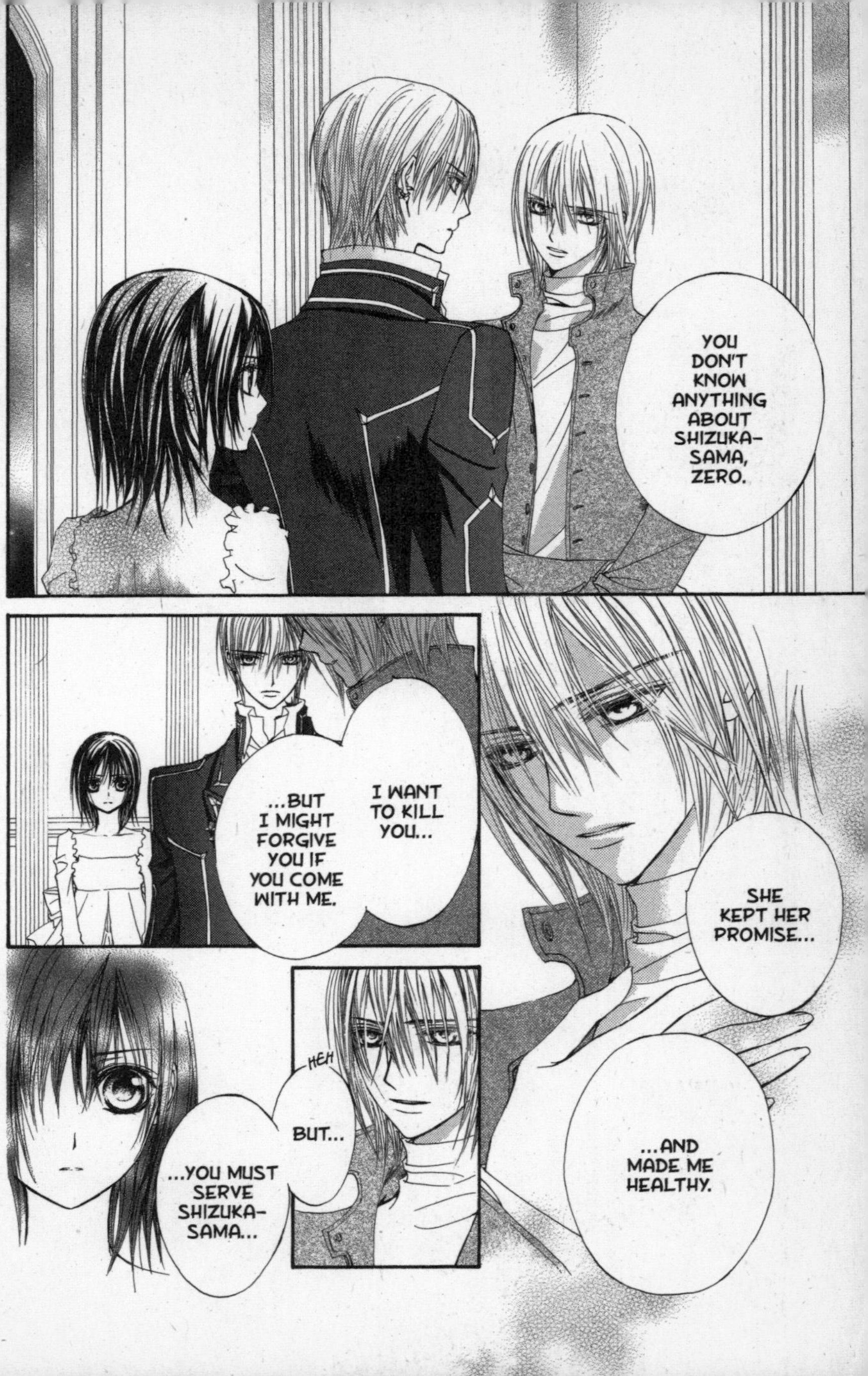
YOU DON'T KNOW ANYTHING ABOUT SHIZUKA-SAMA, ZERO.
SHE KEPT HER PROMISE...
...AND MADE ME HEALTHY.
I WANT TO KILL YOU...
...BUT I MIGHT FORGIVE YOU IF YOU COME WITH ME.
HEH
BUT...
...YOU MUST SERVE SHIZUKA-SAMA...

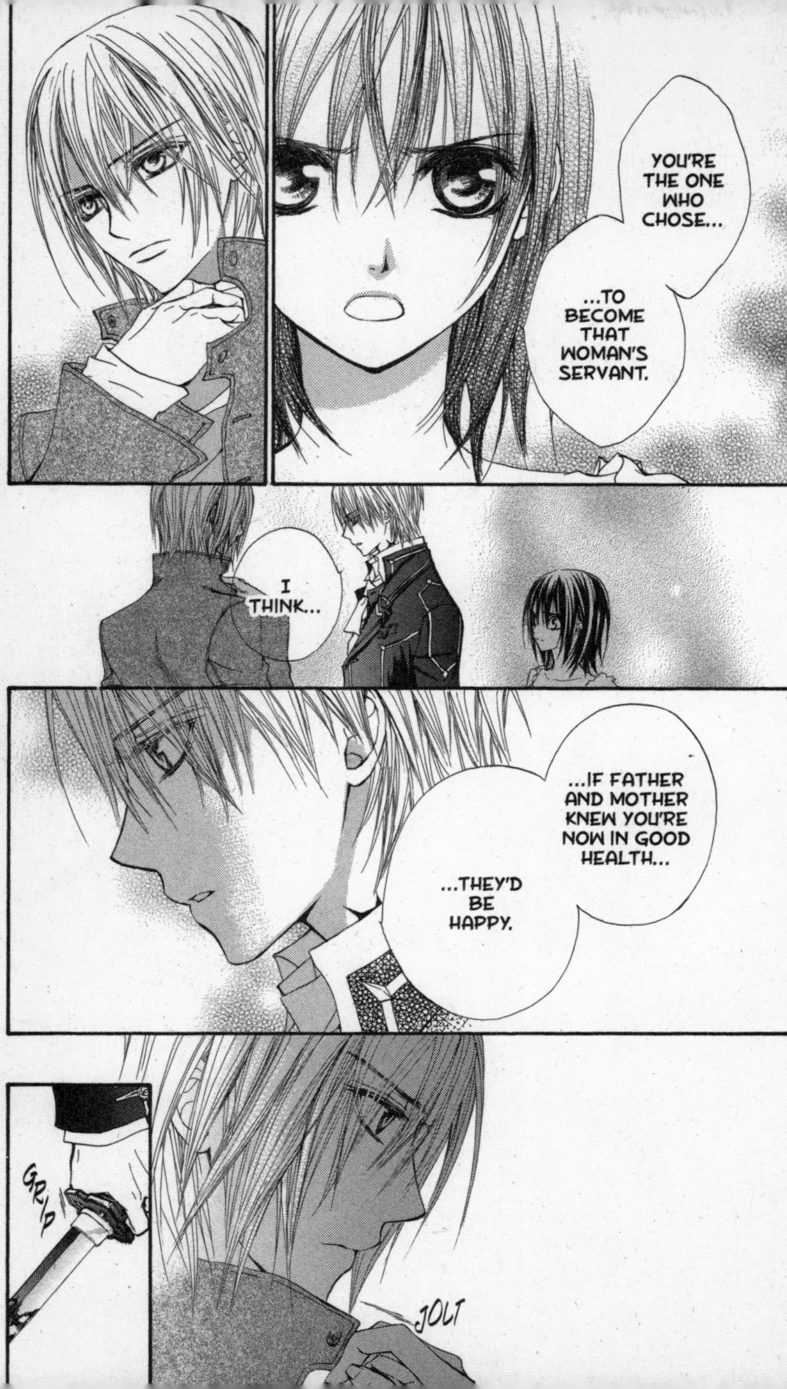
YOU'RE THE ONE WHO CHOSE...
...TO BECOME THAT WOMAN'S SERVANT.
I THINK...
...IF FATHER AND MOTHER KNEW YOU'RE NOW IN GOOD HEALTH...
...THEY'D BE HAPPY.
GRIP
JOLT

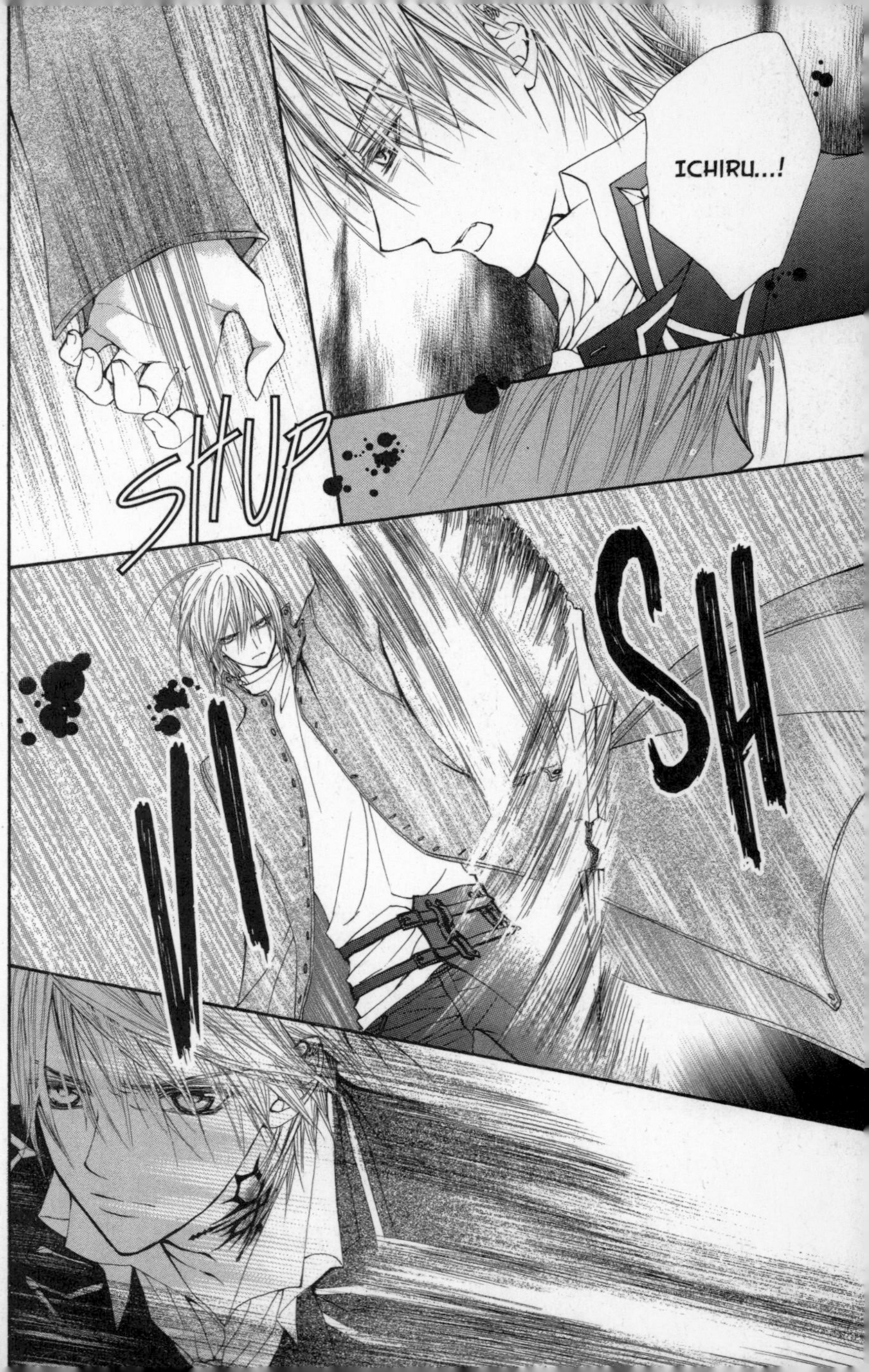
ICHIRU...!
SHUP
VI
SH

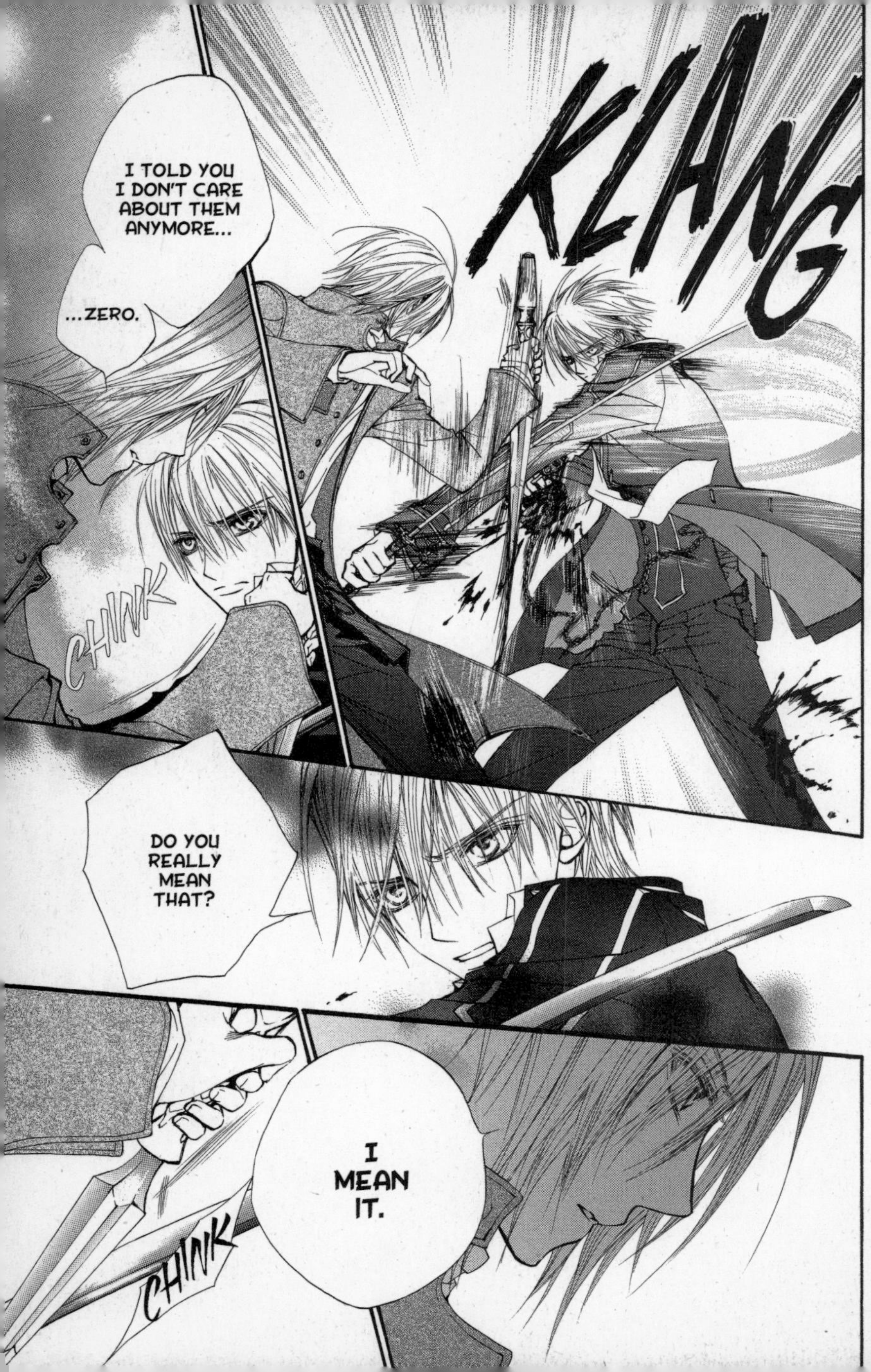
KLANG
I TOLD YOU I DON'T CARE ABOUT THEM ANYMORE...
...ZERO.
CHINK
DO YOU REALLY MEAN THAT?
I MEAN IT.
CHINK

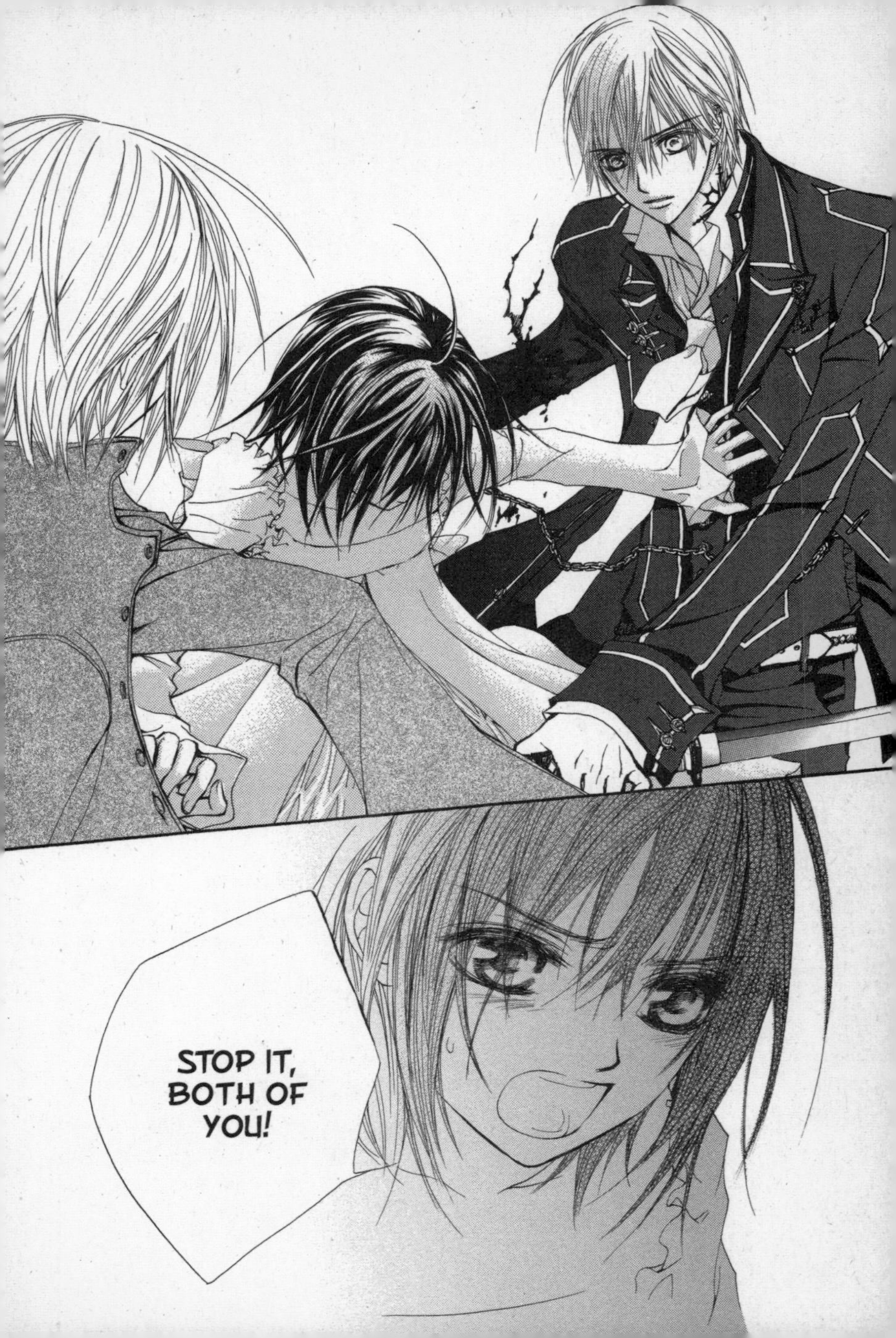
STOP IT, BOTH OF YOU!

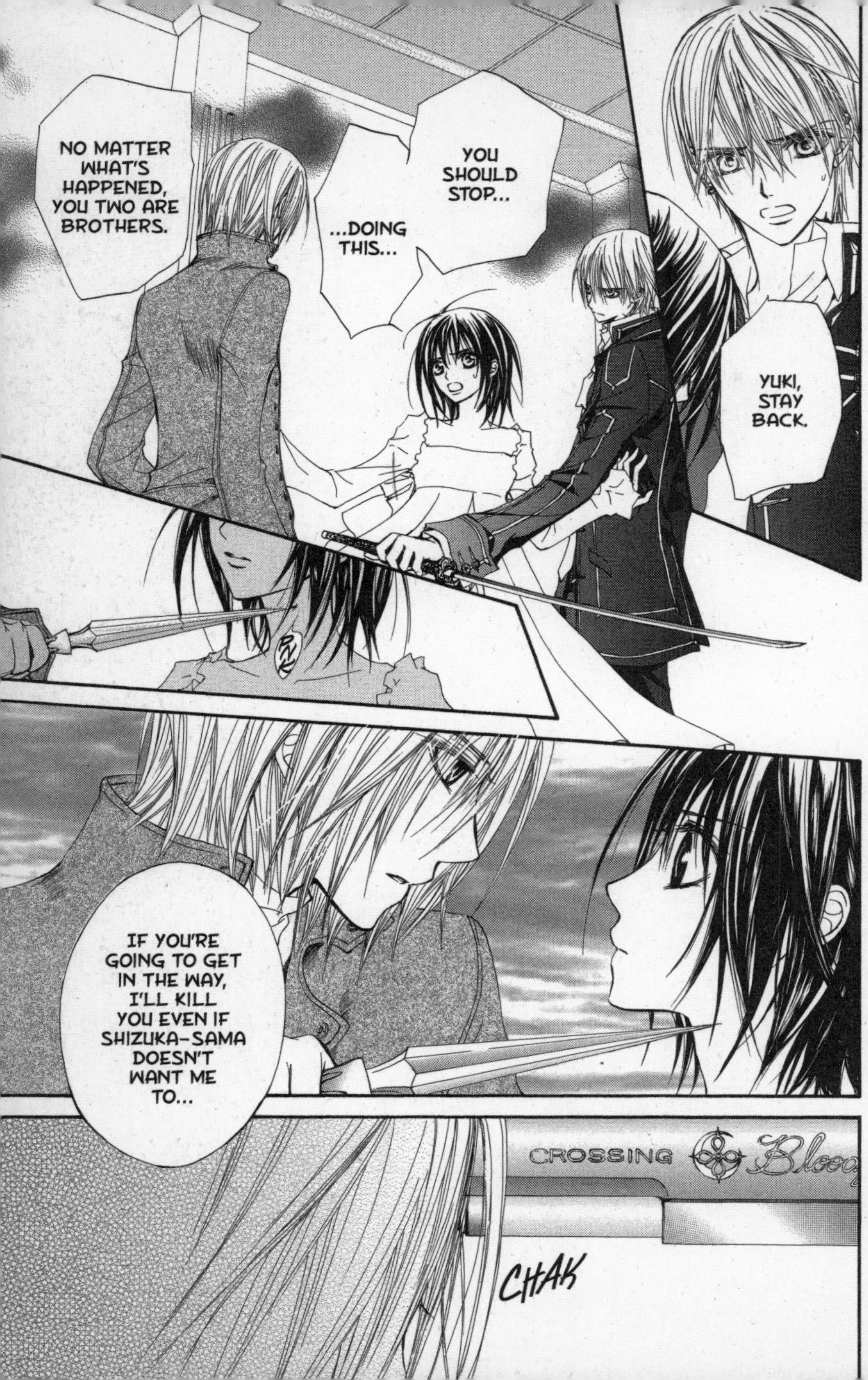
YUKI, STAY BACK.
YOU SHOULD STOP...
...DOING THIS...
NO MATTER WHAT'S HAPPENED, YOU TWO ARE BROTHERS.
IF YOU'RE GOING TO GET IN THE WAY, I'LL KILL YOU EVEN IF SHIZUKA-SAMA DOESN'T WANT ME TO...
CROSSING
CHAK

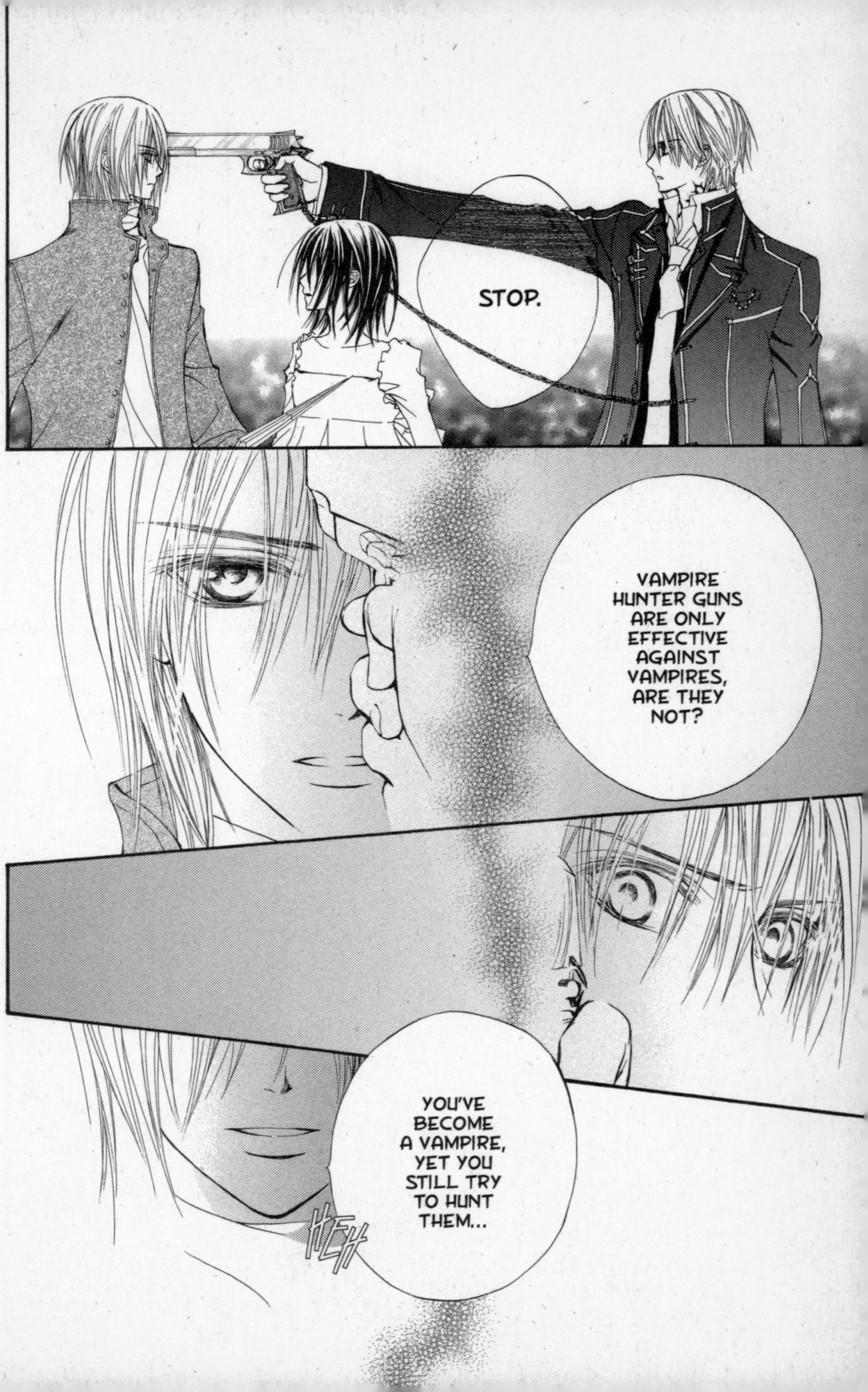
STOP.
VAMPIRE HUNTER GUNS ARE ONLY EFFECTIVE AGAINST VAMPIRES, ARE THEY NOT?
YOU'VE BECOME A VAMPIRE, YET YOU STILL TRY TO HUNT THEM...
HEH

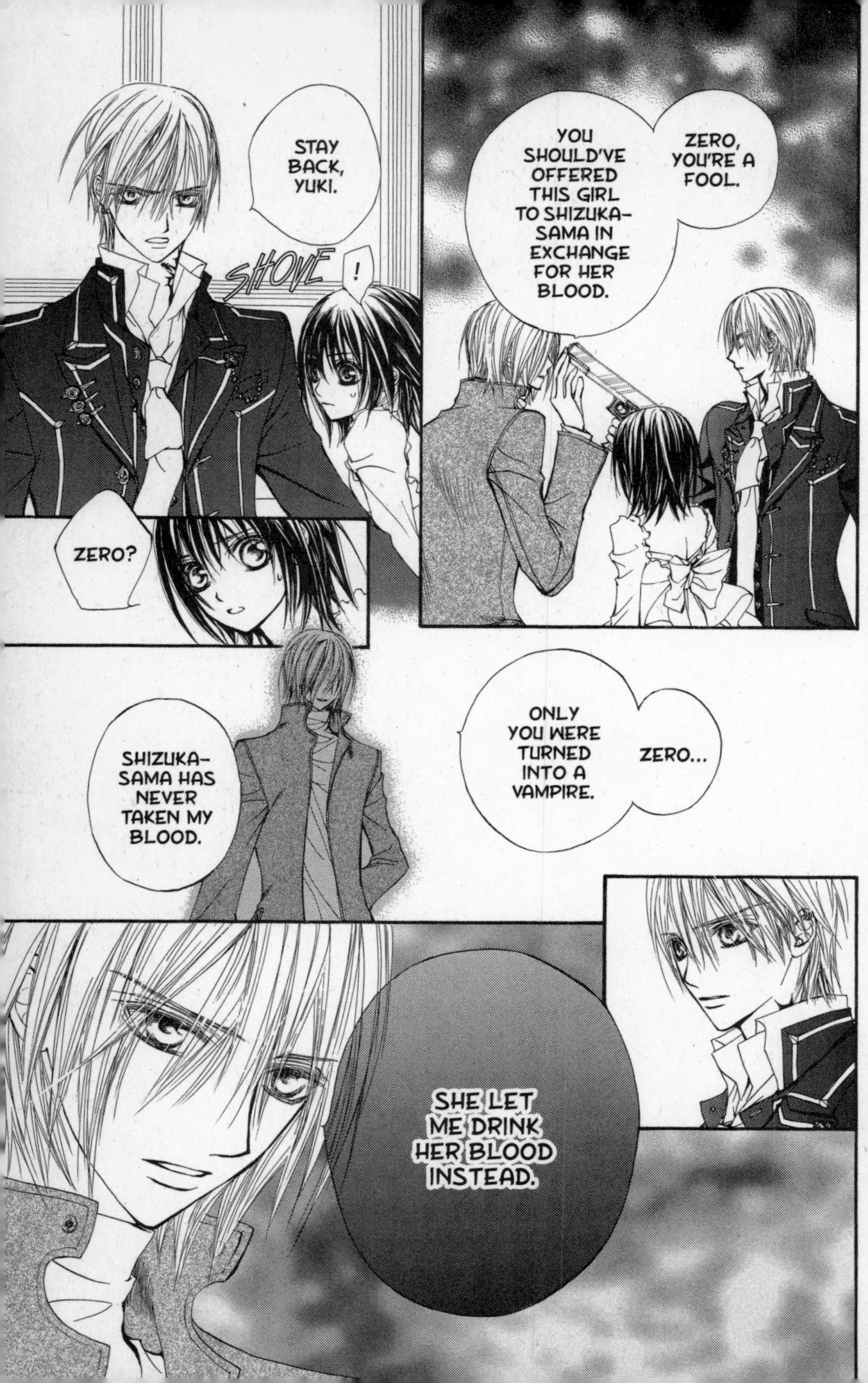
ZERO, YOU'RE A FOOL.
YOU SHOULD'VE OFFERED THIS GIRL TO SHIZUKA-SAMA IN EXCHANGE FOR HER BLOOD.
STAY BACK, YUKI.
SHOVE
!
ZERO?
ZERO...
ONLY YOU WERE TURNED INTO A VAMPIRE.
SHIZUKA-SAMA HAS NEVER TAKEN MY BLOOD.
SHE LET ME DRINK HER BLOOD INSTEAD.

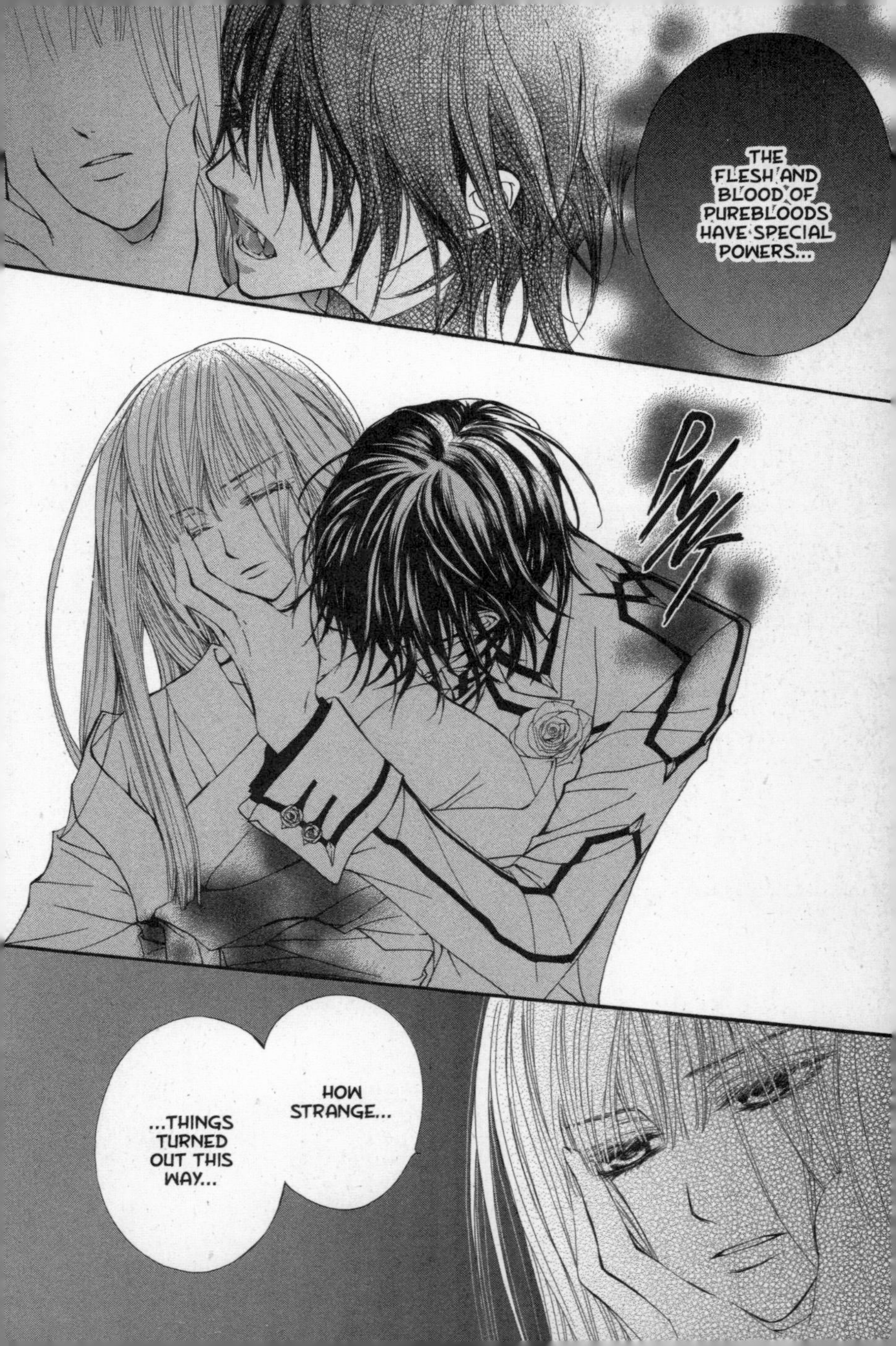
THE FLESH AND BLOOD OF PUREBLOODS HAVE SPECIAL POWERS...
HOW STRANGE...
...THINGS TURNED OUT THIS WAY...

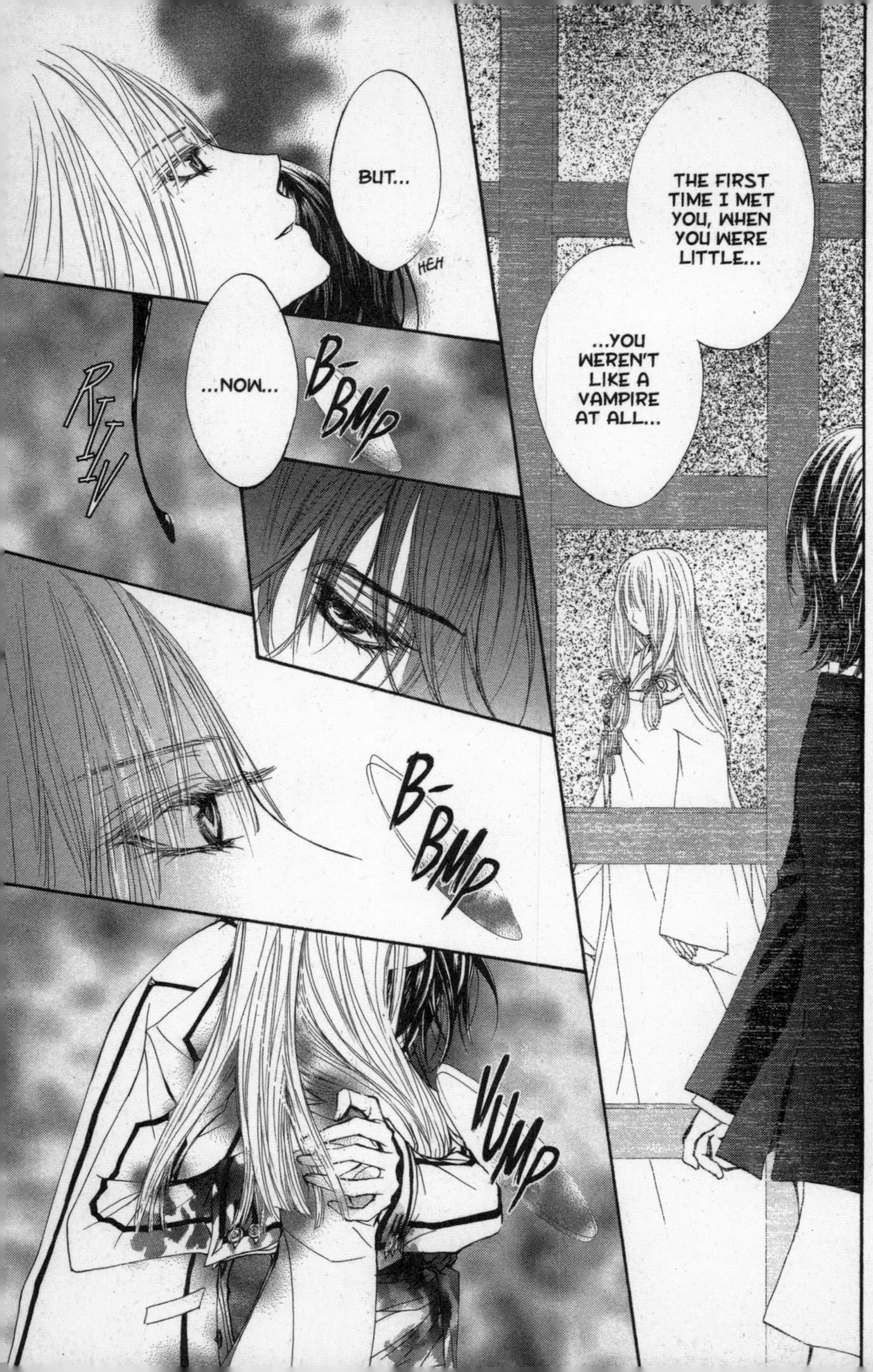
THE FIRST TIME I MET YOU, WHEN YOU WERE LITTLE...
...YOU WEREN'T LIKE A VAMPIRE AT ALL...
BUT...
HEH
B-BMP
...NOW...
RIIN
B-BMP
VUMP

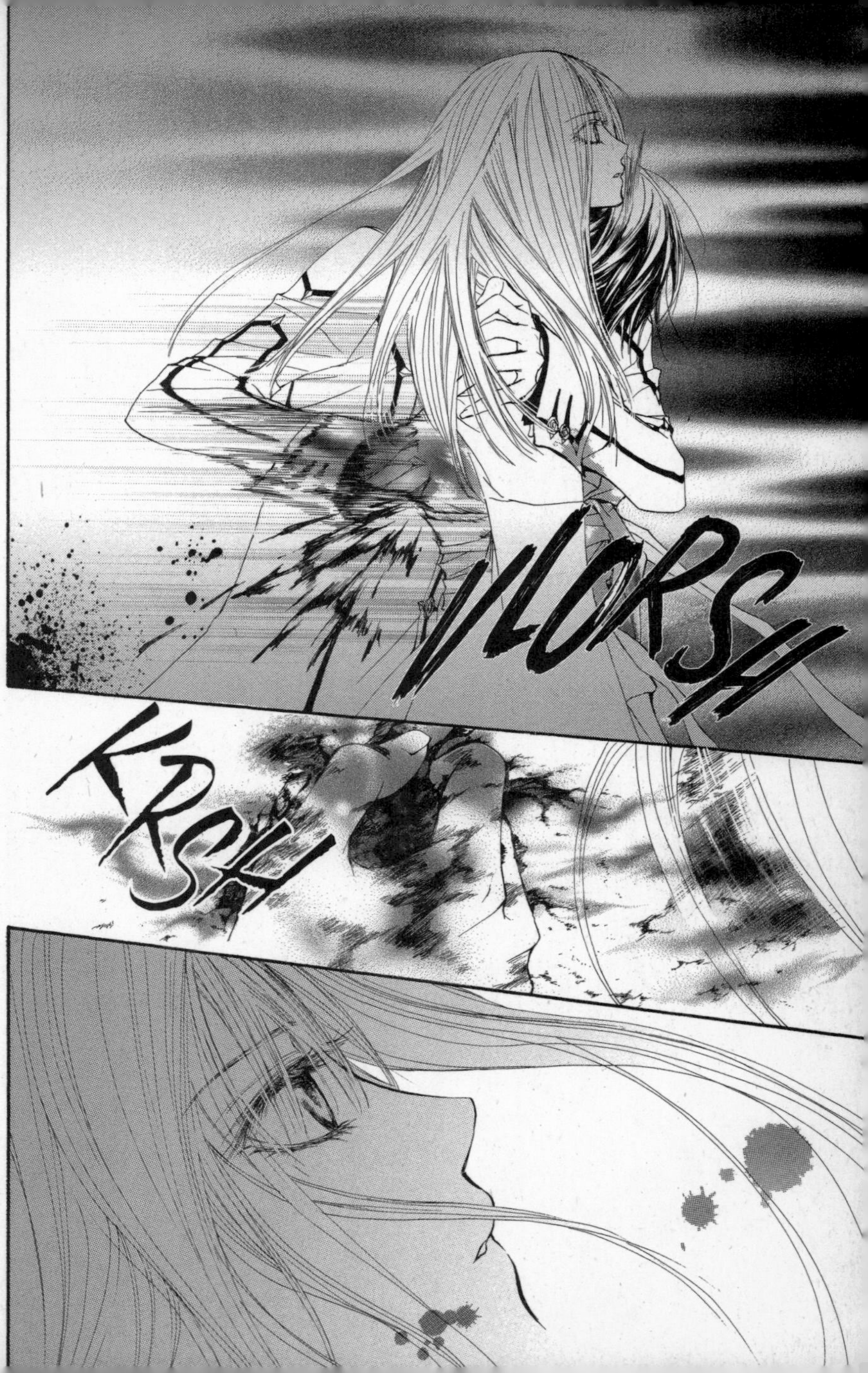
VWORSH
KRSH

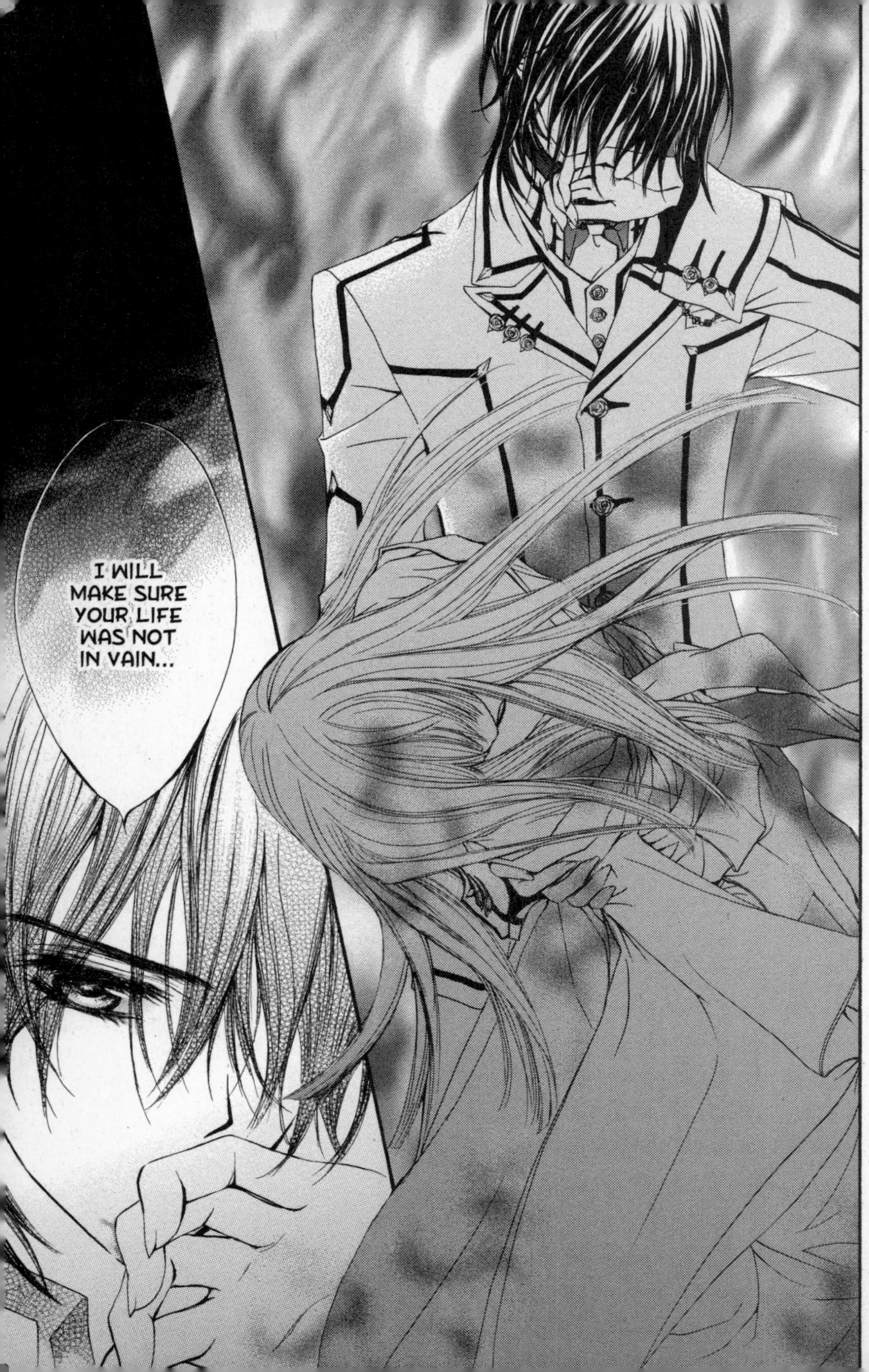
I WILL MAKE SURE YOUR LIFE WAS NOT IN VAIN...

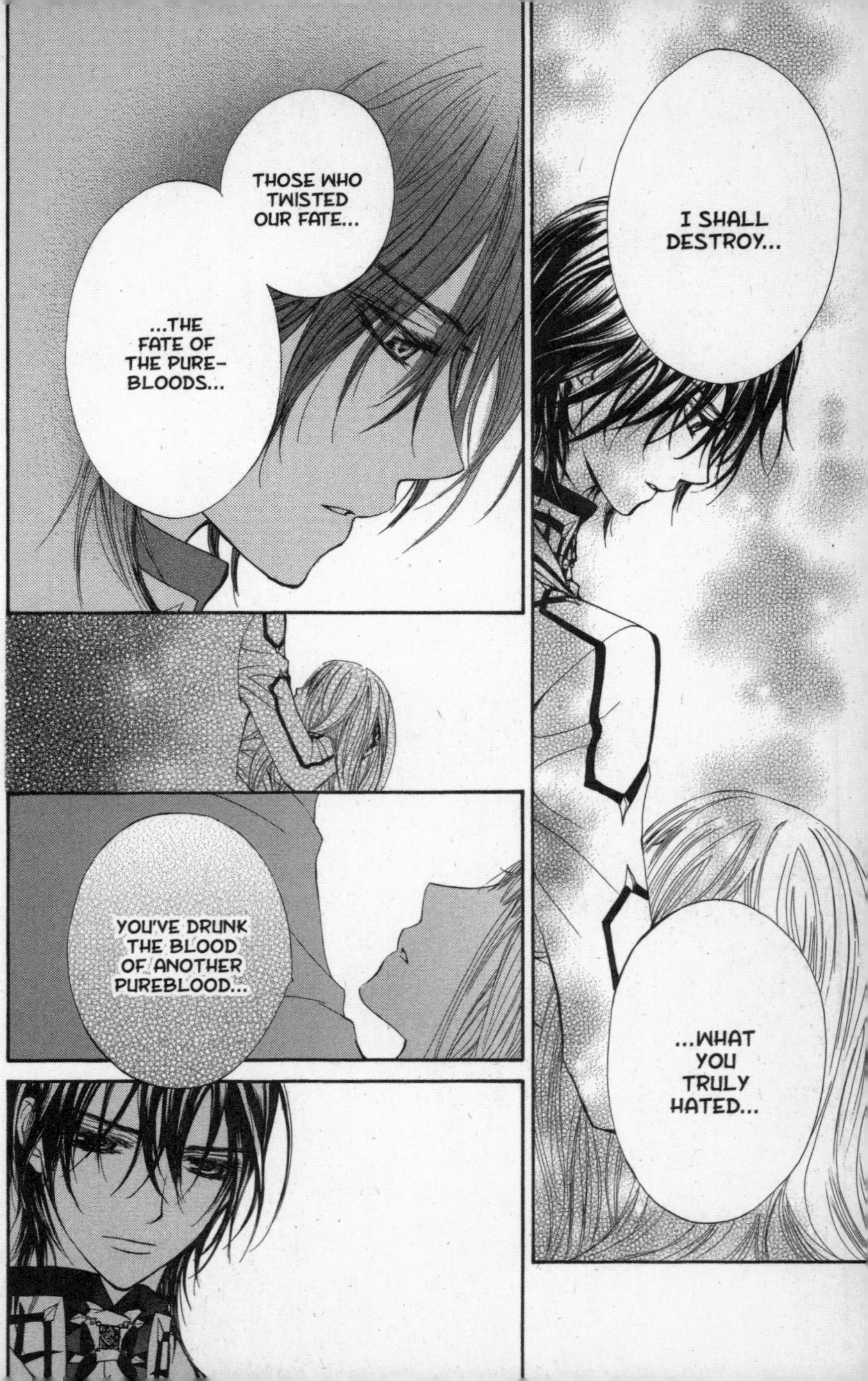
I SHALL DESTROY...
...WHAT YOU TRULY HATED...
THOSE WHO TWISTED OUR FATE...
...THE FATE OF THE PURE-BLOODS...
YOU'VE DRUNK THE BLOOD OF ANOTHER PUREBLOOD...

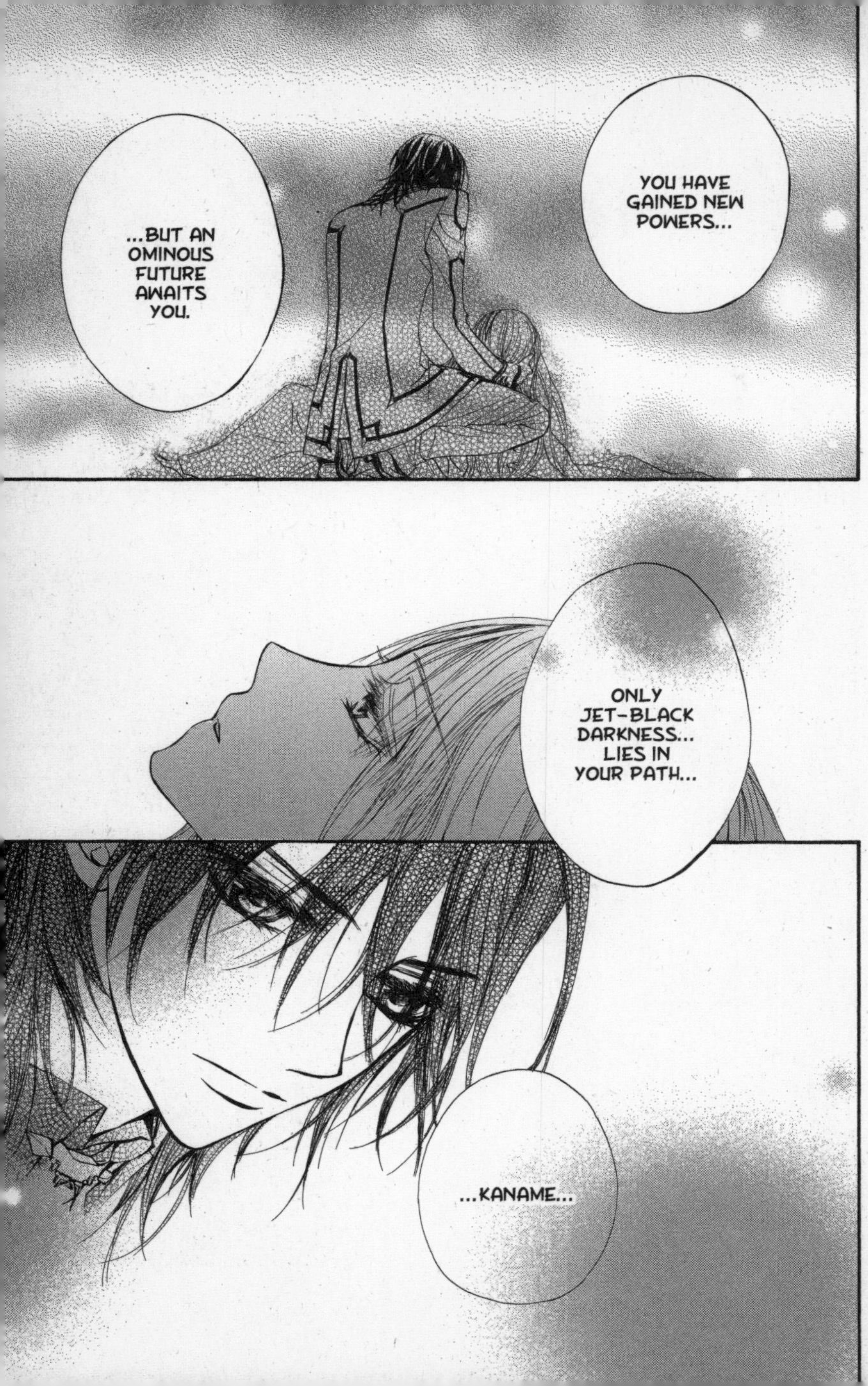
YOU HAVE GAINED NEW POWERS...
...BUT AN OMINOUS FUTURE AWAITS YOU.
ONLY JET-BLACK DARKNESS... LIES IN YOUR PATH...
...KANAME...

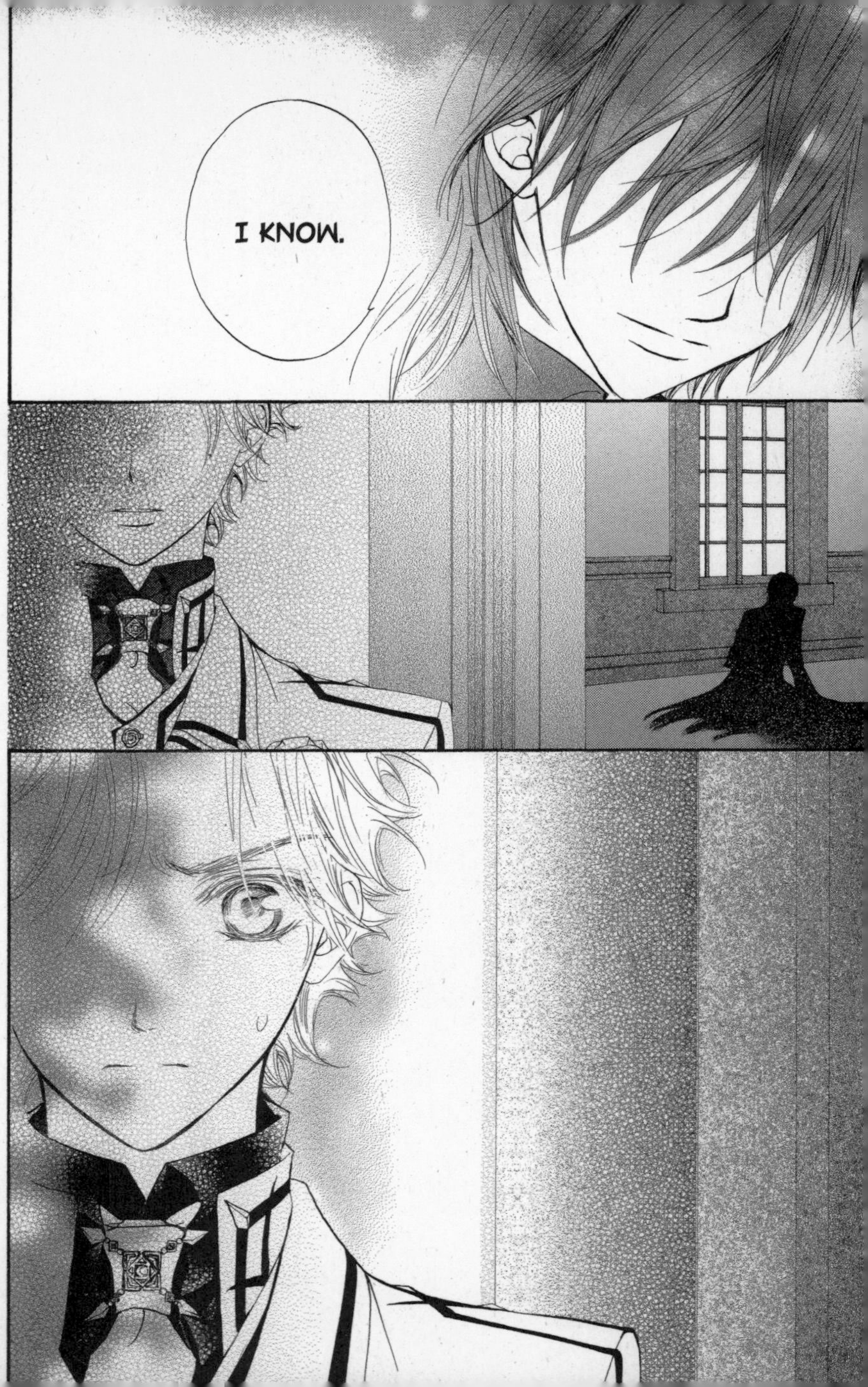
I KNOW.

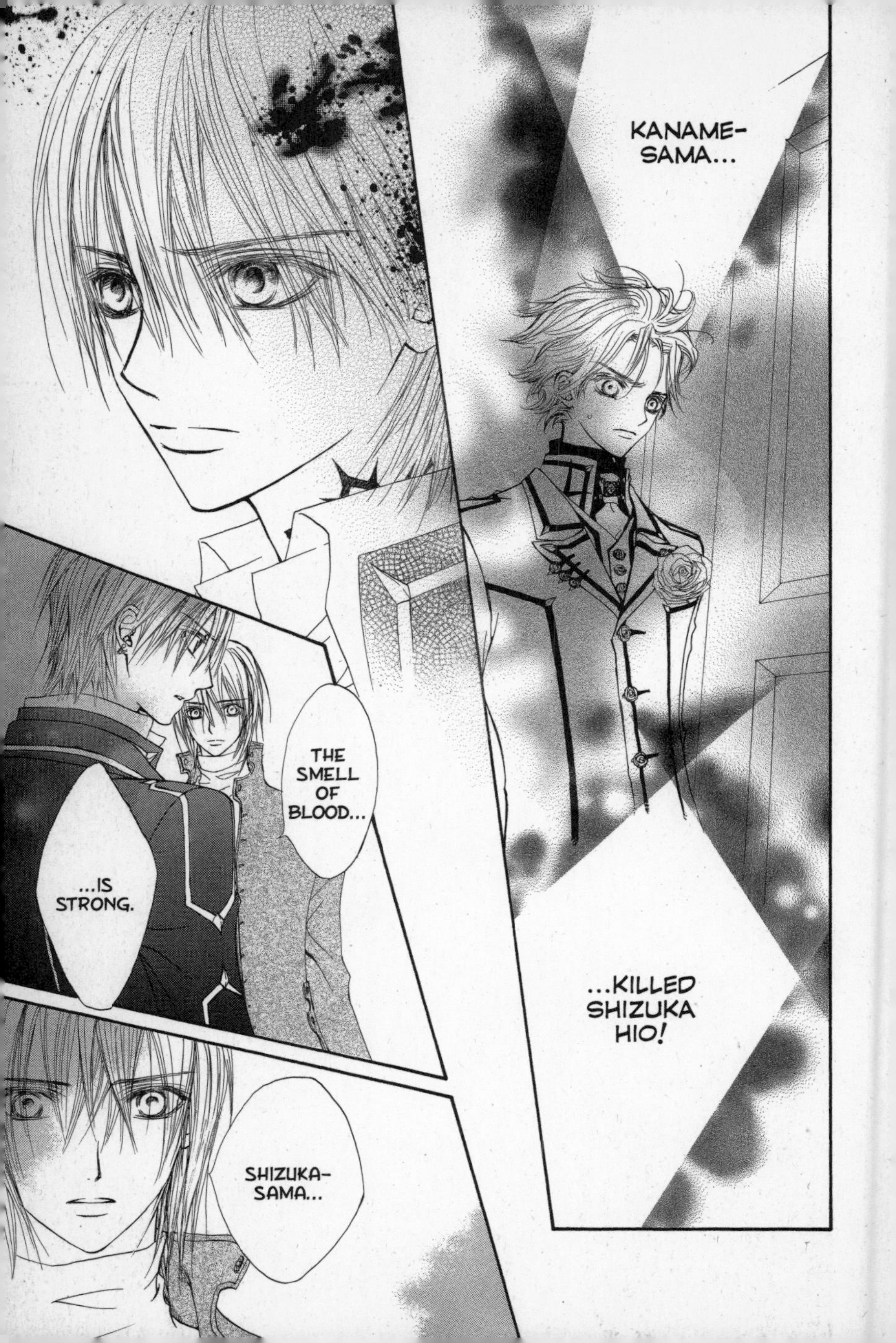
KANAME-SAMA...
...KILLED SHIZUKA HIO!
THE SMELL OF BLOOD...
...IS STRONG.
SHIZUKA-SAMA...

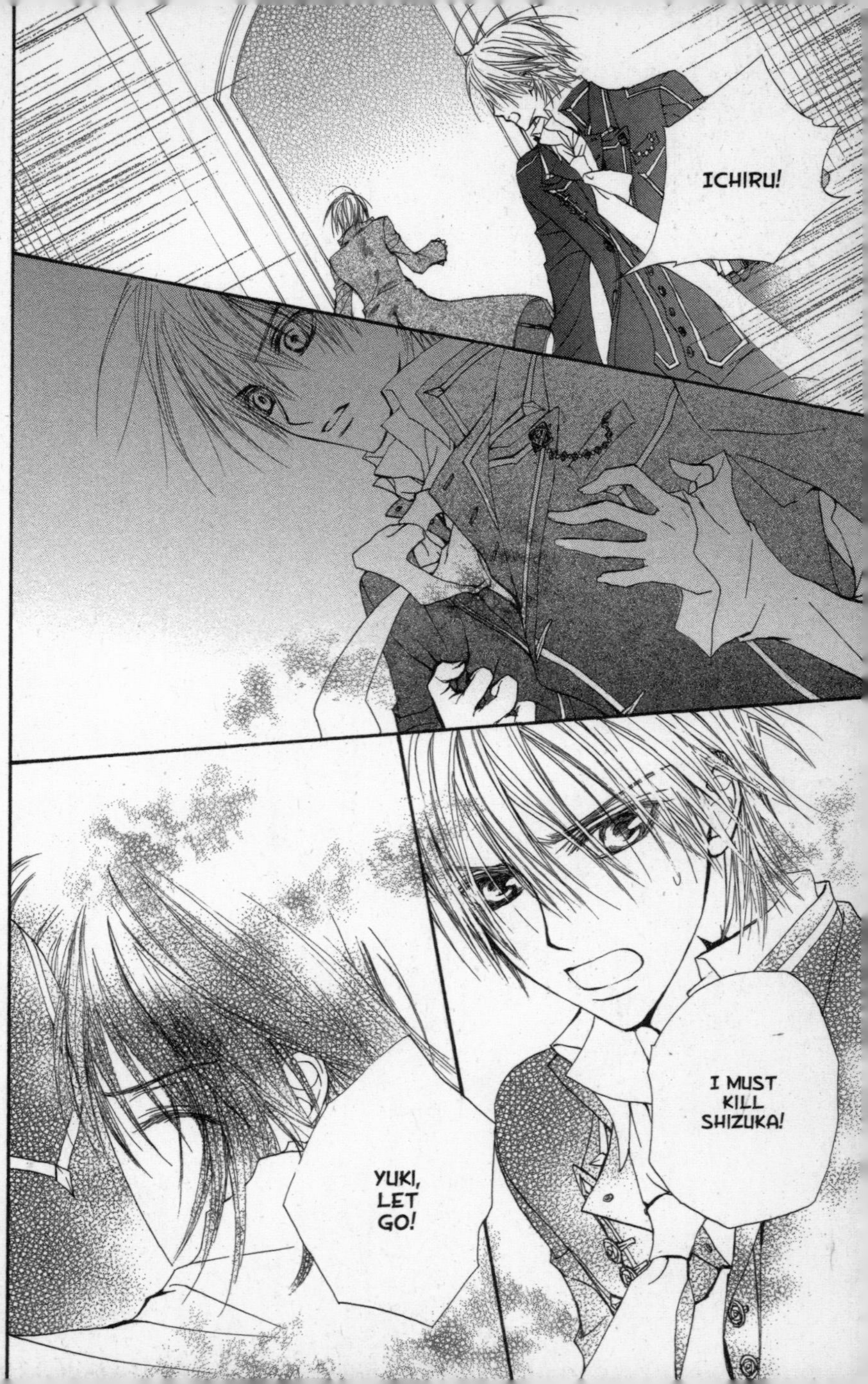
ICHIRU!
I MUST KILL SHIZUKA!
YUKI, LET GO!

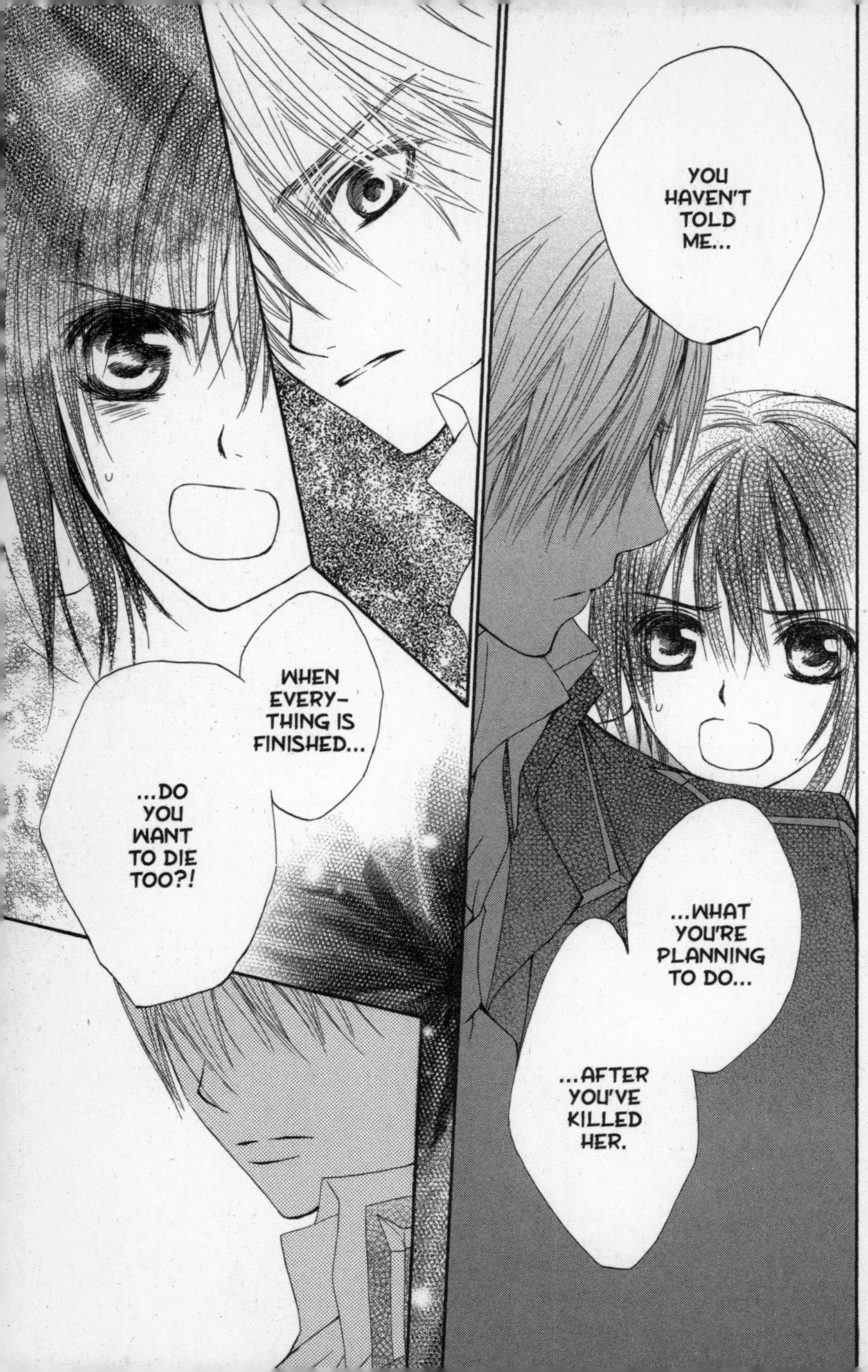
YOU HAVEN'T TOLD ME...
...WHAT YOU'RE PLANNING TO DO...
...AFTER YOU'VE KILLED HER.
WHEN EVERY-THING IS FINISHED...
...DO YOU WANT TO DIE TOO?!

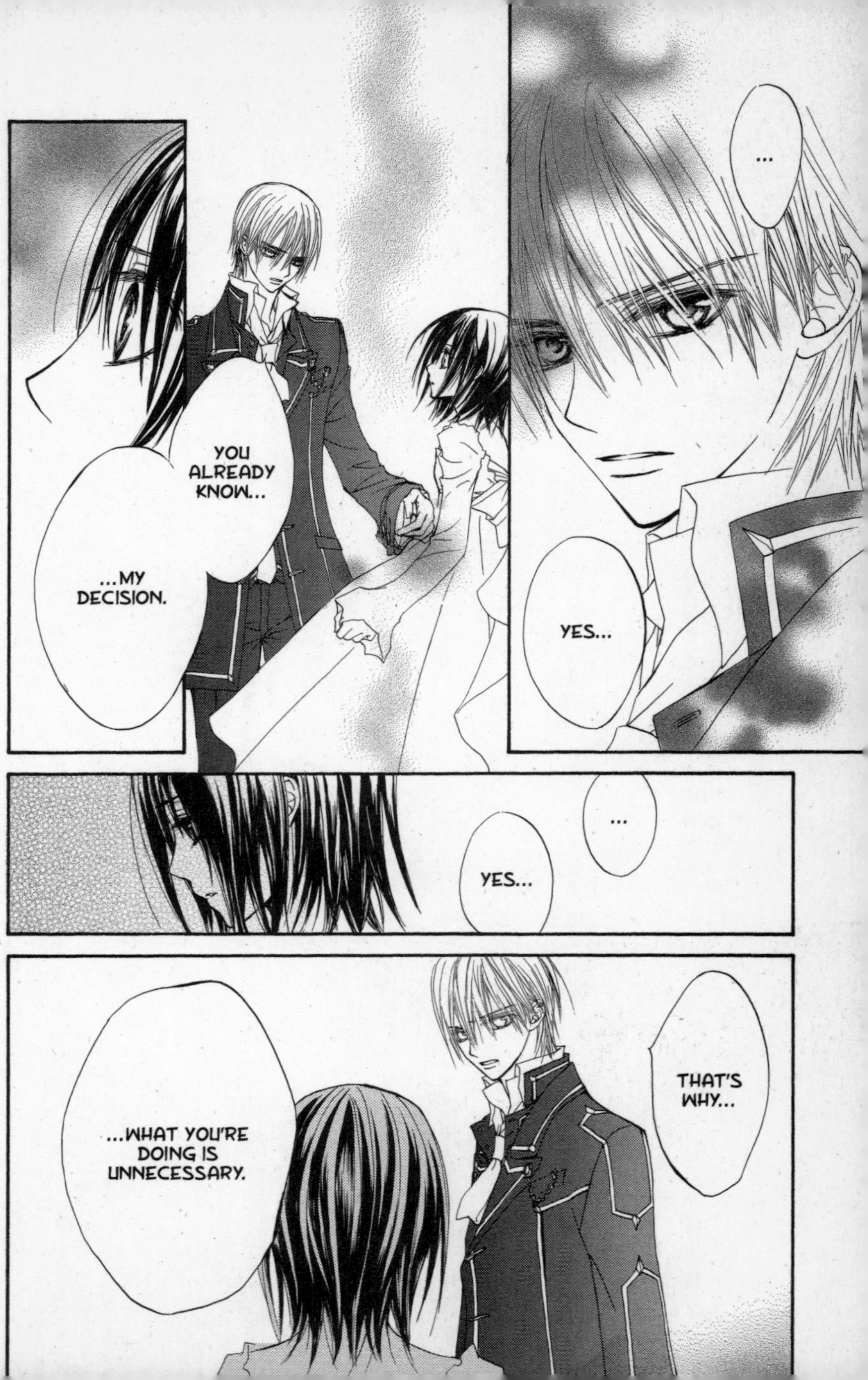
...
YES...
YOU ALREADY KNOW...
...MY DECISION.
...
YES...
THAT'S WHY...
...WHAT YOU'RE DOING IS UNNECESSARY.

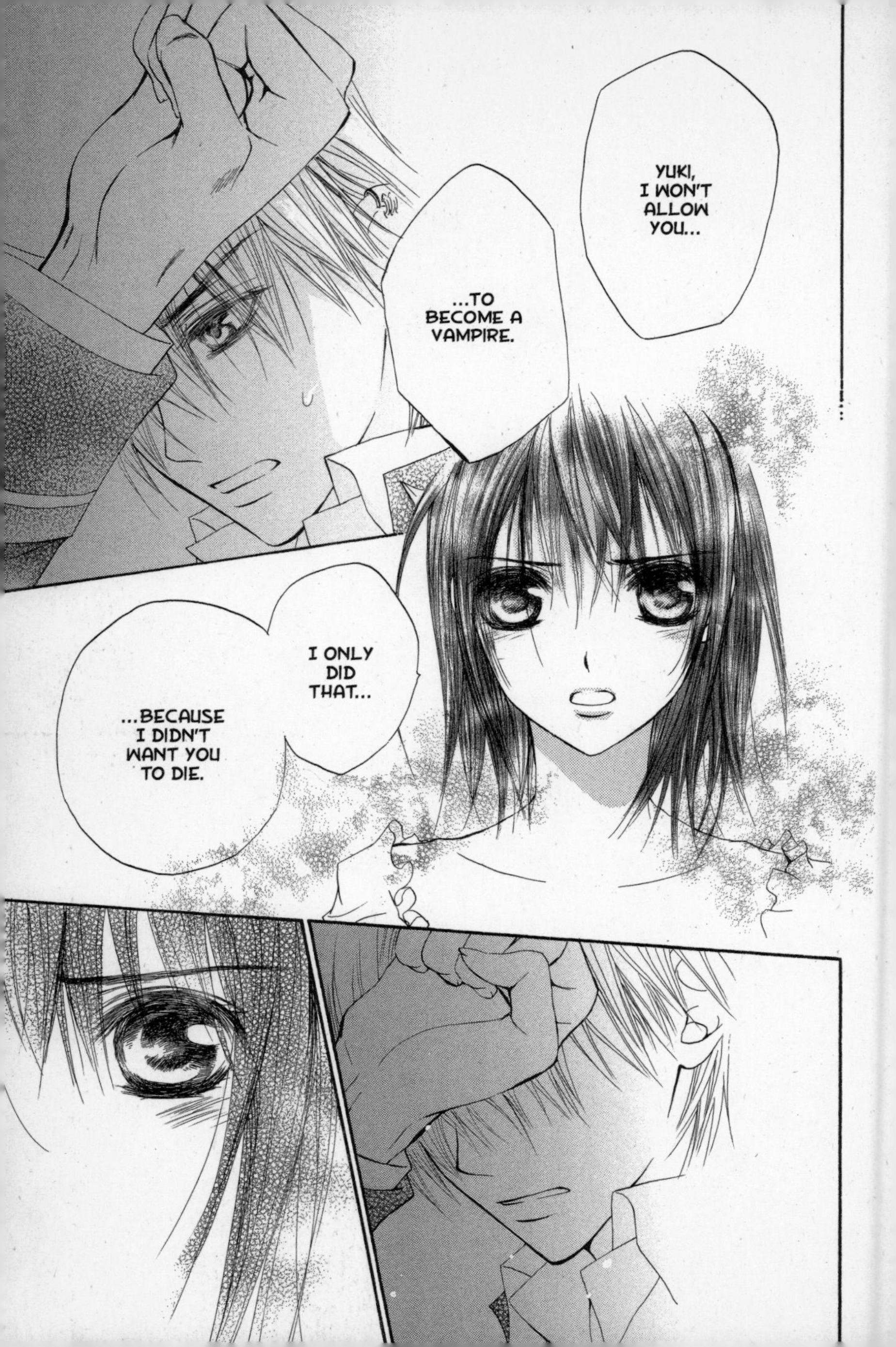
YUKI, I WON'T ALLOW YOU...
...TO BECOME A VAMPIRE.
I ONLY DID THAT...
...BECAUSE I DIDN'T WANT YOU TO DIE.

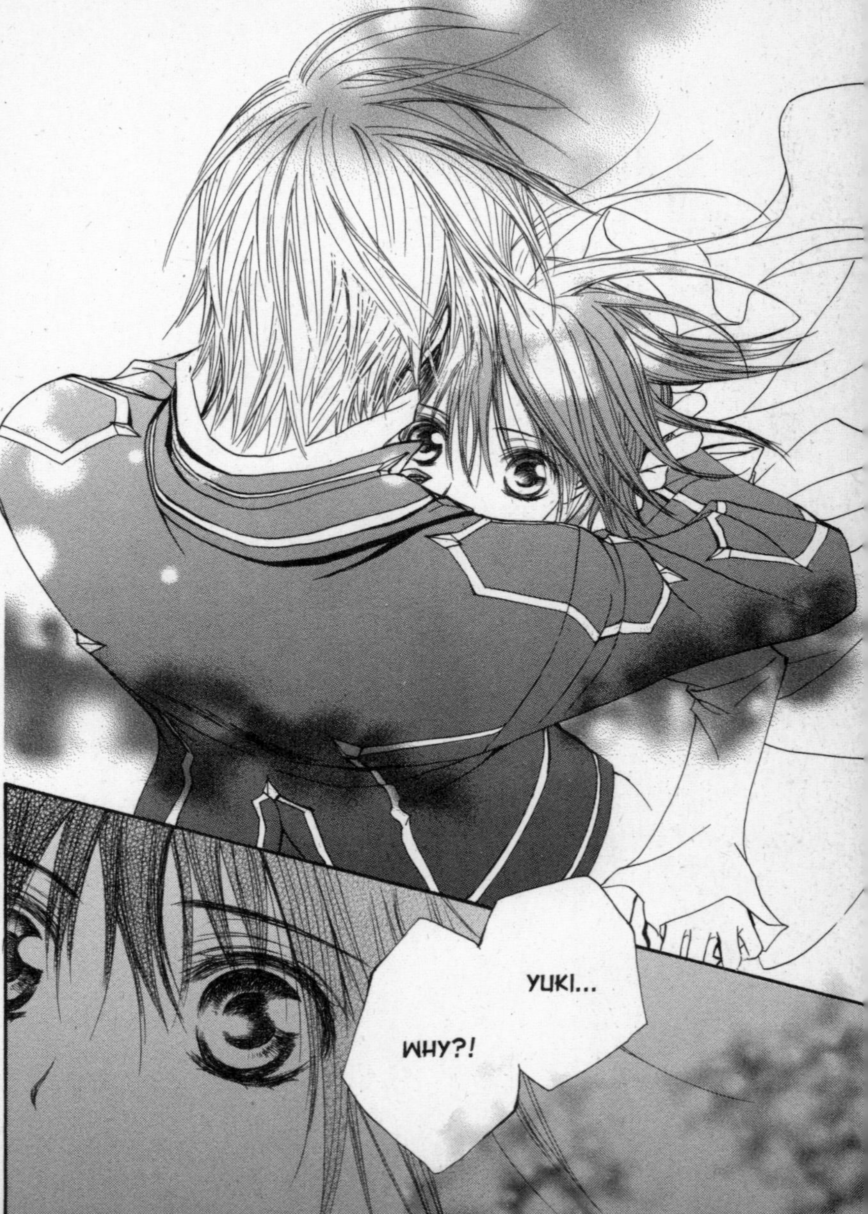
YUKI...
WHY?!

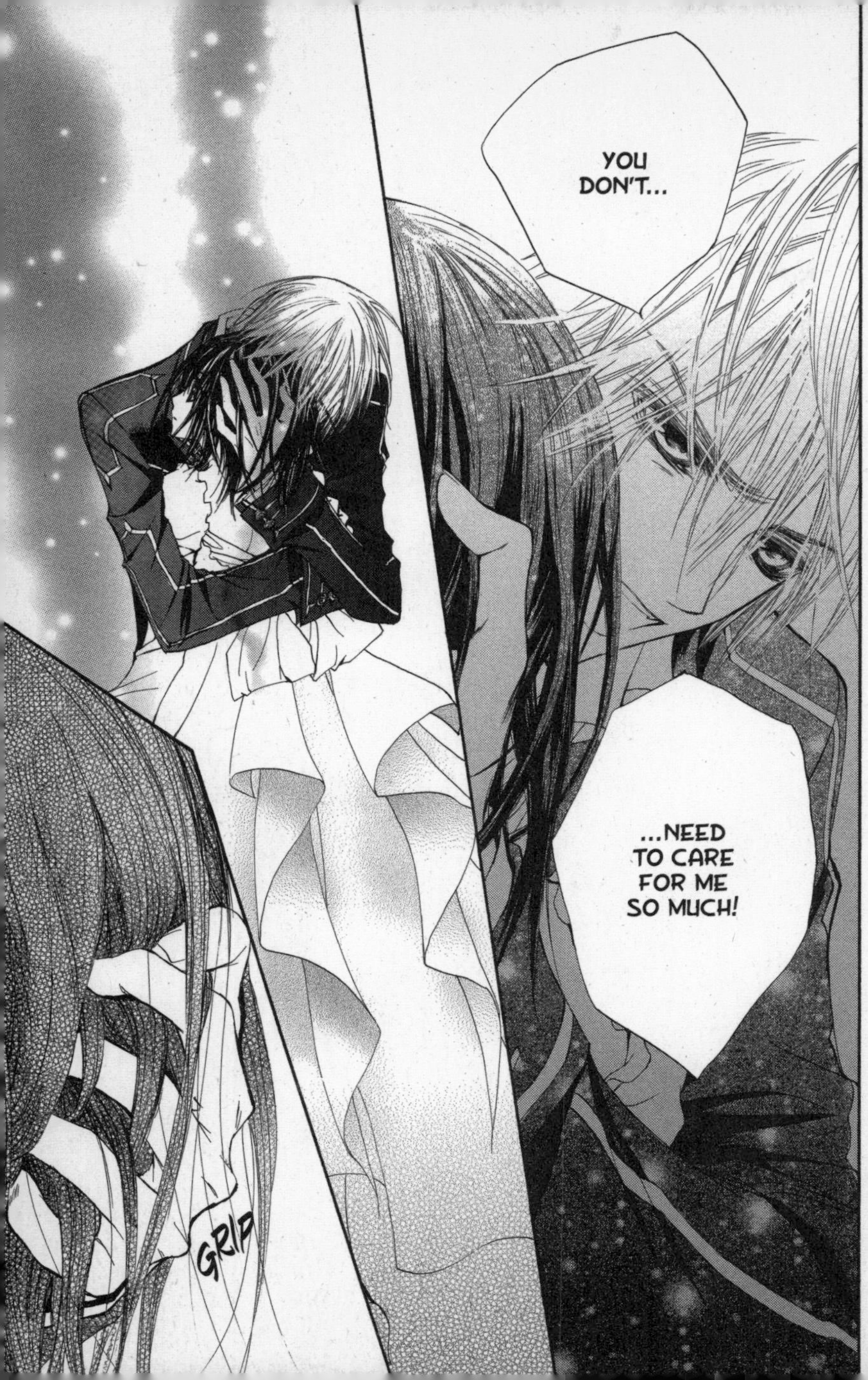
YOU DON'T...
...NEED TO CARE FOR ME SO MUCH!
GRIP

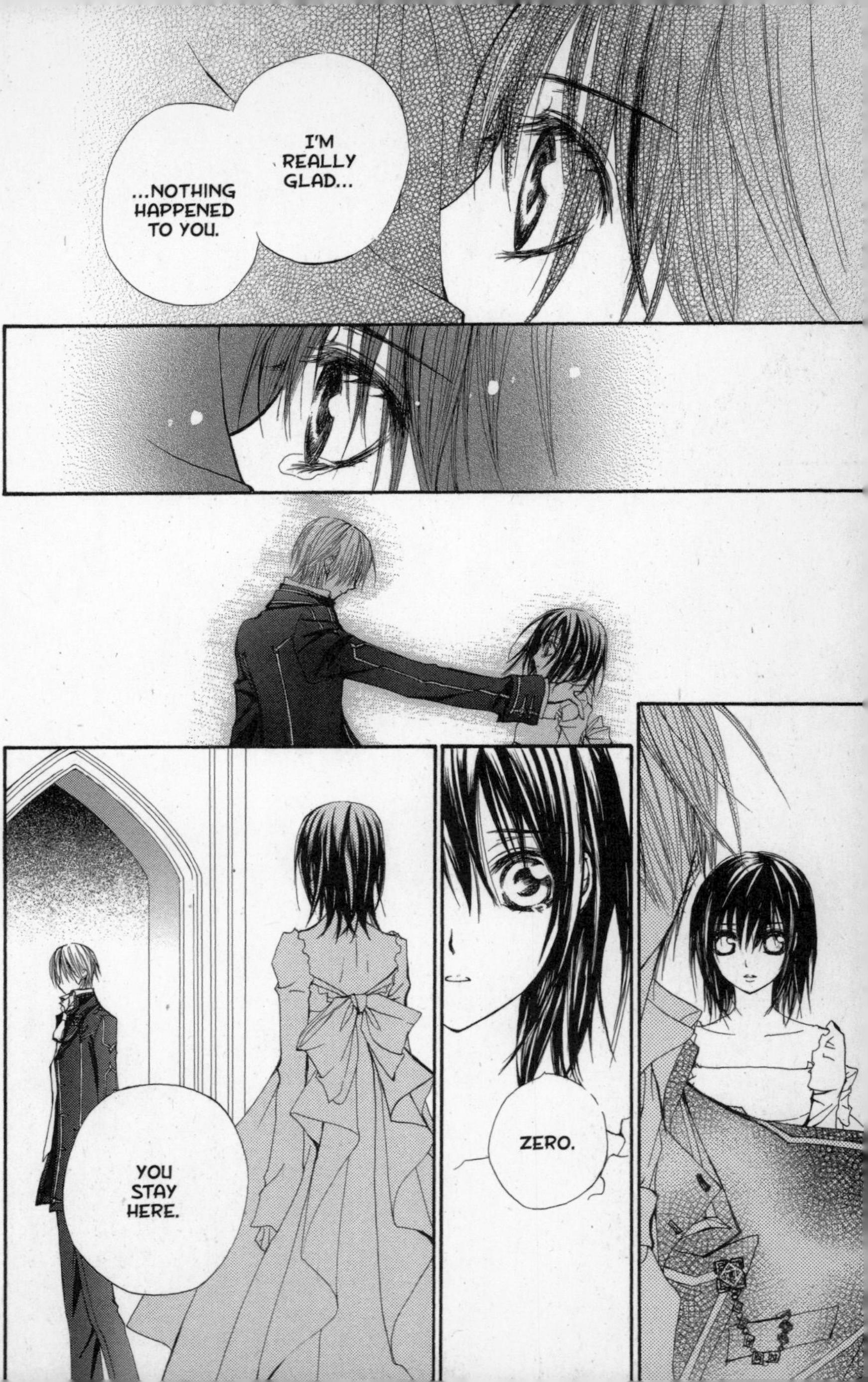
I'M REALLY GLAD...
...NOTHING HAPPENED TO YOU.
ZERO.
YOU STAY HERE.

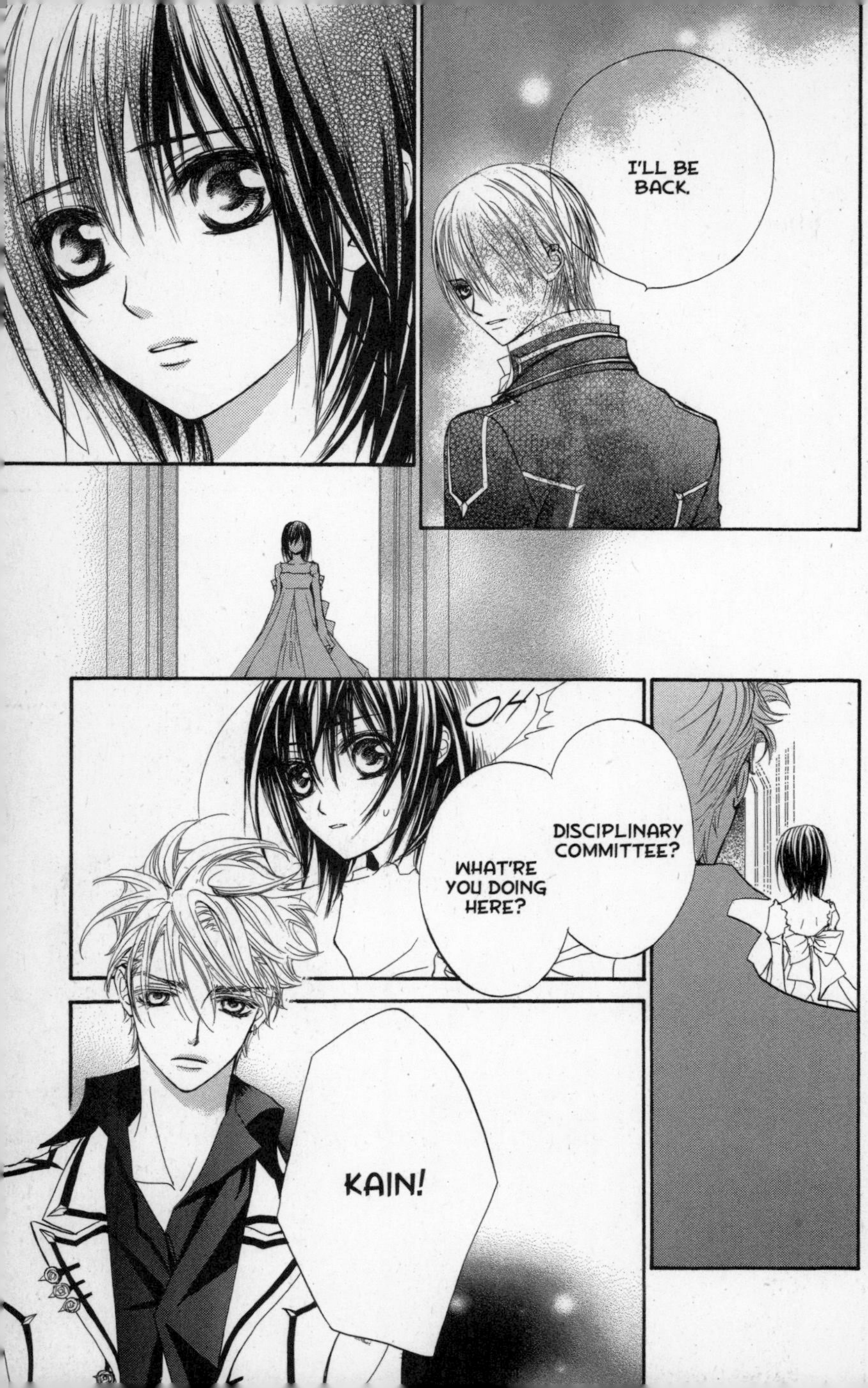
I'LL BE BACK.
OH
DISCIPLINARY COMMITTEE? WHAT'RE YOU DOING HERE?
KAIN!

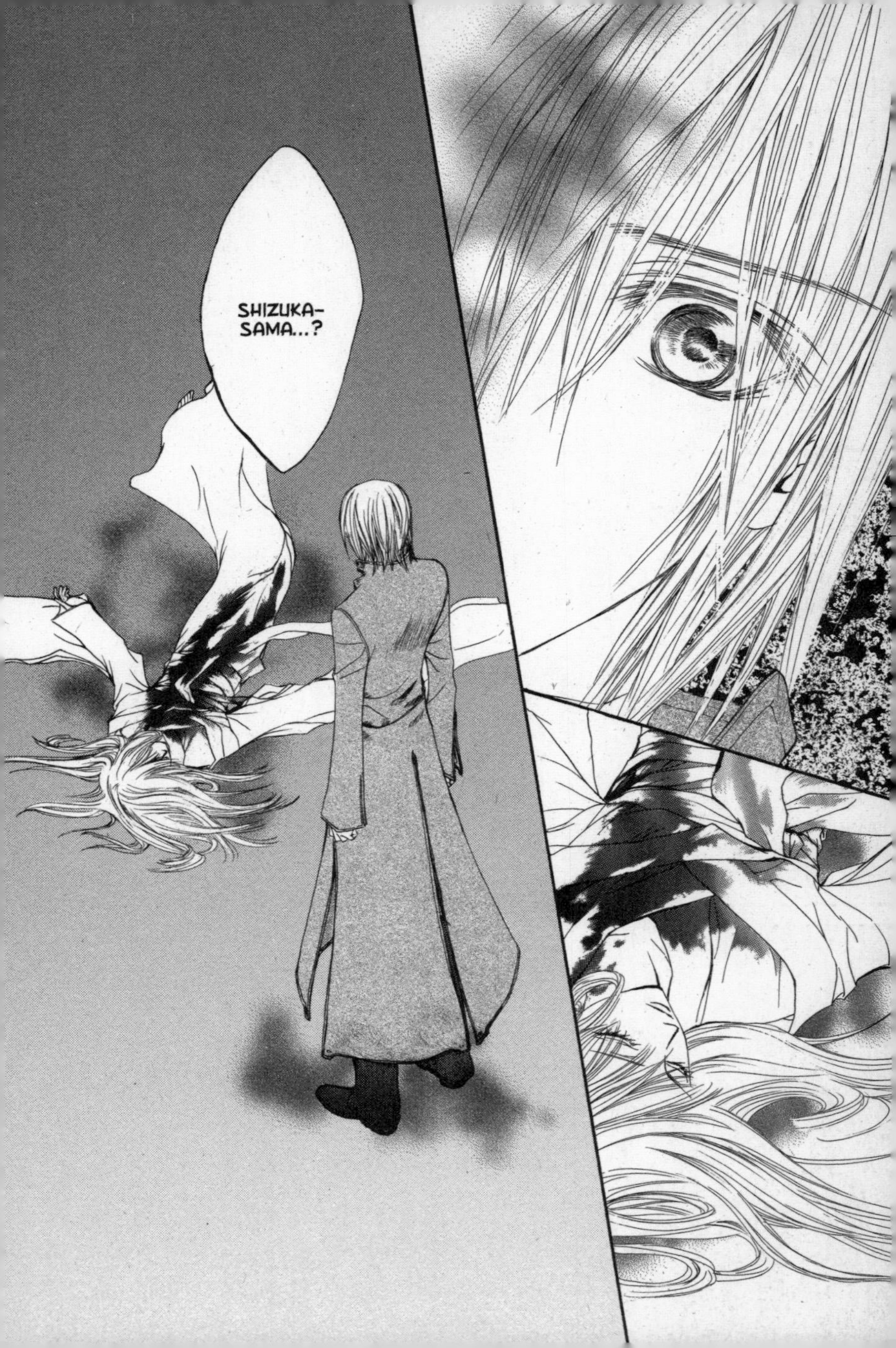
SHIZUKA-SAMA...?

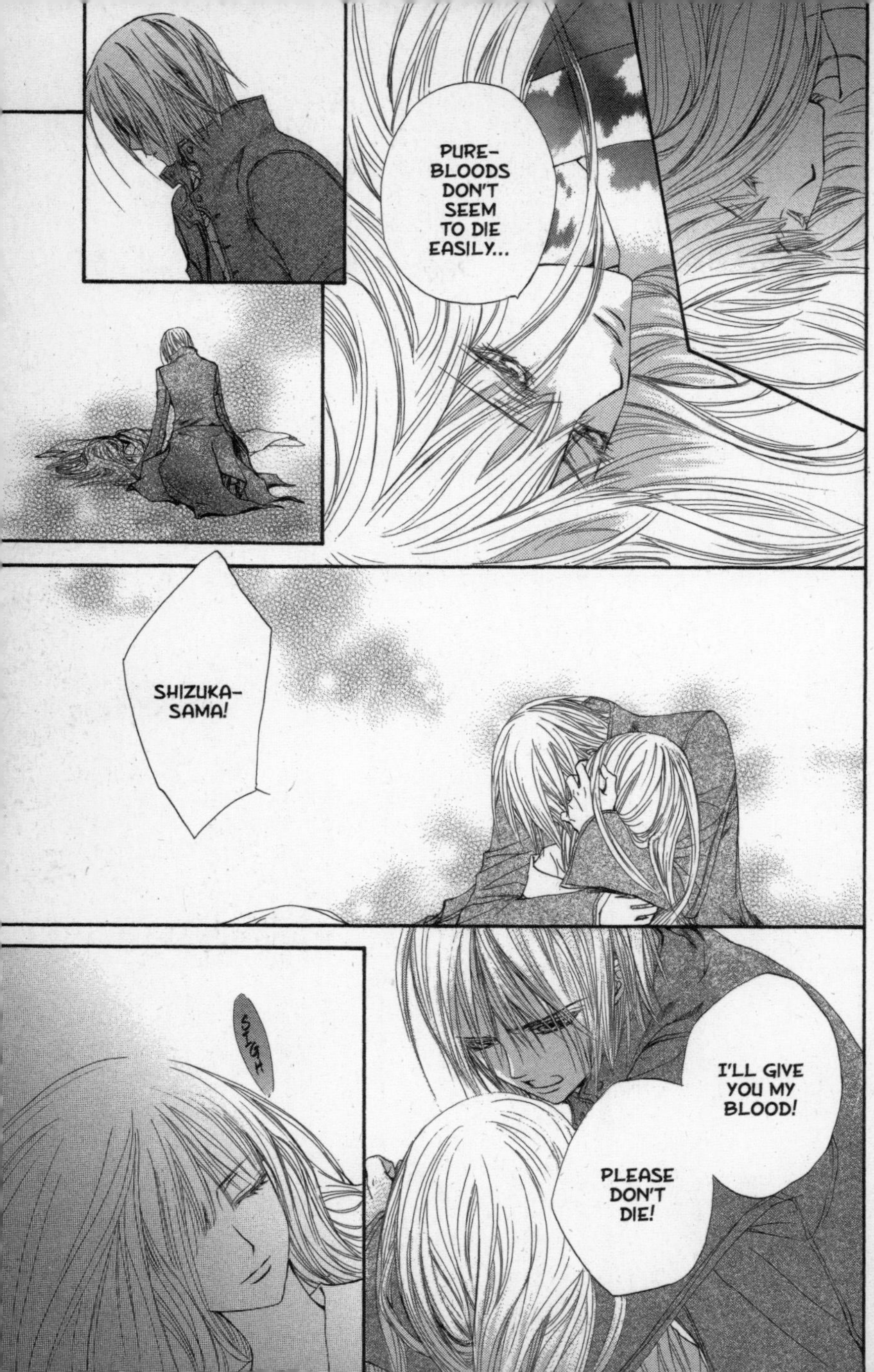
PURE-BLOODS DON'T SEEM TO DIE EASILY...
SHIZUKA-SAMA!
I'LL GIVE YOU MY BLOOD!
PLEASE DON'T DIE!
SIGH

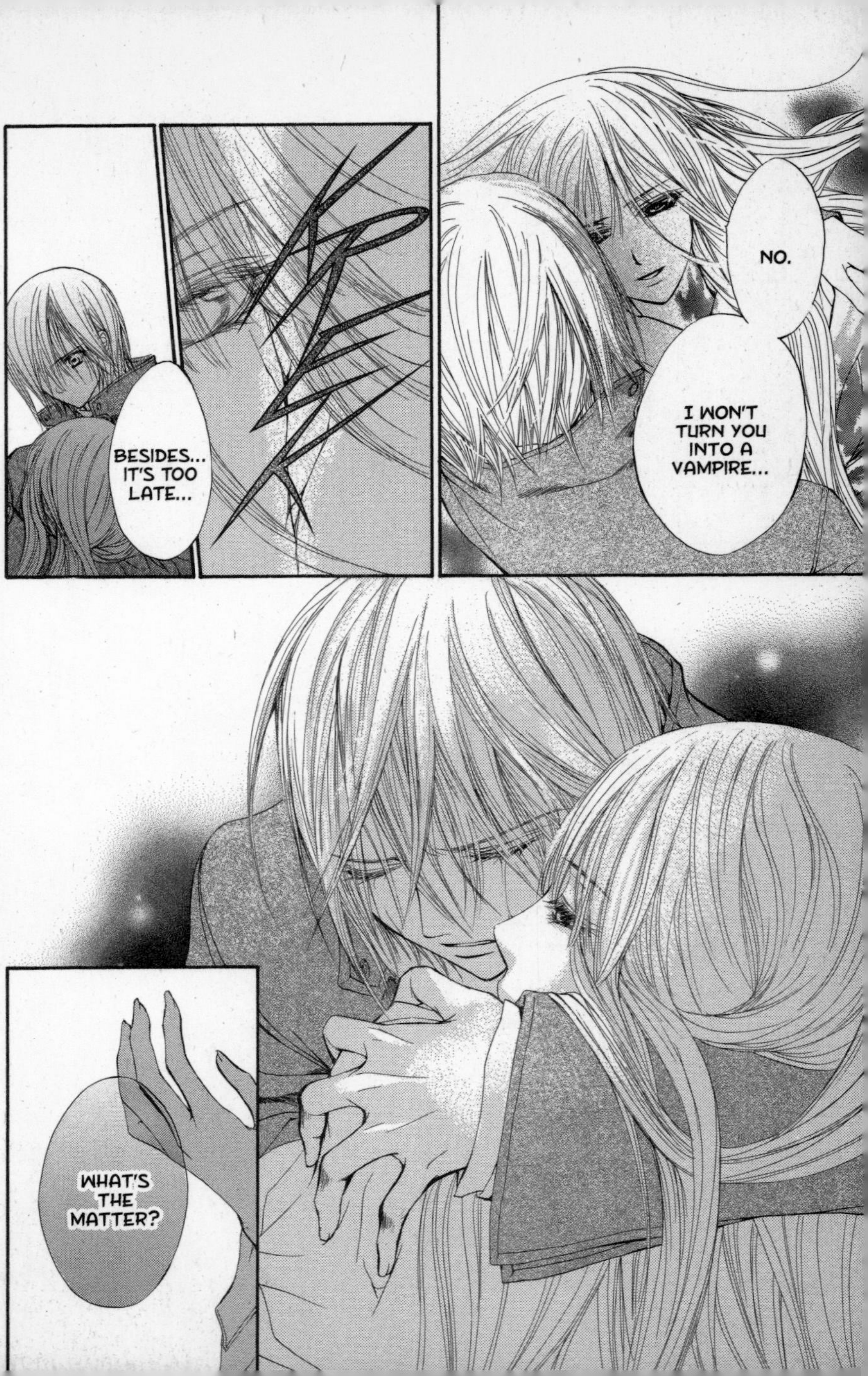
NO.
I WON'T TURN YOU INTO A VAMPIRE...
BESIDES... IT'S TOO LATE...
WHAT'S THE MATTER?

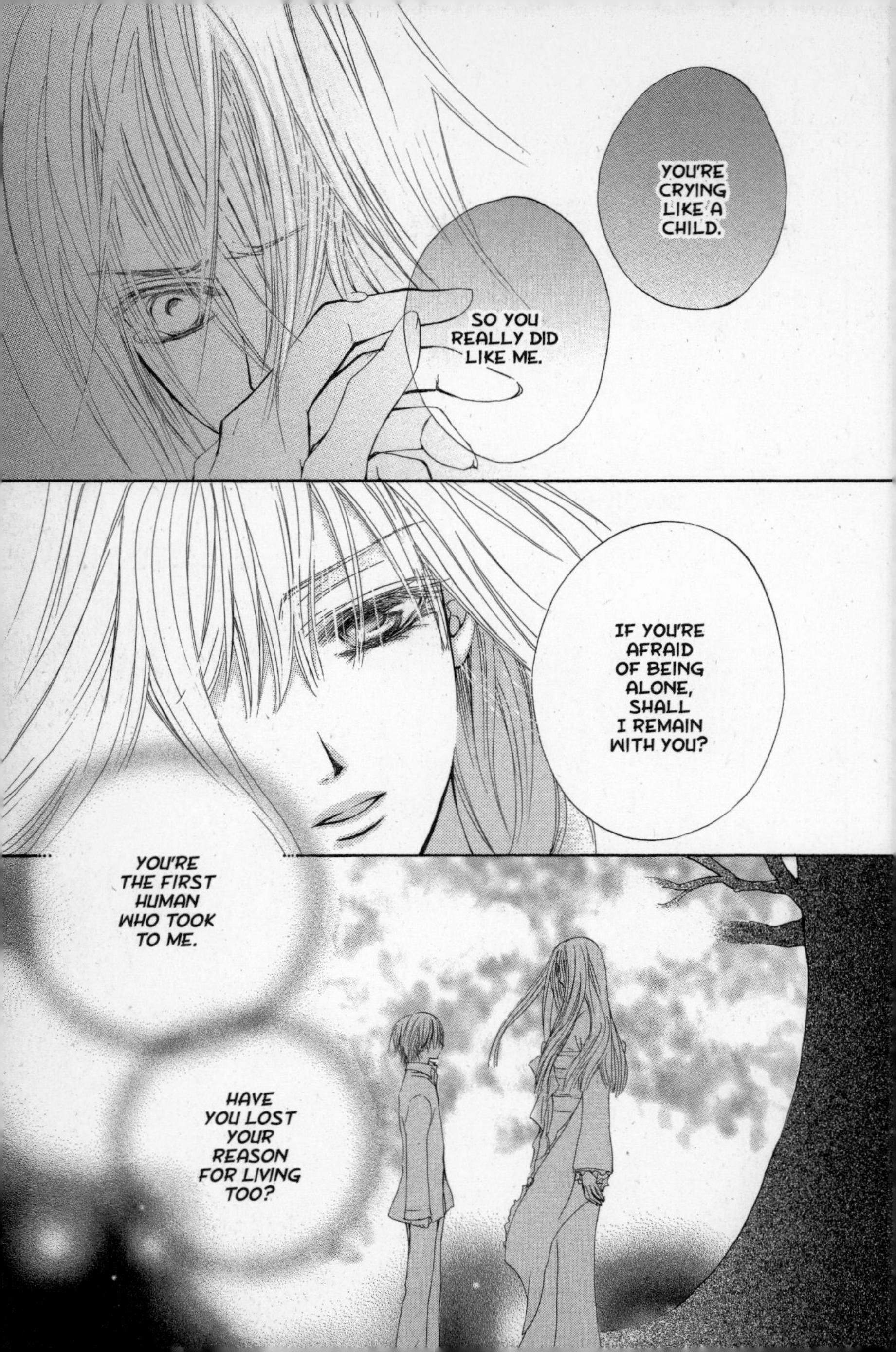
YOU'RE CRYING LIKE A CHILD.
SO YOU REALLY DID LIKE ME.
IF YOU'RE AFRAID OF BEING ALONE, SHALL I REMAIN WITH YOU?
YOU'RE THE FIRST HUMAN WHO TOOK TO ME.
HAVE YOU LOST YOUR REASON FOR LIVING TOO?

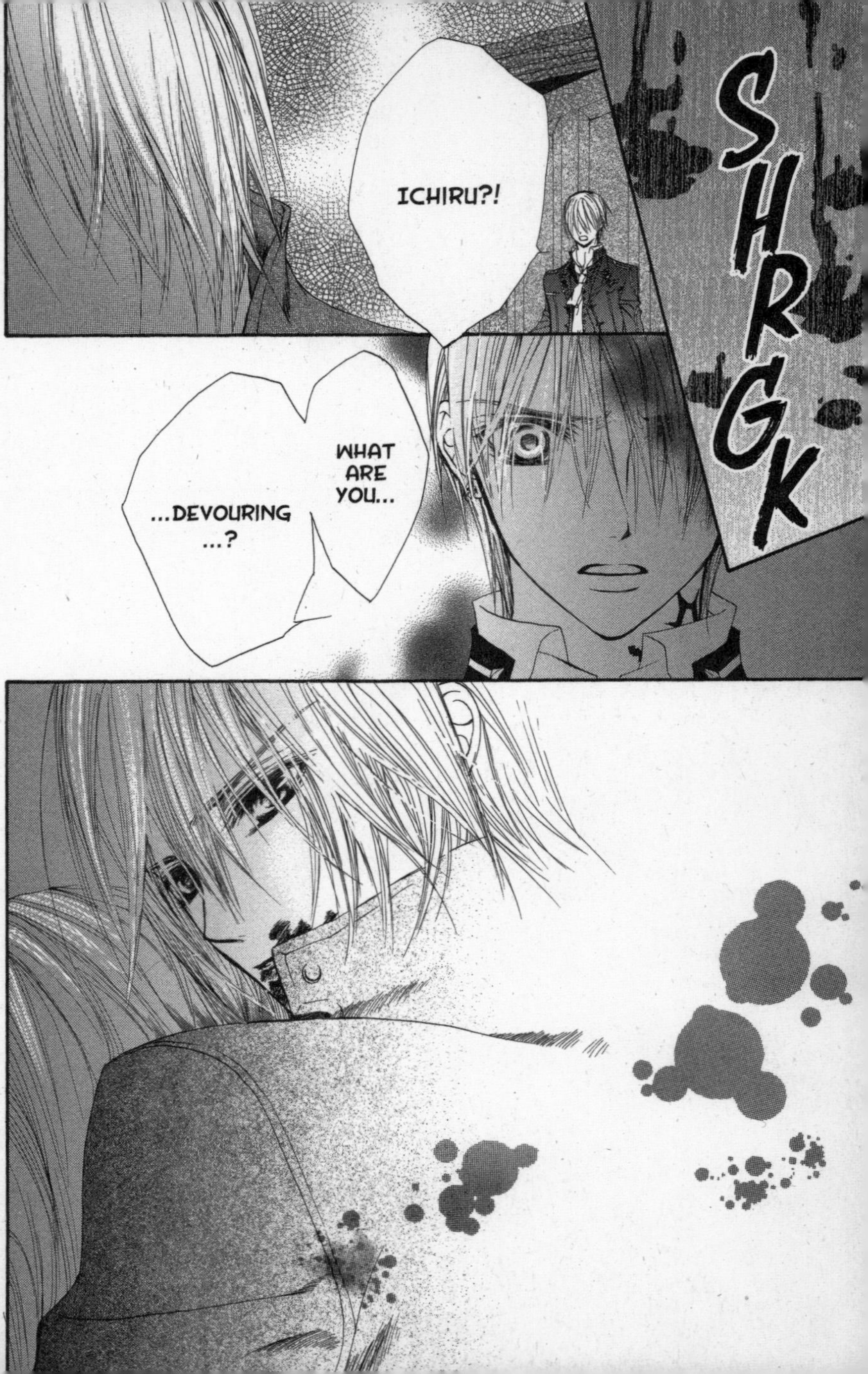
SHRGK
ICHIRU?!
WHAT ARE YOU...
...DEVOURING ...?

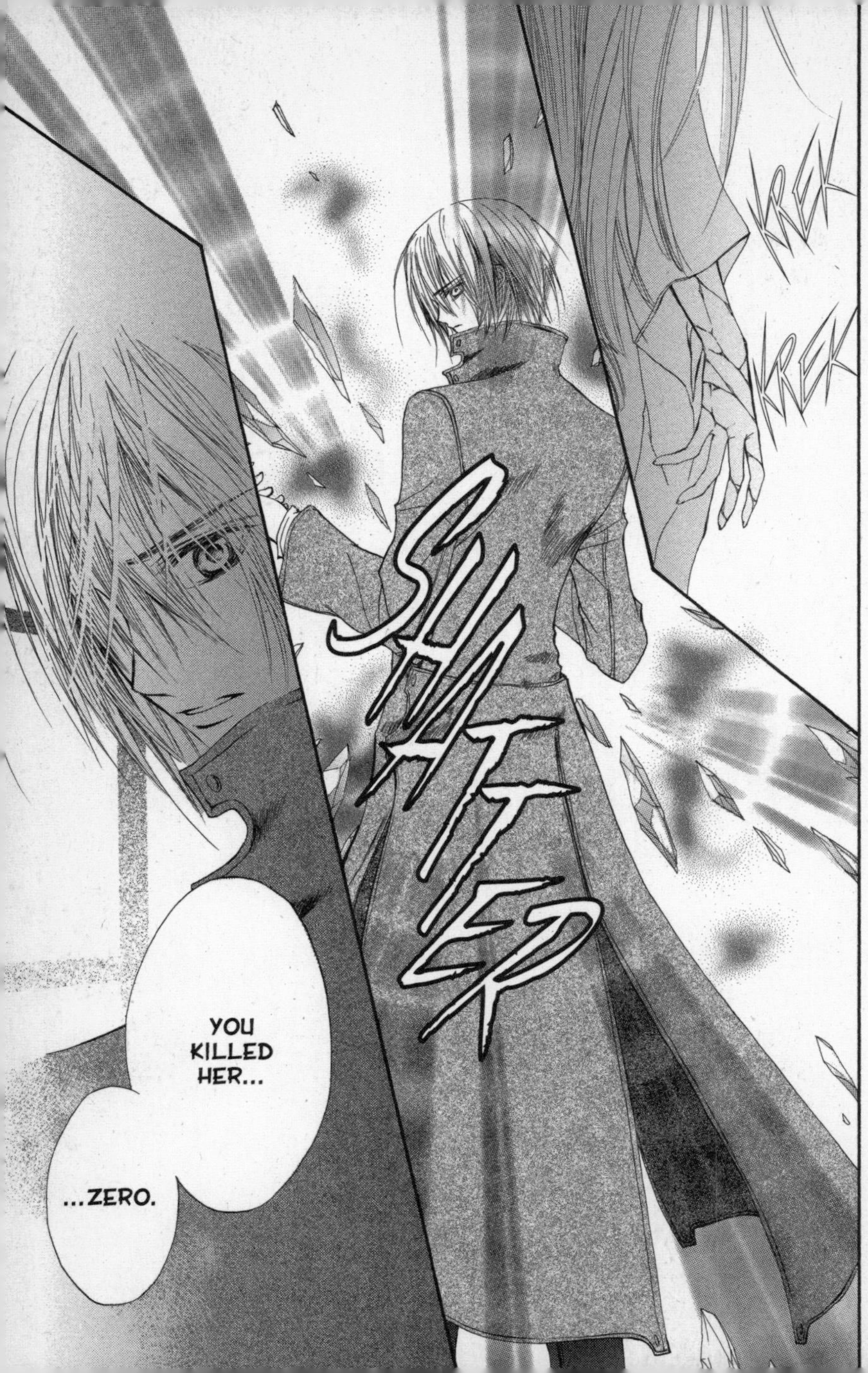
KREK
KREK
SHATTER
YOU KILLED HER...
...ZERO.

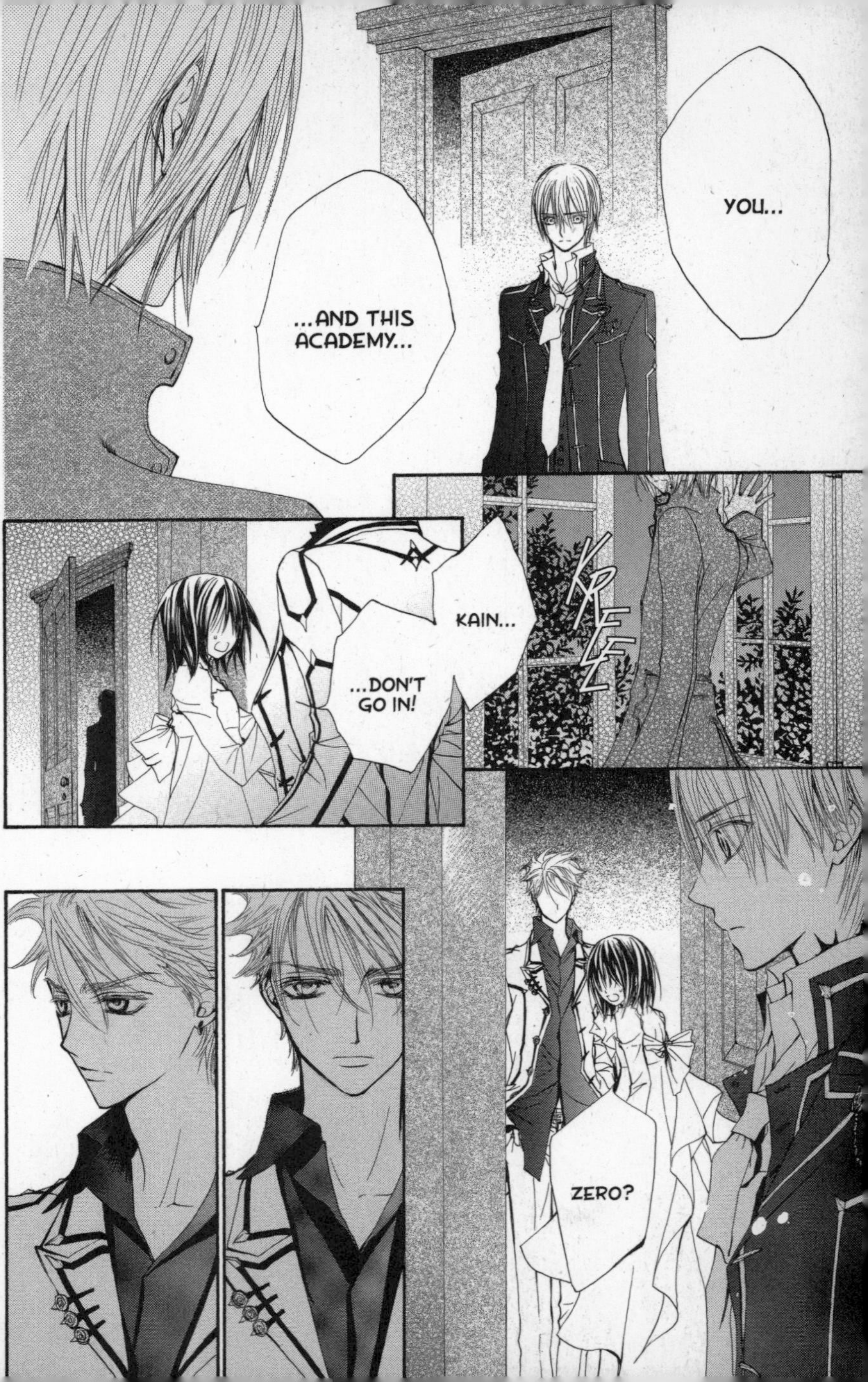
YOU...
...AND THIS ACADEMY...
KREEE
KAIN...
...DON'T GO IN!
ZERO?

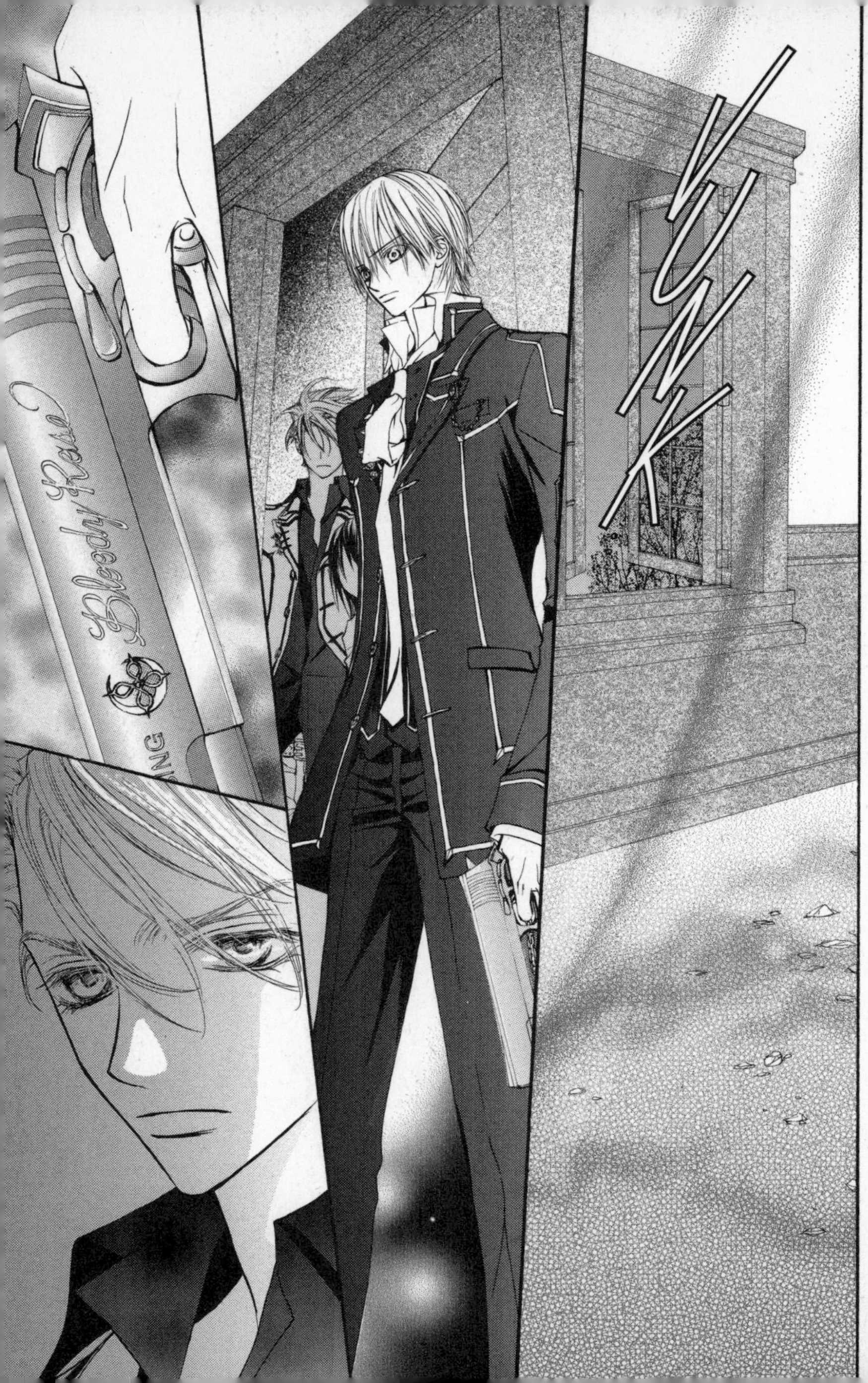
VUNK
Bloody Rose

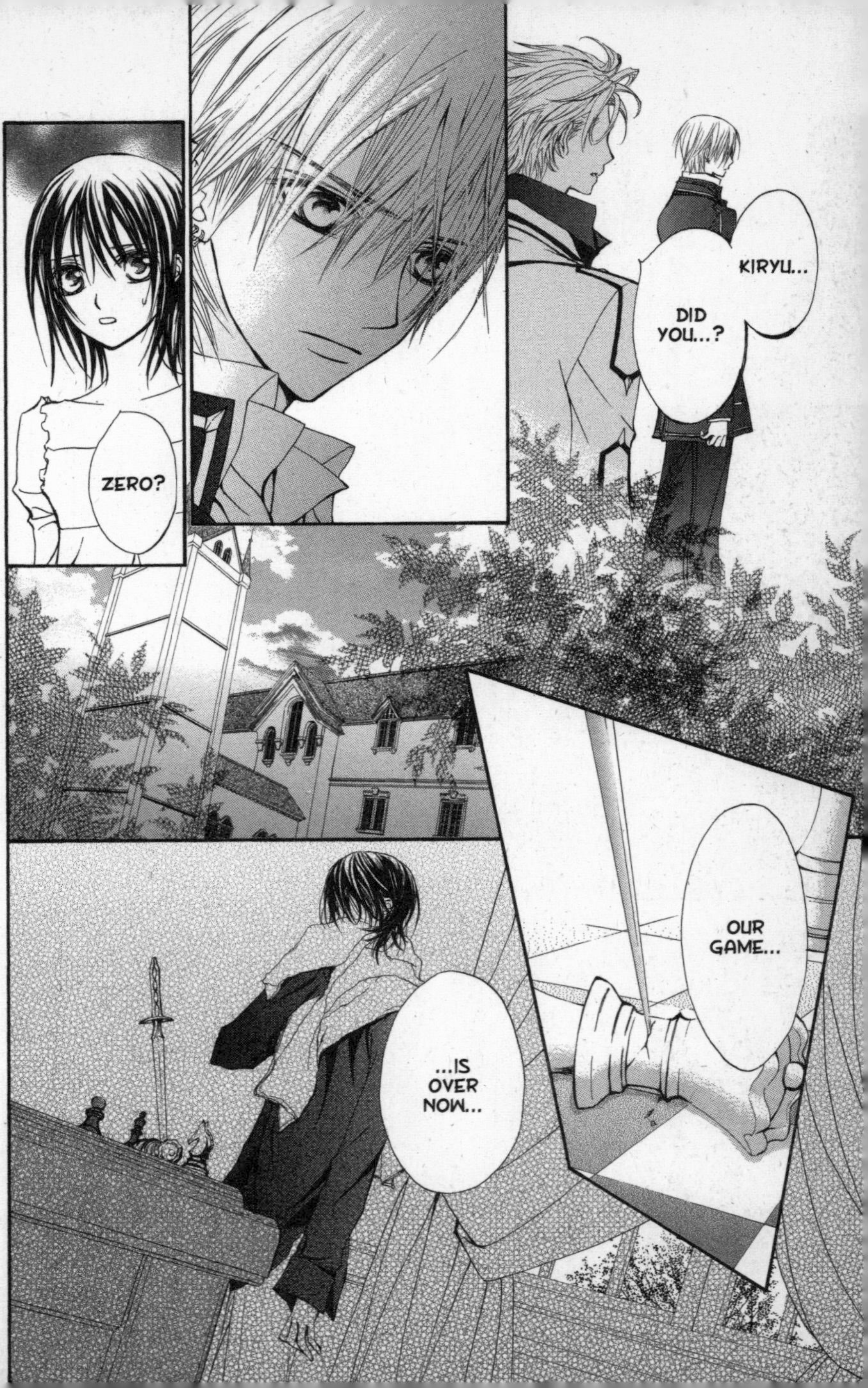
KIRYU...
DID YOU...?
ZERO?
OUR GAME...
...IS OVER NOW...

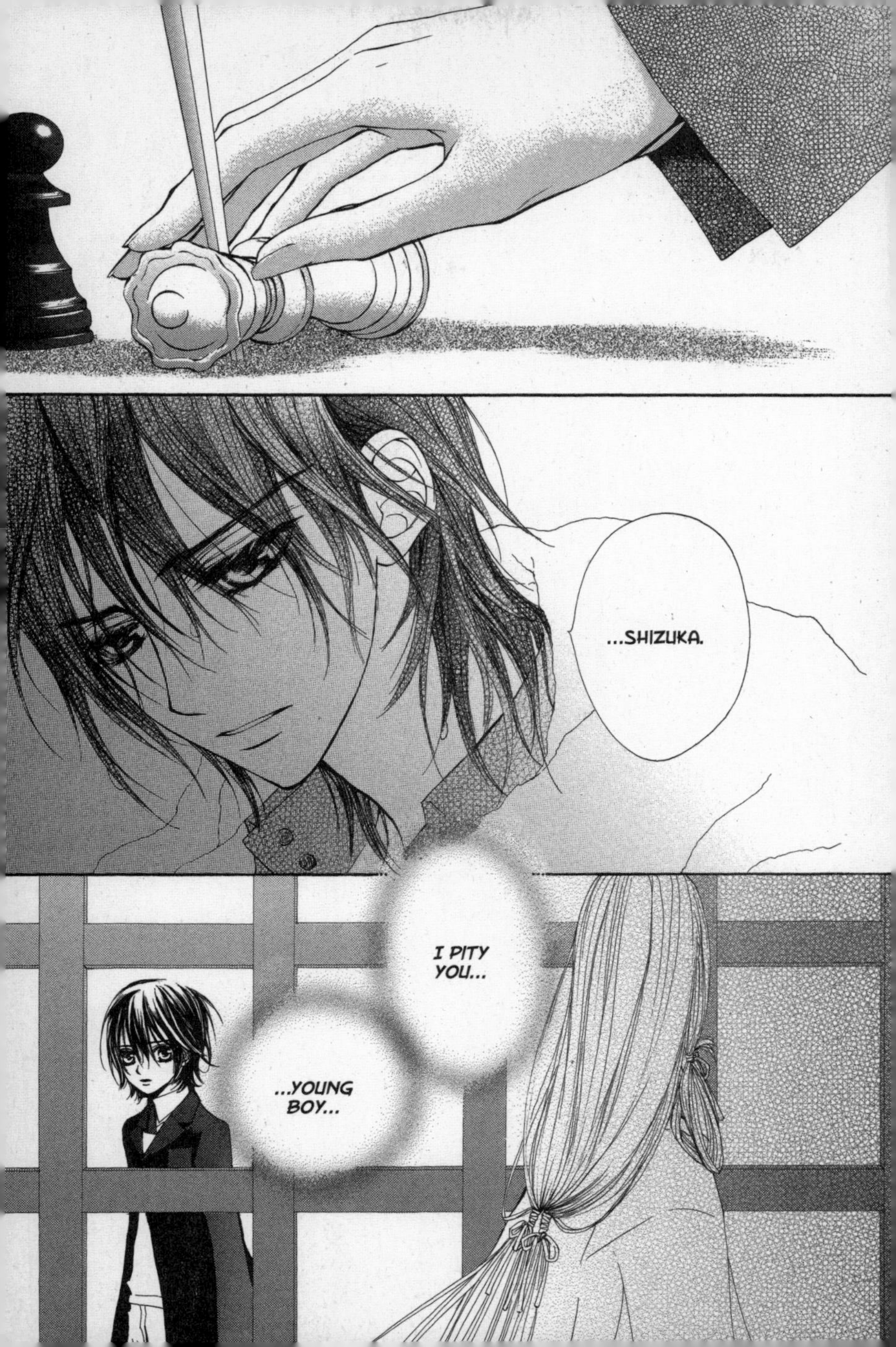
...SHIZUKA.
I PITY YOU...
...YOUNG BOY...

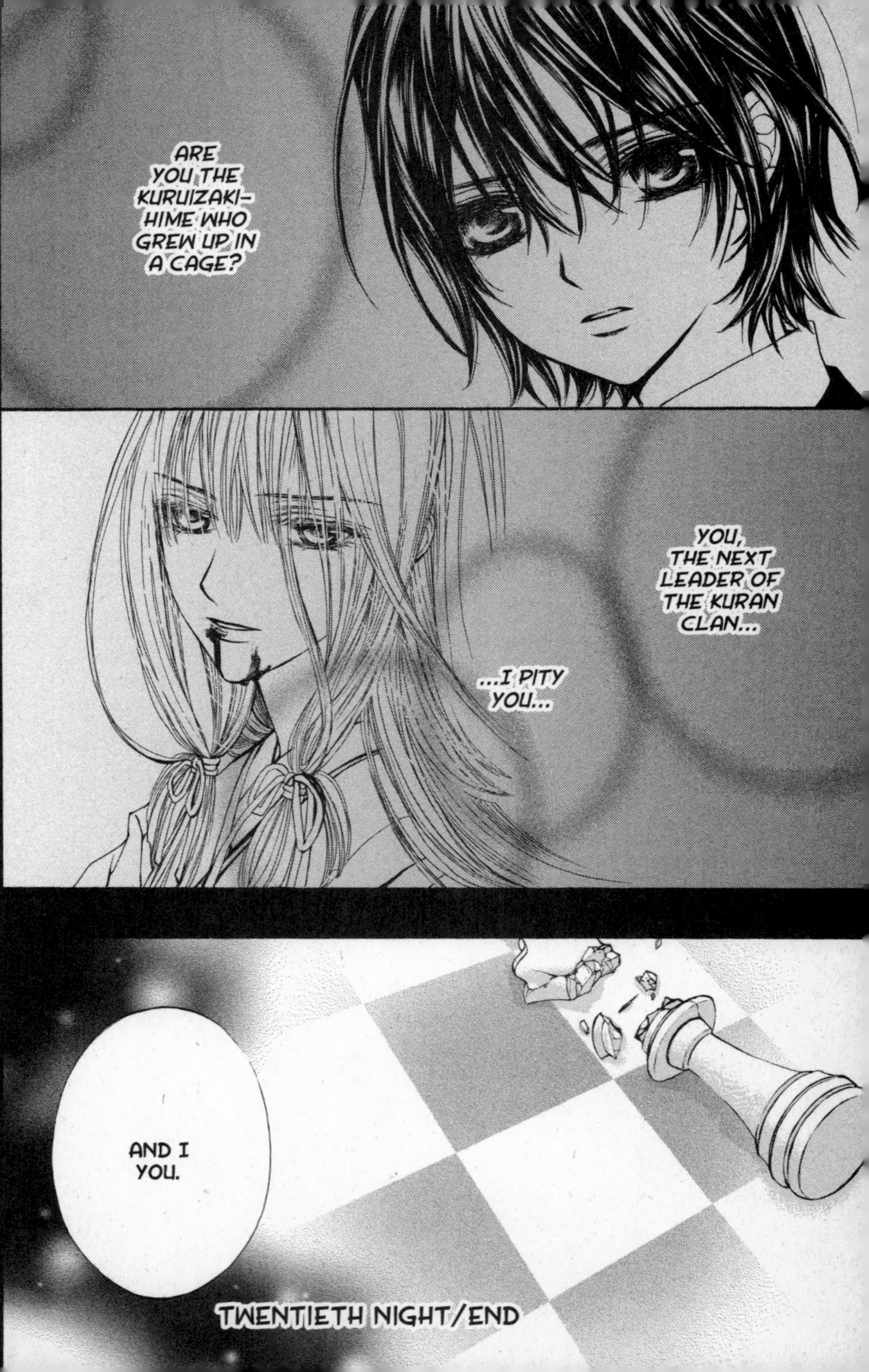
ARE YOU THE KURUIZAKI-HIME WHO GREW UP IN A CAGE?
YOU, THE NEXT LEADER OF THE KURAN CLAN...
...I PITY YOU...
AND I YOU.
TWENTIETH NIGHT/END

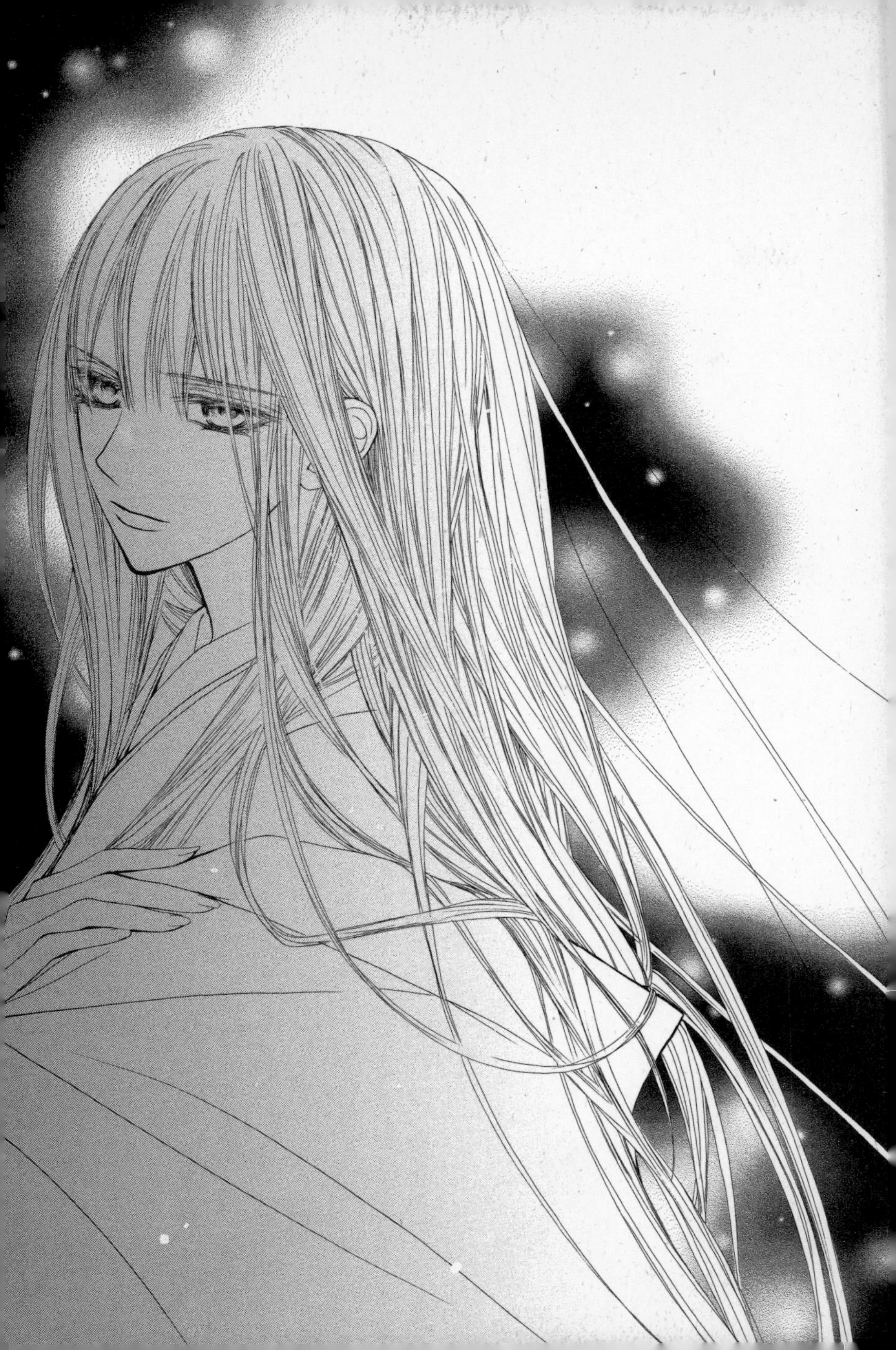

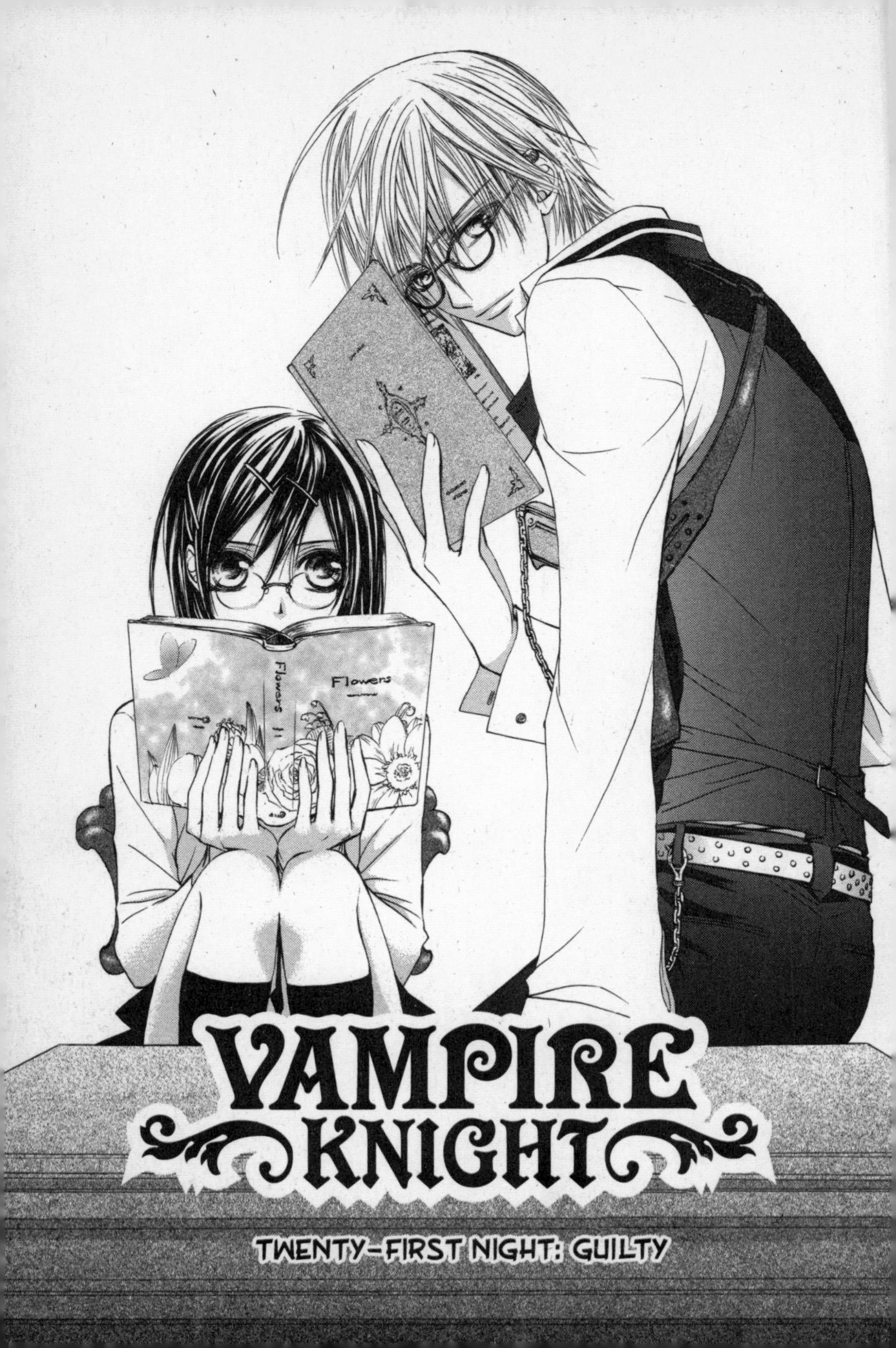
Flowers
Flowers
VAMPIRE KNIGHT
TWENTY-FIRST NIGHT: GUILTY

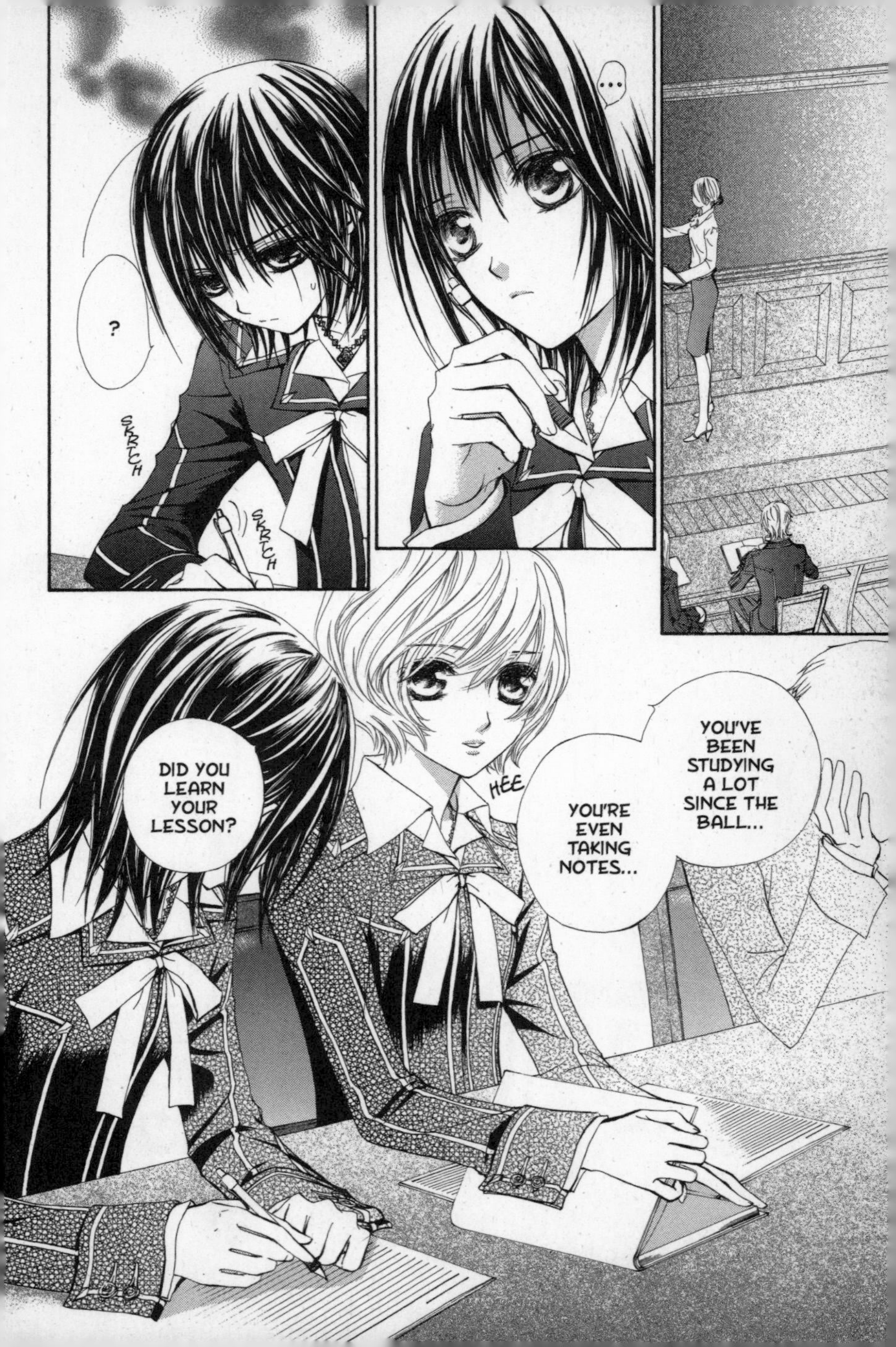
...
?
SKRTCH
SKRTCH
YOU'VE BEEN STUDYING A LOT SINCE THE BALL...
YOU'RE EVEN TAKING NOTES...
HEE
DID YOU LEARN YOUR LESSON?

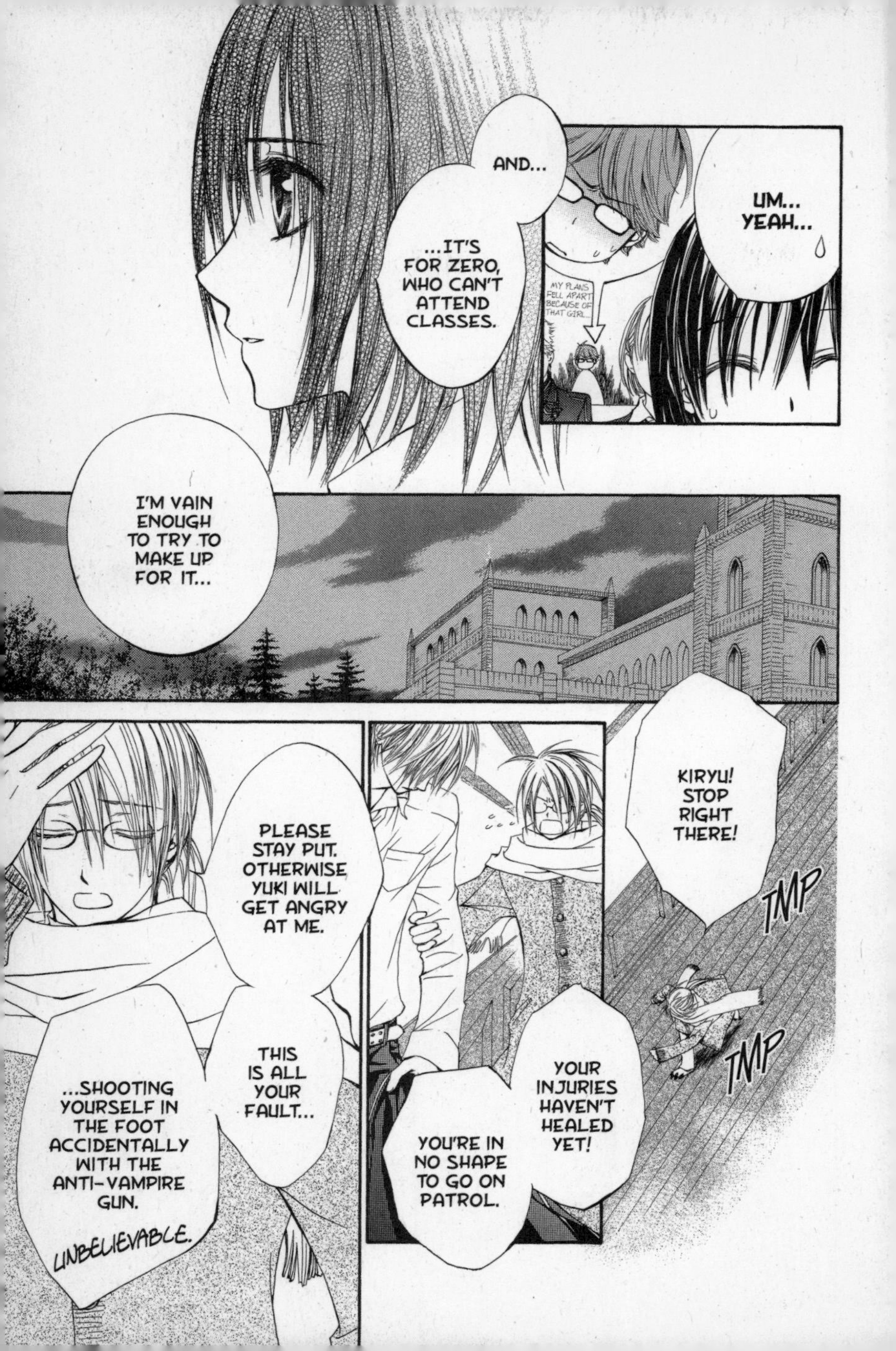
AND...
...IT'S FOR ZERO, WHO CAN'T ATTEND CLASSES.
UM... YEAH...
MY PLANS FELL APART BECAUSE OF THAT GIRL...
I'M VAIN ENOUGH TO TRY TO MAKE UP FOR IT...
KIRYU! STOP RIGHT THERE!
TMP
TMP
YOUR INJURIES HAVEN'T HEALED YET!
YOU'RE IN NO SHAPE TO GO ON PATROL.
PLEASE STAY PUT. OTHERWISE YUKI WILL GET ANGRY AT ME.
THIS IS ALL YOUR FAULT...
...SHOOTING YOURSELF IN THE FOOT ACCIDENTALLY WITH THE ANTI-VAMPIRE GUN.
UNBELIEVABLE.

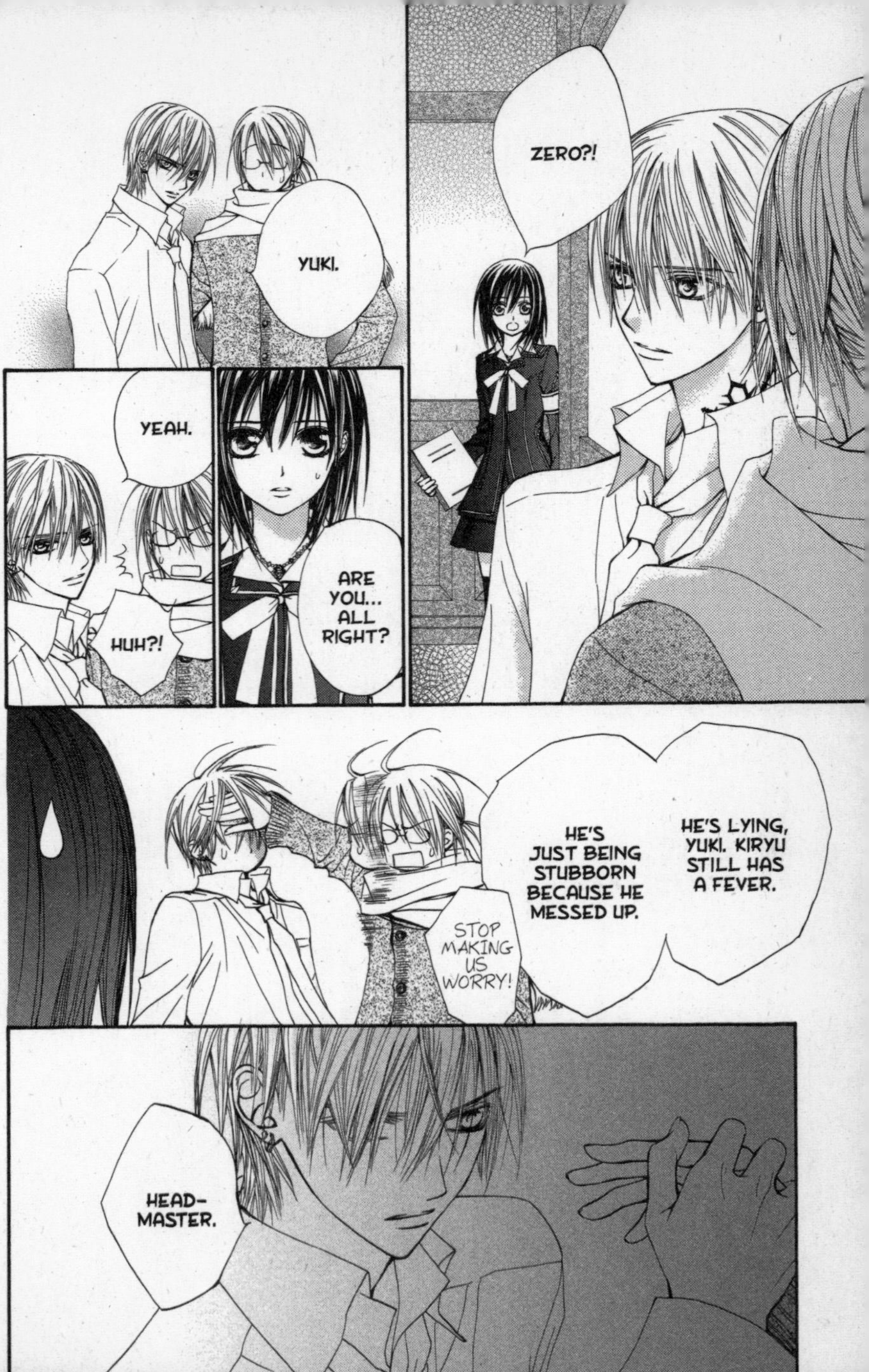
ZERO?!
YUKI.
ARE YOU... ALL RIGHT?
YEAH.
HUH?!
HE'S LYING, YUKI. KIRYU STILL HAS A FEVER.
HE'S JUST BEING STUBBORN BECAUSE HE MESSED UP.
STOP MAKING US WORRY!
HEAD-MASTER.

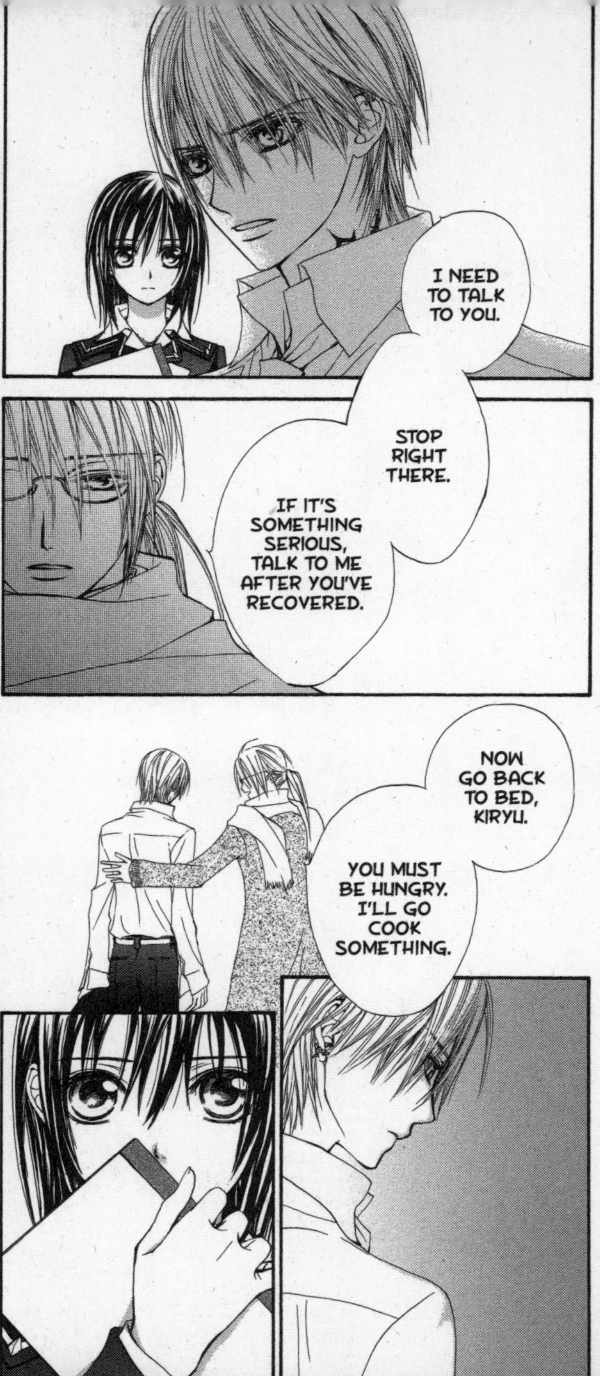
I NEED TO TALK TO YOU.
STOP RIGHT THERE.
IF IT'S SOMETHING SERIOUS, TALK TO ME AFTER YOU'VE RECOVERED.
NOW GO BACK TO BED, KIRYU.
YOU MUST BE HUNGRY. I'LL GO COOK SOMETHING.

III

Ahhh. I have to do my best with what's going on in the manga...

Every single time, things never go smoothly.

Various things...
Various things...

And when I get stuck, I still talk about MeruPuri with my editor. The last time I counted, it was translated and published in 15 countries.

I'm really interested in the cultural differences in those countries. Kiss scenes were made fuzzy in one, and a school PTA added MeruPuri to the recommended reading list for children's books. (This would never happen in Japan!!) Due to those small launches overseas, VIZ Media invited me to the U.S last year, and I had a chance to meet with readers there.

↓(continues)

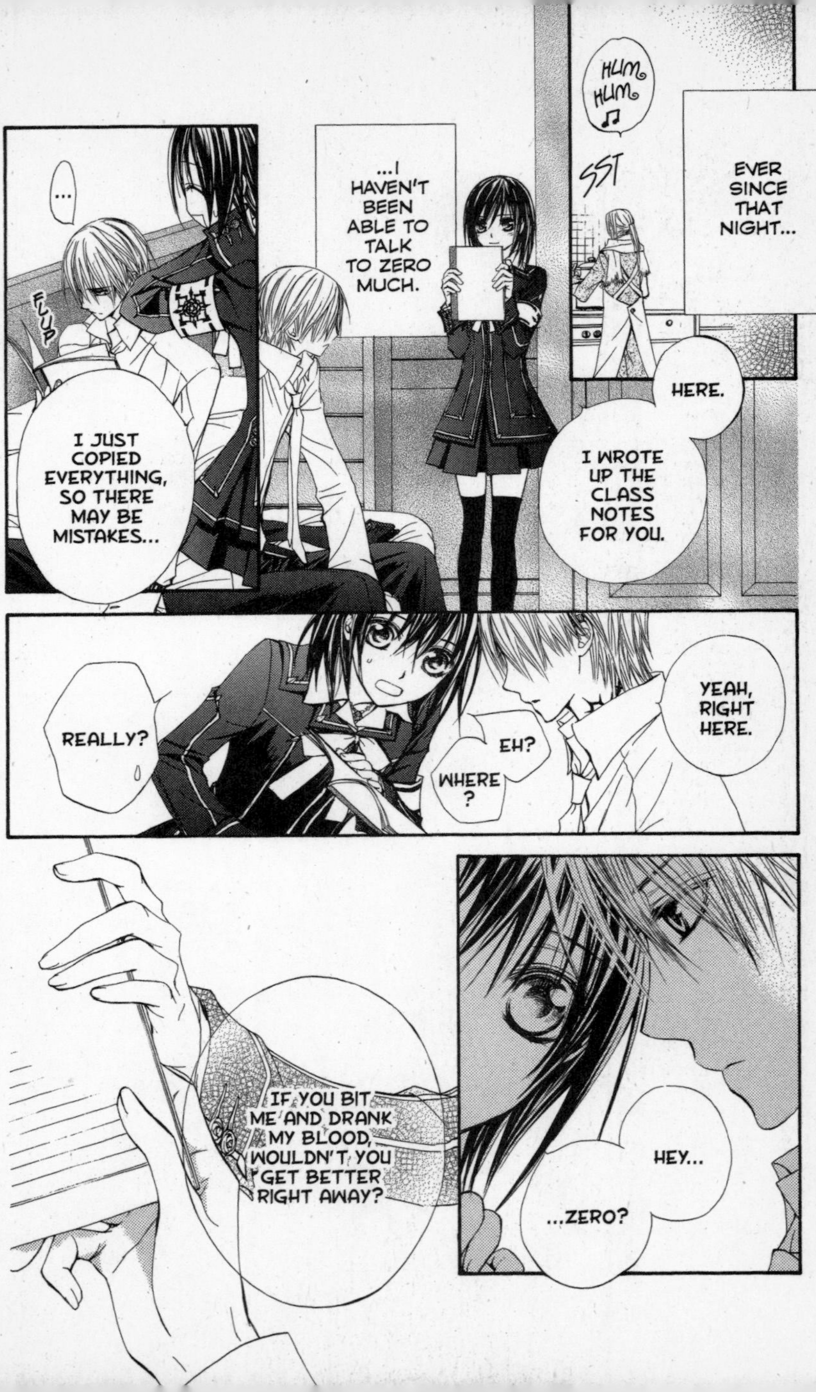
HUM HUM ♫
SST
EVER SINCE THAT NIGHT...
...I HAVEN'T BEEN ABLE TO TALK TO ZERO MUCH.
HERE.
I WROTE UP THE CLASS NOTES FOR YOU.
...
FLUP
I JUST COPIED EVERYTHING, SO THERE MAY BE MISTAKES...
YEAH, RIGHT HERE.
EH?
WHERE?
REALLY?
HEY...
...ZERO?
IF YOU BIT ME AND DRANK MY BLOOD, WOULDN'T YOU GET BETTER RIGHT AWAY?

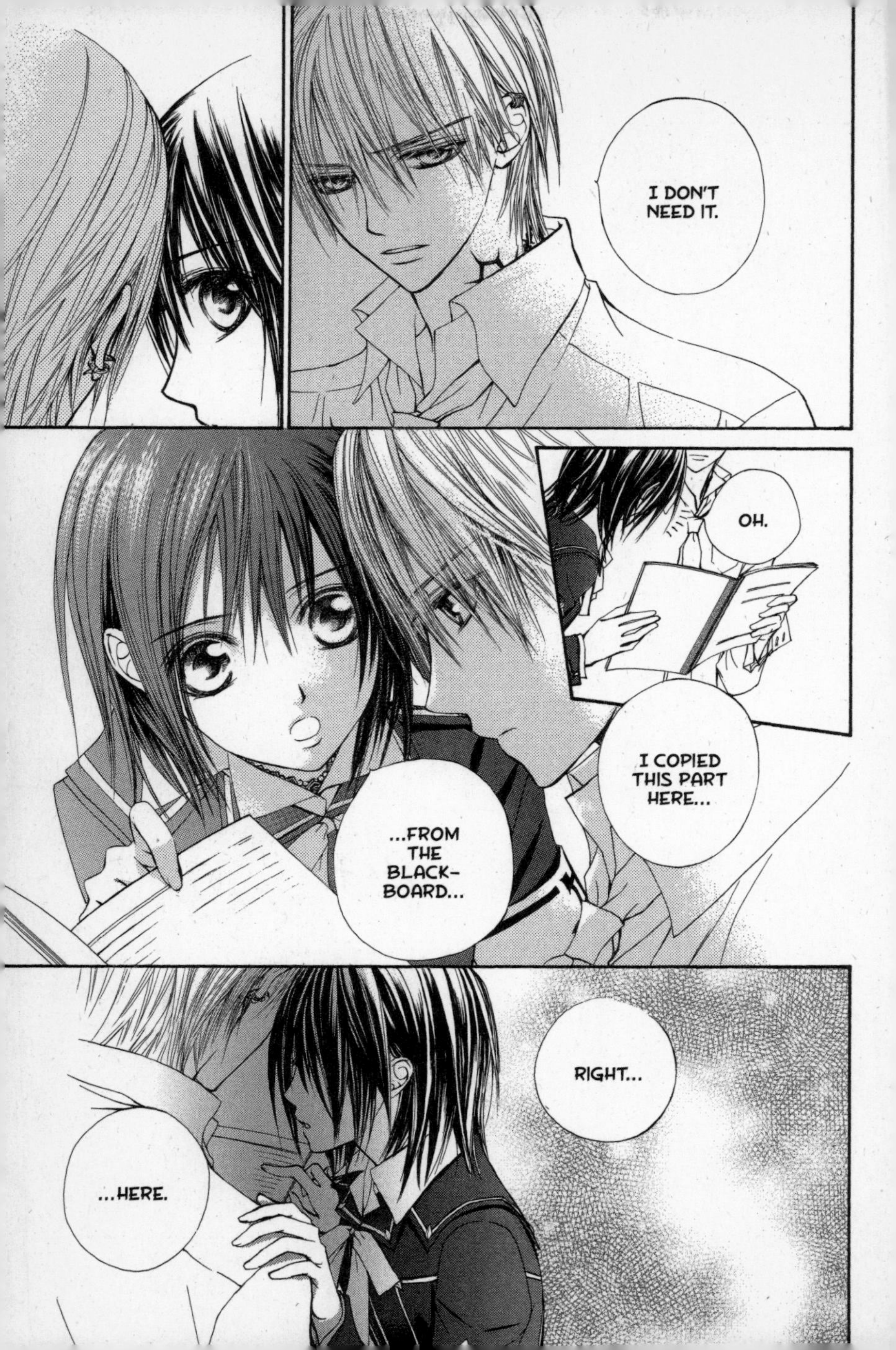
I DON'T NEED IT.
OH.
I COPIED THIS PART HERE...
...FROM THE BLACK-BOARD...
RIGHT...
...HERE.

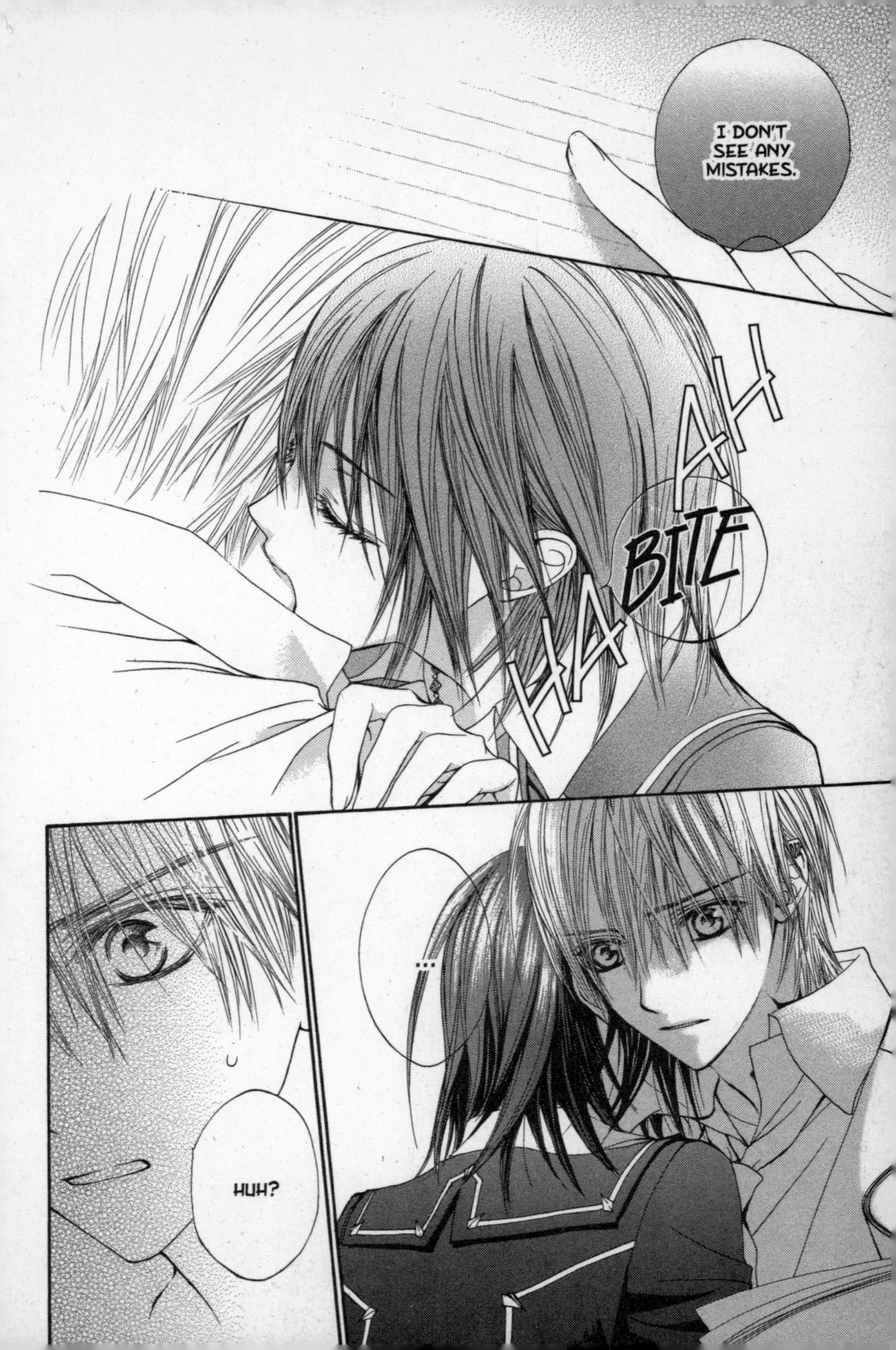

I DON'T SEE ANY MISTAKES.
HAAH
BITE
...
HUH?

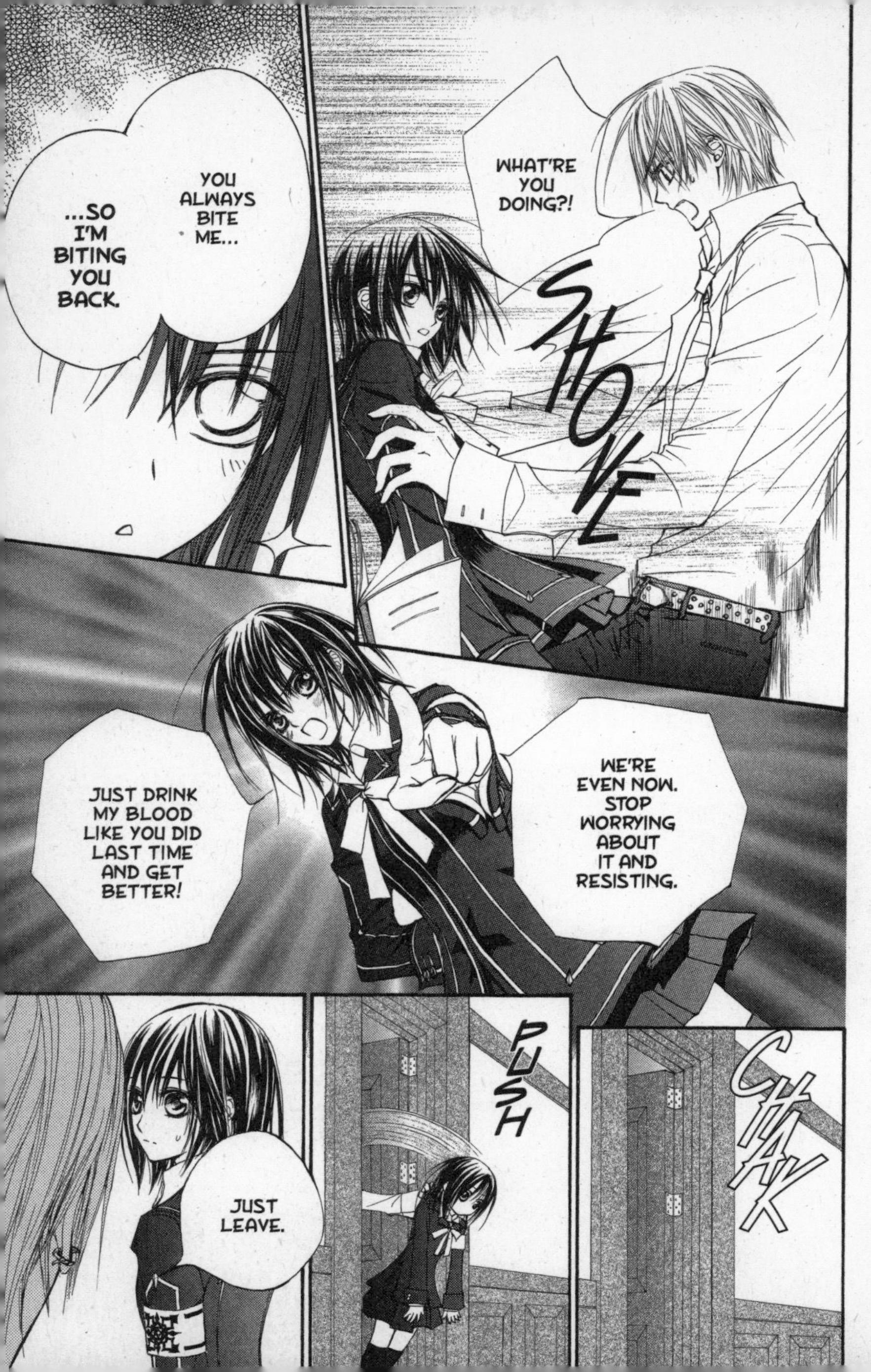
WHAT'RE YOU DOING?!
SHOVE
YOU ALWAYS BITE ME...
...SO I'M BITING YOU BACK.
WE'RE EVEN NOW. STOP WORRYING ABOUT IT AND RESISTING.
JUST DRINK MY BLOOD LIKE YOU DID LAST TIME AND GET BETTER!
CHAK
PUSH
JUST LEAVE.

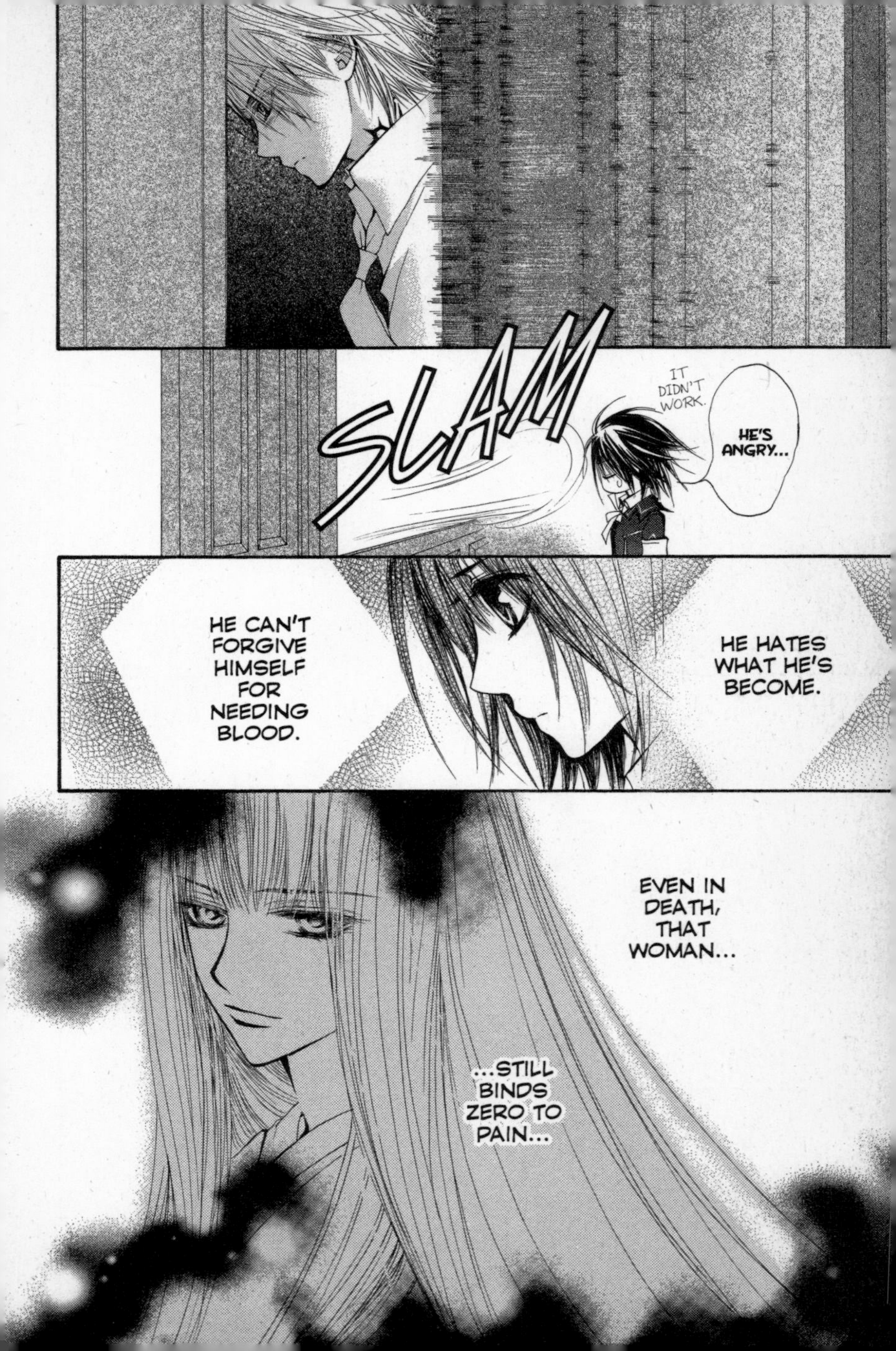
HE'S ANGRY...
IT DIDN'T WORK.
SLAM
HE HATES WHAT HE'S BECOME.
HE CAN'T FORGIVE HIMSELF FOR NEEDING BLOOD.
EVEN IN DEATH, THAT WOMAN...
...STILL BINDS ZERO TO PAIN...

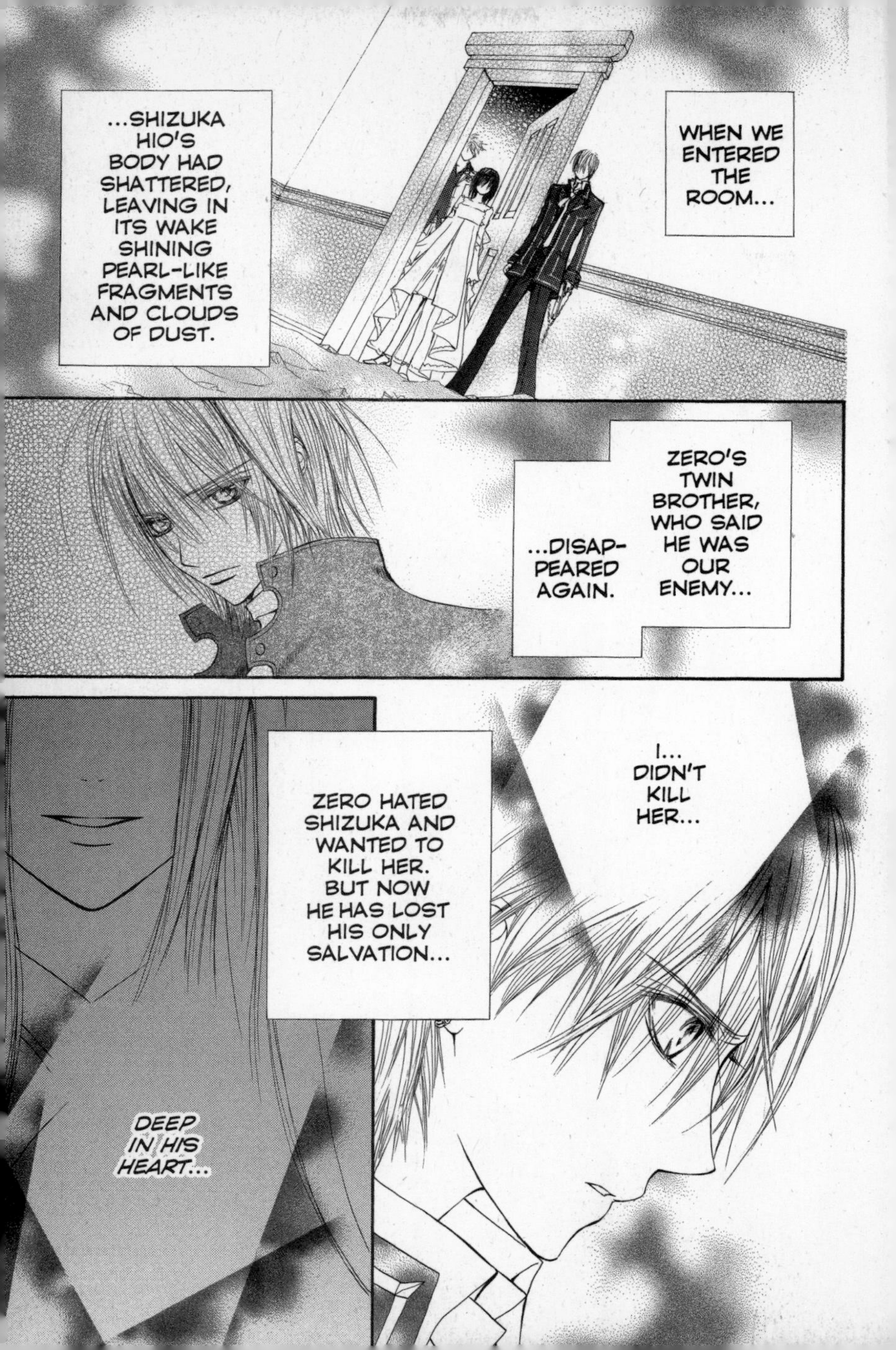
WHEN WE ENTERED THE ROOM...
...SHIZUKA HIO'S BODY HAD SHATTERED, LEAVING IN ITS WAKE SHINING PEARL-LIKE FRAGMENTS AND CLOUDS OF DUST.
ZERO'S TWIN BROTHER, WHO SAID HE WAS OUR ENEMY...
...DISAPPEARED AGAIN.
I... DIDN'T KILL HER...
ZERO HATED SHIZUKA AND WANTED TO KILL HER. BUT NOW HE HAS LOST HIS ONLY SALVATION...
DEEP IN HIS HEART...

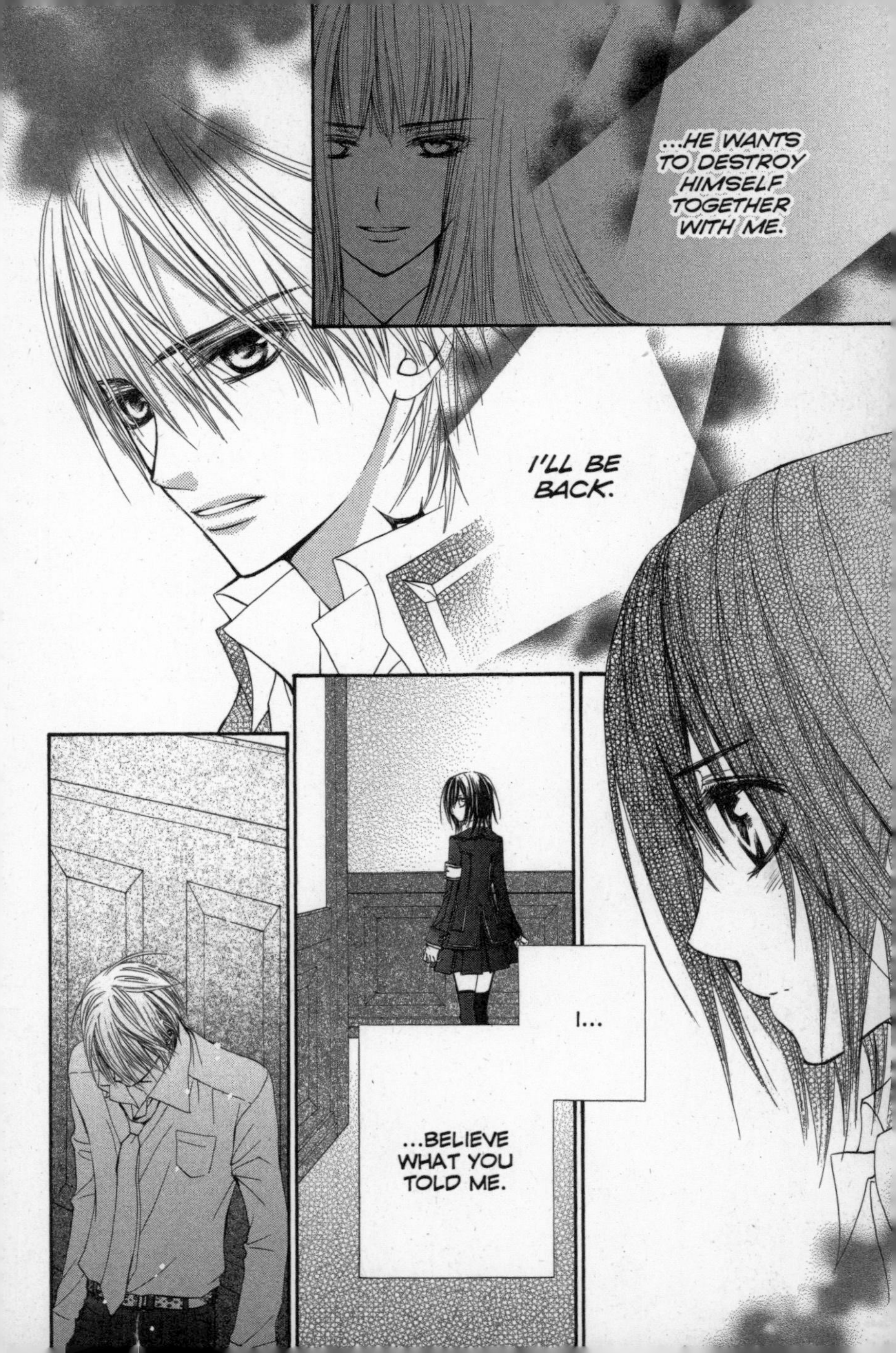
...HE WANTS TO DESTROY HIMSELF TOGETHER WITH ME.
I'LL BE BACK.
I...
...BELIEVE WHAT YOU TOLD ME.

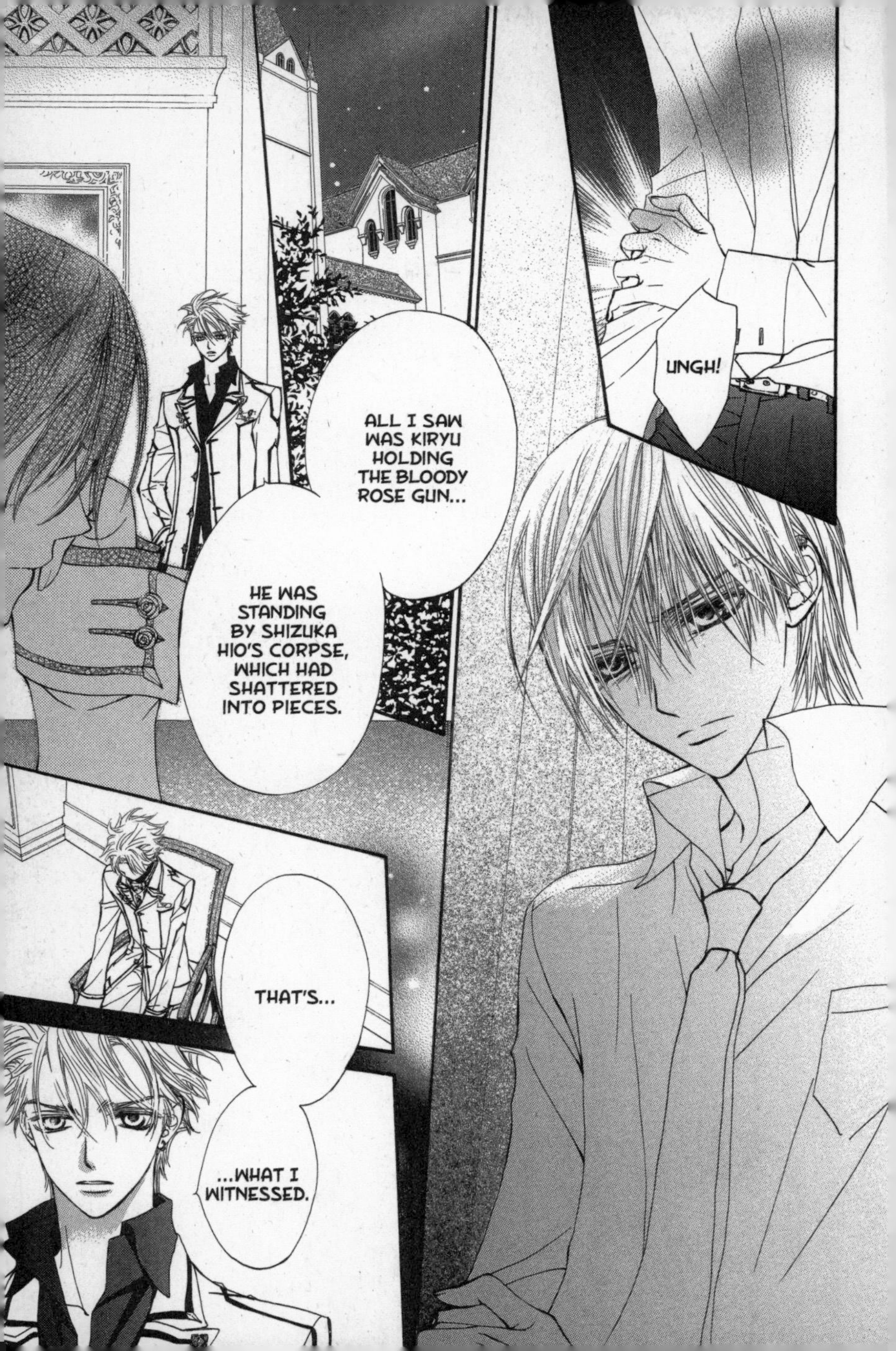
UNGH!
ALL I SAW WAS KIRYU HOLDING THE BLOODY ROSE GUN...
HE WAS STANDING BY SHIZUKA HIO'S CORPSE, WHICH HAD SHATTERED INTO PIECES.
THAT'S...
...WHAT I WITNESSED.

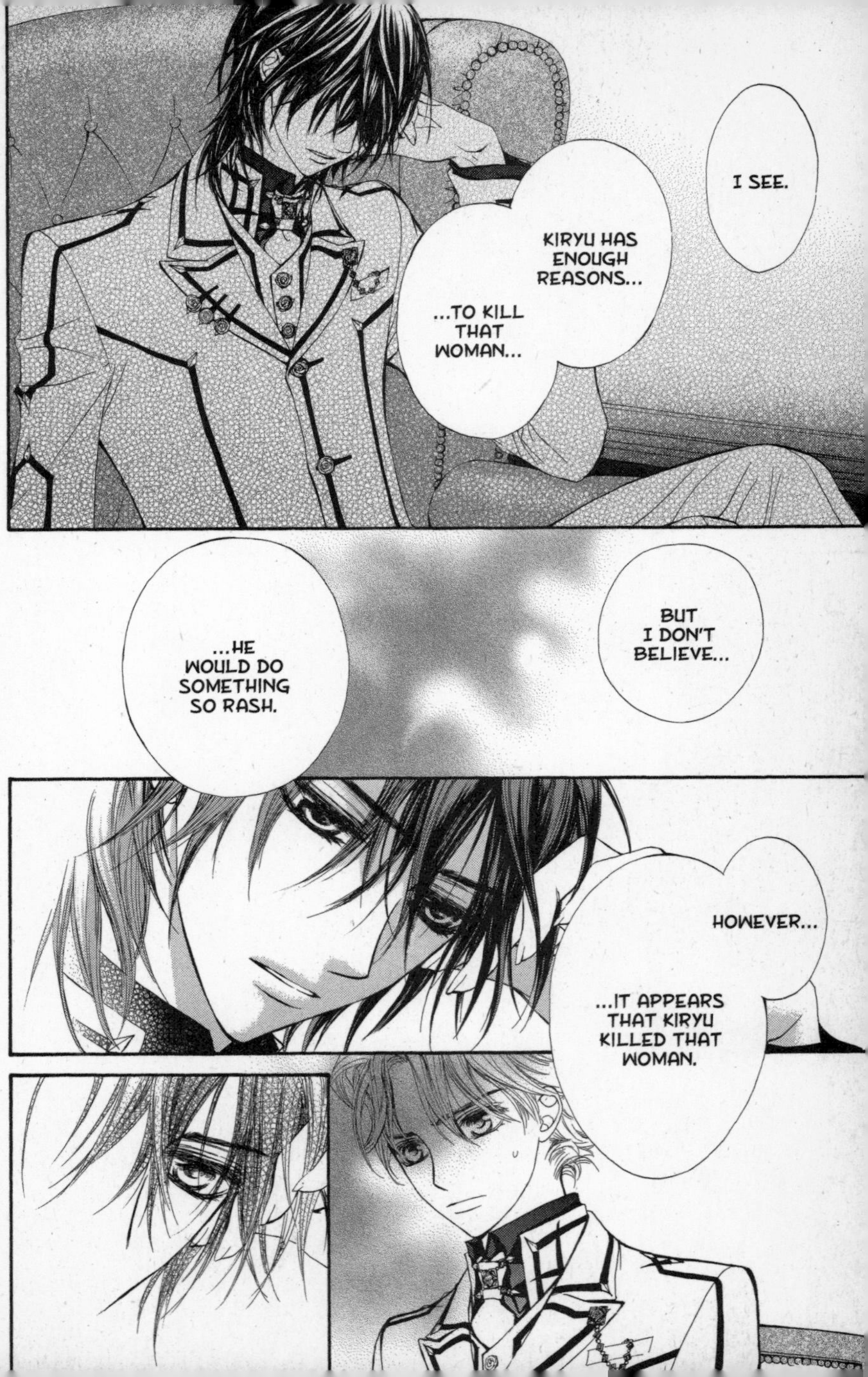
I SEE.
KIRYU HAS ENOUGH REASONS...
...TO KILL THAT WOMAN...
BUT I DON'T BELIEVE...
...HE WOULD DO SOMETHING SO RASH.
HOWEVER...
...IT APPEARS THAT KIRYU KILLED THAT WOMAN.

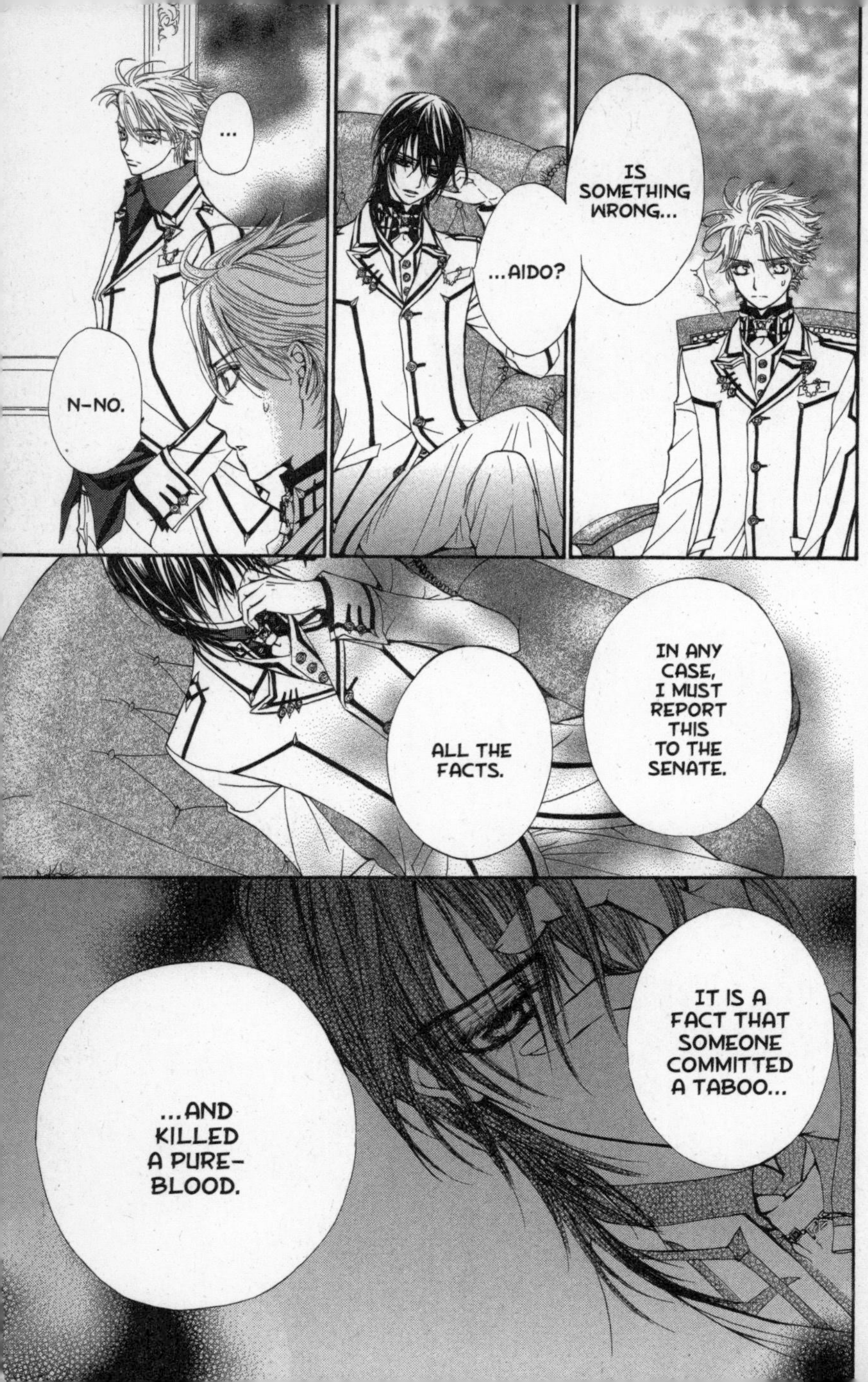
IS SOMETHING WRONG...
...AIDO?
...
N-NO.
IN ANY CASE, I MUST REPORT THIS TO THE SENATE.
ALL THE FACTS.
IT IS A FACT THAT SOMEONE COMMITTED A TABOO...
...AND KILLED A PURE-BLOOD.

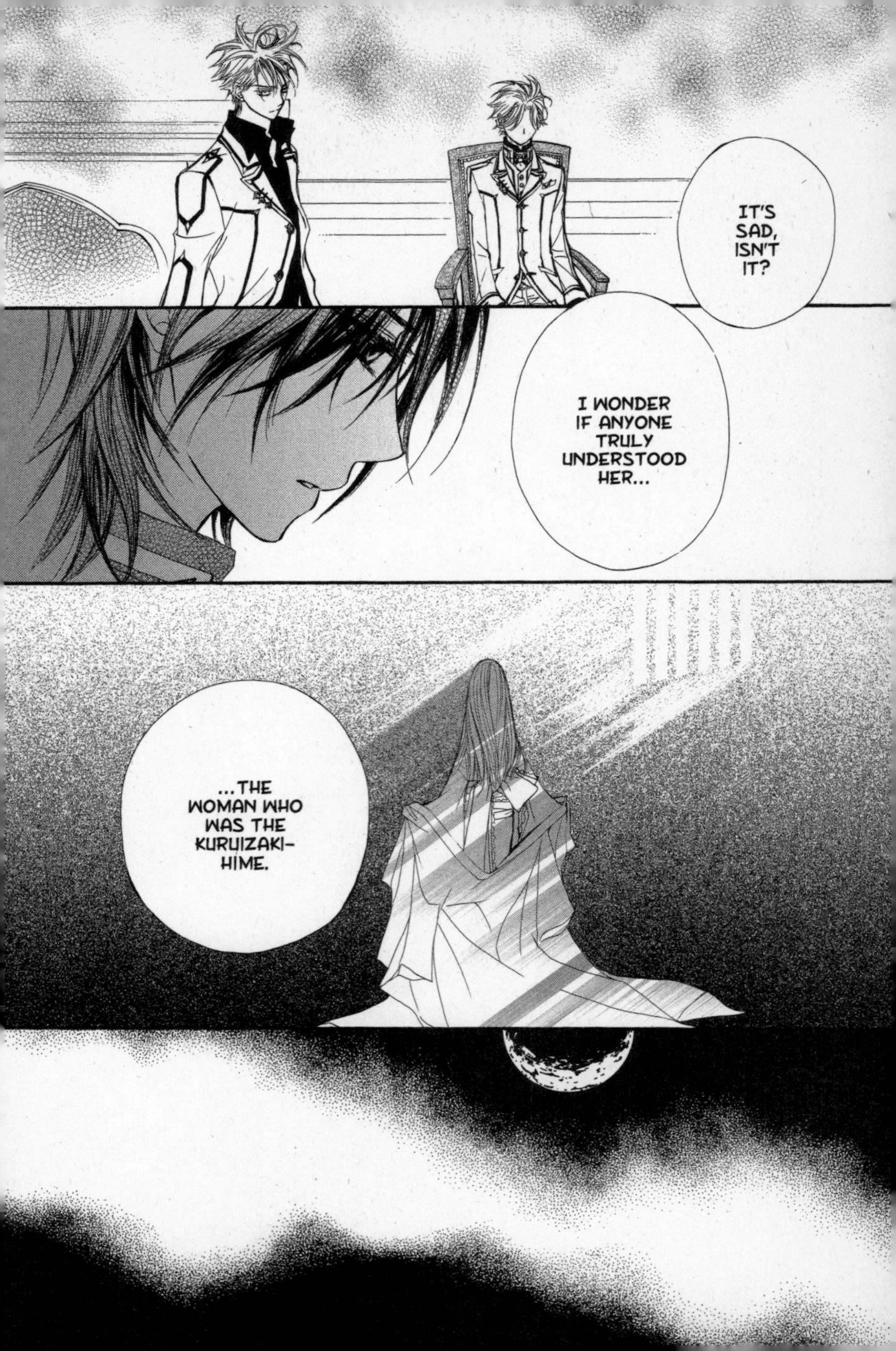
IT'S SAD, ISN'T IT?
I WONDER IF ANYONE TRULY UNDERSTOOD HER...
...THE WOMAN WHO WAS THE KURUIZAKI-HIME.

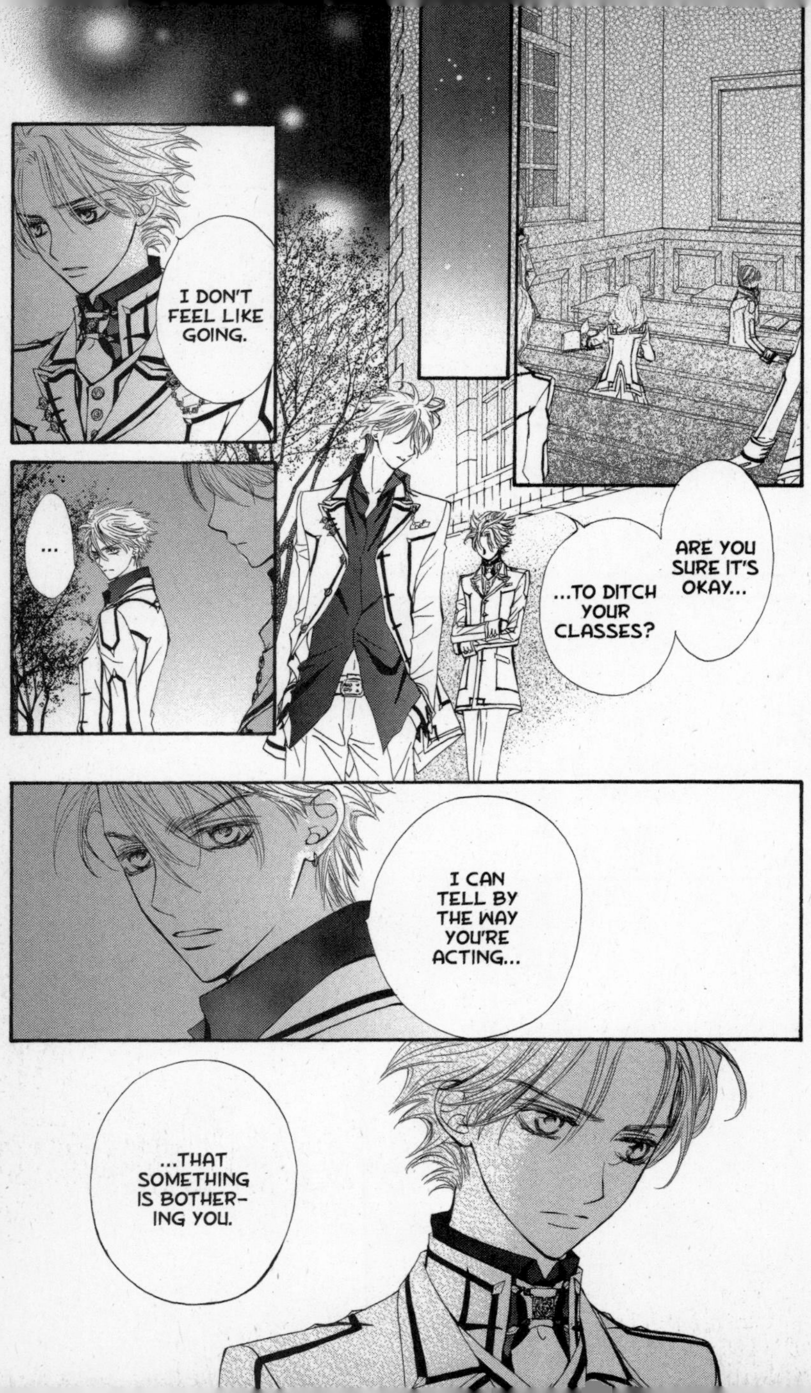
ARE YOU SURE IT'S OKAY...
...TO DITCH YOUR CLASSES?
I DON'T FEEL LIKE GOING.
...
I CAN TELL BY THE WAY YOU'RE ACTING...
...THAT SOMETHING IS BOTHER-ING YOU.

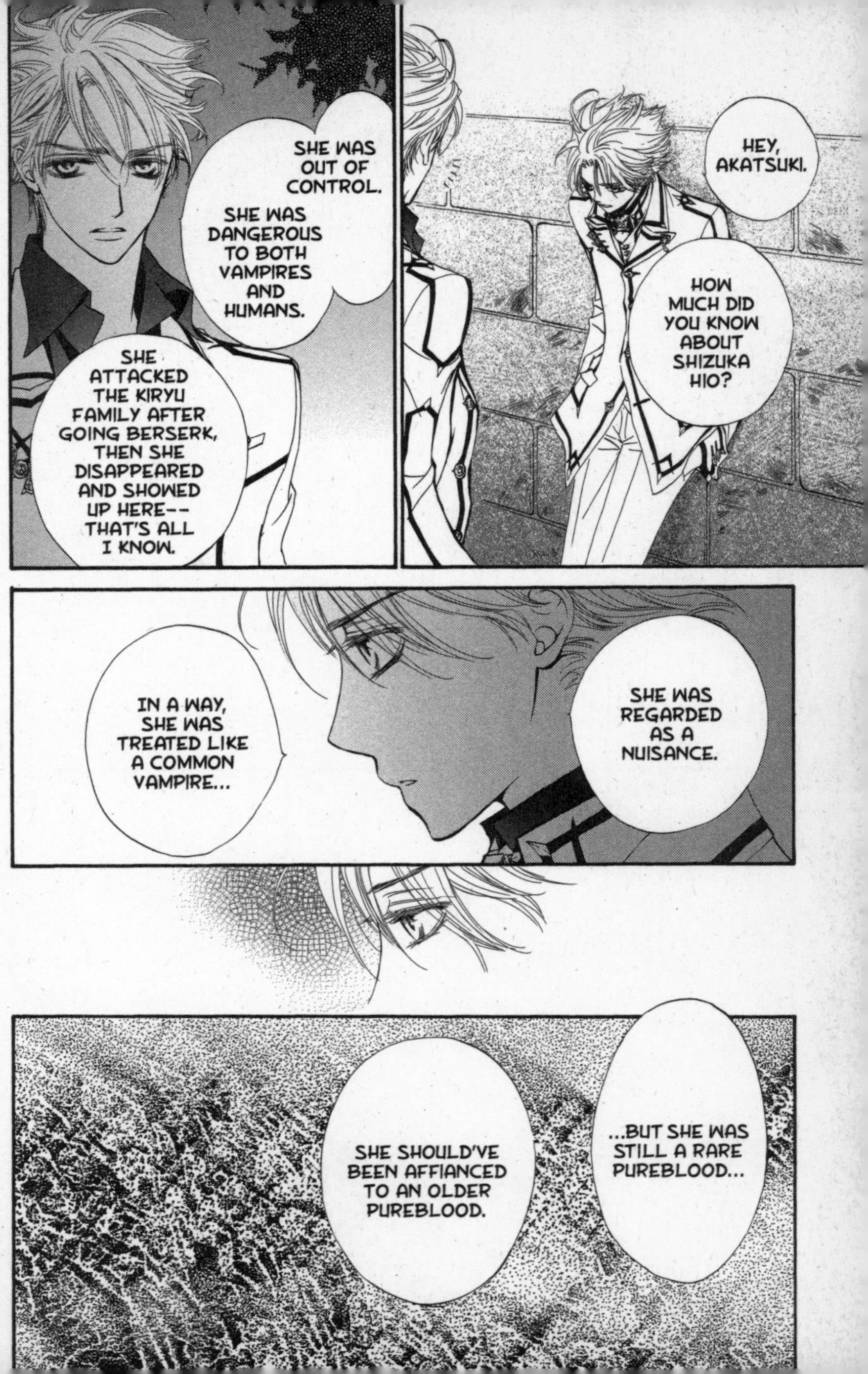
HEY, AKATSUKI.
HOW MUCH DID YOU KNOW ABOUT SHIZUKA HIO?
SHE WAS OUT OF CONTROL.
SHE WAS DANGEROUS TO BOTH VAMPIRES AND HUMANS.
SHE ATTACKED THE KIRYU FAMILY AFTER GOING BERSERK, THEN SHE DISAPPEARED AND SHOWED UP HERE--THAT'S ALL I KNOW.
SHE WAS REGARDED AS A NUISANCE.
IN A WAY, SHE WAS TREATED LIKE A COMMON VAMPIRE...
...BUT SHE WAS STILL A RARE PUREBLOOD...
SHE SHOULD'VE BEEN AFFIANCED TO AN OLDER PUREBLOOD.

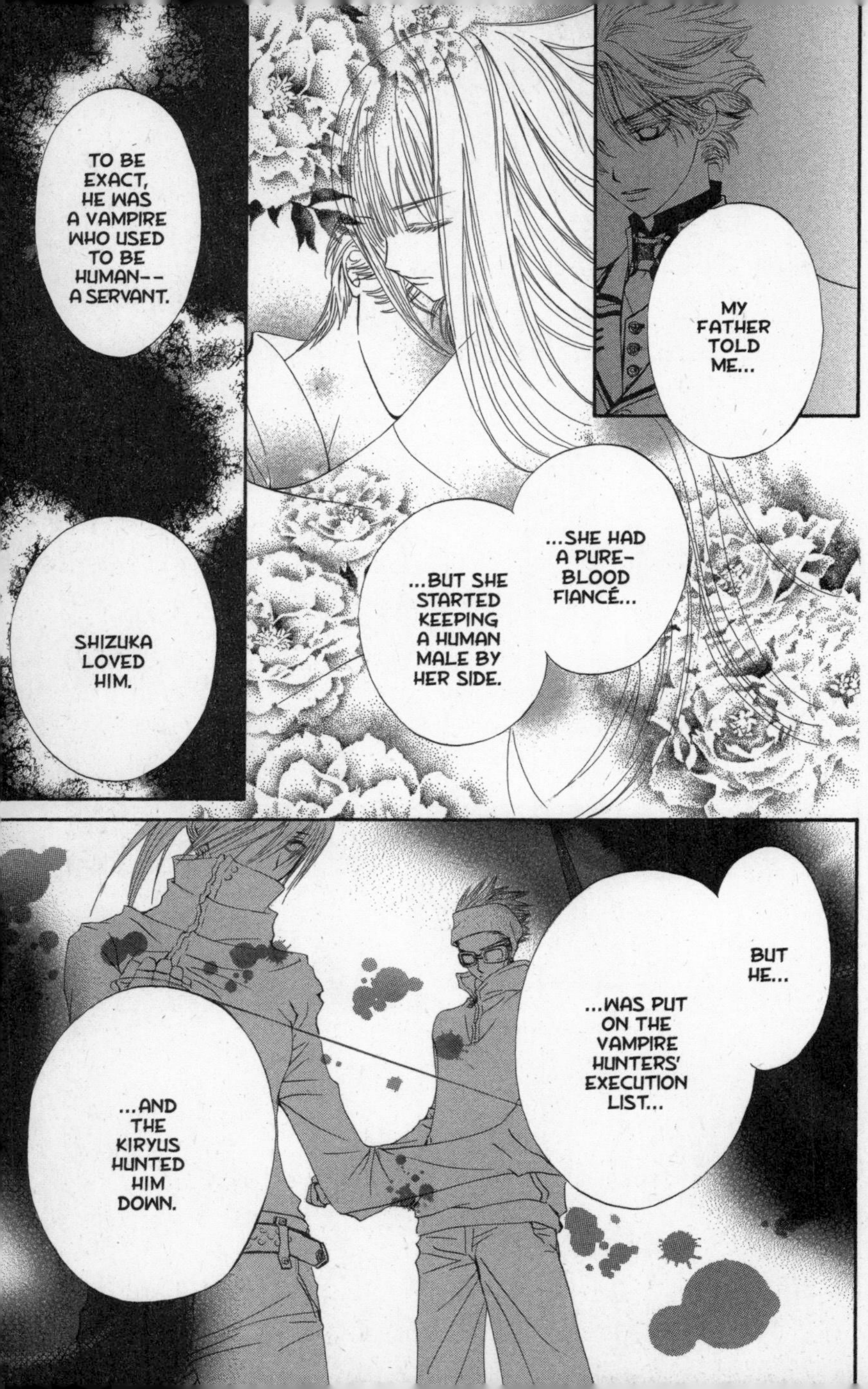
MY FATHER TOLD ME...
...SHE HAD A PURE-BLOOD FIANCÉ...
...BUT SHE STARTED KEEPING A HUMAN MALE BY HER SIDE.
TO BE EXACT, HE WAS A VAMPIRE WHO USED TO BE HUMAN-- A SERVANT.
SHIZUKA LOVED HIM.
BUT HE...
...WAS PUT ON THE VAMPIRE HUNTERS' EXECUTION LIST...
...AND THE KIRYUS HUNTED HIM DOWN.

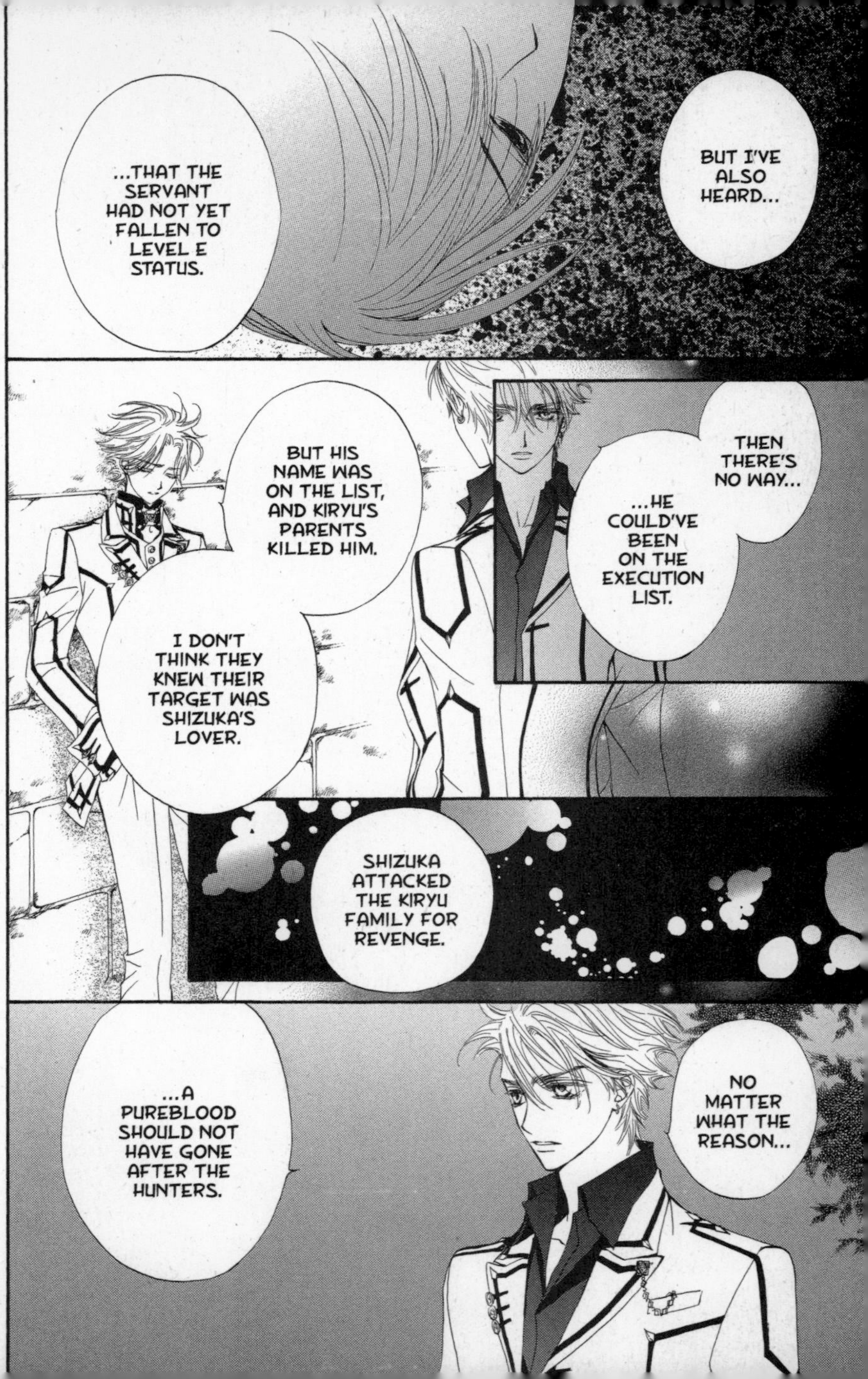
BUT I'VE ALSO HEARD...
...THAT THE SERVANT HAD NOT YET FALLEN TO LEVEL E STATUS.
THEN THERE'S NO WAY...
...HE COULD'VE BEEN ON THE EXECUTION LIST.
BUT HIS NAME WAS ON THE LIST, AND KIRYU'S PARENTS KILLED HIM.
I DON'T THINK THEY KNEW THEIR TARGET WAS SHIZUKA'S LOVER.
SHIZUKA ATTACKED THE KIRYU FAMILY FOR REVENGE.
NO MATTER WHAT THE REASON...
...A PUREBLOOD SHOULD NOT HAVE GONE AFTER THE HUNTERS.

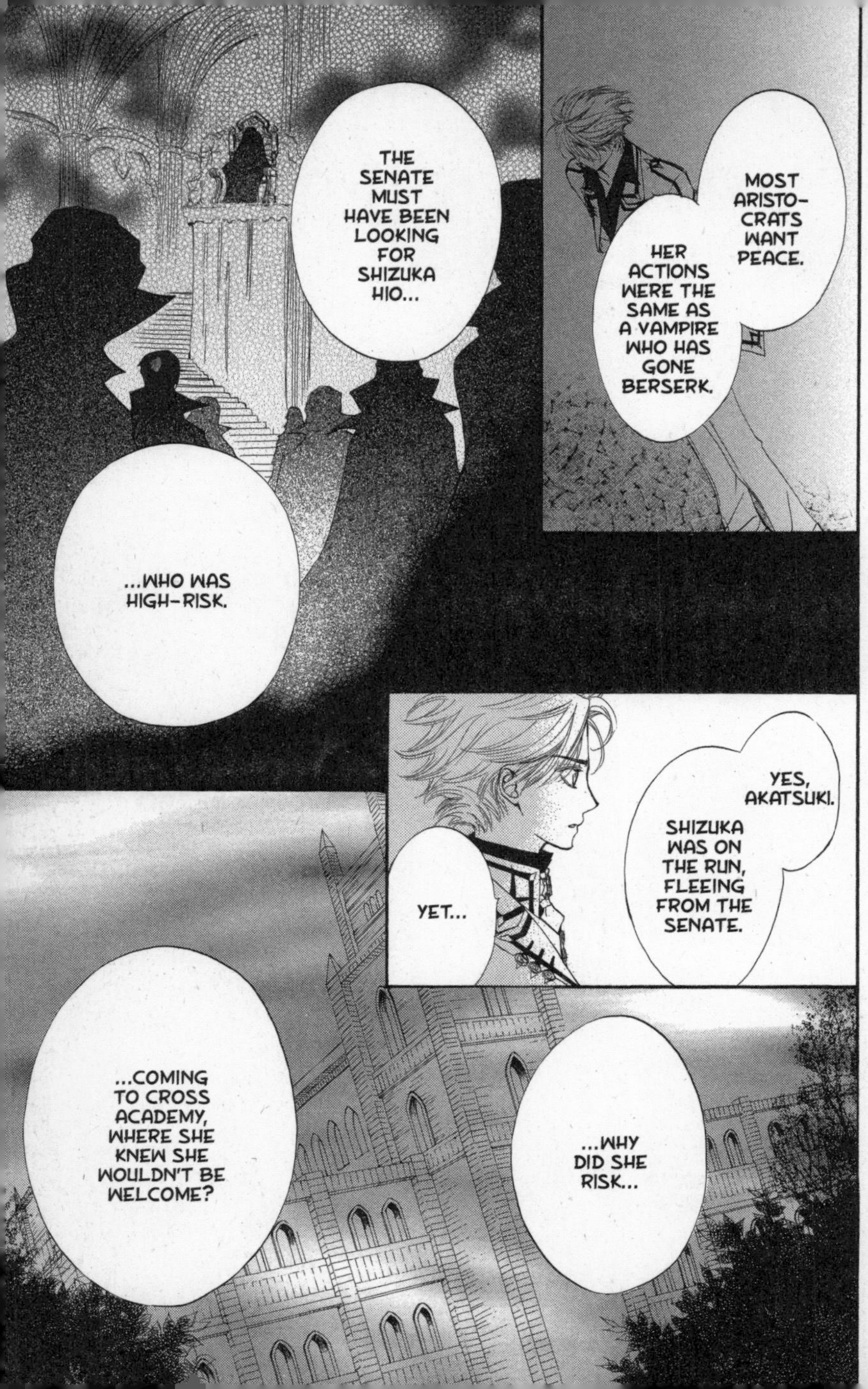
MOST ARISTOCRATS WANT PEACE.
HER ACTIONS WERE THE SAME AS A VAMPIRE WHO HAS GONE BERSERK.
THE SENATE MUST HAVE BEEN LOOKING FOR SHIZUKA HIO...
...WHO WAS HIGH-RISK.
YES, AKATSUKI.
SHIZUKA WAS ON THE RUN, FLEEING FROM THE SENATE.
YET...
...WHY DID SHE RISK...
...COMING TO CROSS ACADEMY, WHERE SHE KNEW SHE WOULDN'T BE WELCOME?

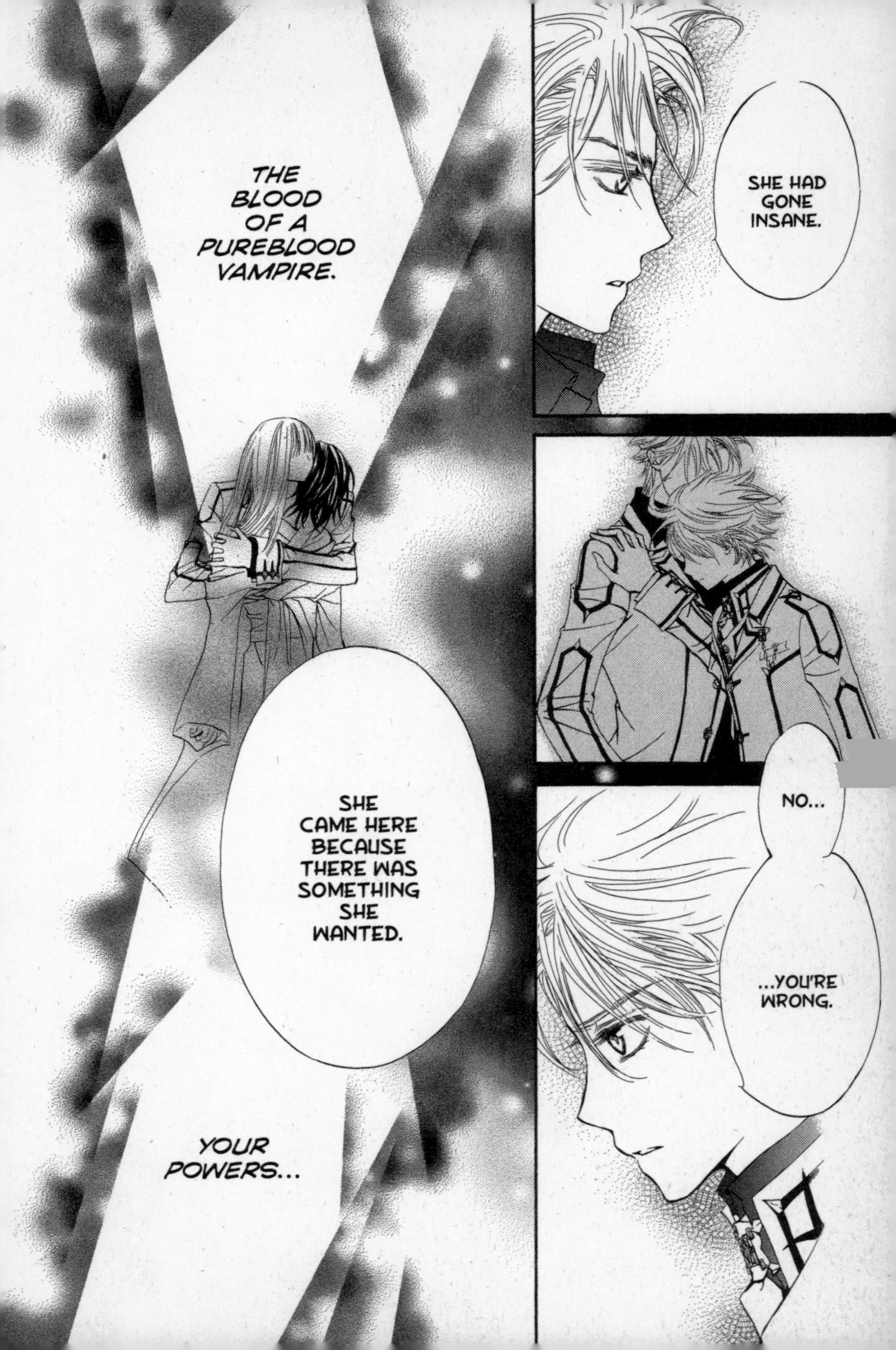
SHE HAD GONE INSANE.
NO...
...YOU'RE WRONG.
THE BLOOD OF A PUREBLOOD VAMPIRE.
SHE CAME HERE BECAUSE THERE WAS SOMETHING SHE WANTED.
YOUR POWERS...

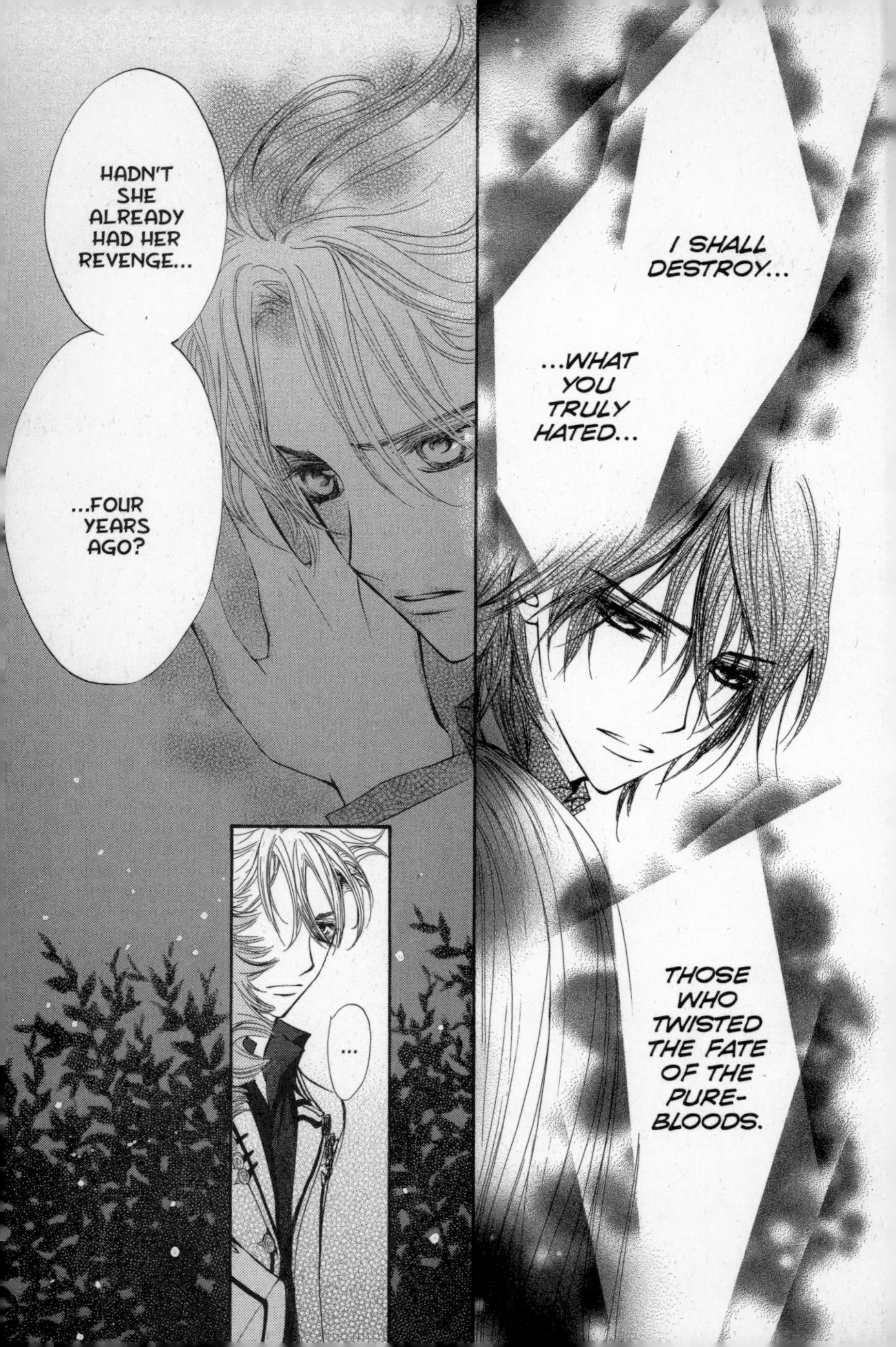
I SHALL DESTROY...
...WHAT YOU TRULY HATED...
THOSE WHO TWISTED THE FATE OF THE PURE-BLOODS.
HADN'T SHE ALREADY HAD HER REVENGE...
...FOUR YEARS AGO?
...

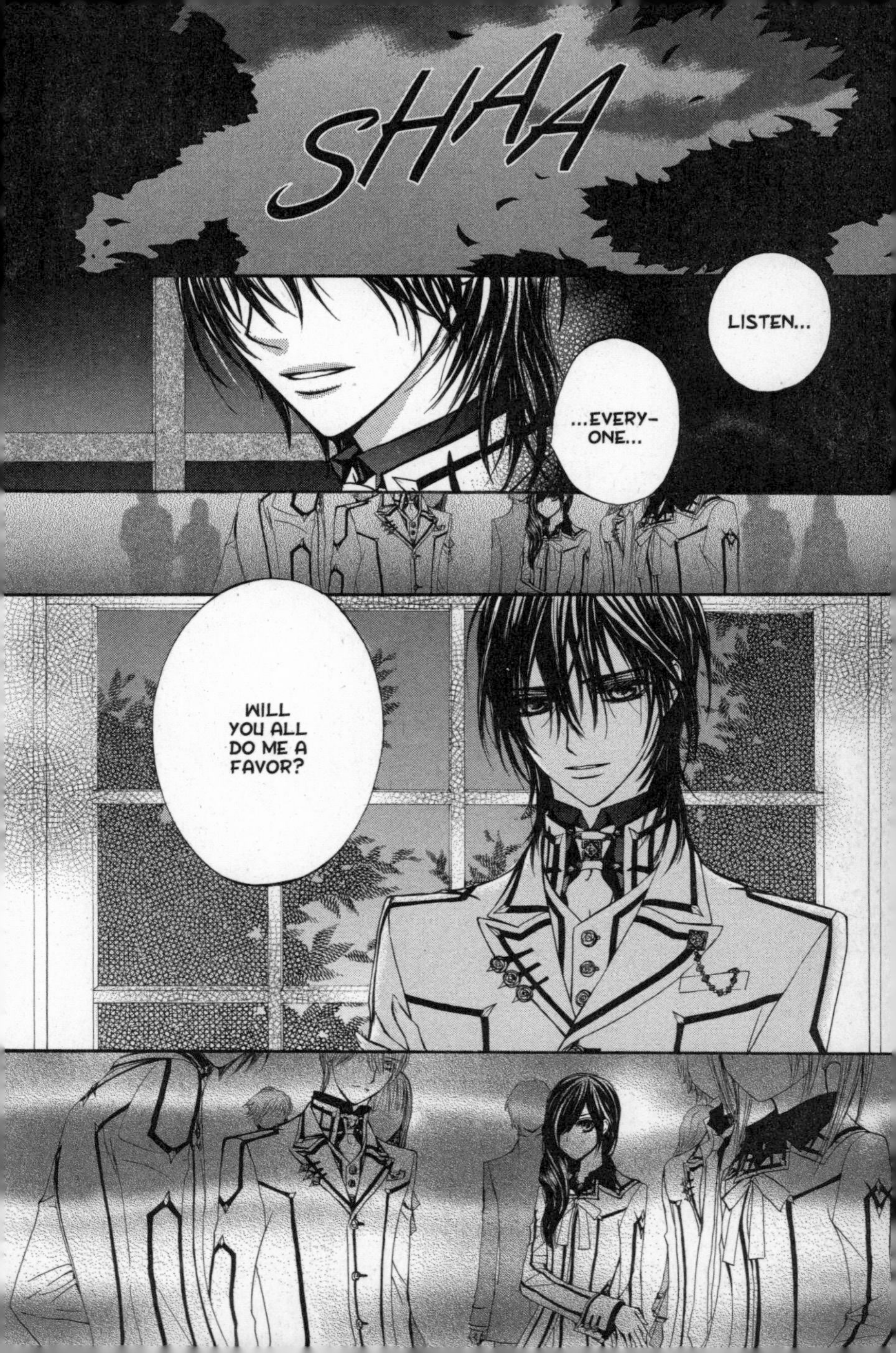
SHAA
LISTEN...
...EVERY-ONE...
WILL YOU ALL DO ME A FAVOR?

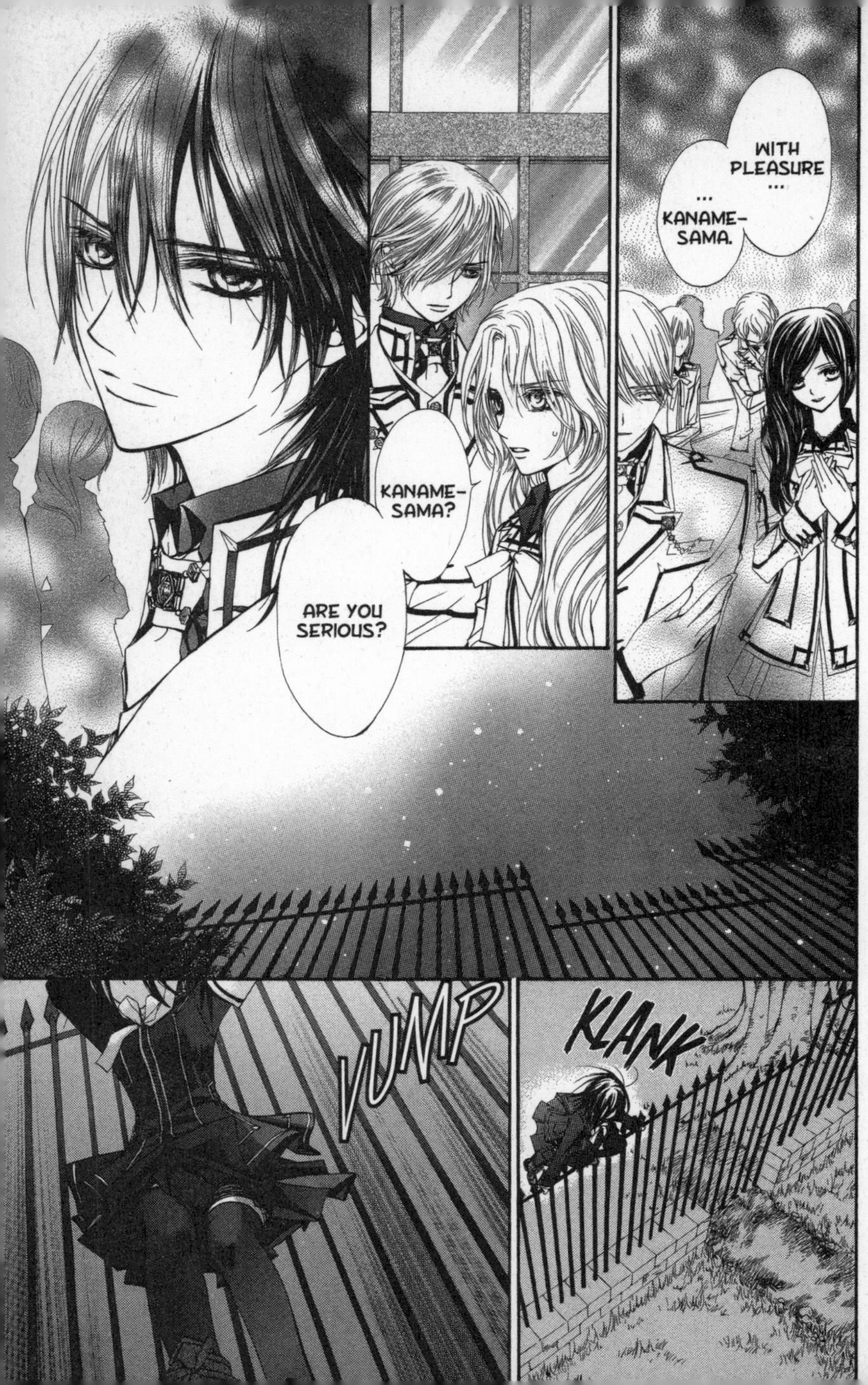
WITH PLEASURE ... ... KANAME-SAMA.
KANAME-SAMA? ARE YOU SERIOUS?
KLANK
VUMP

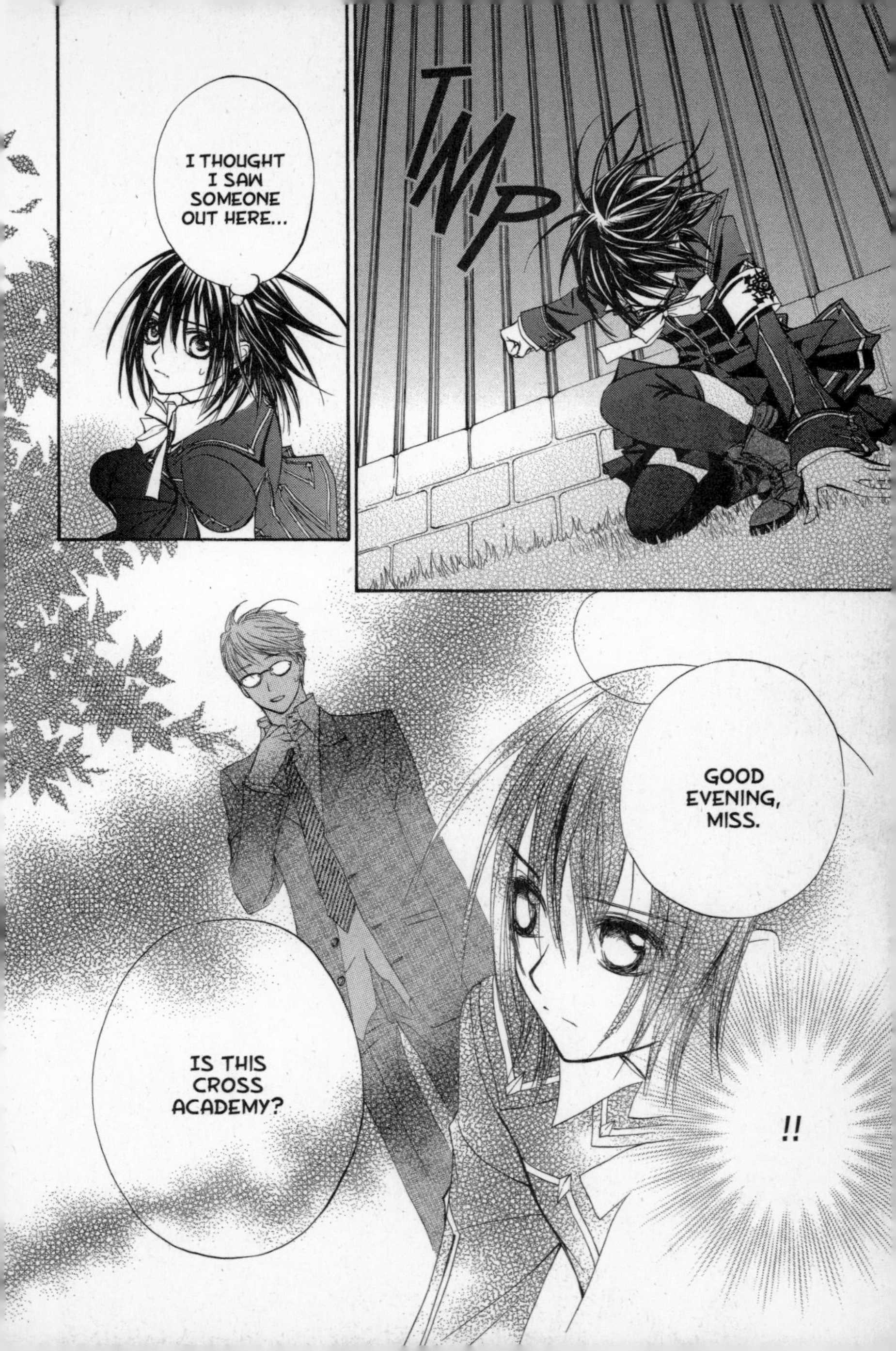
TMP
I THOUGHT I SAW SOMEONE OUT HERE...
GOOD EVENING, MISS.
!!
IS THIS CROSS ACADEMY?

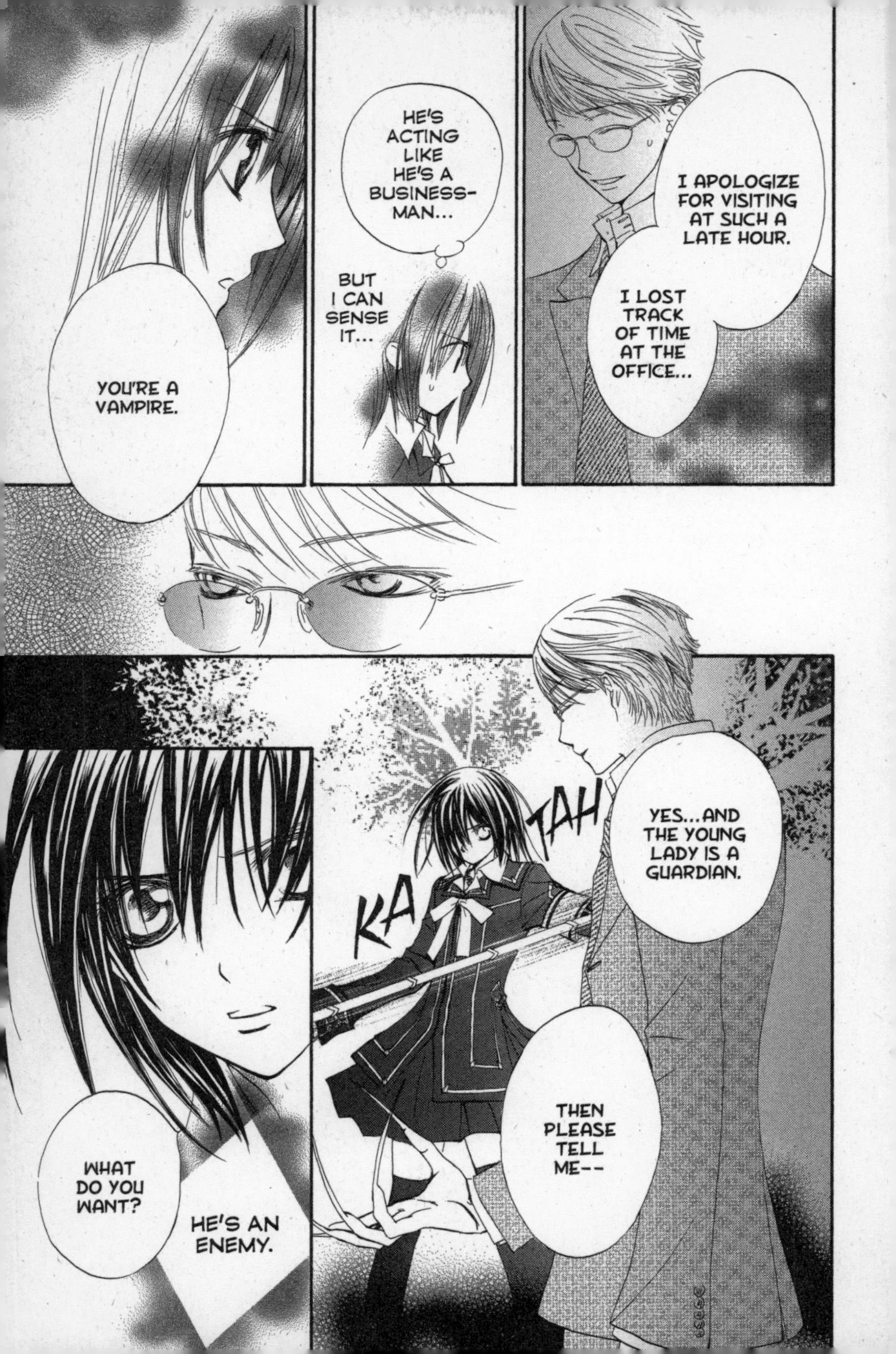
I APOLOGIZE FOR VISITING AT SUCH A LATE HOUR.
I LOST TRACK OF TIME AT THE OFFICE...
HE'S ACTING LIKE HE'S A BUSINESS-MAN...
BUT I CAN SENSE IT...
YOU'RE A VAMPIRE.
YES...AND THE YOUNG LADY IS A GUARDIAN.
KA TAH
THEN PLEASE TELL ME--
WHAT DO YOU WANT?
HE'S AN ENEMY.

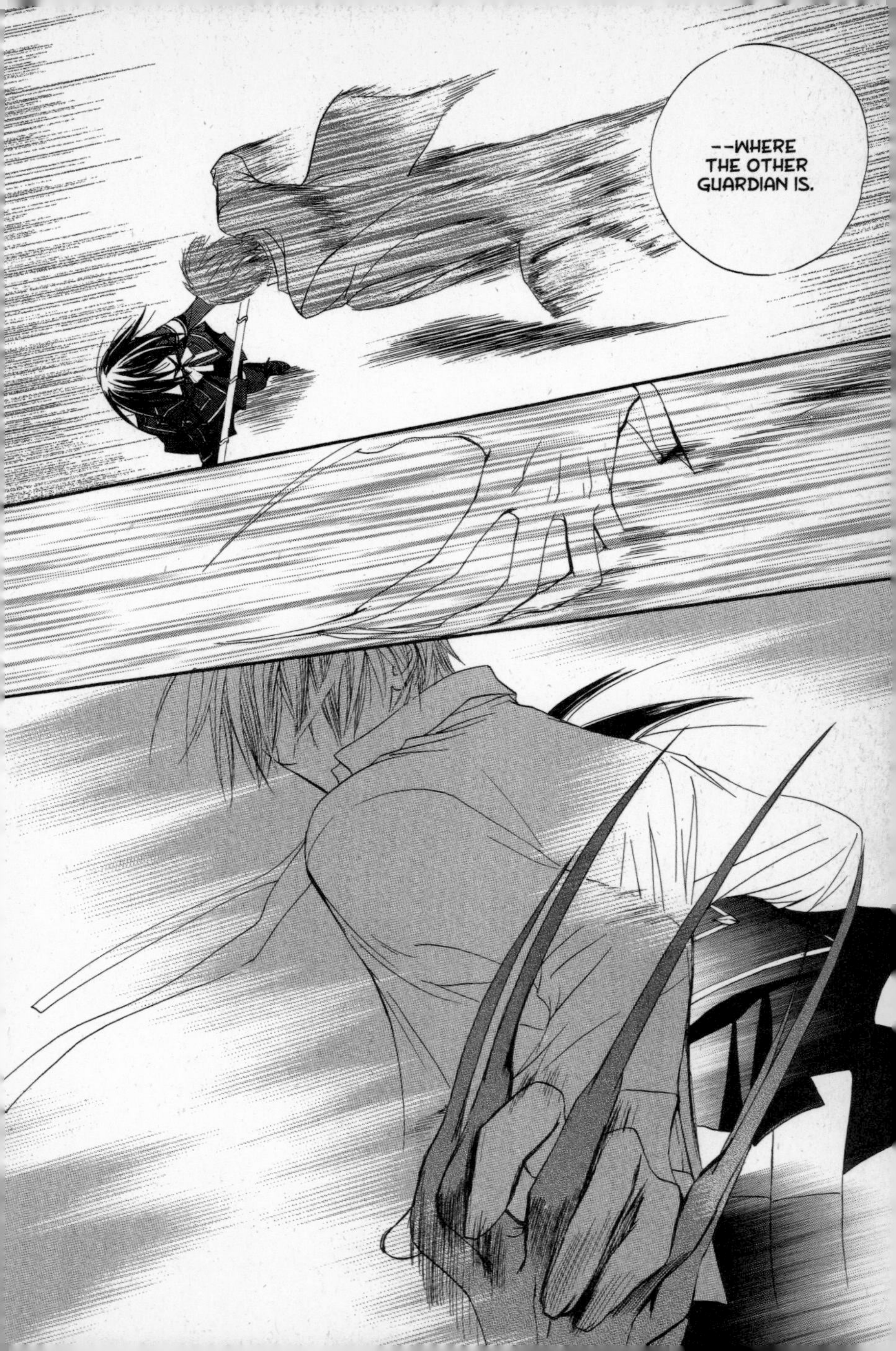
--WHERE THE OTHER GUARDIAN IS.

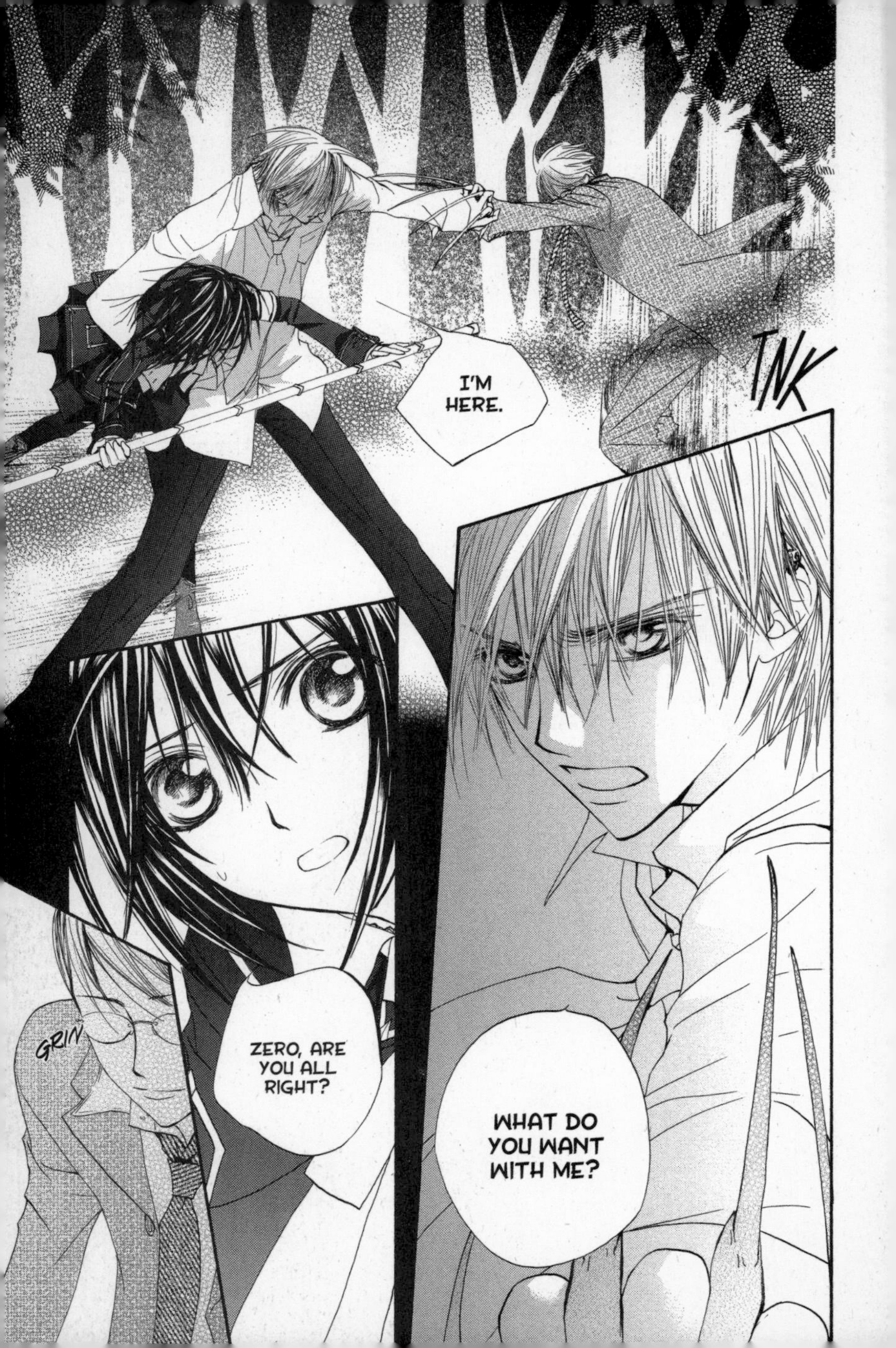
TNK
I'M HERE.
WHAT DO YOU WANT WITH ME?
ZERO, ARE YOU ALL RIGHT?
GRIN

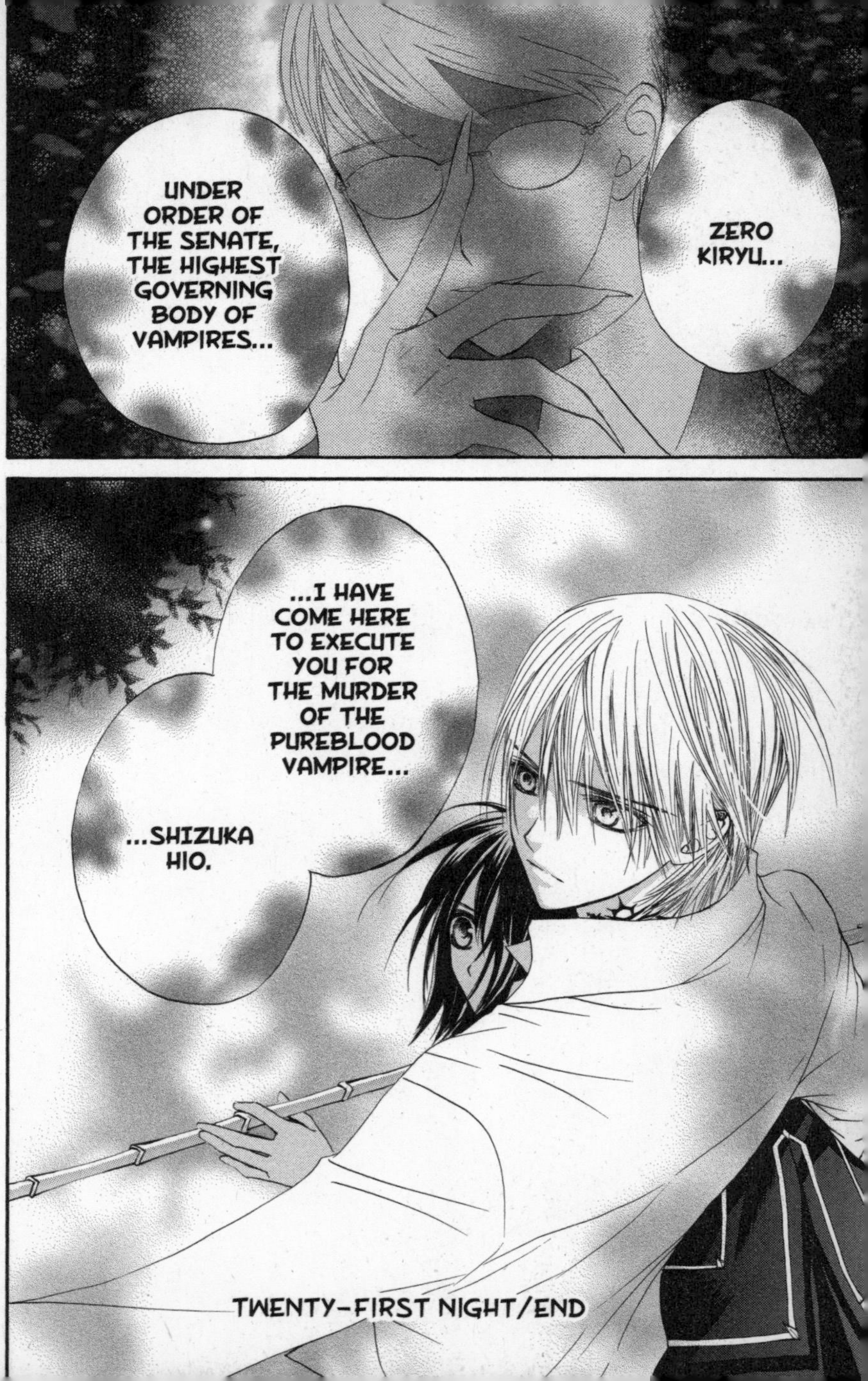
ZERO KIRYU...
UNDER ORDER OF THE SENATE, THE HIGHEST GOVERNING BODY OF VAMPIRES...
...I HAVE COME HERE TO EXECUTE YOU FOR THE MURDER OF THE PUREBLOOD VAMPIRE...
...SHIZUKA HIO.
TWENTY-FIRST NIGHT/END

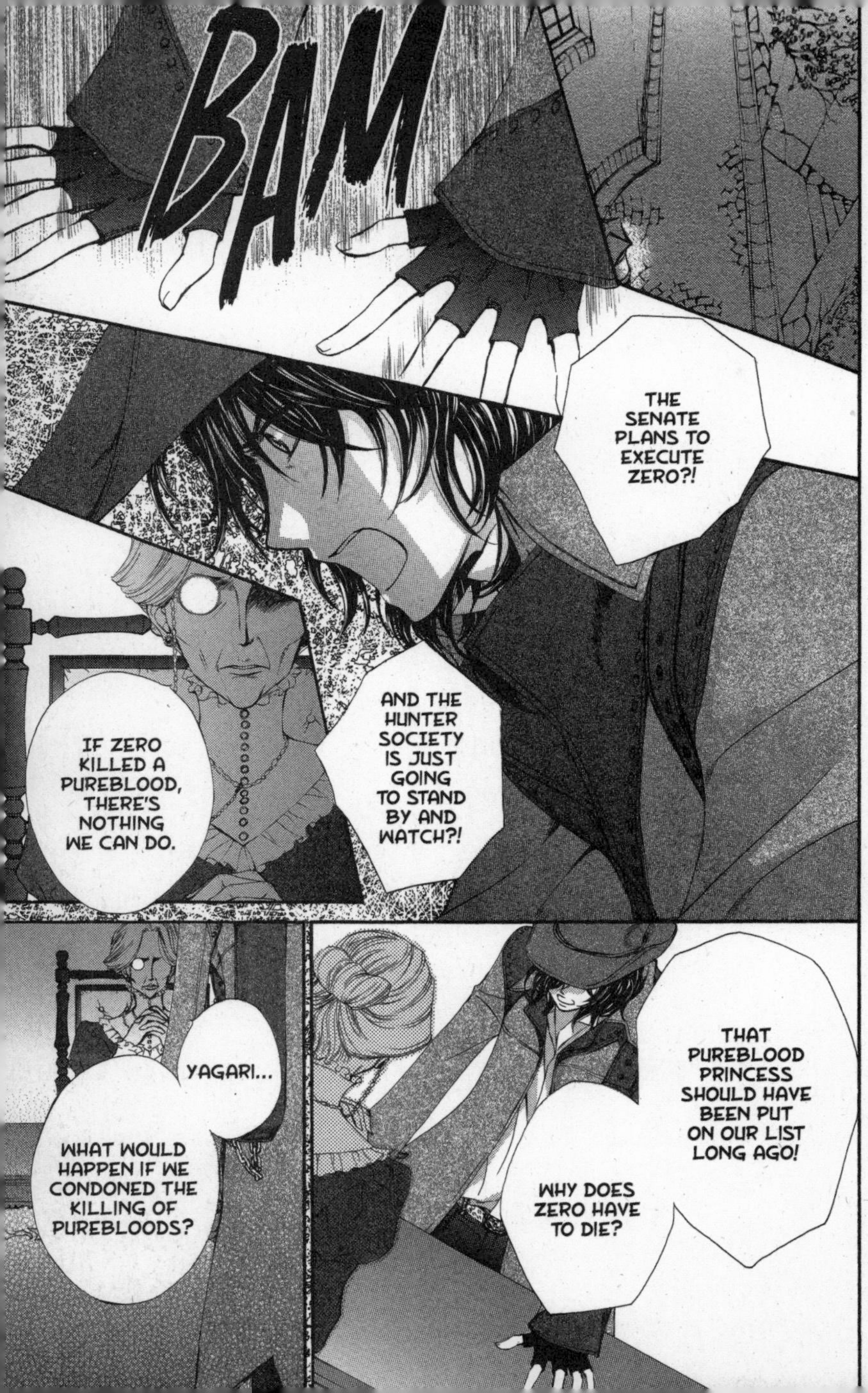
BAM
THE SENATE PLANS TO EXECUTE ZERO?!
AND THE HUNTER SOCIETY IS JUST GOING TO STAND BY AND WATCH?!
IF ZERO KILLED A PUREBLOOD, THERE'S NOTHING WE CAN DO.
THAT PUREBLOOD PRINCESS SHOULD HAVE BEEN PUT ON OUR LIST LONG AGO!
WHY DOES ZERO HAVE TO DIE?
YAGARI...
WHAT WOULD HAPPEN IF WE CONDONED THE KILLING OF PUREBLOODS?

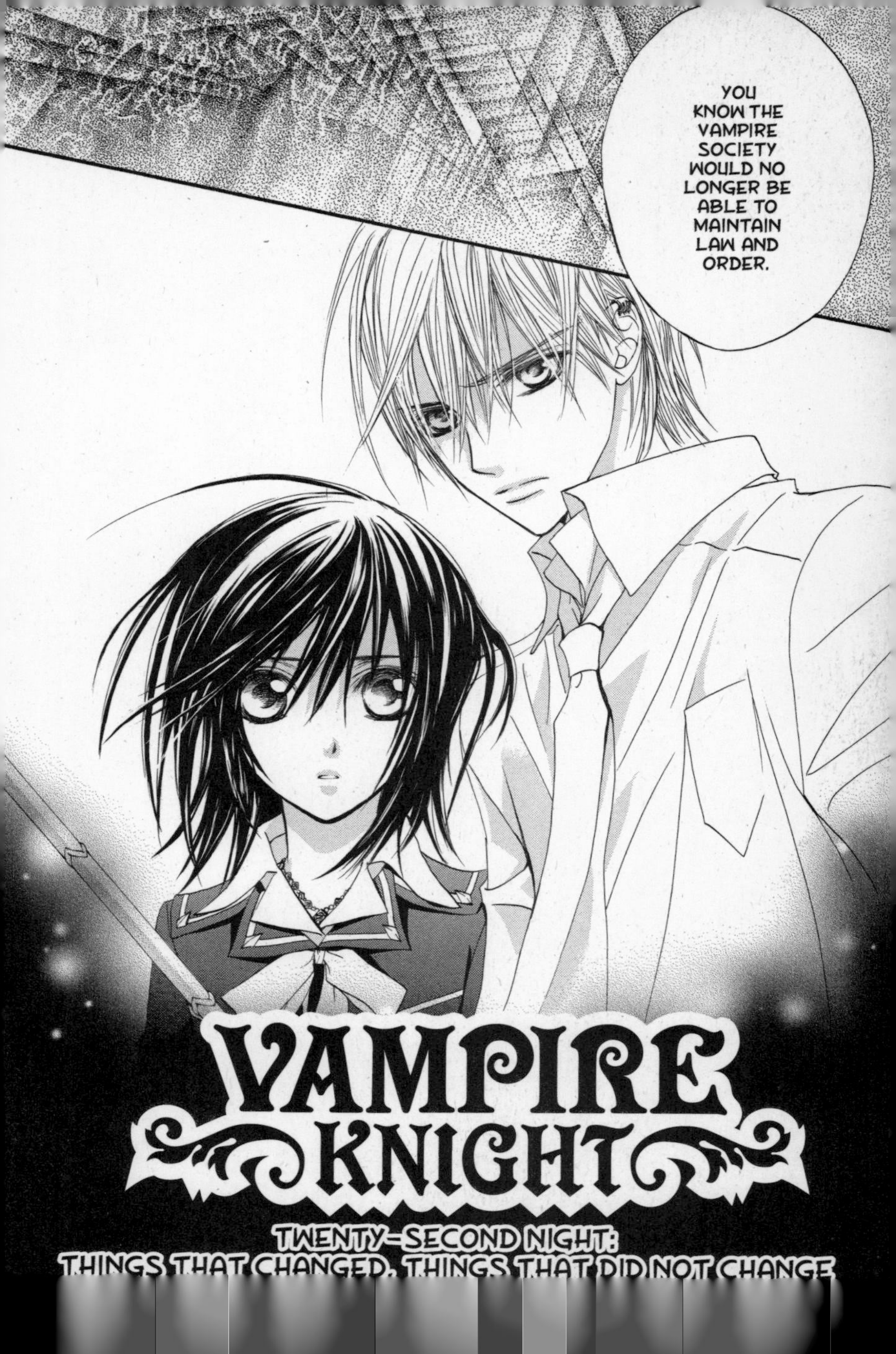
YOU KNOW THE VAMPIRE SOCIETY WOULD NO LONGER BE ABLE TO MAINTAIN LAW AND ORDER.
VAMPIRE KNIGHT
TWENTY-SECOND NIGHT:
THINGS THAT CHANGED, THINGS THAT DID NOT CHANGE

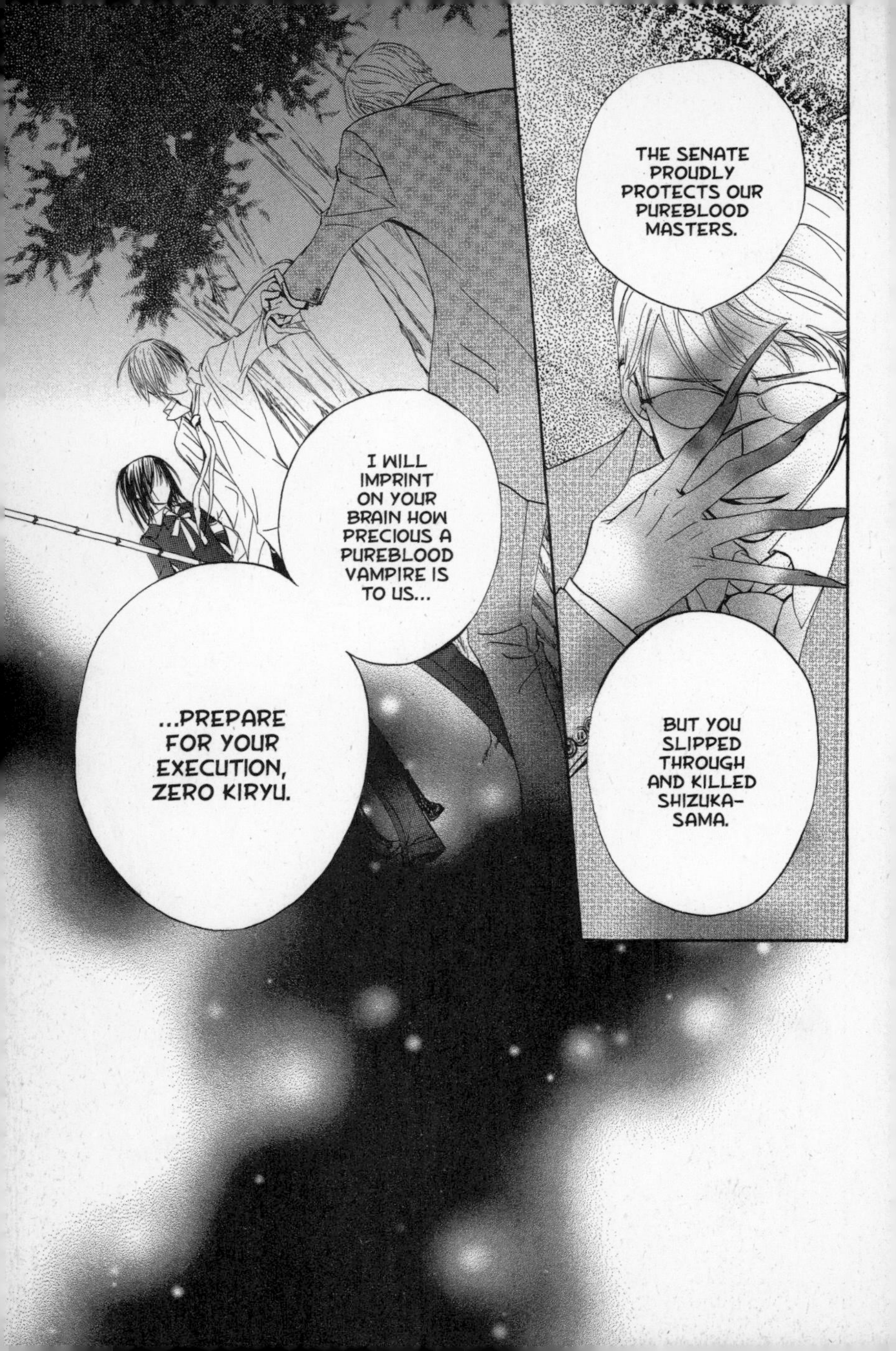
THE SENATE PROUDLY PROTECTS OUR PUREBLOOD MASTERS.
BUT YOU SLIPPED THROUGH AND KILLED SHIZUKA-SAMA.
I WILL IMPRINT ON YOUR BRAIN HOW PRECIOUS A PUREBLOOD VAMPIRE IS TO US...
...PREPARE FOR YOUR EXECUTION, ZERO KIRYU.

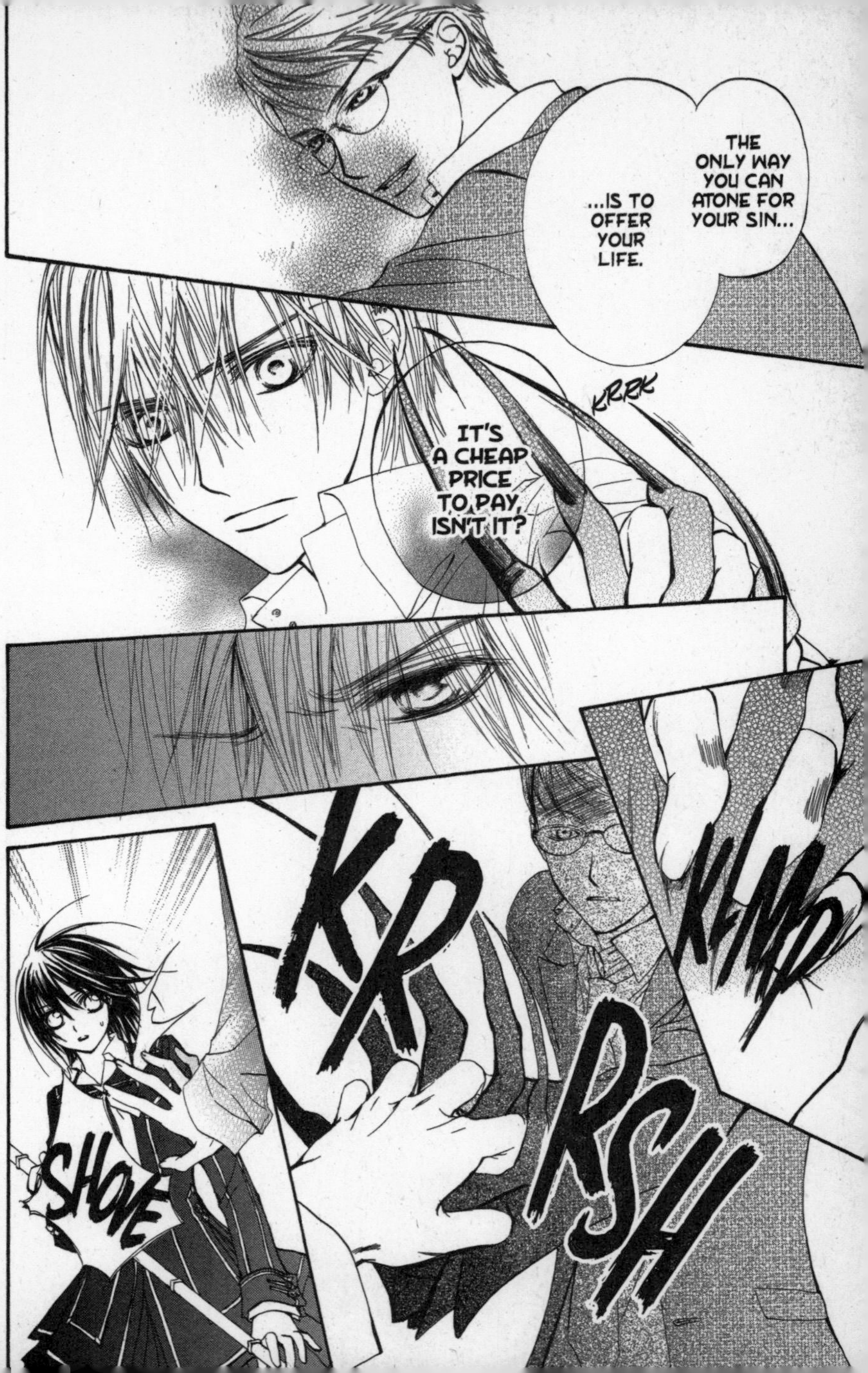
THE ONLY WAY YOU CAN ATONE FOR YOUR SIN...
...IS TO OFFER YOUR LIFE.
KRRK
IT'S A CHEAP PRICE TO PAY, ISN'T IT?
KR
RSH
SHOVE

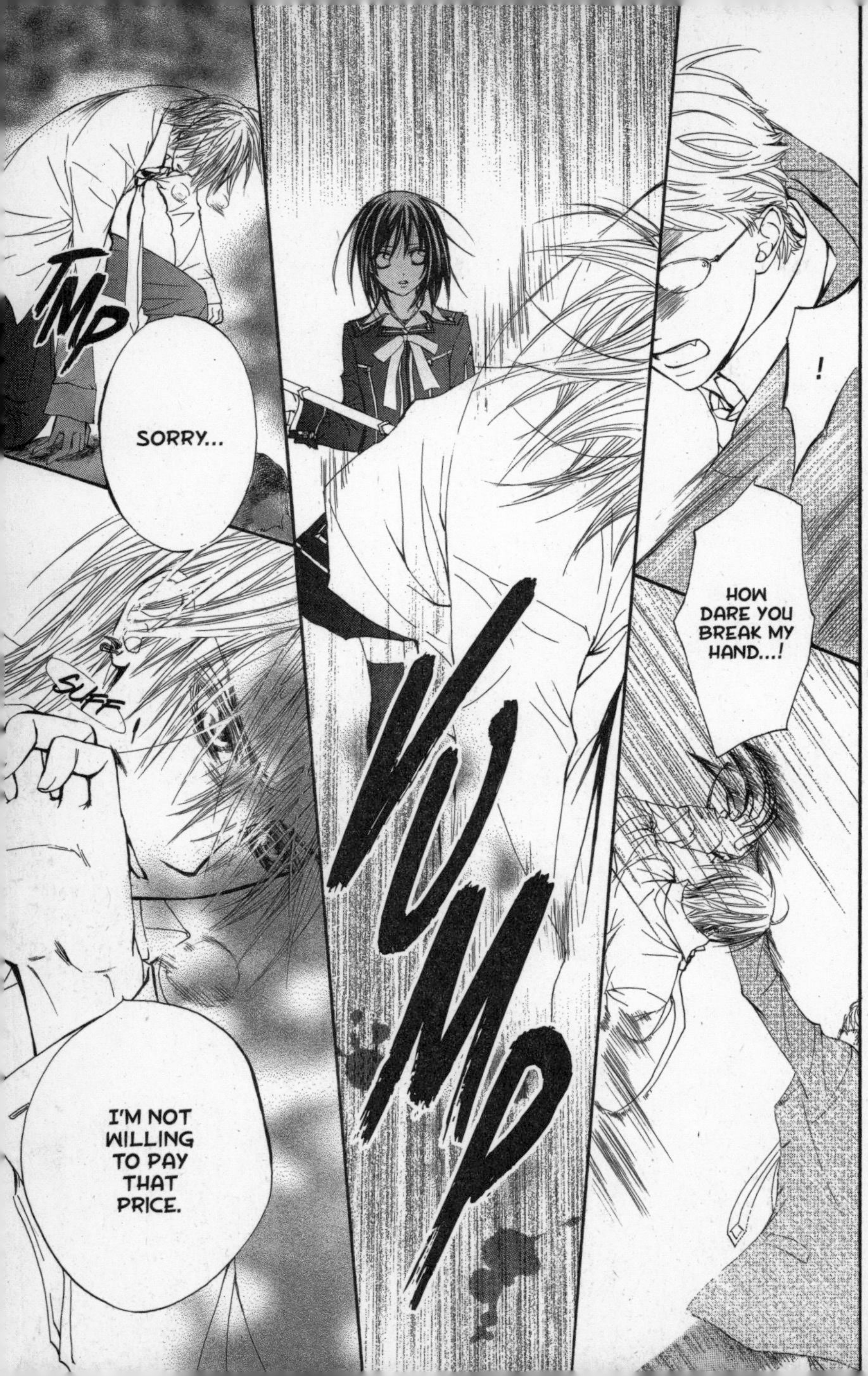
!
HOW DARE YOU BREAK MY HAND...!
WUMP
TMP
SORRY...
I'M NOT WILLING TO PAY THAT PRICE.

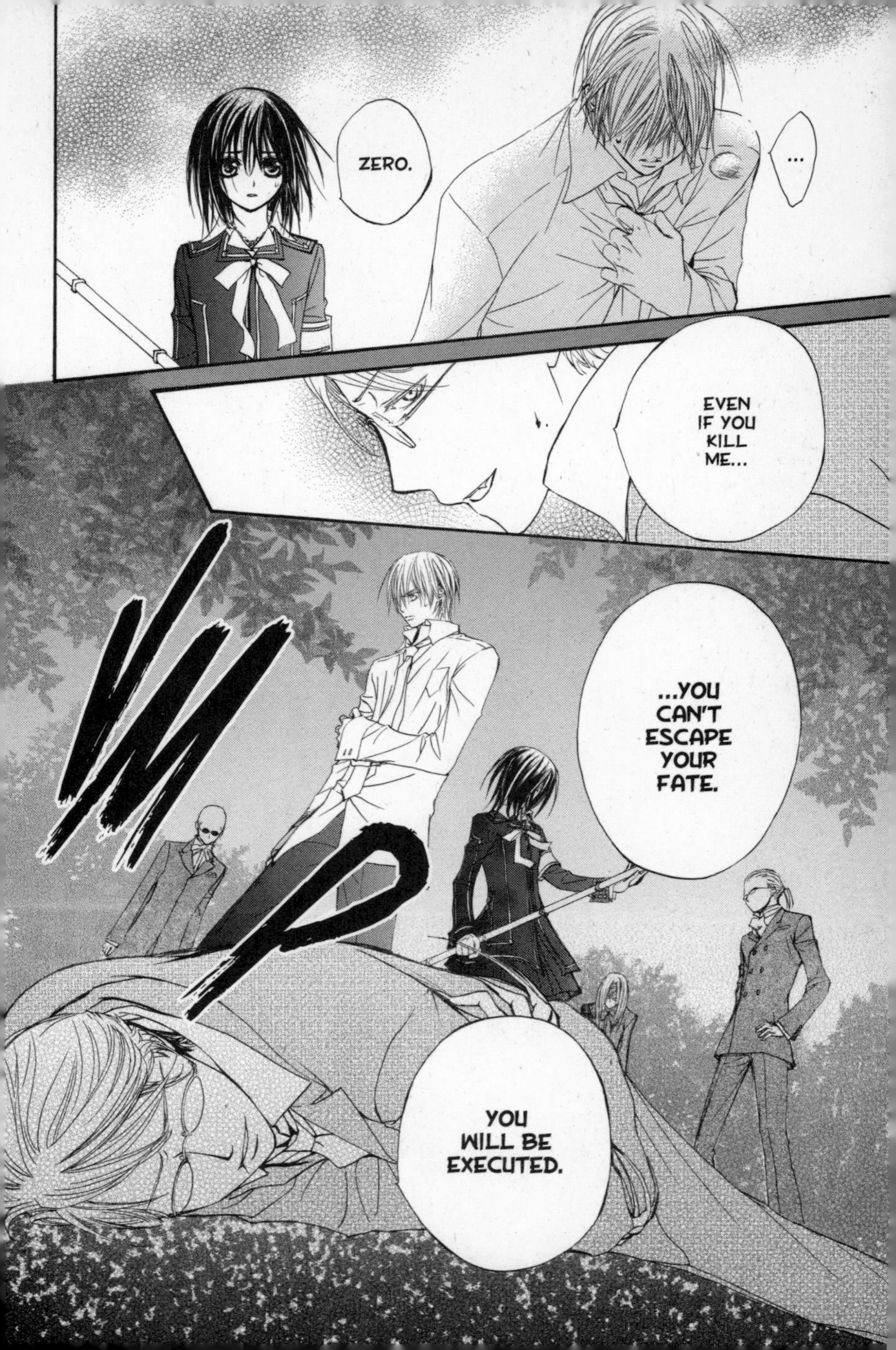
ZERO.
...
EVEN IF YOU KILL ME...
...YOU CAN'T ESCAPE YOUR FATE.
WP
YOU WILL BE EXECUTED.

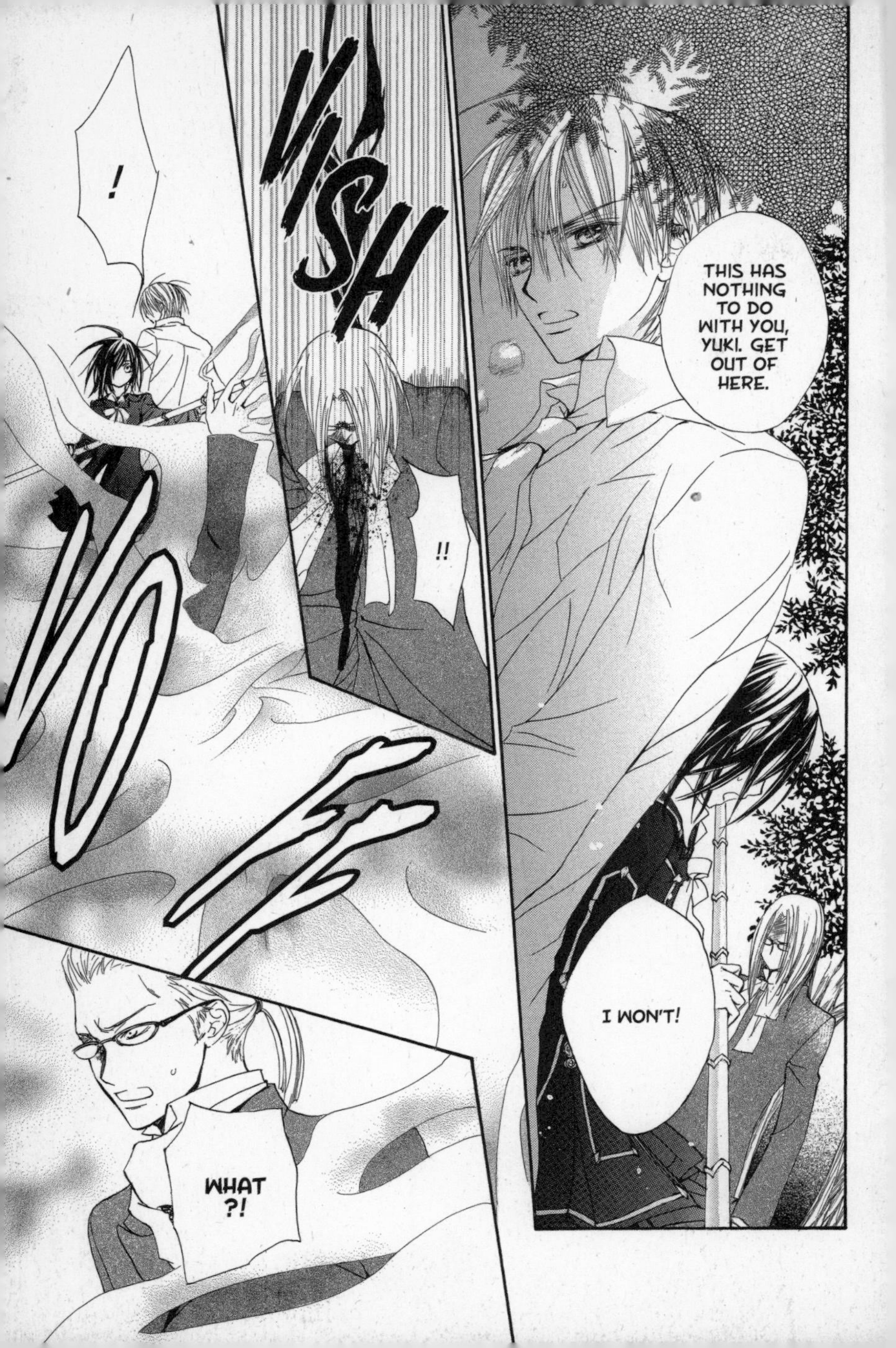
THIS HAS NOTHING TO DO WITH YOU, YUKI. GET OUT OF HERE.
I WON'T!
!!
!
WHAT ?!

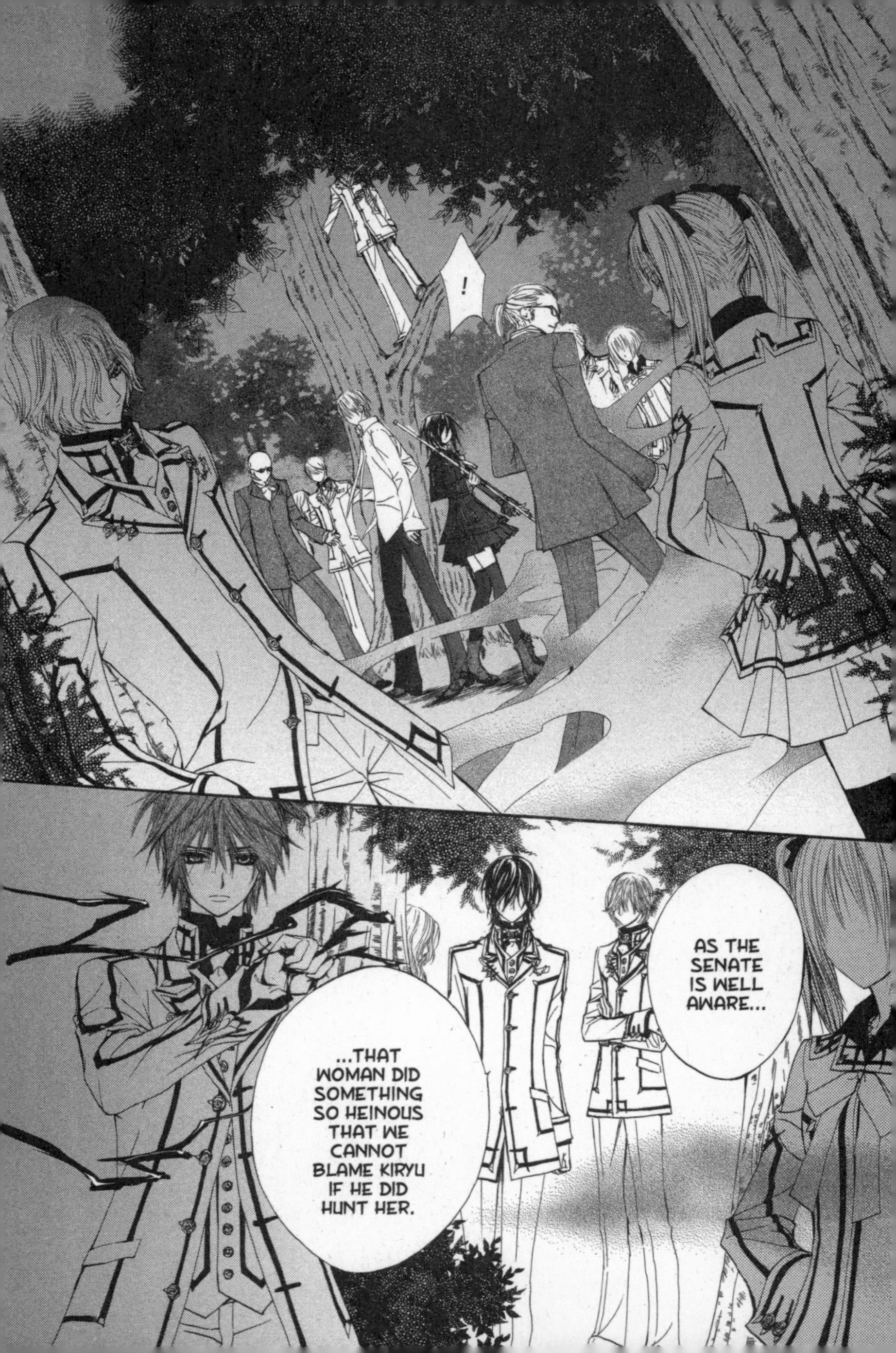
!
AS THE SENATE IS WELL AWARE...
...THAT WOMAN DID SOMETHING SO HEINOUS THAT WE CANNOT BLAME KIRYU IF HE DID HUNT HER.

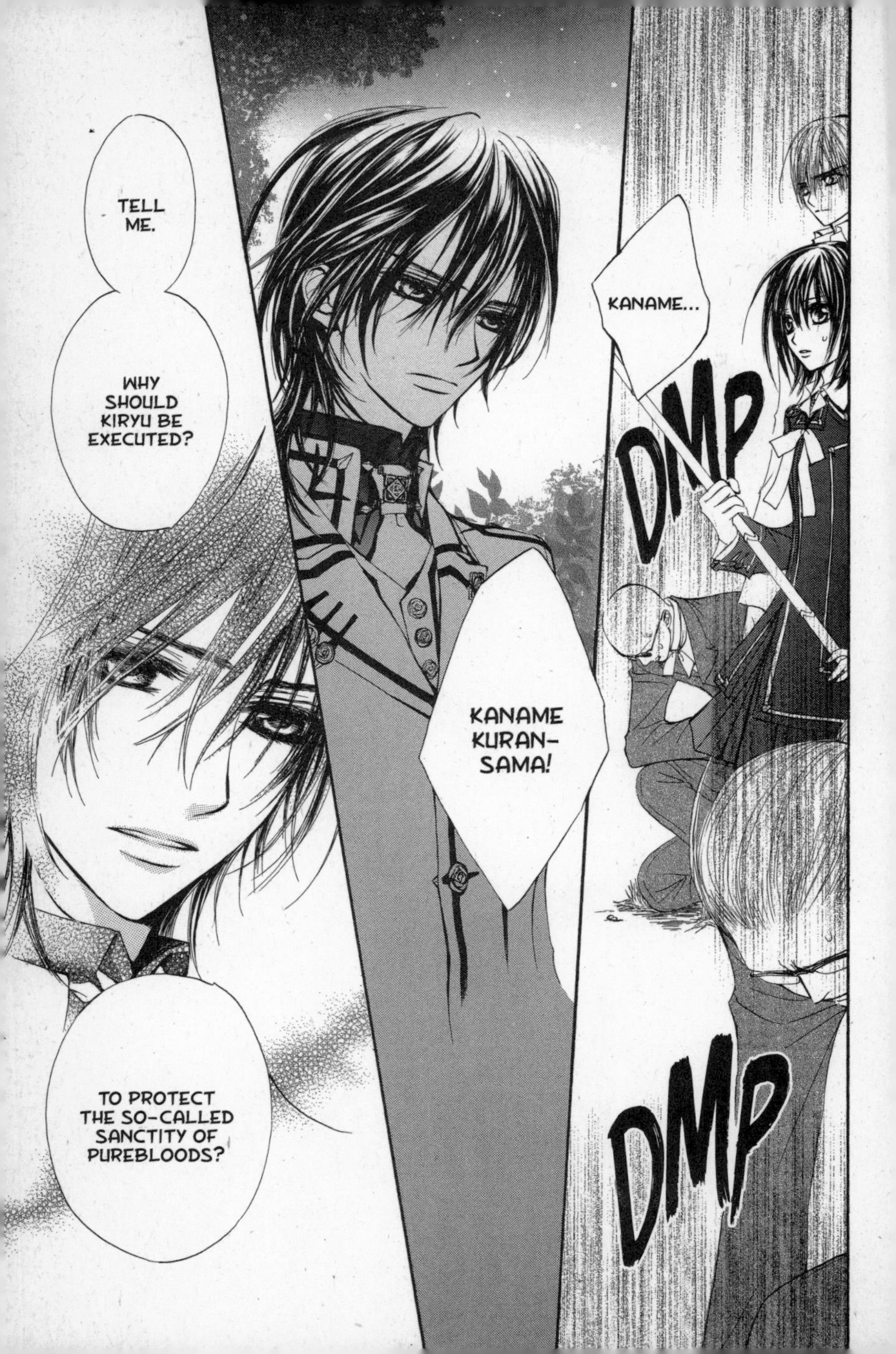
KANAME...
DMP
DMP
KANAME KURAN-SAMA!
TELL ME.
WHY SHOULD KIRYU BE EXECUTED?
TO PROTECT THE SO-CALLED SANCTITY OF PUREBLOODS?

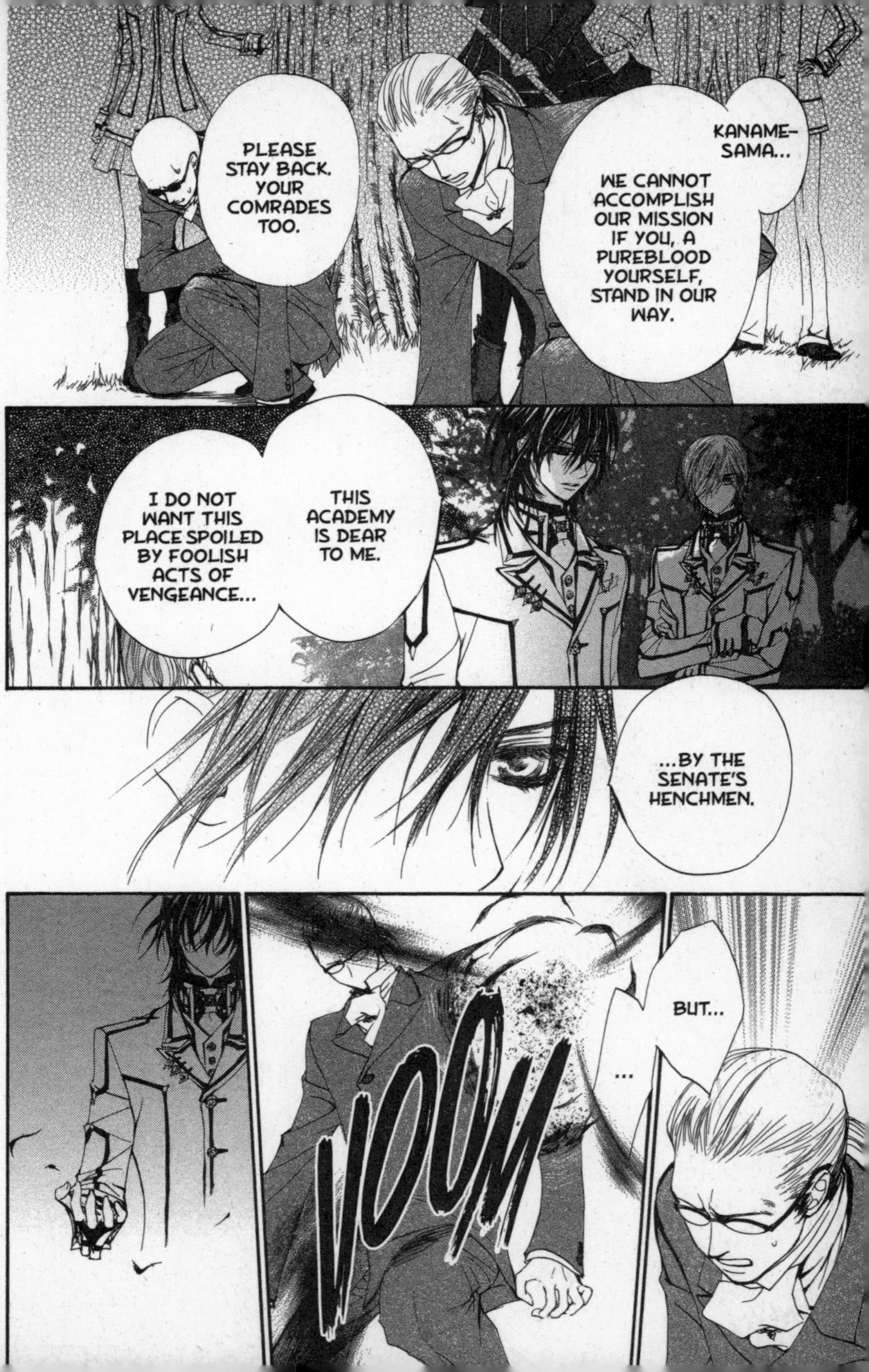
KANAME-SAMA...
WE CANNOT ACCOMPLISH OUR MISSION IF YOU, A PUREBLOOD YOURSELF, STAND IN OUR WAY.
PLEASE STAY BACK. YOUR COMRADES TOO.
THIS ACADEMY IS DEAR TO ME.
I DO NOT WANT THIS PLACE SPOILED BY FOOLISH ACTS OF VENGEANCE...
...BY THE SENATE'S HENCHMEN.
BUT...
...
VOOM

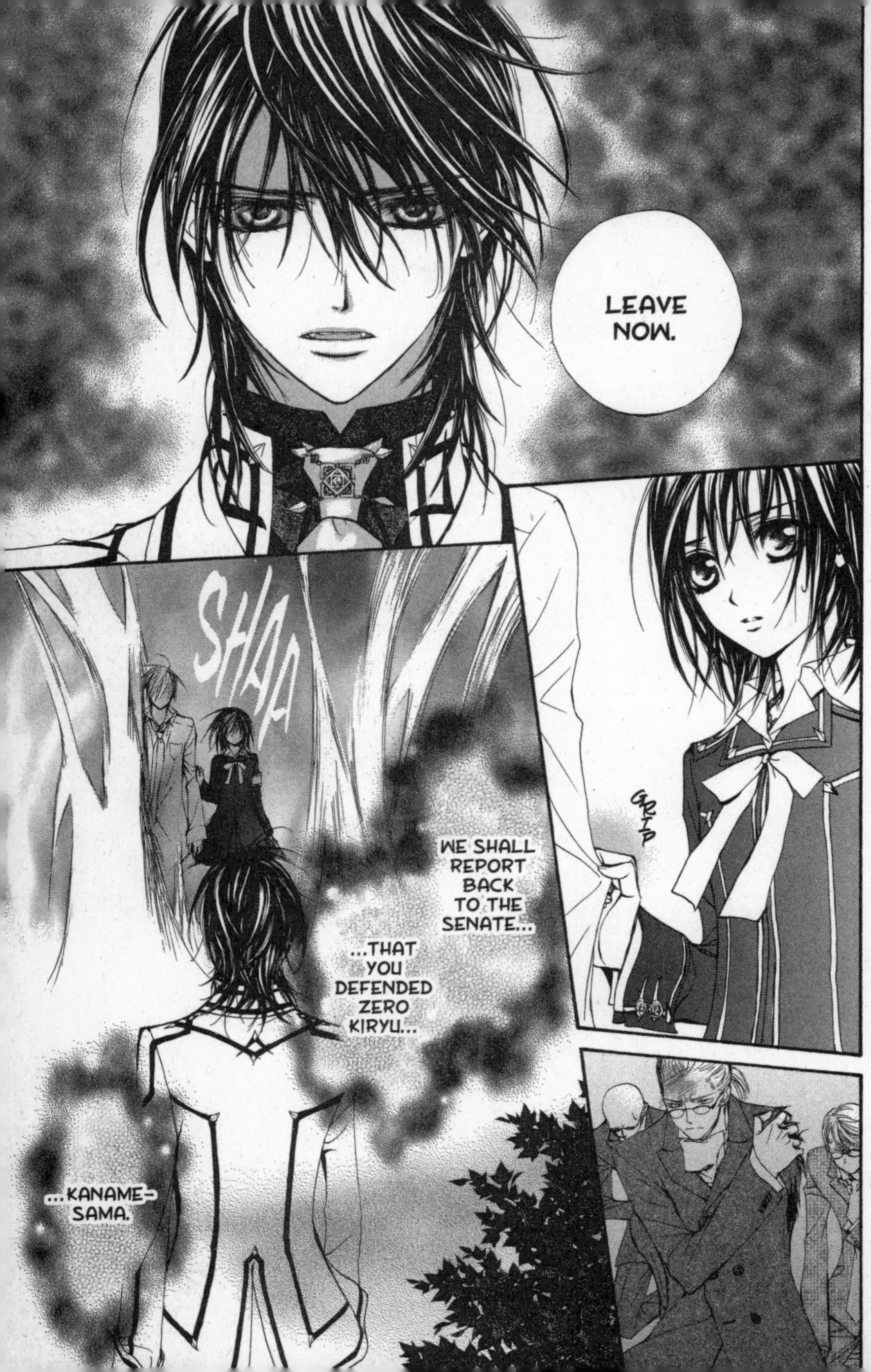
LEAVE NOW.
GRIP
SHAA
WE SHALL REPORT BACK TO THE SENATE...
...THAT YOU DEFENDED ZERO KIRYU...
...KANAME-SAMA.

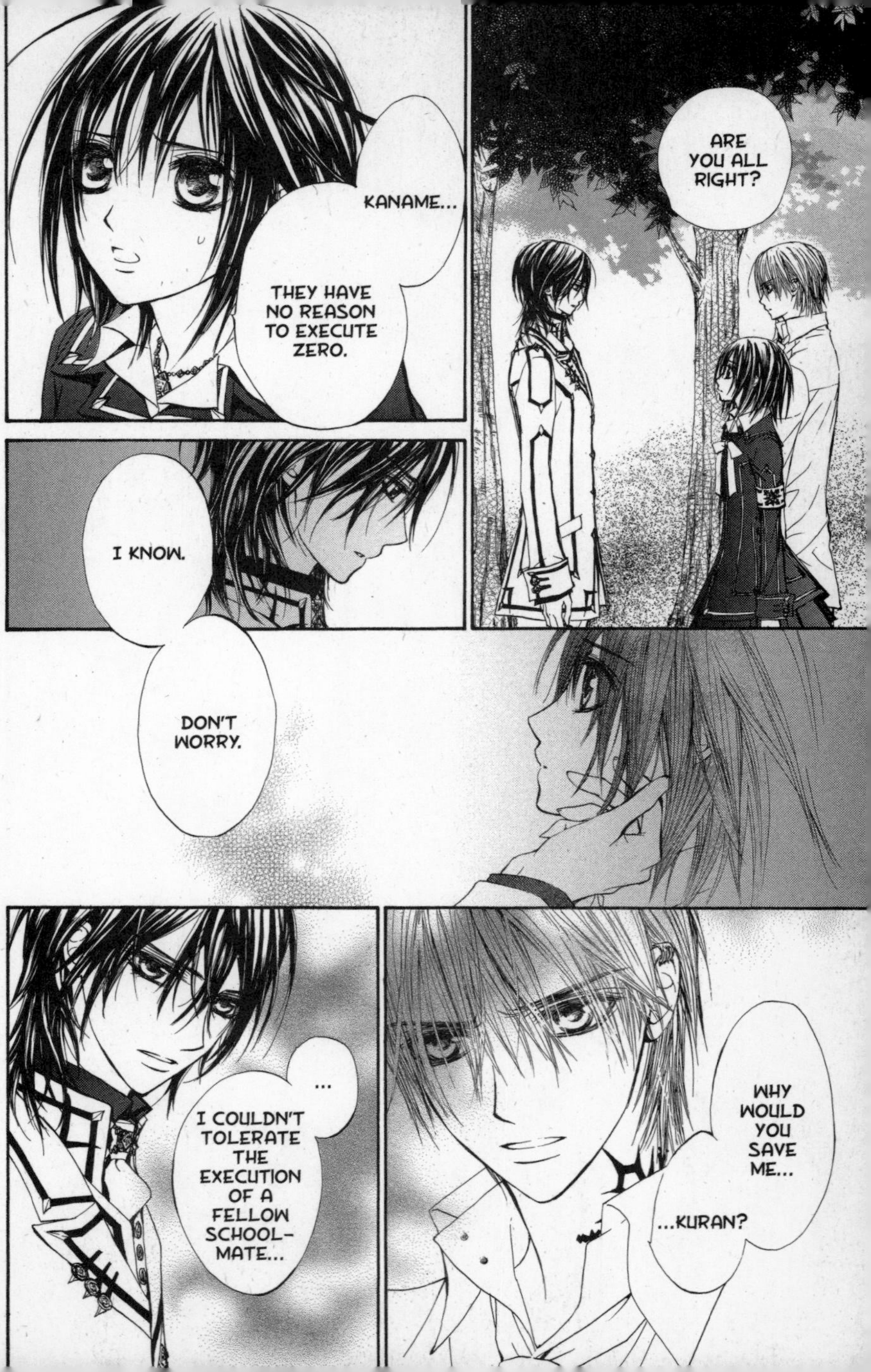
ARE YOU ALL RIGHT?
KANAME...
THEY HAVE NO REASON TO EXECUTE ZERO.
I KNOW.
DON'T WORRY.
WHY WOULD YOU SAVE ME...
...KURAN?
...
I COULDN'T TOLERATE THE EXECUTION OF A FELLOW SCHOOL-MATE...

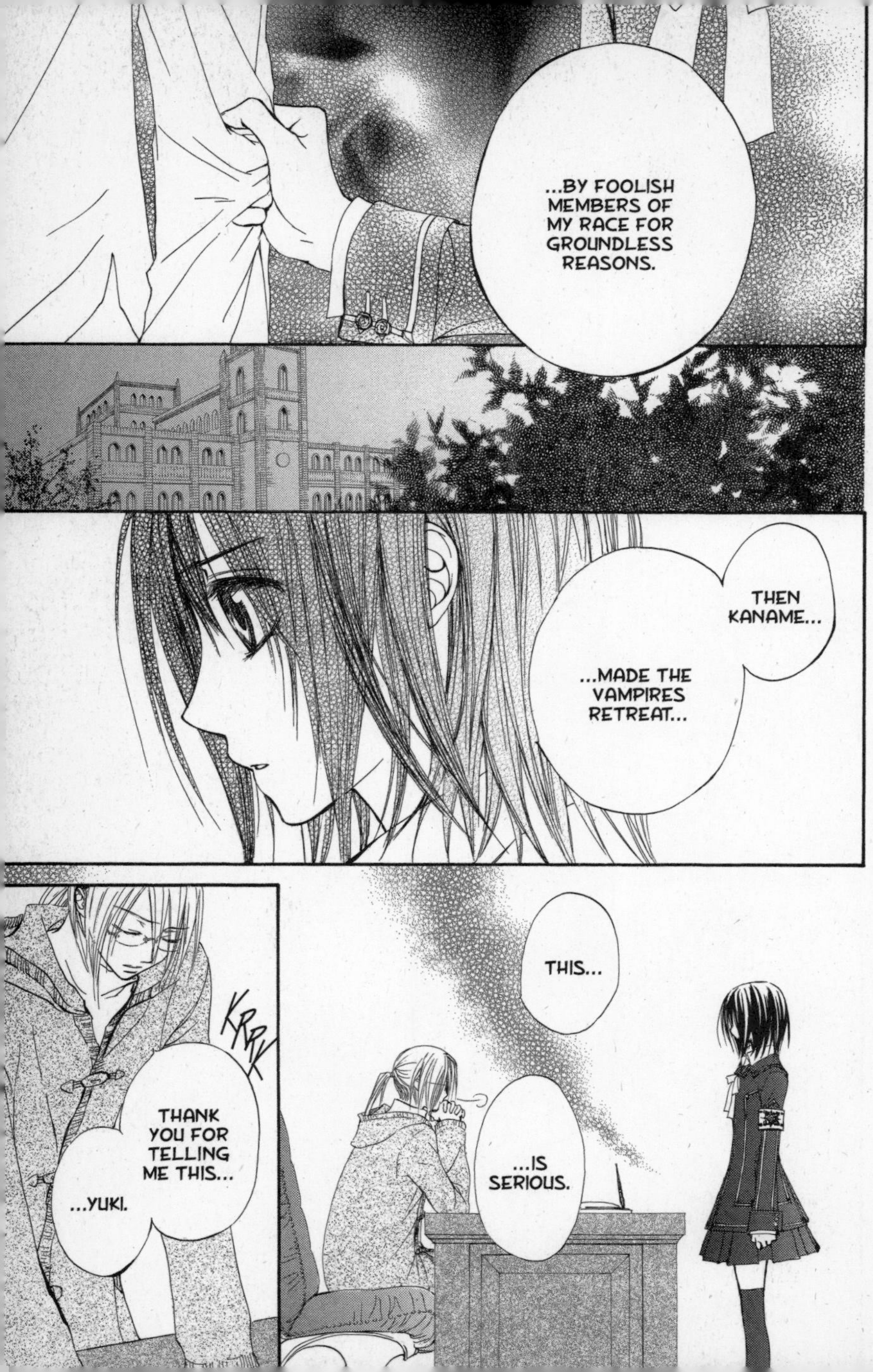
...BY FOOLISH MEMBERS OF MY RACE FOR GROUNDLESS REASONS.
THEN KANAME...
...MADE THE VAMPIRES RETREAT...
THIS...
...IS SERIOUS.
KRRK
THANK YOU FOR TELLING ME THIS...
...YUKI.

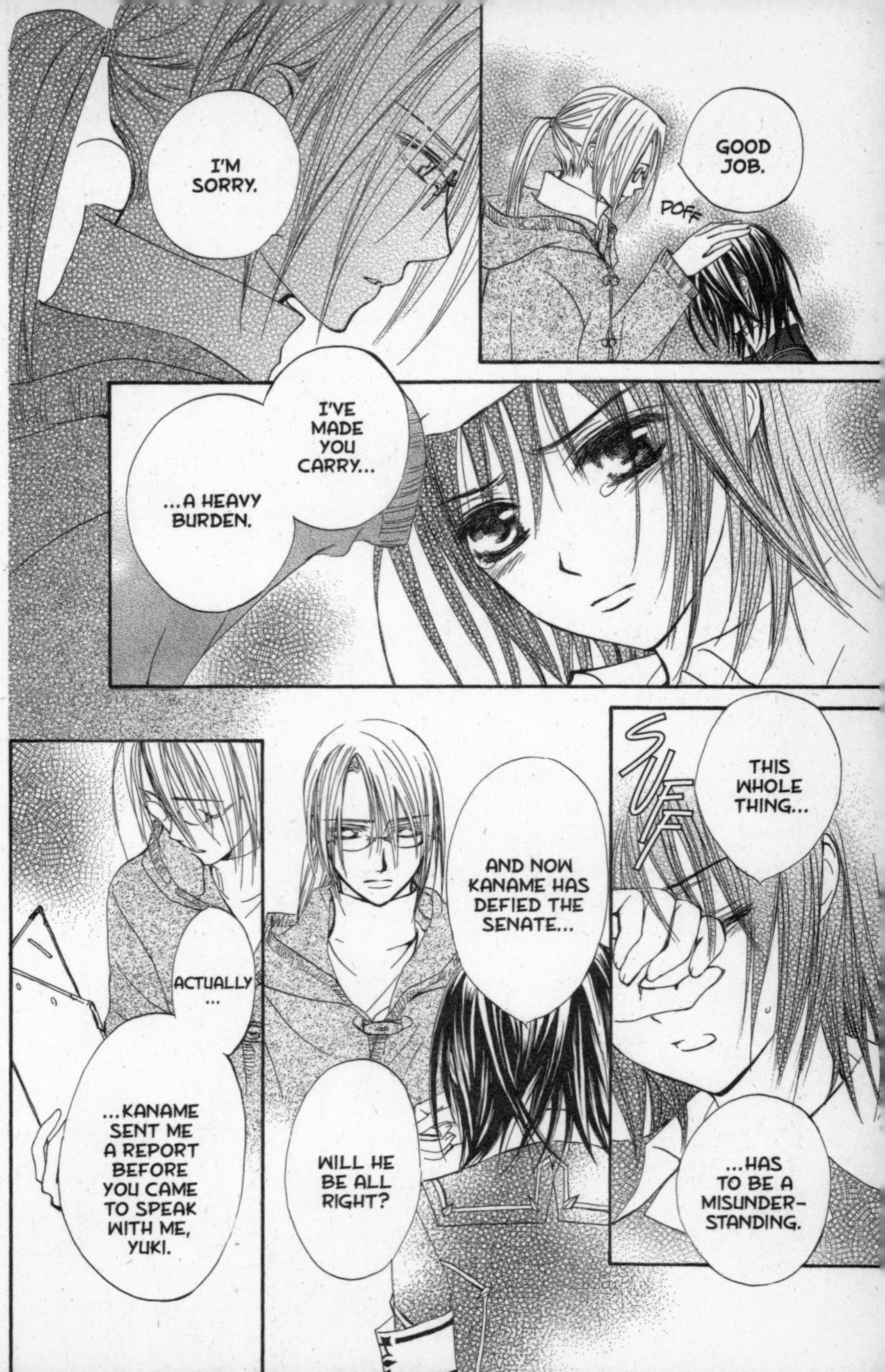
GOOD JOB.
POFF
I'M SORRY.
I'VE MADE YOU CARRY...
...A HEAVY BURDEN.
SUFF
THIS WHOLE THING...
...HAS TO BE A MISUNDER-STANDING.
AND NOW KANAME HAS DEFIED THE SENATE...
WILL HE BE ALL RIGHT?
ACTUALLY...
...KANAME SENT ME A REPORT BEFORE YOU CAME TO SPEAK WITH ME, YUKI.

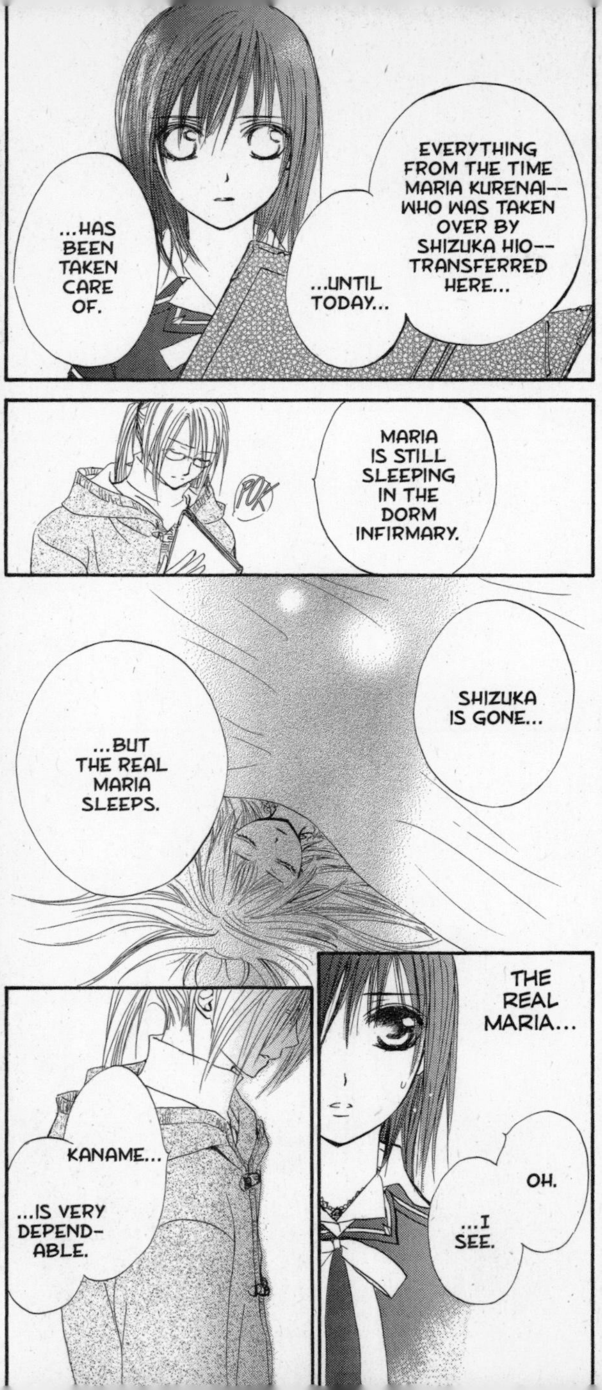
EVERYTHING FROM THE TIME MARIA KURENAI-- WHO WAS TAKEN OVER BY SHIZUKA HIO-- TRANSFERRED HERE...
...UNTIL TODAY...
...HAS BEEN TAKEN CARE OF.
MARIA IS STILL SLEEPING IN THE DORM INFIRMARY.
POK
SHIZUKA IS GONE...
...BUT THE REAL MARIA SLEEPS.
THE REAL MARIA...
OH.
...I SEE.
KANAME...
...IS VERY DEPEND-ABLE.

IV

I heard lots of interesting stories from the people in VIZ Media's Shojo Beat department. I learned a lot. I understood that American girls enjoy shojo manga the same way that Japanese girls do. Woo!

I'd like to use this space to give my heartfelt thanks to everyone at Shojo Beat. Thank you very much! I will take English conversation lessons!! ? [And I'll keep working on improving my Japanese! —Ed.]

I'm really happy I can connect to various places in the world through shojo manga. ♡

(Extra: At a large bookstore that they took me to in the U.S., I bought a huge book on weaponry for reference material—the book is not sold in Japan. The young man at the store, wearing wild-looking clothes, grumbled, "Oh, crazy!" [wry smile] Having him say this to me face-to-face was actually refreshing...)

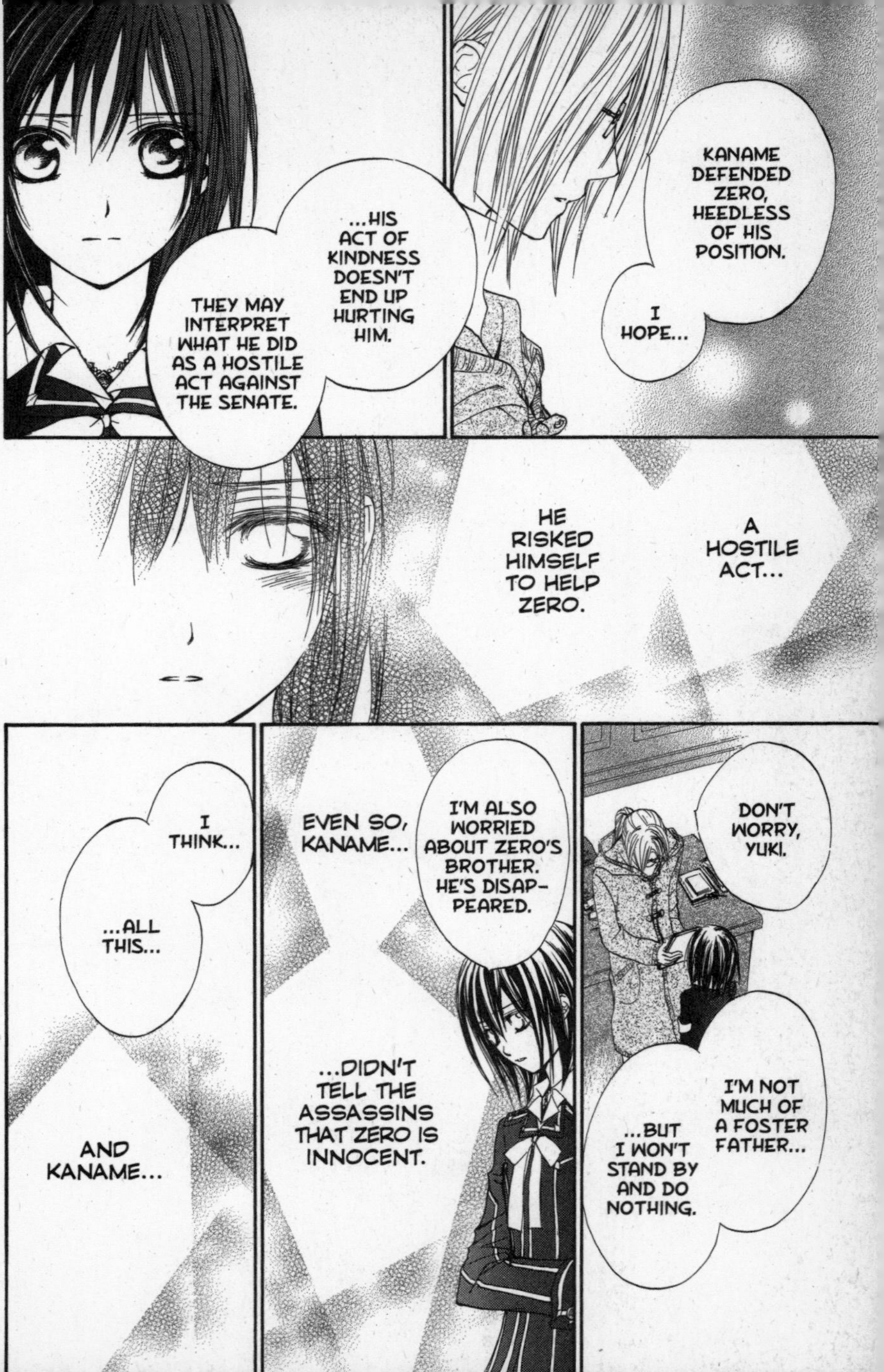
KANAME DEFENDED ZERO, HEEDLESS OF HIS POSITION.
I HOPE...
...HIS ACT OF KINDNESS DOESN'T END UP HURTING HIM.
THEY MAY INTERPRET WHAT HE DID AS A HOSTILE ACT AGAINST THE SENATE.
A HOSTILE ACT...
HE RISKED HIMSELF TO HELP ZERO.
DON'T WORRY, YUKI.
I'M NOT MUCH OF A FOSTER FATHER...
...BUT I WON'T STAND BY AND DO NOTHING.
I'M ALSO WORRIED ABOUT ZERO'S BROTHER. HE'S DISAP-PEARED.
EVEN SO, KANAME...
...DIDN'T TELL THE ASSASSINS THAT ZERO IS INNOCENT.
I THINK...
...ALL THIS...
AND KANAME...

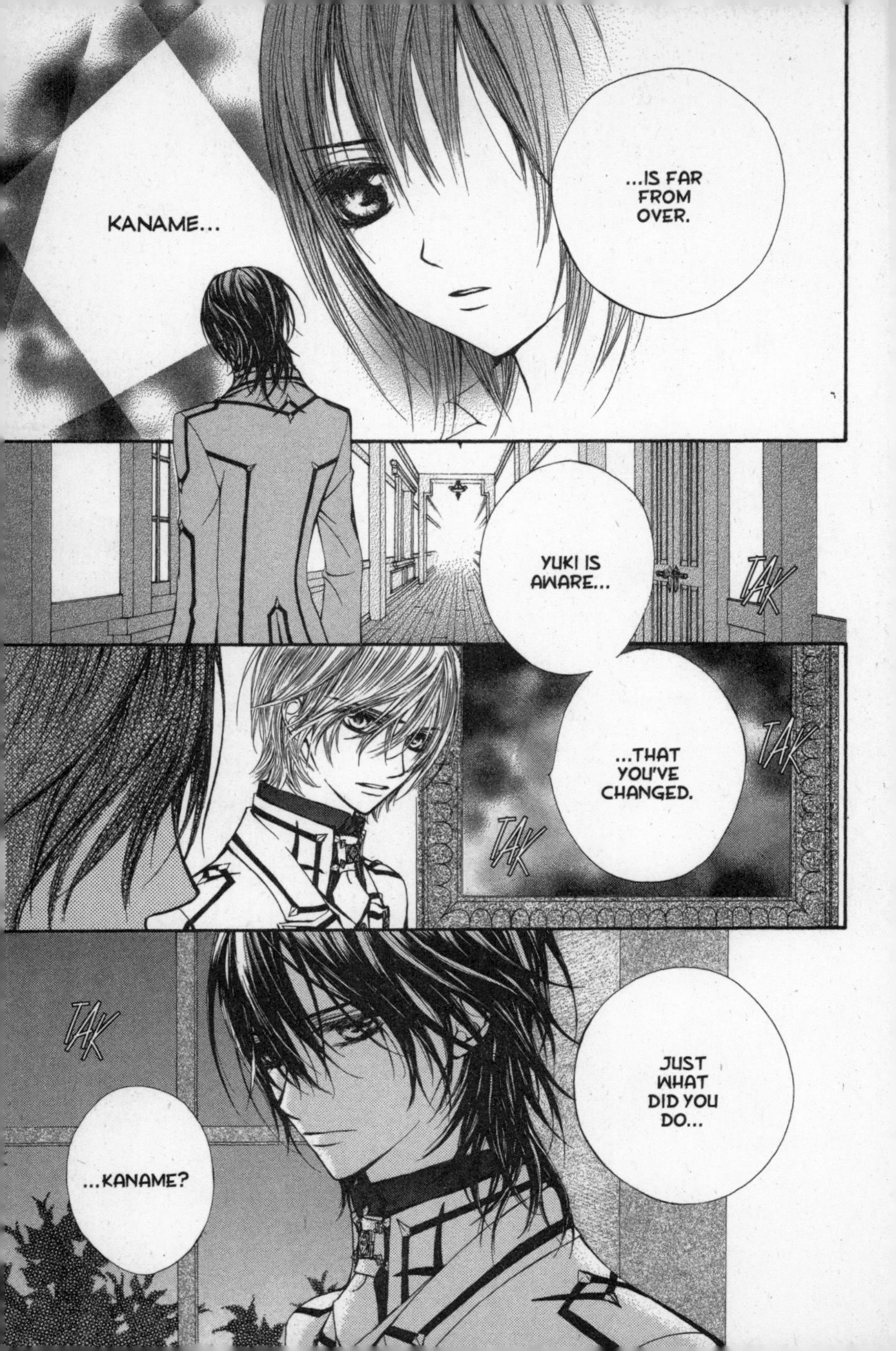
...IS FAR FROM OVER.
KANAME...
TAK
YUKI IS AWARE...
TAK
...THAT YOU'VE CHANGED.
TAK
JUST WHAT DID YOU DO...
TAK
...KANAME?

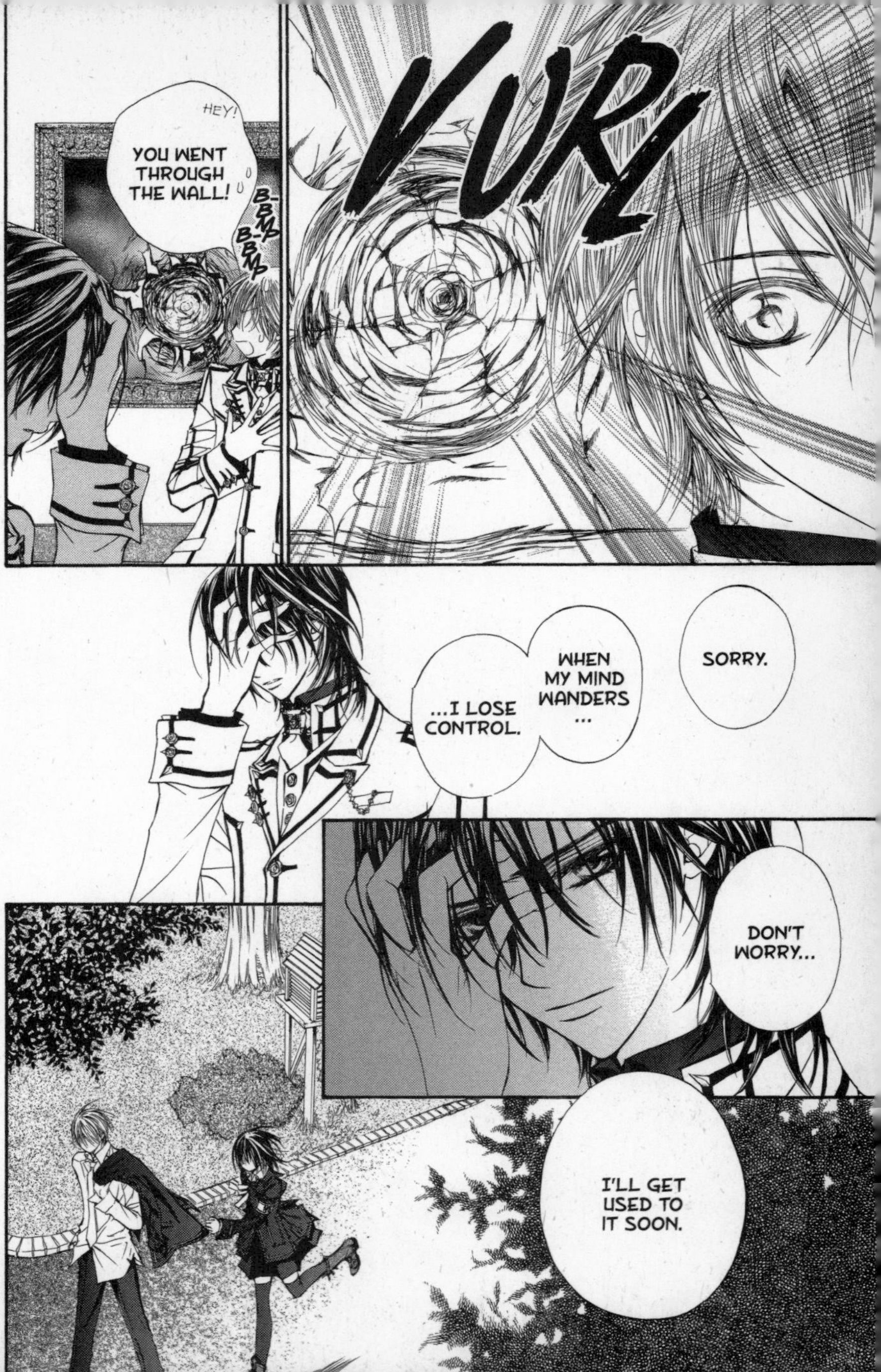
VUR
HEY!
YOU WENT THROUGH THE WALL!
B-BMP B-BMP
SORRY.
WHEN MY MIND WANDERS...
...I LOSE CONTROL.
DON'T WORRY...
I'LL GET USED TO IT SOON.

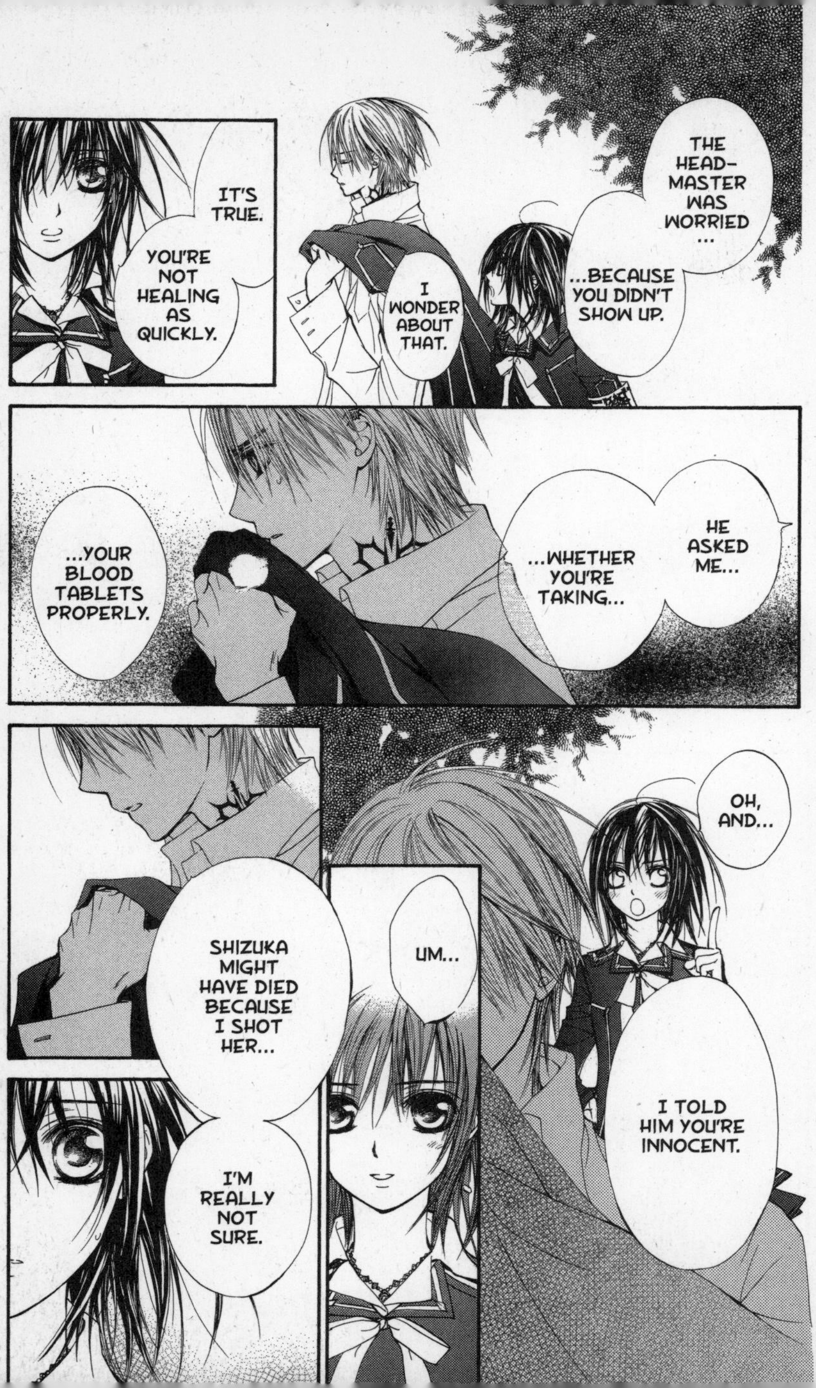
THE HEAD-MASTER WAS WORRIED...
...BECAUSE YOU DIDN'T SHOW UP.
I WONDER ABOUT THAT.
IT'S TRUE.
YOU'RE NOT HEALING AS QUICKLY.
HE ASKED ME...
...WHETHER YOU'RE TAKING...
...YOUR BLOOD TABLETS PROPERLY.
OH, AND...
I TOLD HIM YOU'RE INNOCENT.
UM...
SHIZUKA MIGHT HAVE DIED BECAUSE I SHOT HER...
I'M REALLY NOT SURE.

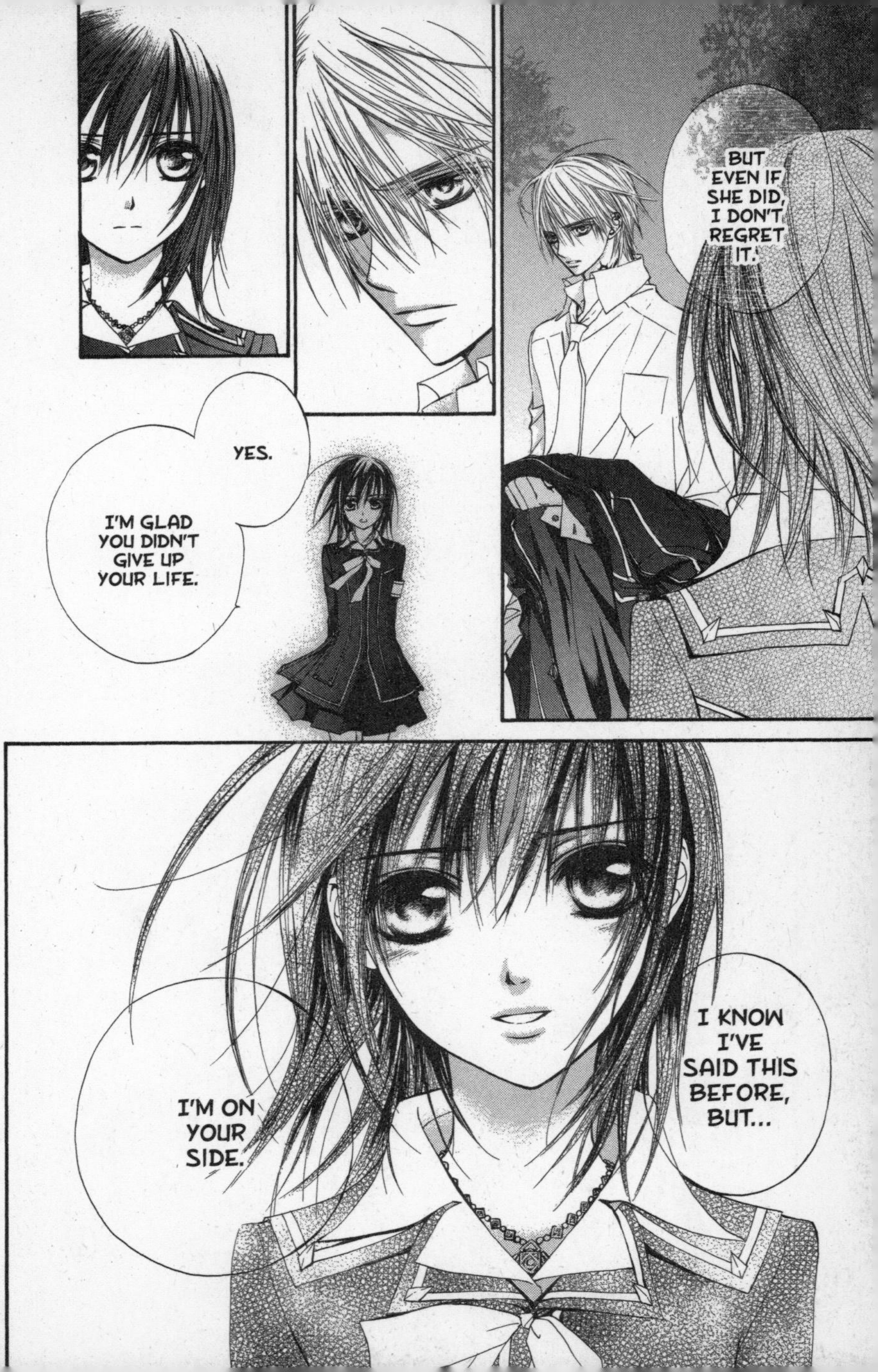
BUT EVEN IF SHE DID, I DON'T REGRET IT.
YES.
I'M GLAD YOU DIDN'T GIVE UP YOUR LIFE.
I KNOW I'VE SAID THIS BEFORE, BUT...
I'M ON YOUR SIDE.

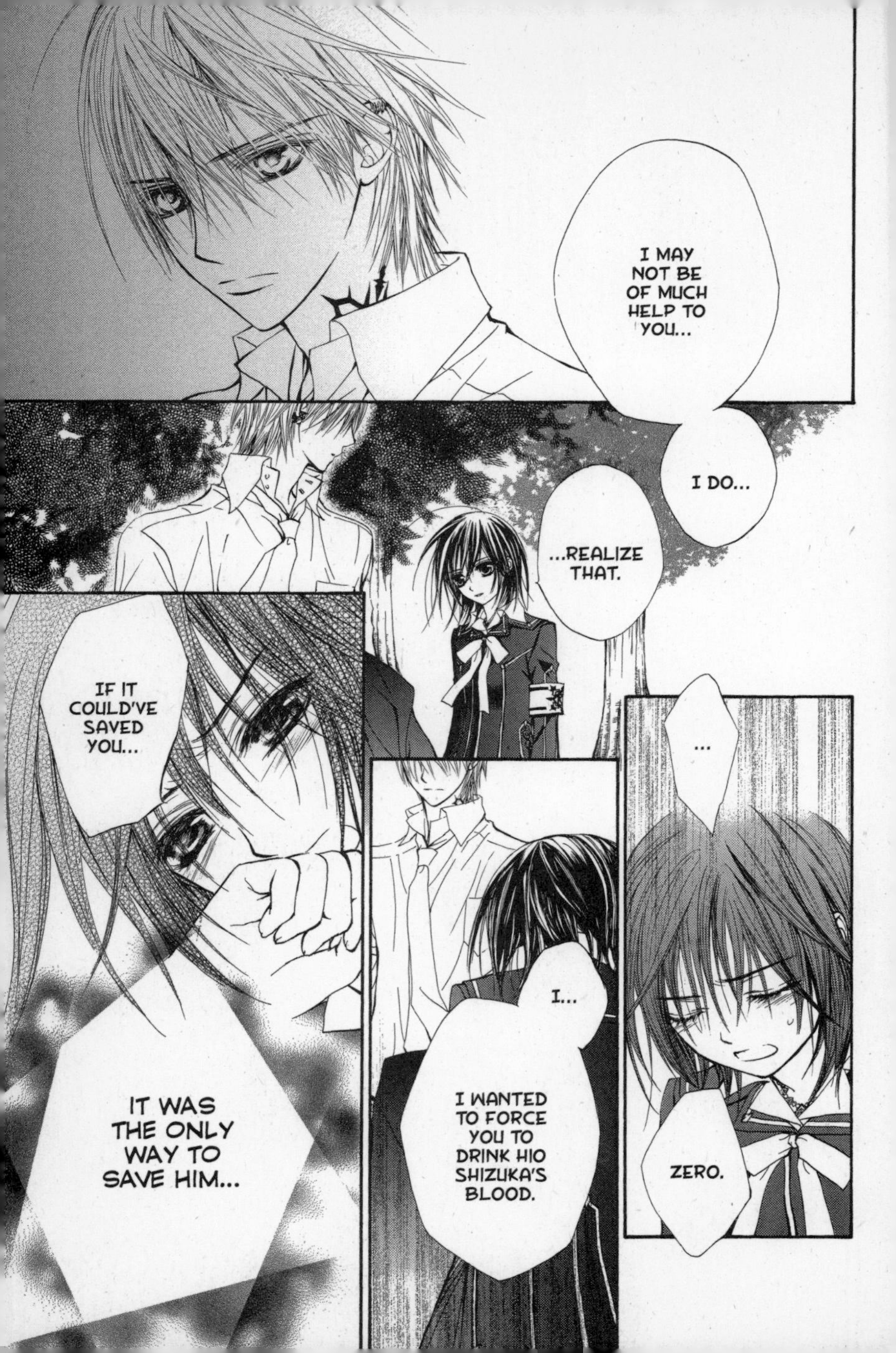
I MAY NOT BE OF MUCH HELP TO YOU...
I DO...
...REALIZE THAT.
...
ZERO.
I...
I WANTED TO FORCE YOU TO DRINK HIO SHIZUKA'S BLOOD.
IF IT COULD'VE SAVED YOU...
IT WAS THE ONLY WAY TO SAVE HIM...

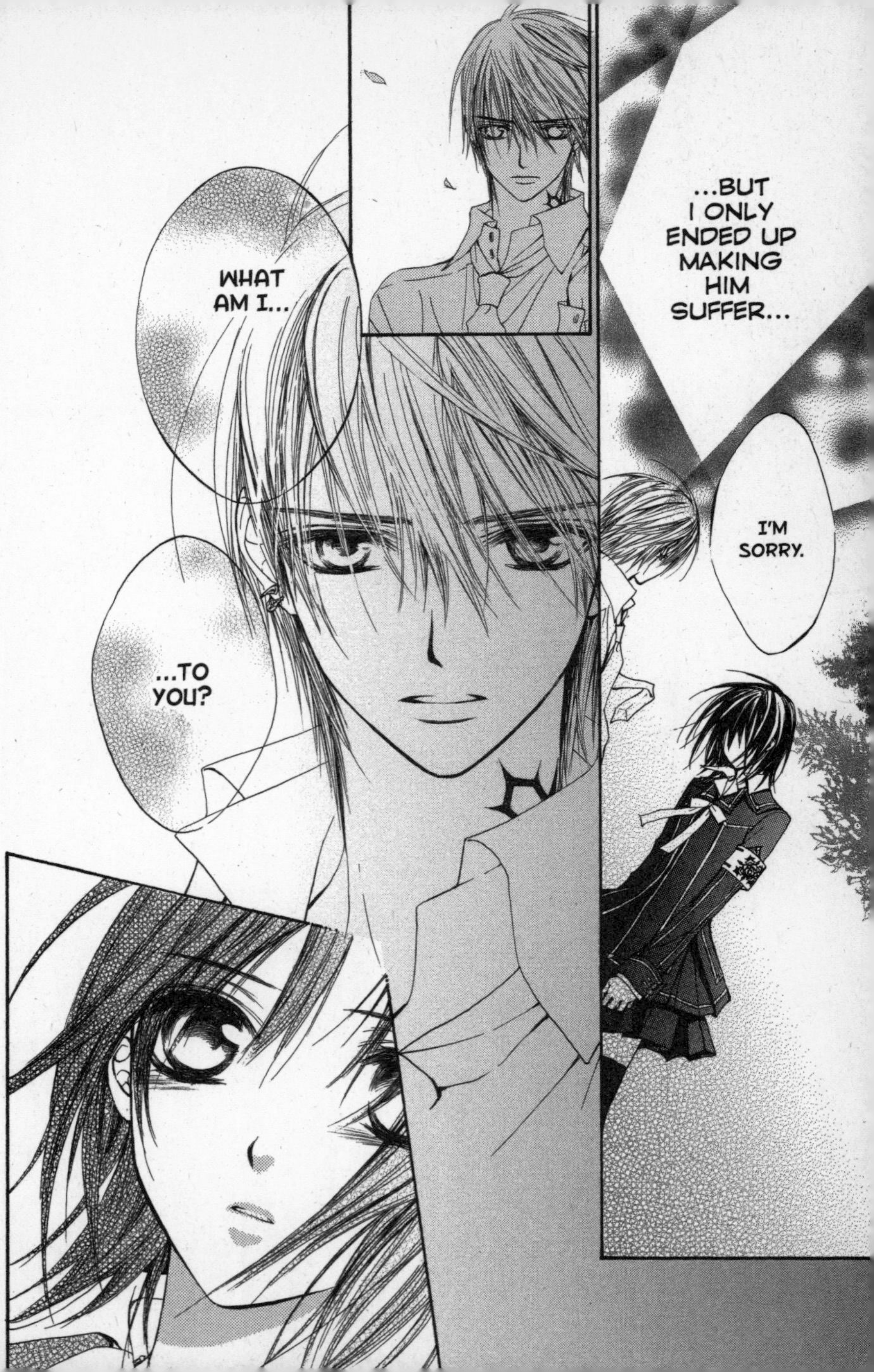
...BUT I ONLY ENDED UP MAKING HIM SUFFER...
I'M SORRY.
WHAT AM I...
...TO YOU?

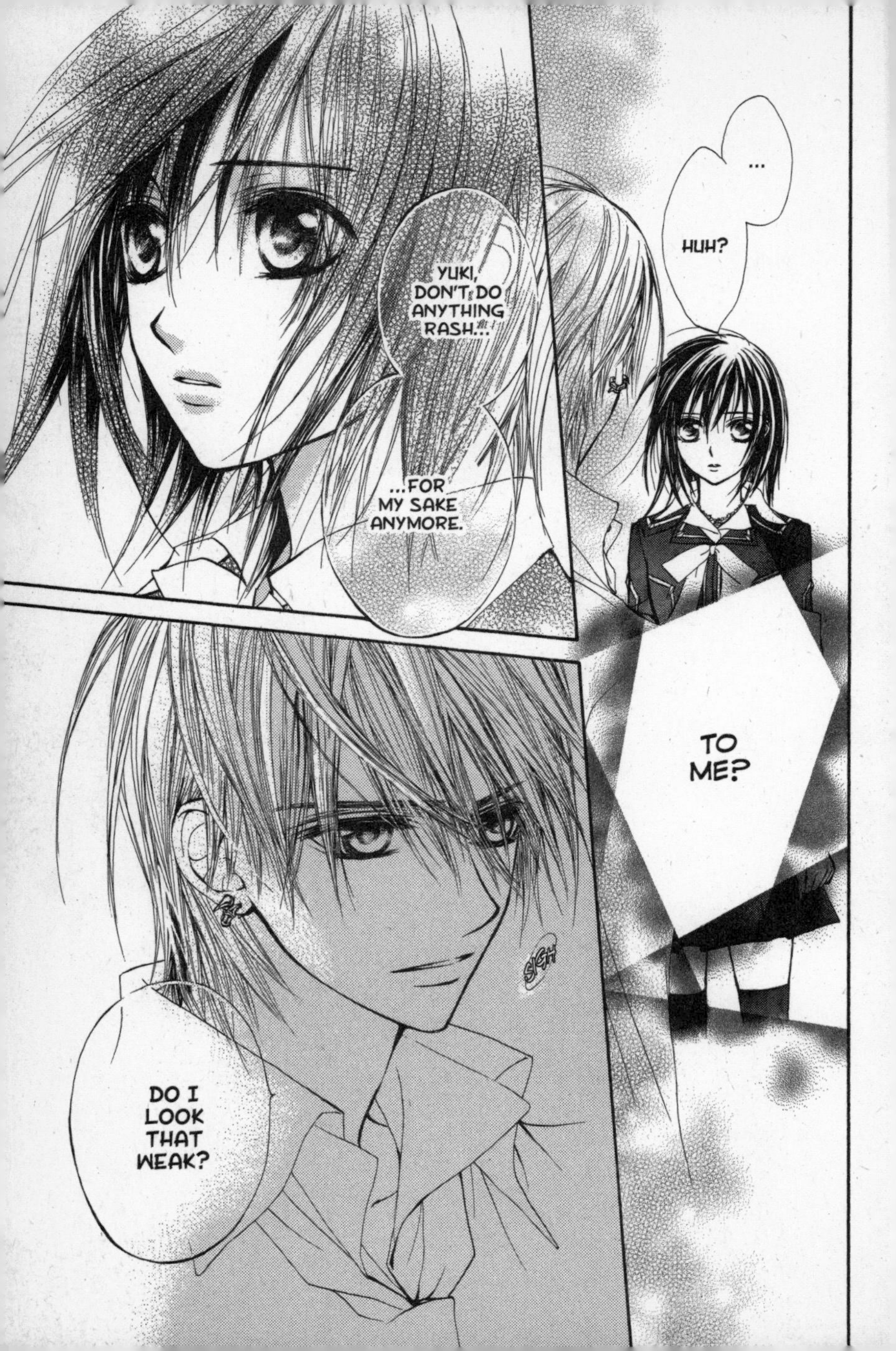
...
HUH?
TO ME?
YUKI, DON'T DO ANYTHING RASH...
...FOR MY SAKE ANYMORE.
SIGH
DO I LOOK THAT WEAK?

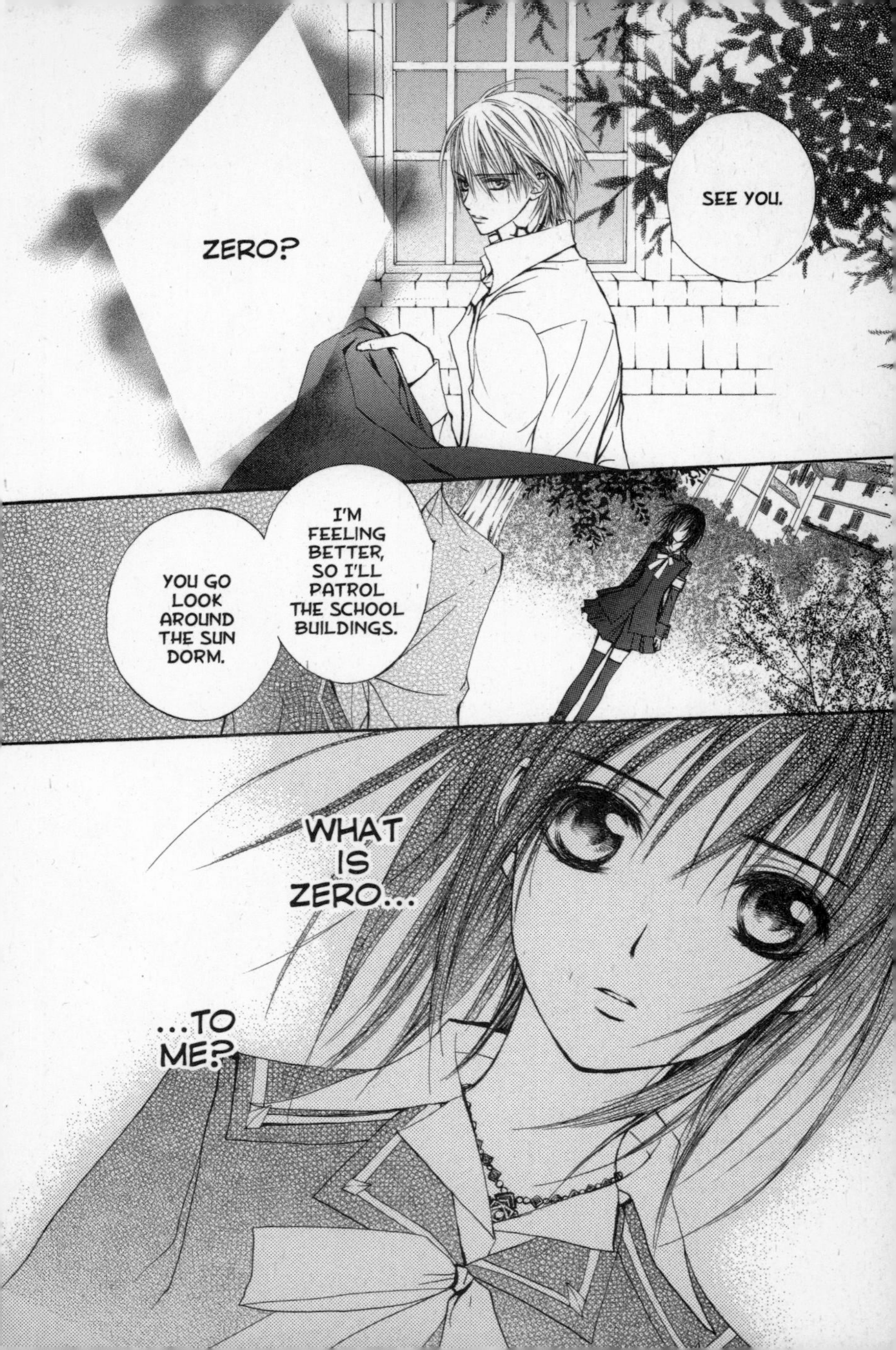
SEE YOU.
ZERO?
I'M FEELING BETTER, SO I'LL PATROL THE SCHOOL BUILDINGS.
YOU GO LOOK AROUND THE SUN DORM.
WHAT IS ZERO...
...TO ME?

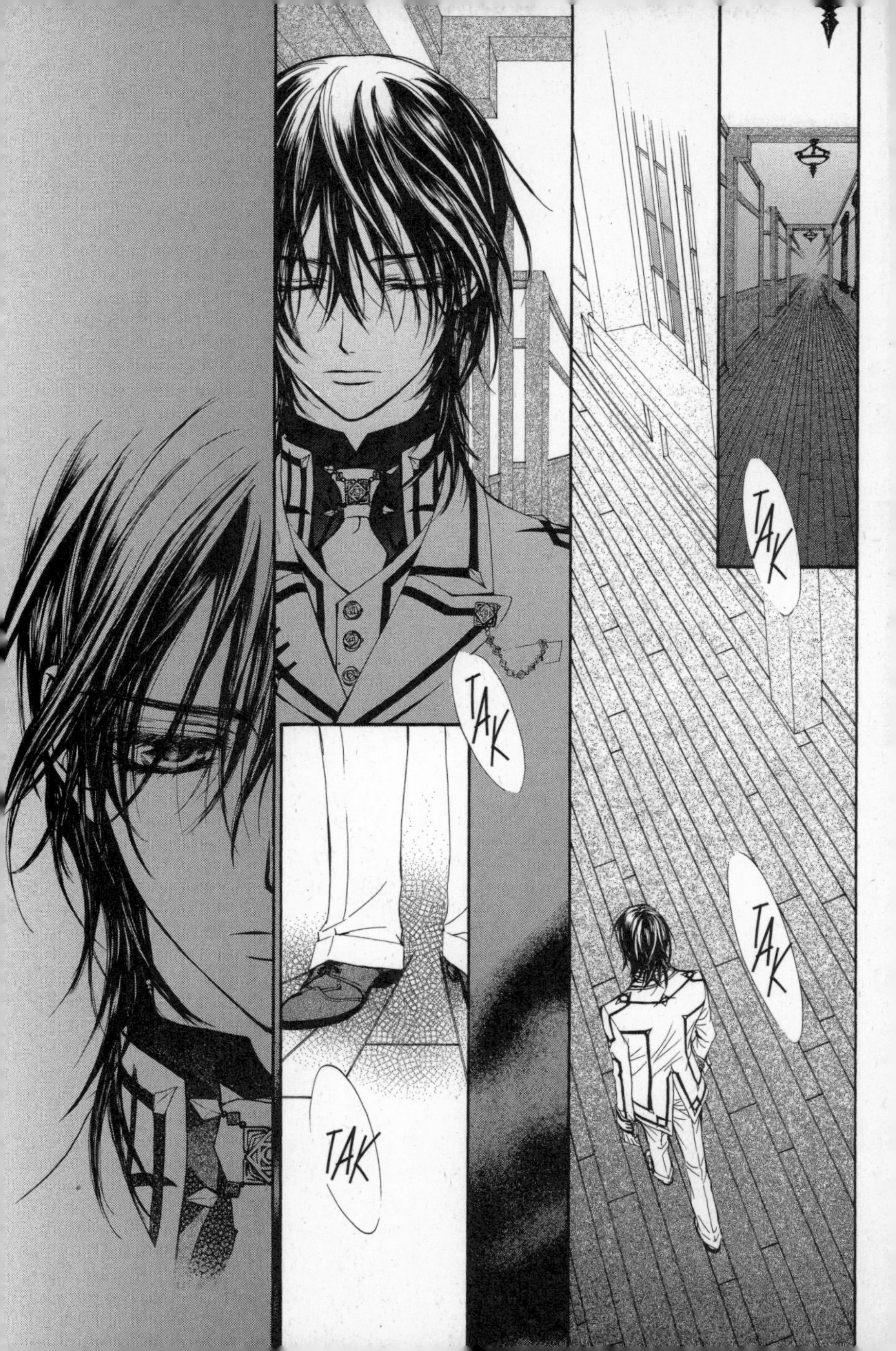
TAK
TAK
TAK
TAK

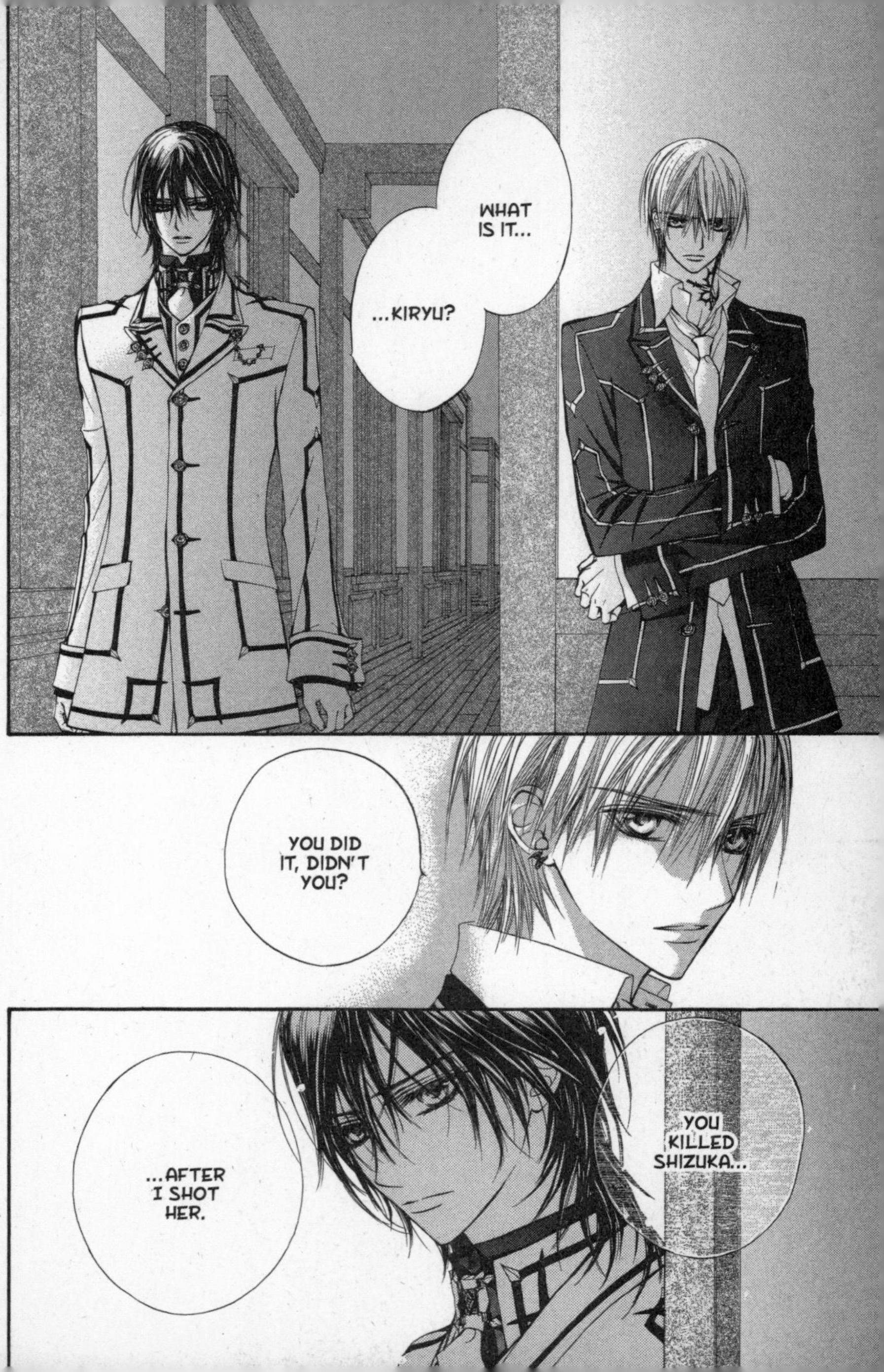
WHAT IS IT...
...KIRYU?
YOU DID IT, DIDN'T YOU?
YOU KILLED SHIZUKA...
...AFTER I SHOT HER.

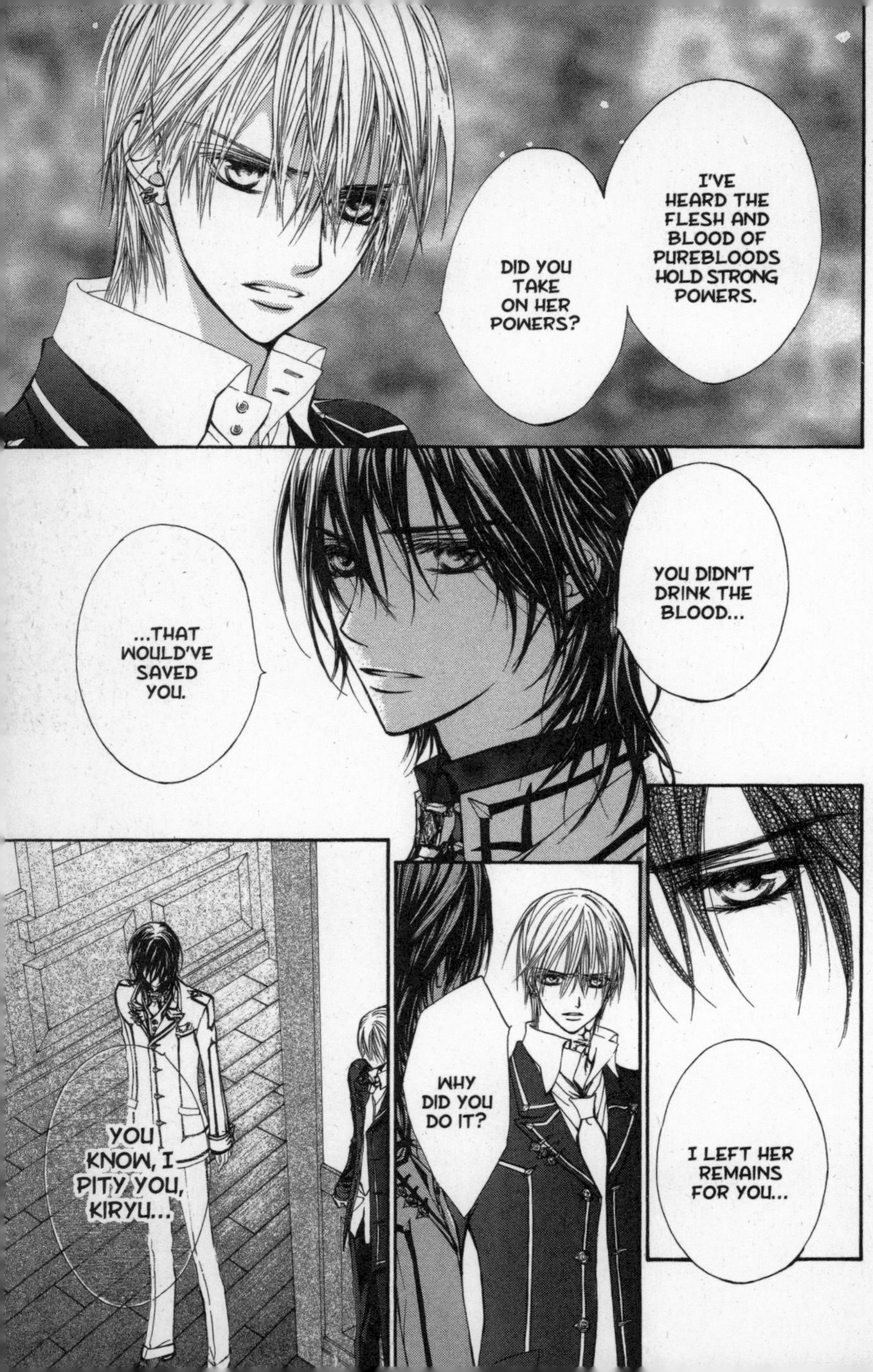
I'VE HEARD THE FLESH AND BLOOD OF PUREBLOODS HOLD STRONG POWERS.
DID YOU TAKE ON HER POWERS?
YOU DIDN'T DRINK THE BLOOD...
...THAT WOULD'VE SAVED YOU.
I LEFT HER REMAINS FOR YOU...
WHY DID YOU DO IT?
YOU KNOW, I PITY YOU, KIRYU...

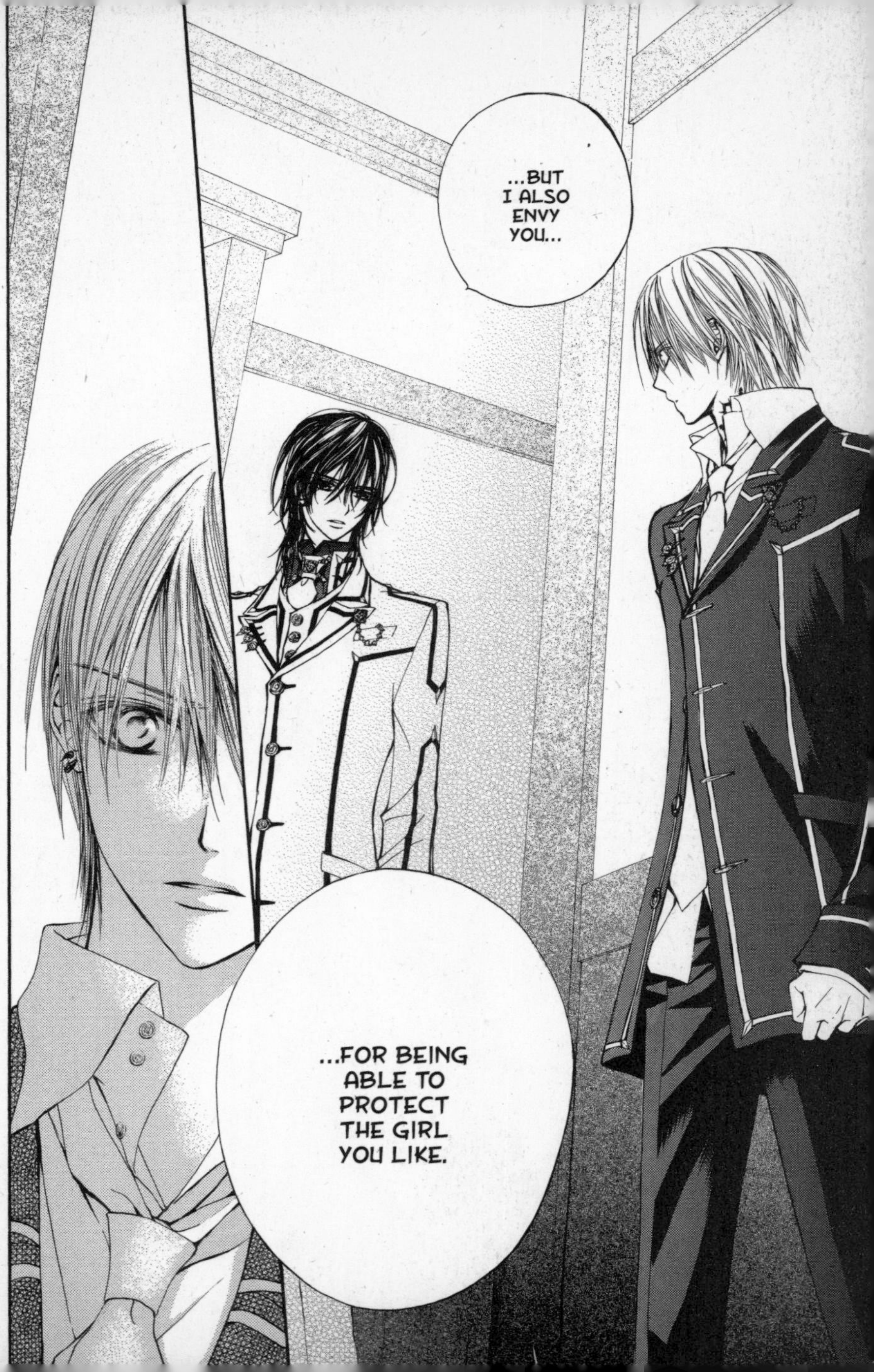
...BUT I ALSO ENVY YOU...
...FOR BEING ABLE TO PROTECT THE GIRL YOU LIKE.

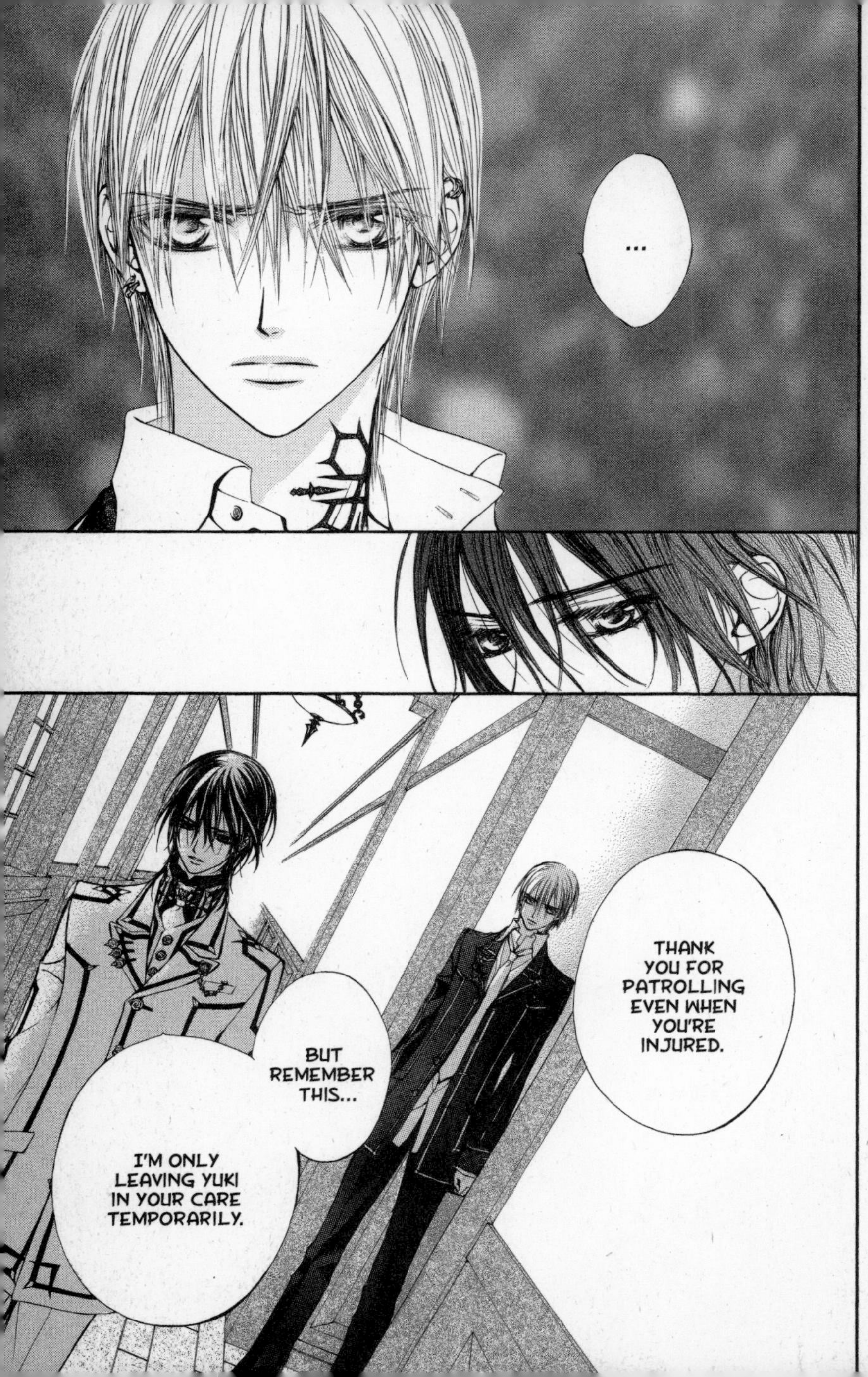
...
THANK YOU FOR PATROLLING EVEN WHEN YOU'RE INJURED.
BUT REMEMBER THIS...
I'M ONLY LEAVING YUKI IN YOUR CARE TEMPORARILY.

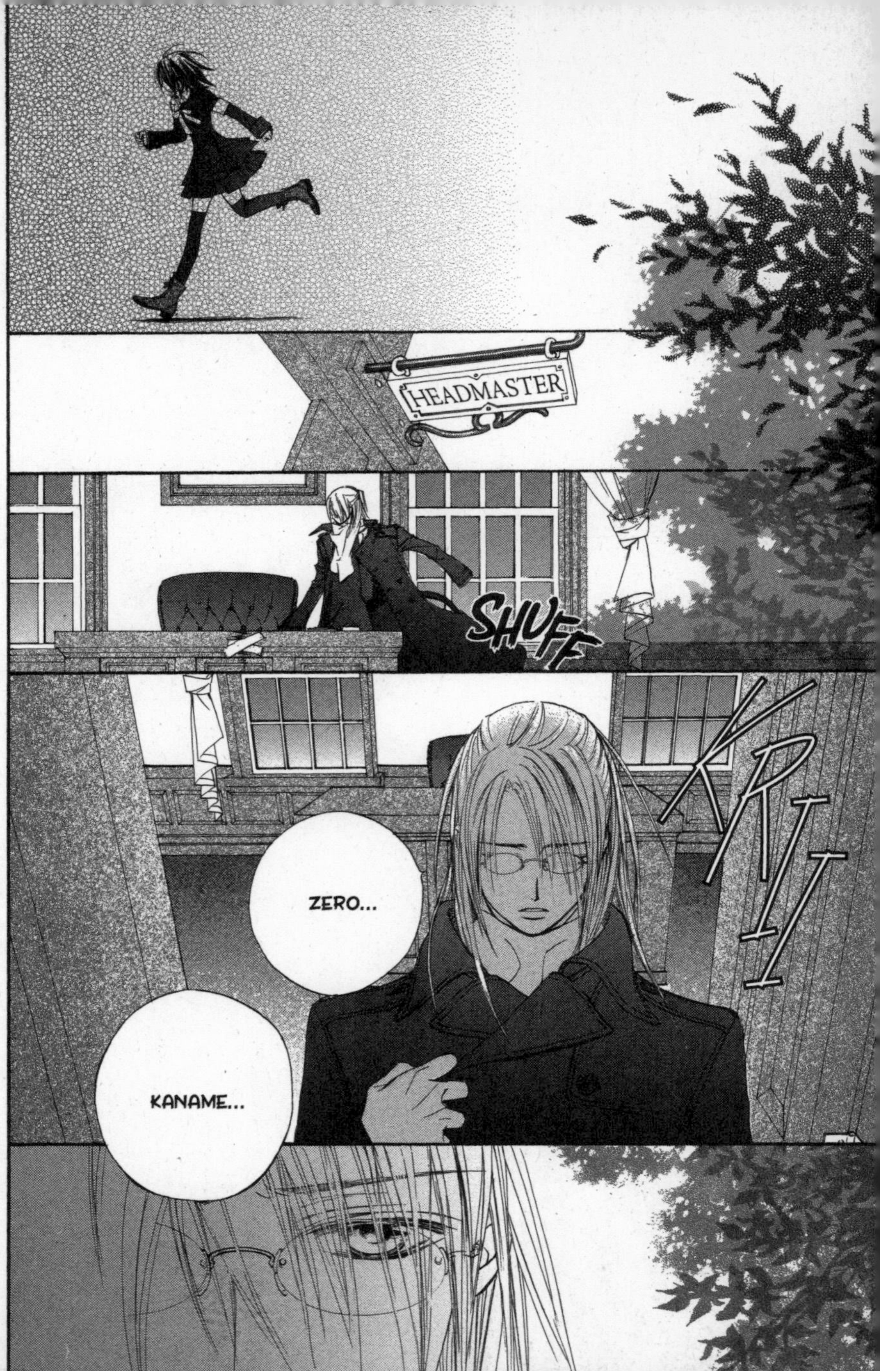
HEADMASTER
SHUFF
KRII
ZERO...
KANAME...

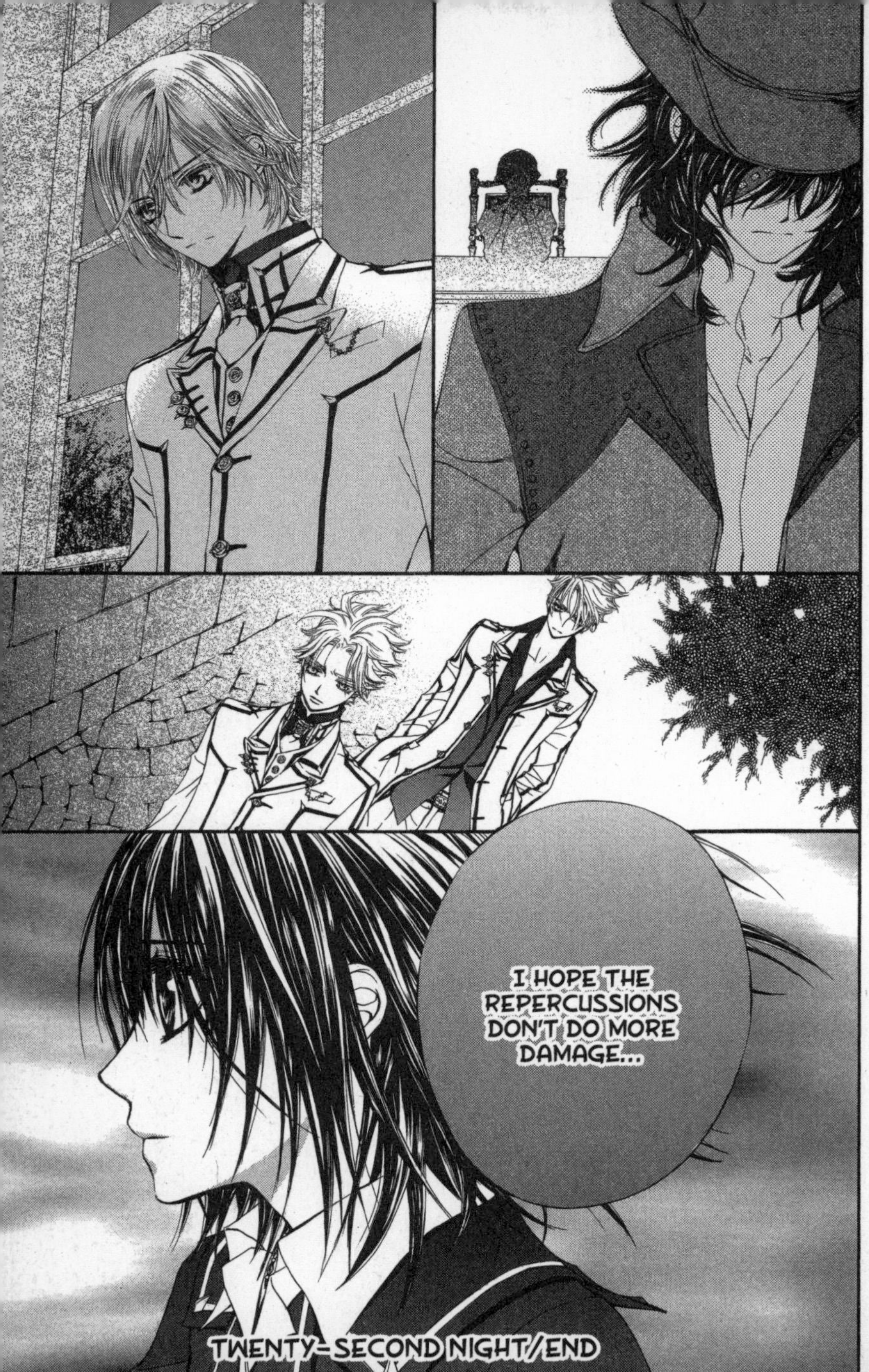
I HOPE THE REPERCUSSIONS DON'T DO MORE DAMAGE...
TWENTY-SECOND NIGHT/END

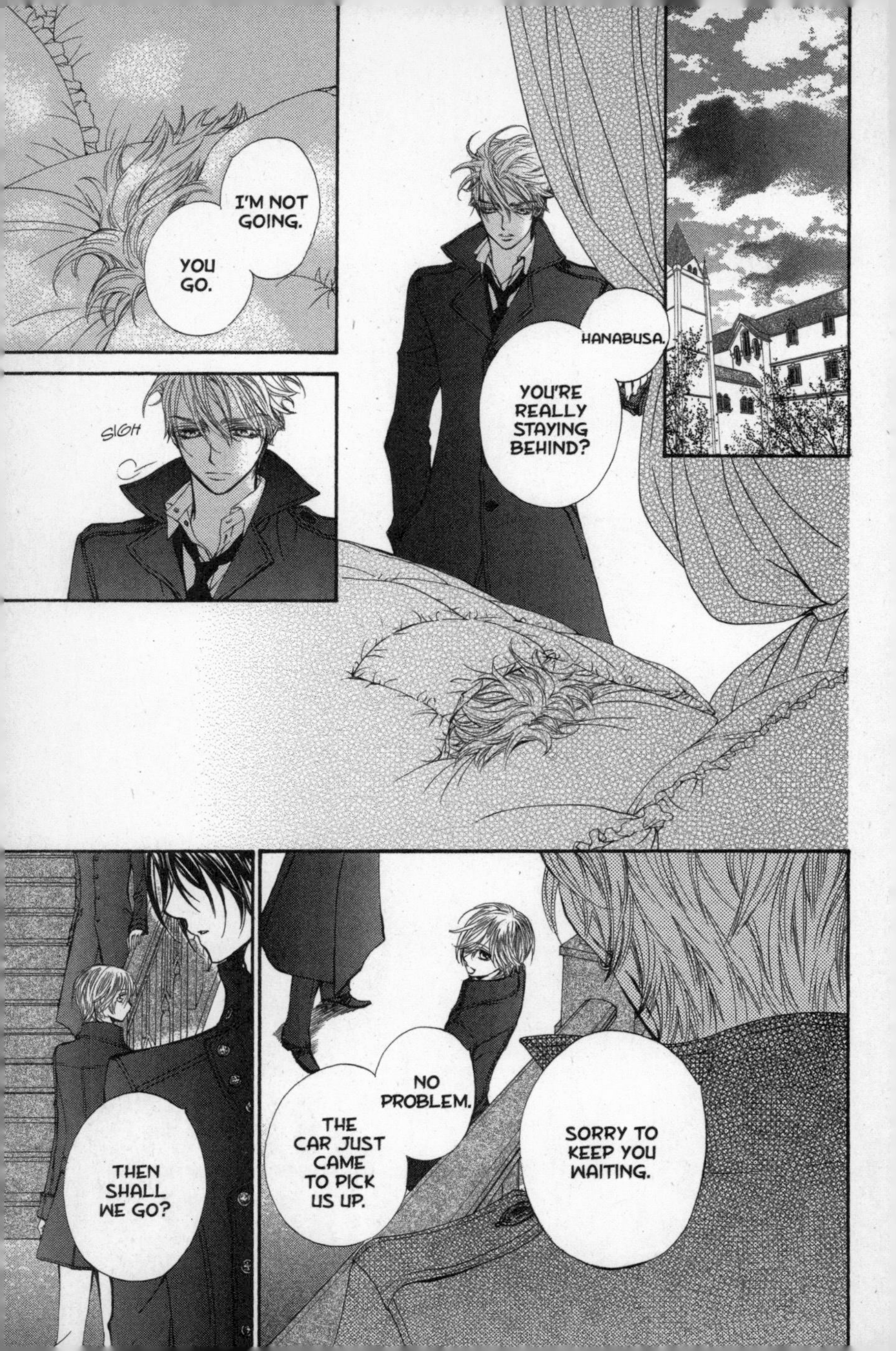
HANABUSA.
YOU'RE REALLY STAYING BEHIND?
I'M NOT GOING.
YOU GO.
SIGH
SORRY TO KEEP YOU WAITING.
NO PROBLEM.
THE CAR JUST CAME TO PICK US UP.
THEN SHALL WE GO?

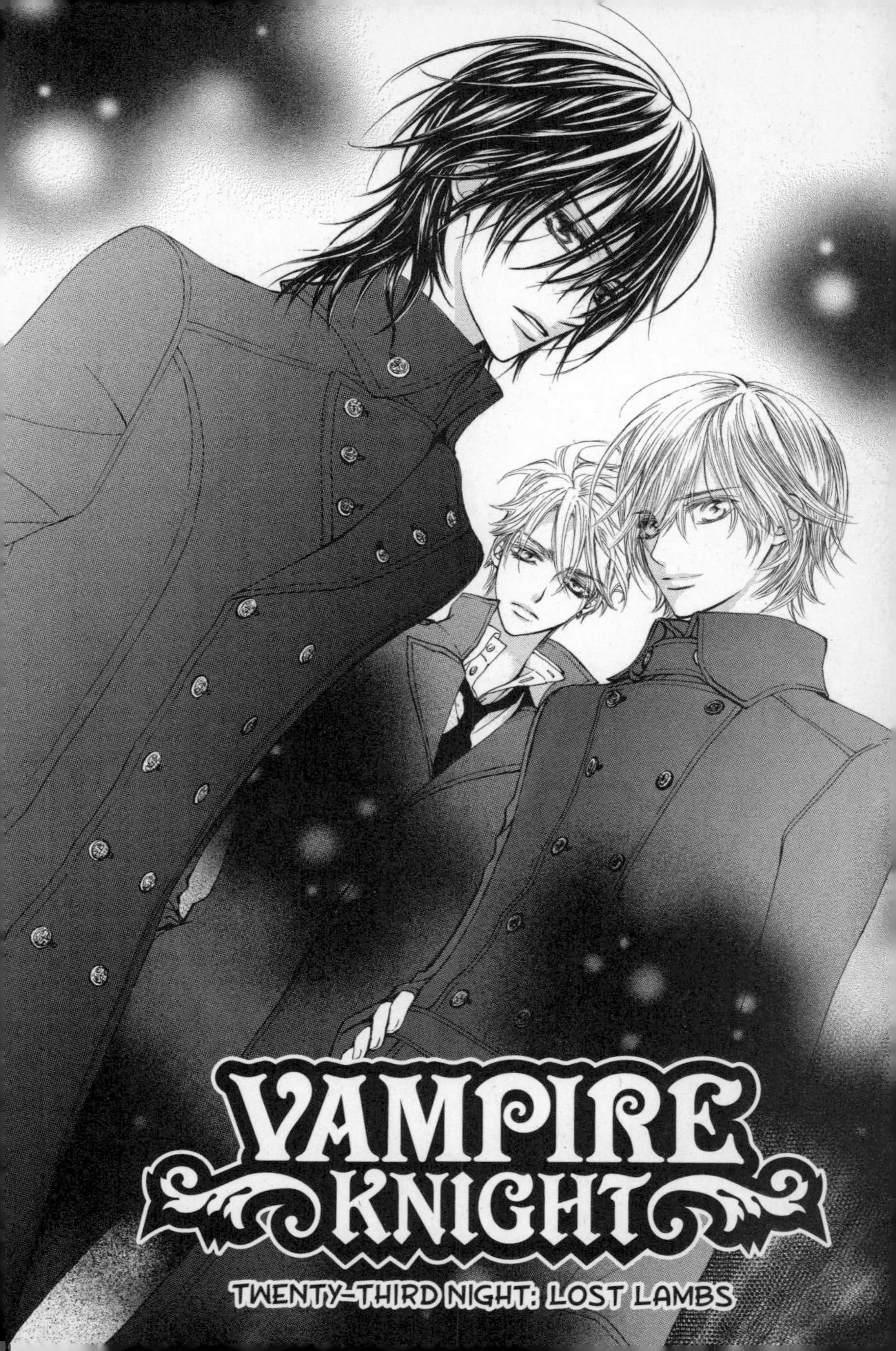
VAMPIRE KNIGHT
TWENTY-THIRD NIGHT: LOST LAMBS

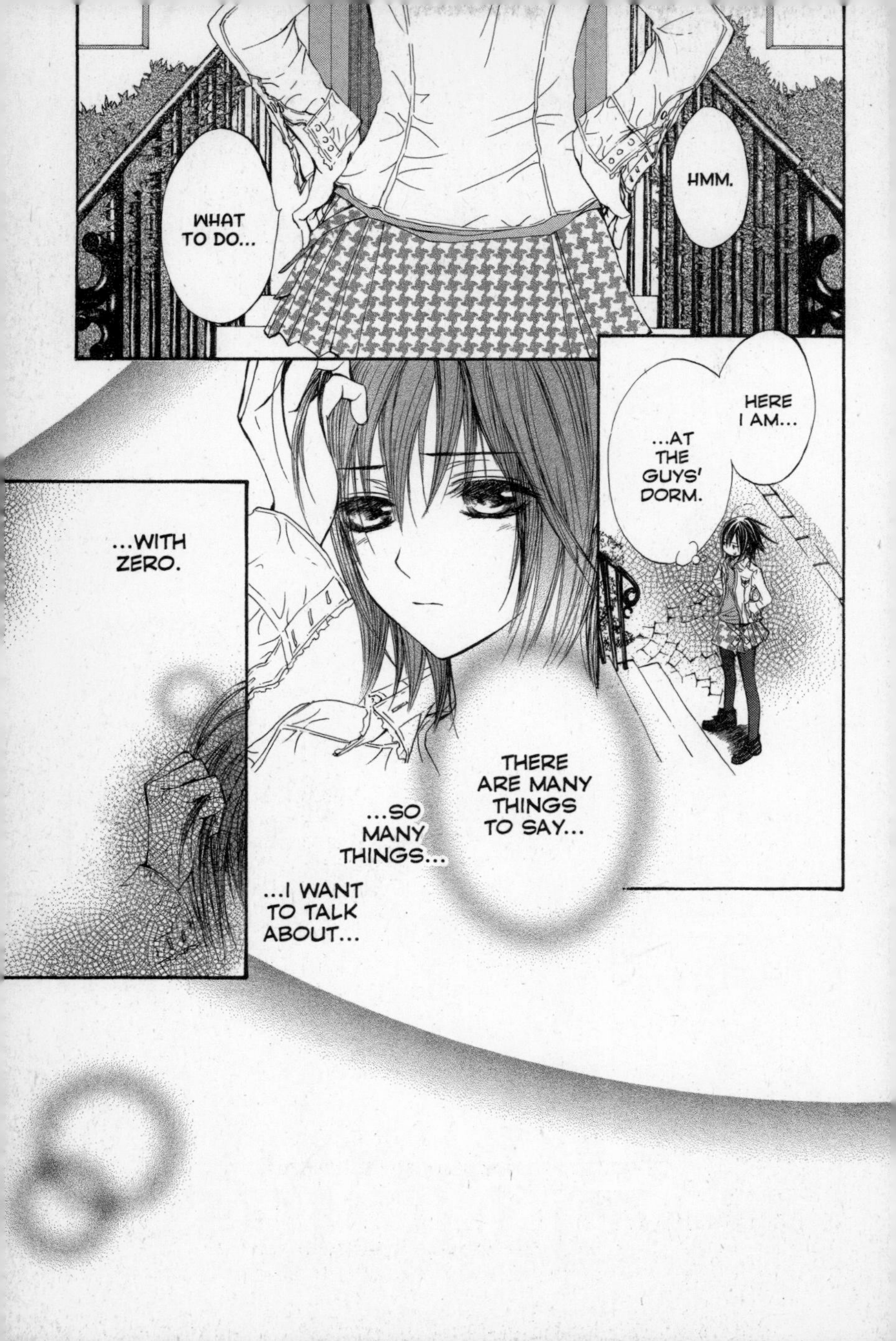
HMM.
WHAT TO DO...
HERE I AM...
...AT THE GUYS' DORM.
...WITH ZERO.
THERE ARE MANY THINGS TO SAY...
...SO MANY THINGS...
...I WANT TO TALK ABOUT...

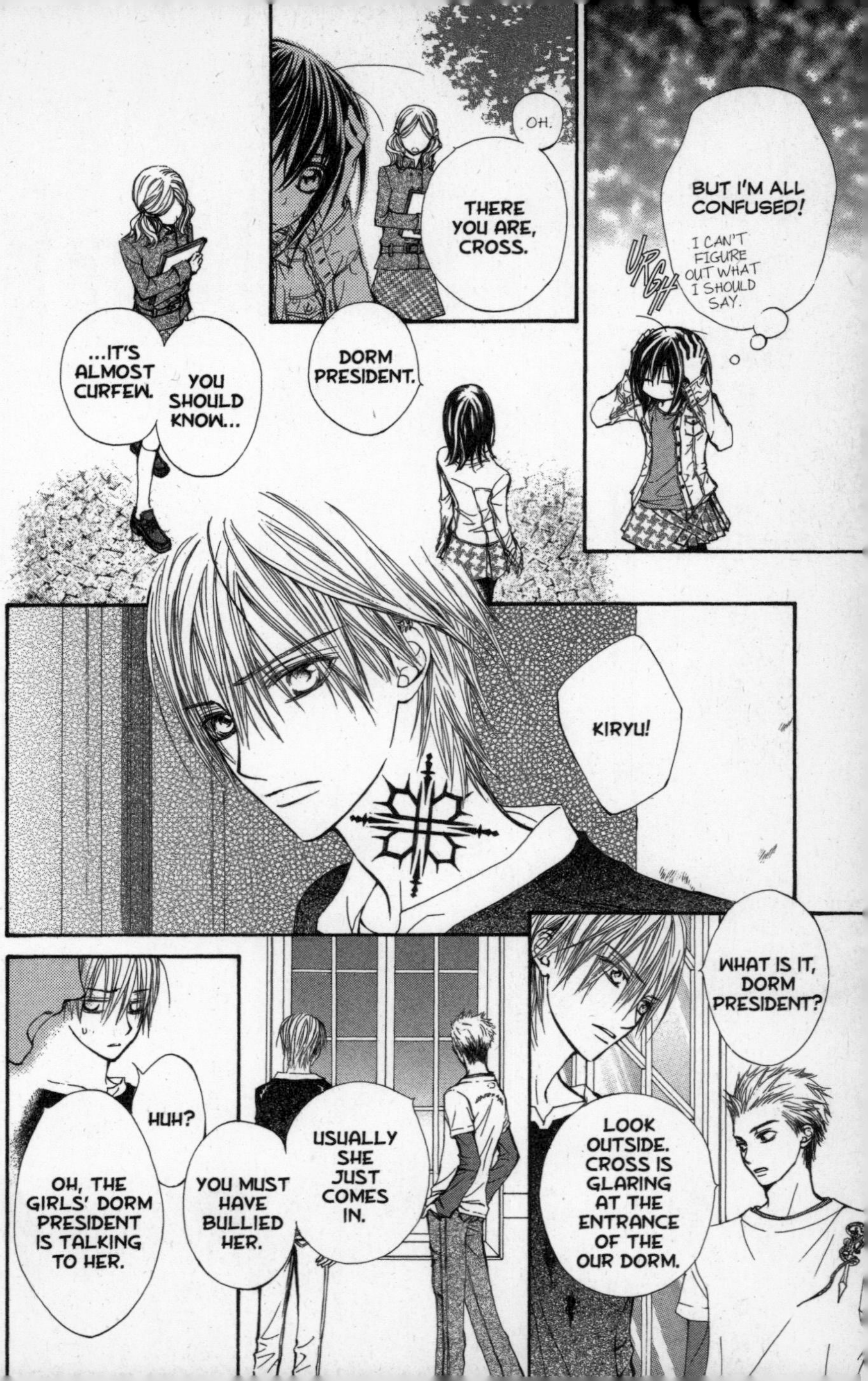
BUT I'M ALL CONFUSED!
URGH
I CAN'T FIGURE OUT WHAT I SHOULD SAY.
OH.
THERE YOU ARE, CROSS.
DORM PRESIDENT.
YOU SHOULD KNOW...
...IT'S ALMOST CURFEW.
KIRYU!
WHAT IS IT, DORM PRESIDENT?
LOOK OUTSIDE. CROSS IS GLARING AT THE ENTRANCE OF THE OUR DORM.
USUALLY SHE JUST COMES IN.
YOU MUST HAVE BULLIED HER.
HUH?
OH, THE GIRLS' DORM PRESIDENT IS TALKING TO HER.

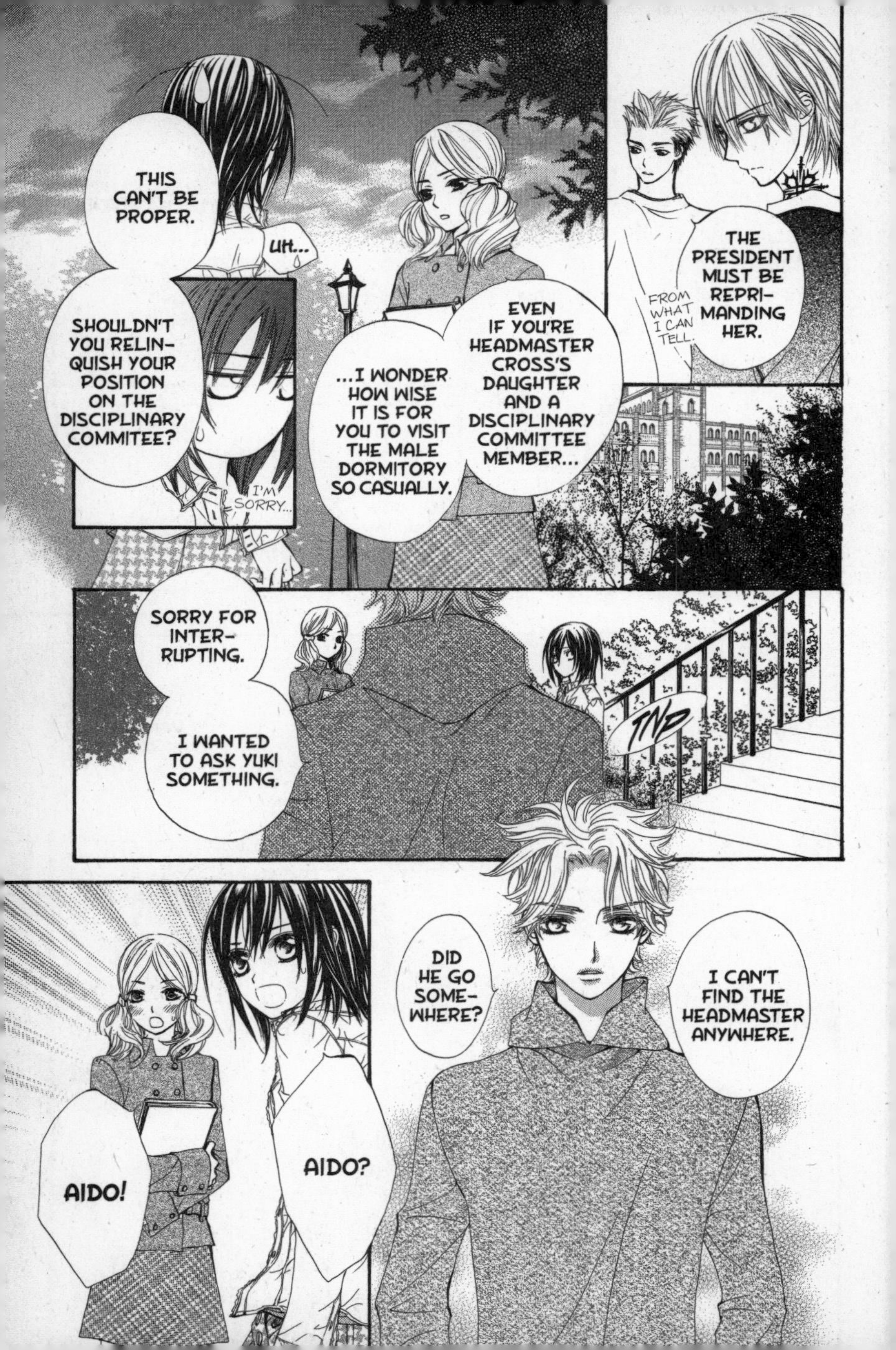
THE PRESIDENT MUST BE REPRI-MANDING HER.
FROM WHAT I CAN TELL.
EVEN IF YOU'RE HEADMASTER CROSS'S DAUGHTER AND A DISCIPLINARY COMMITTEE MEMBER...
...I WONDER HOW WISE IT IS FOR YOU TO VISIT THE MALE DORMITORY SO CASUALLY.
UH...
THIS CAN'T BE PROPER.
SHOULDN'T YOU RELIN-QUISH YOUR POSITION ON THE DISCIPLINARY COMMITEE?
I'M SORRY...
TMP
SORRY FOR INTER-RUPTING.
I WANTED TO ASK YUKI SOMETHING.
I CAN'T FIND THE HEADMASTER ANYWHERE.
DID HE GO SOME-WHERE?
AIDO?
AIDO!

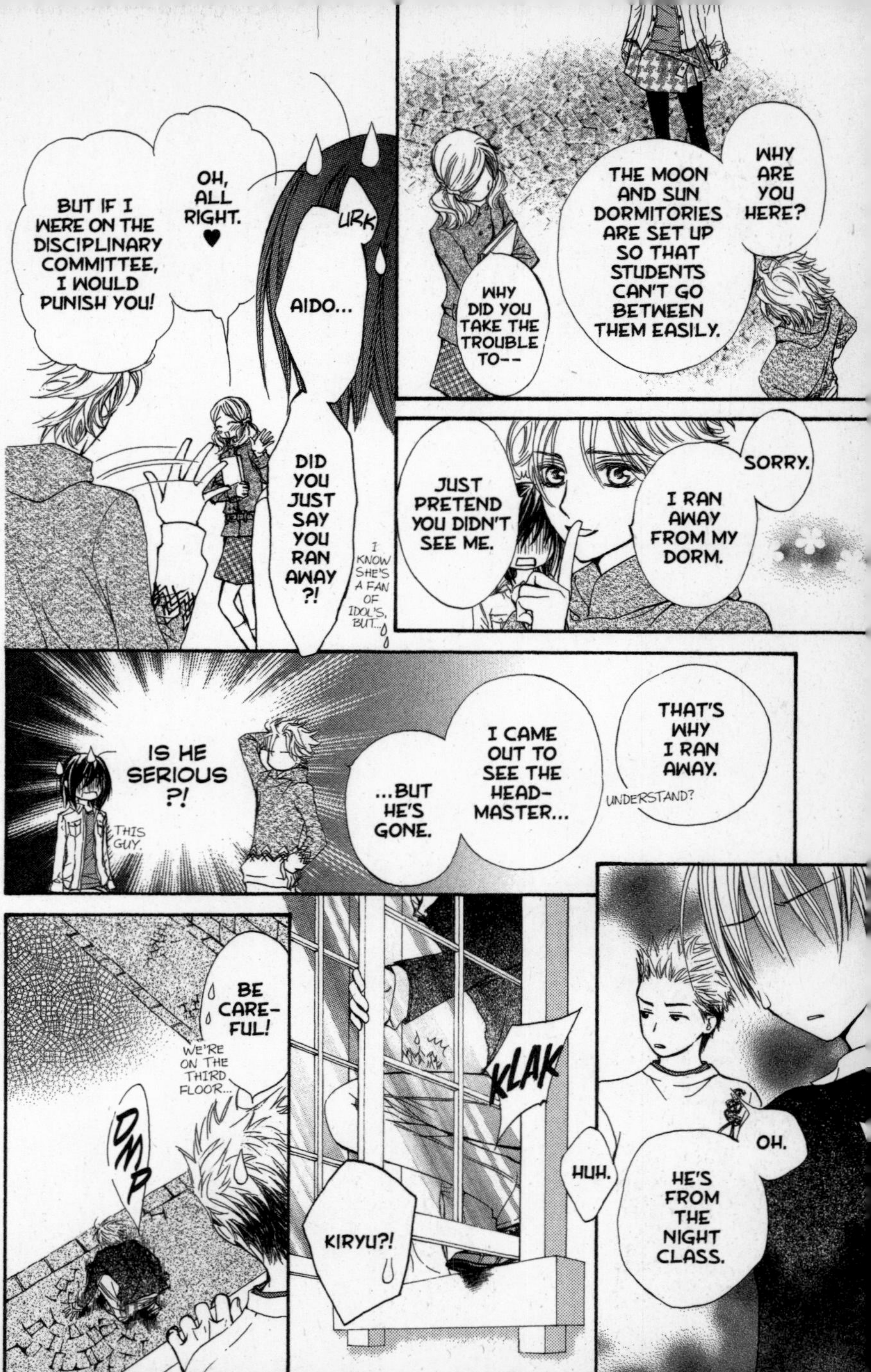
WHY ARE YOU HERE?
THE MOON AND SUN DORMITORIES ARE SET UP SO THAT STUDENTS CAN'T GO BETWEEN THEM EASILY.
WHY DID YOU TAKE THE TROUBLE TO--
SORRY.
I RAN AWAY FROM MY DORM.
JUST PRETEND YOU DIDN'T SEE ME.
URK
OH, ALL RIGHT. ♥
BUT IF I WERE ON THE DISCIPLINARY COMMITTEE, I WOULD PUNISH YOU!
AIDO...
DID YOU JUST SAY YOU RAN AWAY?!
I KNOW SHE'S A FAN OF IDOL'S, BUT...
THAT'S WHY I RAN AWAY.
UNDERSTAND?
I CAME OUT TO SEE THE HEAD-MASTER...
...BUT HE'S GONE.
IS HE SERIOUS?!
THIS GUY.
OH.
HE'S FROM THE NIGHT CLASS.
HUH.
KLAK
KIRYU?!
BE CAREFUL!
WE'RE ON THE THIRD FLOOR...
DMP

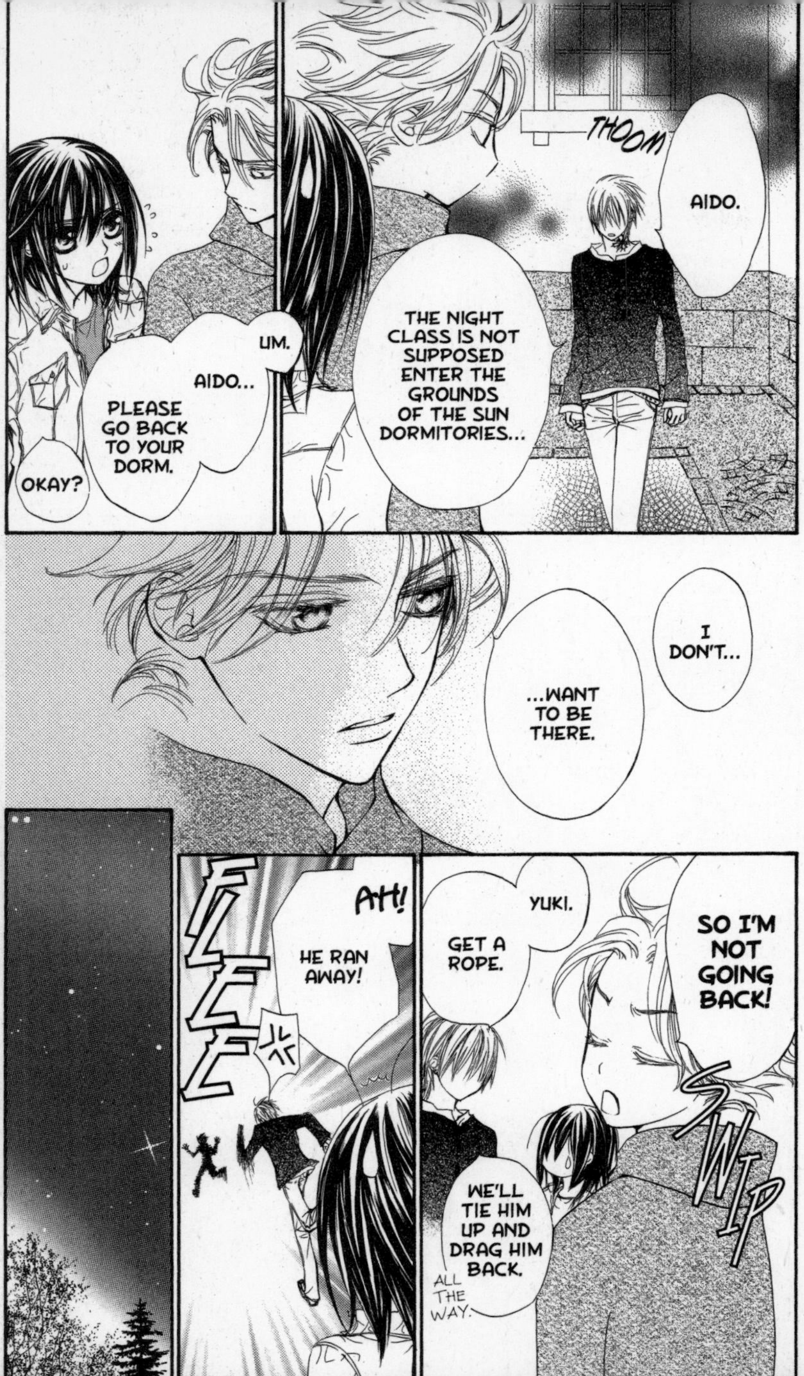
THOOM
AIDO.
THE NIGHT CLASS IS NOT SUPPOSED ENTER THE GROUNDS OF THE SUN DORMITORIES...
UM.
AIDO...
PLEASE GO BACK TO YOUR DORM.
OKAY?
I DON'T...
...WANT TO BE THERE.
SO I'M NOT GOING BACK!
SWIP
YUKI.
GET A ROPE.
WE'LL TIE HIM UP AND DRAG HIM BACK.
ALL THE WAY.
AH!
HE RAN AWAY!
FLEE

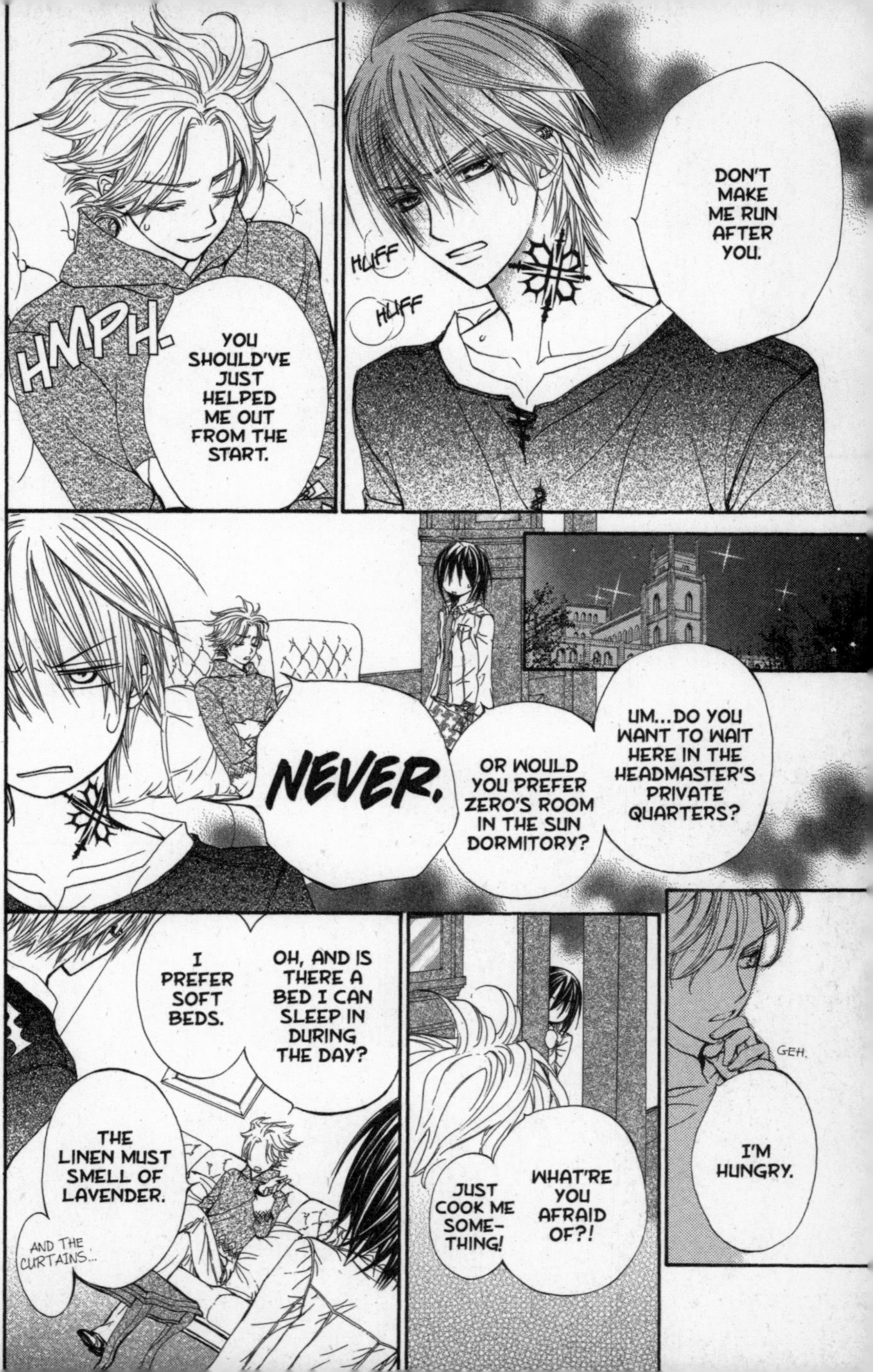
HUFF
HUFF
DON'T MAKE ME RUN AFTER YOU.
HMPH.
YOU SHOULD'VE JUST HELPED ME OUT FROM THE START.
UM...DO YOU WANT TO WAIT HERE IN THE HEADMASTER'S PRIVATE QUARTERS?
OR WOULD YOU PREFER ZERO'S ROOM IN THE SUN DORMITORY?
NEVER.
GEH.
I'M HUNGRY.
WHAT'RE YOU AFRAID OF?!
JUST COOK ME SOME-THING!
OH, AND IS THERE A BED I CAN SLEEP IN DURING THE DAY?
I PREFER SOFT BEDS.
THE LINEN MUST SMELL OF LAVENDER.
AND THE CURTAINS...

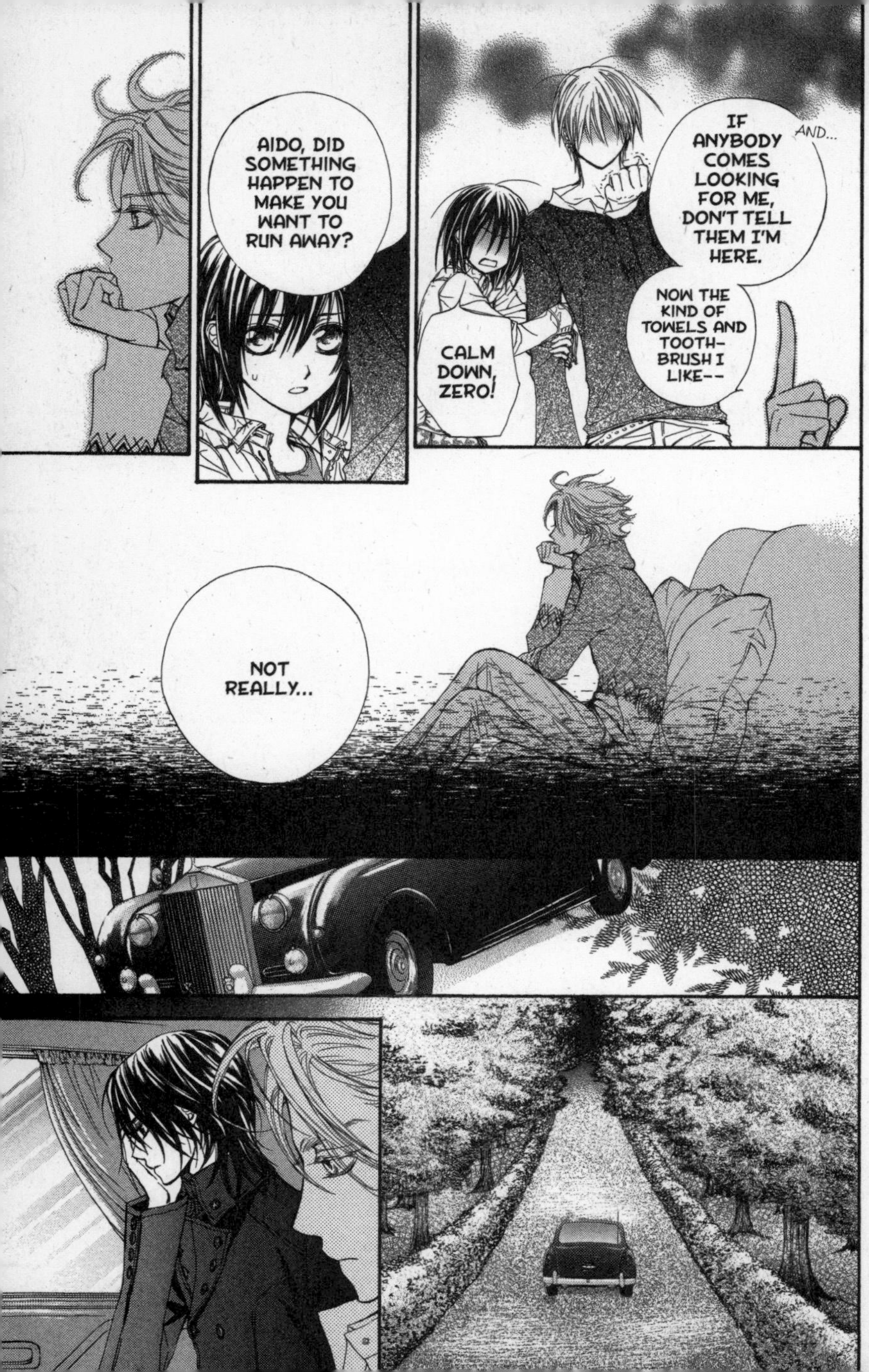
IF ANYBODY COMES LOOKING FOR ME, DON'T TELL THEM I'M HERE.
AND...
NOW THE KIND OF TOWELS AND TOOTH-BRUSH I LIKE--
CALM DOWN, ZERO!
AIDO, DID SOMETHING HAPPEN TO MAKE YOU WANT TO RUN AWAY?
NOT REALLY...

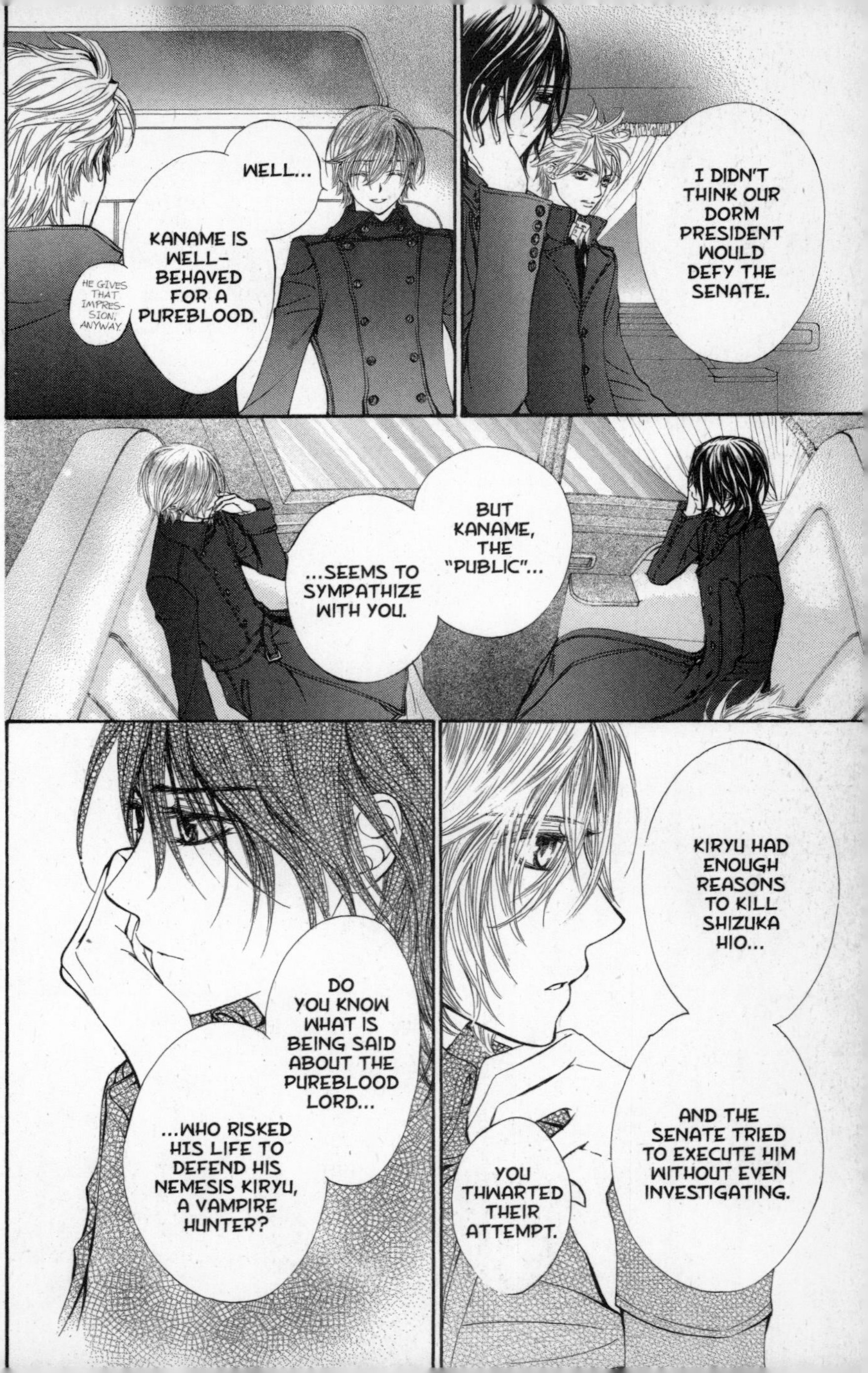
I DIDN'T THINK OUR DORM PRESIDENT WOULD DEFY THE SENATE.
WELL...
KANAME IS WELL-BEHAVED FOR A PUREBLOOD.
HE GIVES THAT IMPRESSION, ANYWAY.
BUT KANAME, THE "PUBLIC"...
...SEEMS TO SYMPATHIZE WITH YOU.
KIRYU HAD ENOUGH REASONS TO KILL SHIZUKA HIO...
AND THE SENATE TRIED TO EXECUTE HIM WITHOUT EVEN INVESTIGATING.
YOU THWARTED THEIR ATTEMPT.
DO YOU KNOW WHAT IS BEING SAID ABOUT THE PUREBLOOD LORD...
...WHO RISKED HIS LIFE TO DEFEND HIS NEMESIS KIRYU, A VAMPIRE HUNTER?

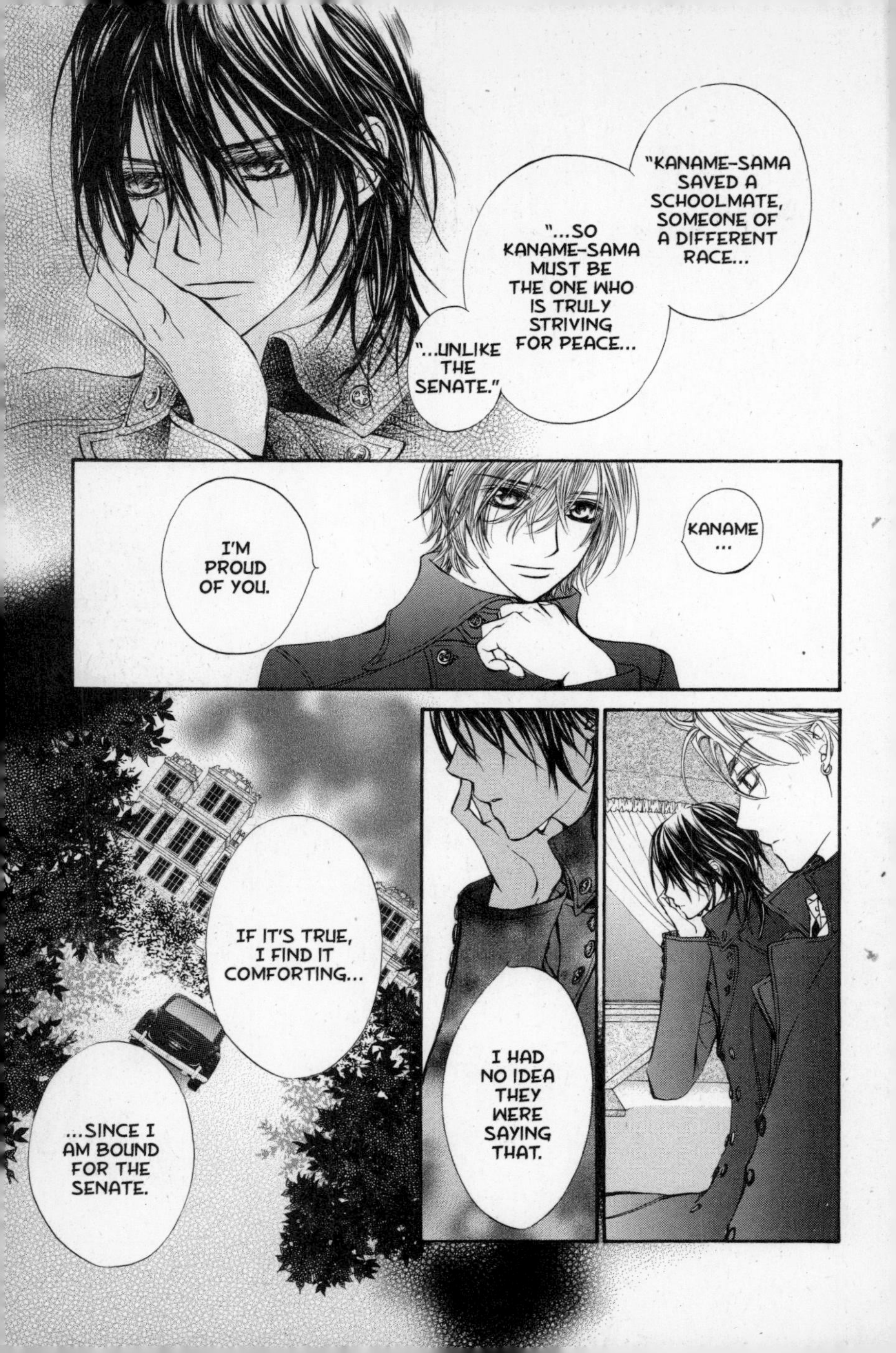
"KANAME-SAMA SAVED A SCHOOLMATE, SOMEONE OF A DIFFERENT RACE...
"...SO KANAME-SAMA MUST BE THE ONE WHO IS TRULY STRIVING FOR PEACE...
"...UNLIKE THE SENATE."
KANAME...
I'M PROUD OF YOU.
I HAD NO IDEA THEY WERE SAYING THAT.
IF IT'S TRUE, I FIND IT COMFORTING...
...SINCE I AM BOUND FOR THE SENATE.

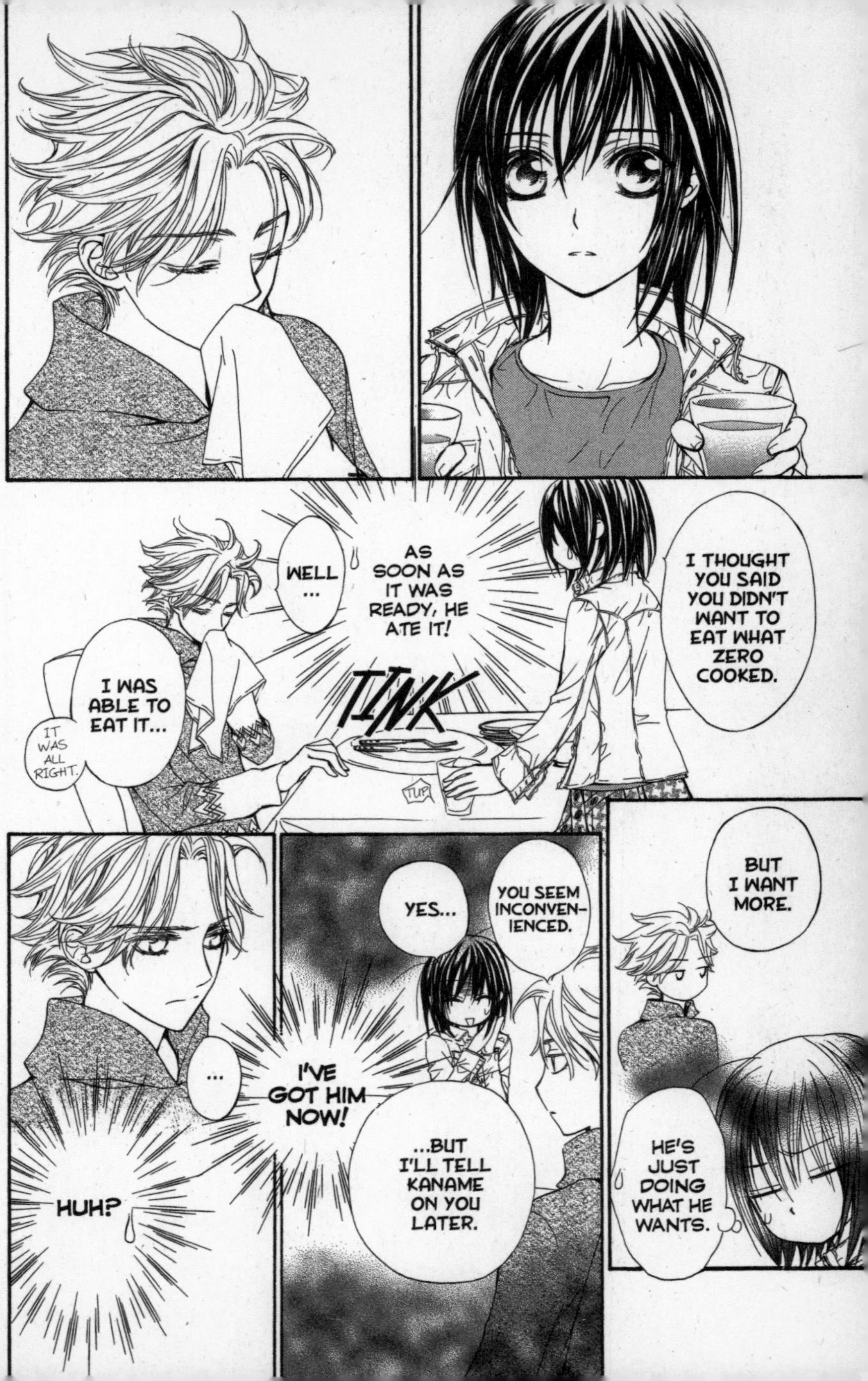
I THOUGHT YOU SAID YOU DIDN'T WANT TO EAT WHAT ZERO COOKED.
AS SOON AS IT WAS READY, HE ATE IT!
WELL...
TINK
TUP
I WAS ABLE TO EAT IT...
IT WAS ALL RIGHT.
BUT I WANT MORE.
HE'S JUST DOING WHAT HE WANTS.
YOU SEEM INCONVENIENCED.
YES...
...BUT I'LL TELL KANAME ON YOU LATER.
I'VE GOT HIM NOW!
...
HUH?

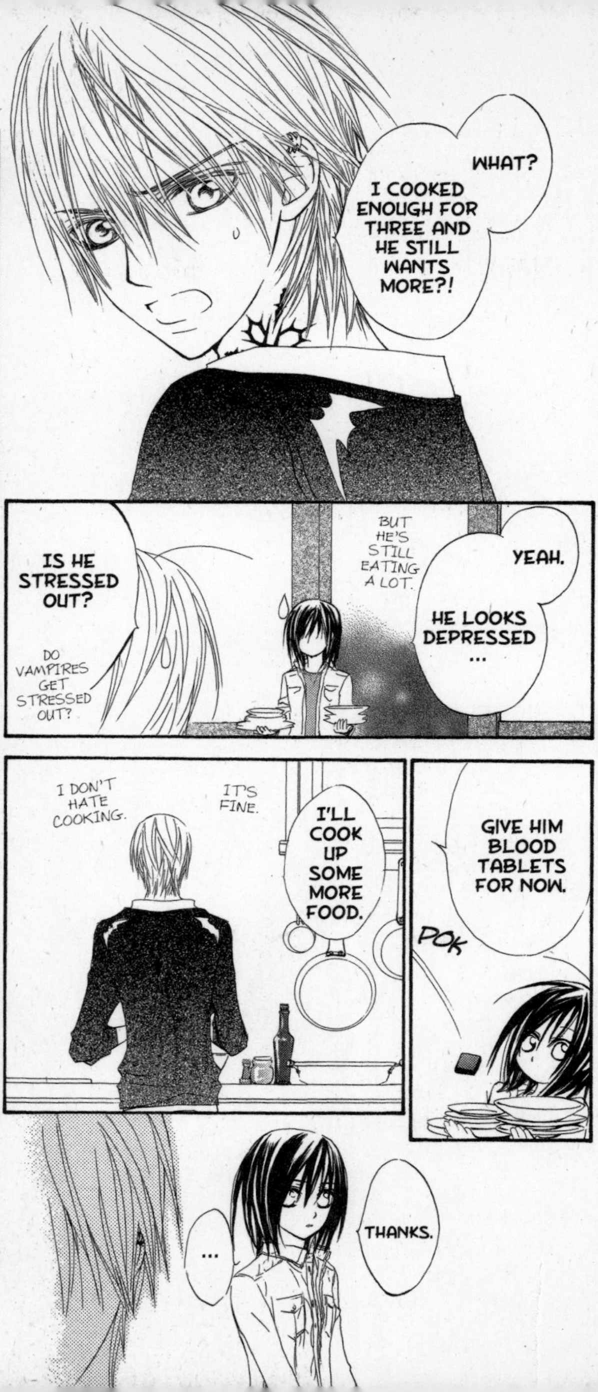
WHAT?
I COOKED ENOUGH FOR THREE AND HE STILL WANTS MORE?!
YEAH.
HE LOOKS DEPRESSED ...
BUT HE'S STILL EATING A LOT.
IS HE STRESSED OUT?
DO VAMPIRES GET STRESSED OUT?
GIVE HIM BLOOD TABLETS FOR NOW.
POK
I'LL COOK UP SOME MORE FOOD.
IT'S FINE.
I DON'T HATE COOKING.
THANKS.
...

V

Here's a collection of the character data that was gathered from zen-ins, events, and articles.

◆Yuki: Probably age 16, 152 cm, blood-type O.

◆Zero: Age 17, 181 cm, blood-type A, silver-gray hair, light purple eyes.

◆Kaname: Age 18 in vampire years, 184 cm, black-gray hair, dark red eyes.

◆Takuma: Age 18 in vampire years, 184 cm.

◆Hanabusa: Age 17 in vampire years, 177 cm.

◆Akatsuki: Age 17 in vampire years, 188 cm.

◆Senri: Age 16 in vampire years, 173 cm.

It's not that I'm being stingy, but there isn't much data on them!! It takes time to determine the hair and eye colors, so I've put it off... I'm really impressed with my editor—she spices up the character introductions in articles by using this data! I thank you!!

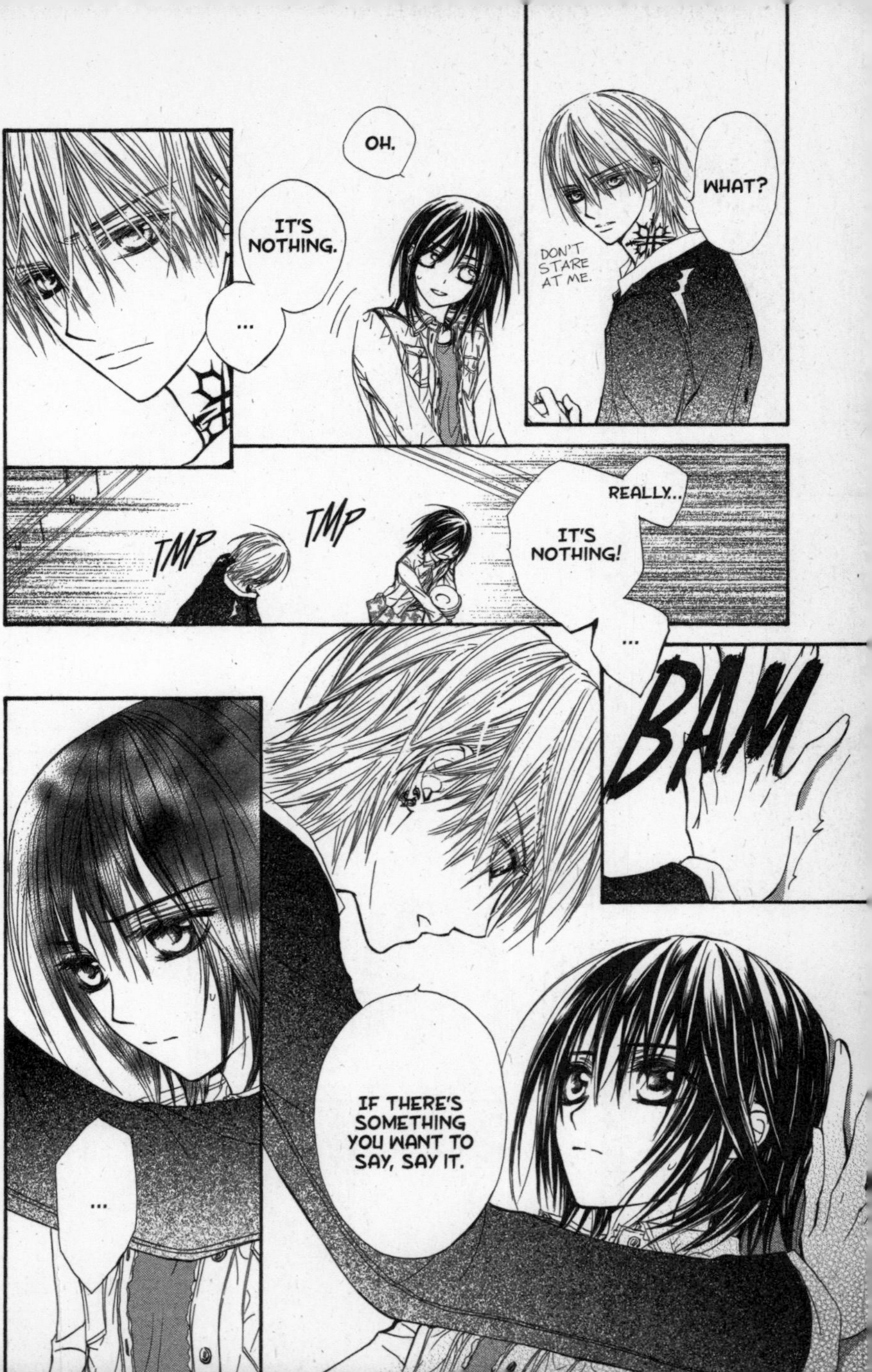
WHAT?
DON'T STARE AT ME.
OH.
IT'S NOTHING.
...
REALLY... IT'S NOTHING!
TMP
TMP
...
BAM
IF THERE'S SOMETHING YOU WANT TO SAY, SAY IT.
...

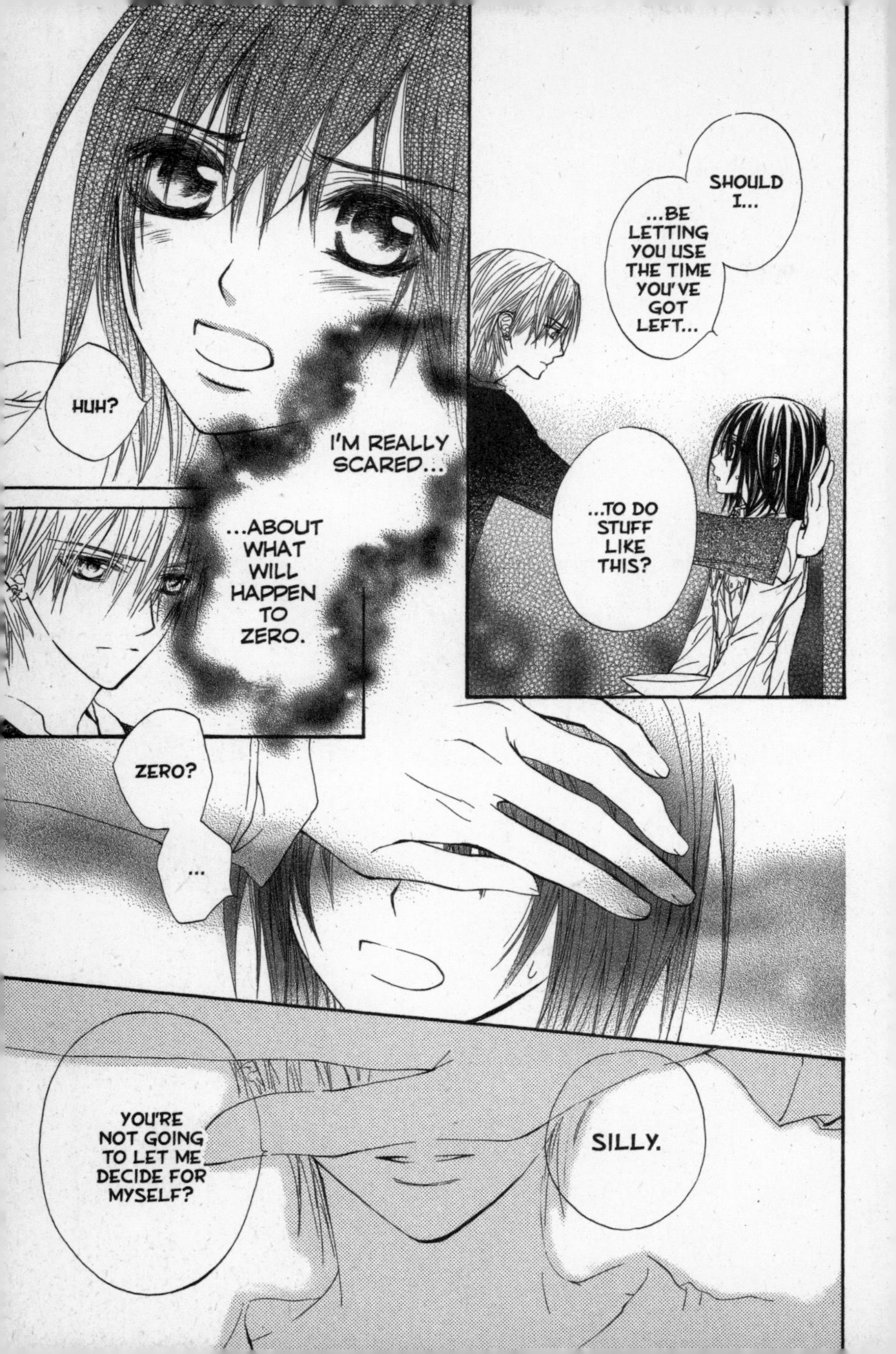
SHOULD I...
...BE LETTING YOU USE THE TIME YOU'VE GOT LEFT...
...TO DO STUFF LIKE THIS?
HUH?
I'M REALLY SCARED...
...ABOUT WHAT WILL HAPPEN TO ZERO.
ZERO?
...
SILLY.
YOU'RE NOT GOING TO LET ME DECIDE FOR MYSELF?

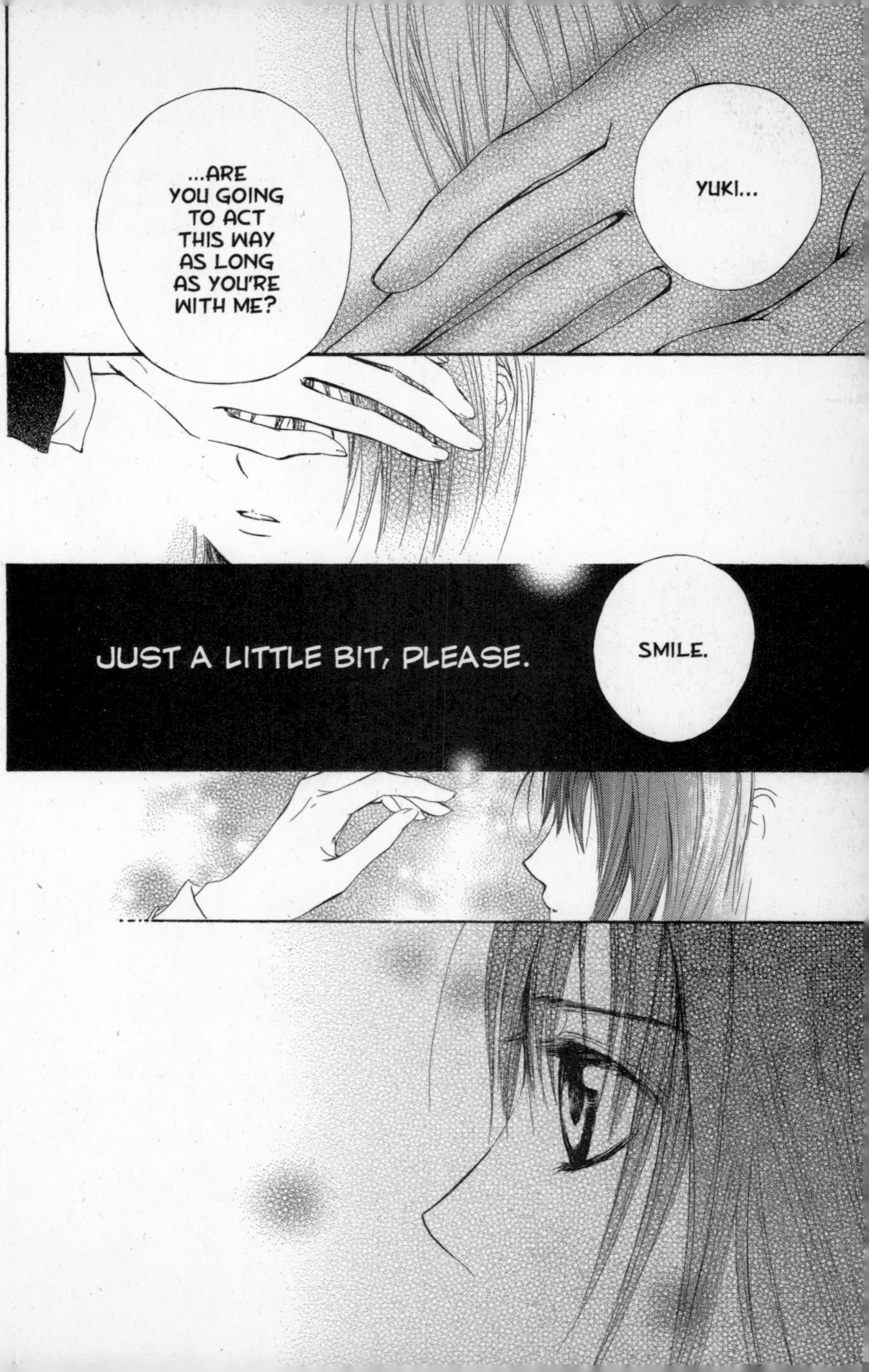
YUKI...
...ARE YOU GOING TO ACT THIS WAY AS LONG AS YOU'RE WITH ME?
SMILE.
JUST A LITTLE BIT, PLEASE.

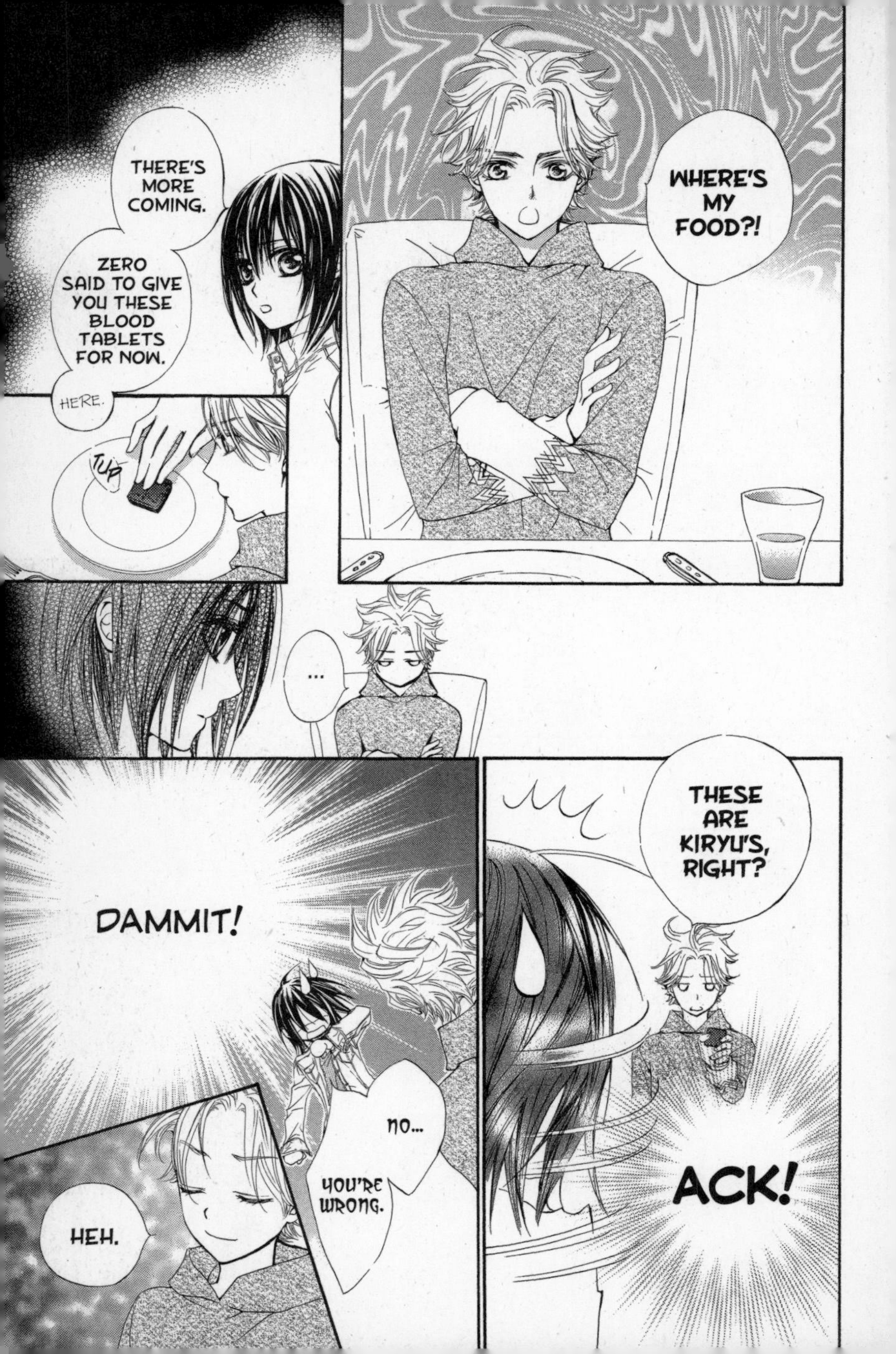
WHERE'S MY FOOD?!
THERE'S MORE COMING.
ZERO SAID TO GIVE YOU THESE BLOOD TABLETS FOR NOW.
HERE.
TUP
...
THESE ARE KIRYU'S, RIGHT?
ACK!
DAMMIT!
NO...
YOU'RE WRONG.
HEH.

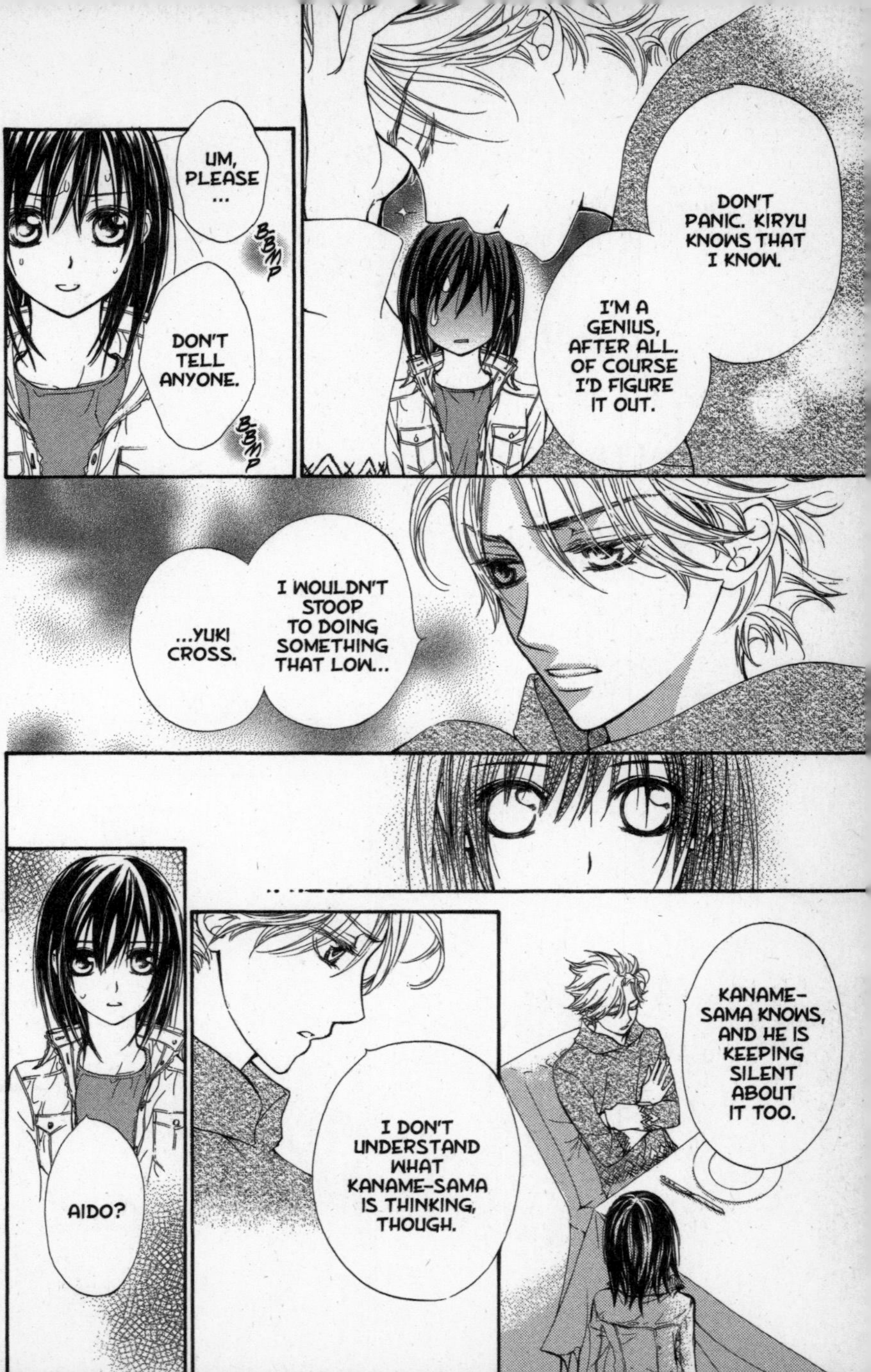
DON'T PANIC. KIRYU KNOWS THAT I KNOW.
I'M A GENIUS, AFTER ALL. OF COURSE I'D FIGURE IT OUT.
UM, PLEASE ...
B-BMP
DON'T TELL ANYONE.
B-BMP
I WOULDN'T STOOP TO DOING SOMETHING THAT LOW...
...YUKI CROSS.
...
KANAME-SAMA KNOWS, AND HE IS KEEPING SILENT ABOUT IT TOO.
I DON'T UNDERSTAND WHAT KANAME-SAMA IS THINKING, THOUGH.
AIDO?

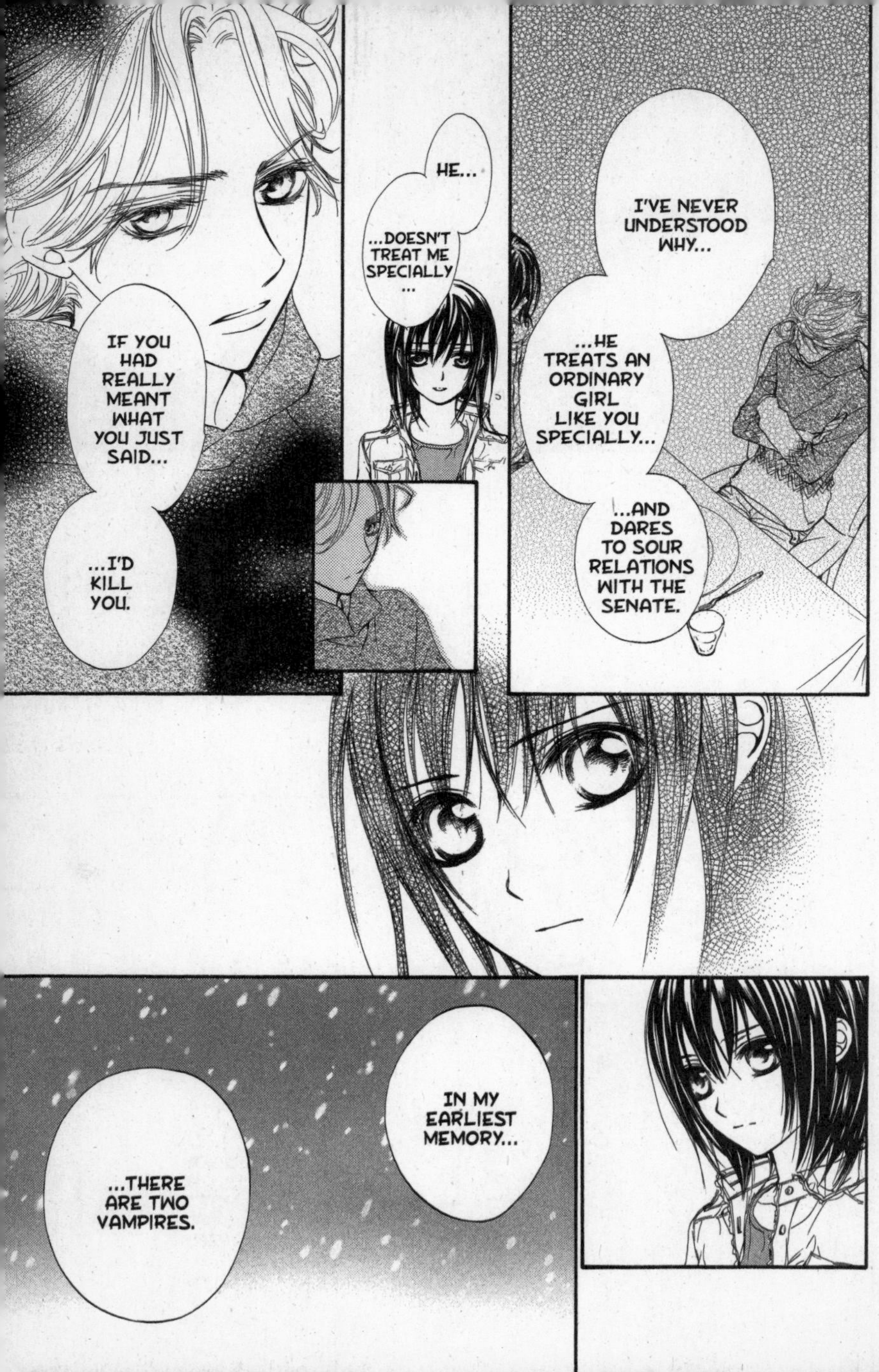
I'VE NEVER UNDERSTOOD WHY...
...HE TREATS AN ORDINARY GIRL LIKE YOU SPECIALLY...
...AND DARES TO SOUR RELATIONS WITH THE SENATE.
HE...
...DOESN'T TREAT ME SPECIALLY ...
IF YOU HAD REALLY MEANT WHAT YOU JUST SAID...
...I'D KILL YOU.
IN MY EARLIEST MEMORY...
...THERE ARE TWO VAMPIRES.

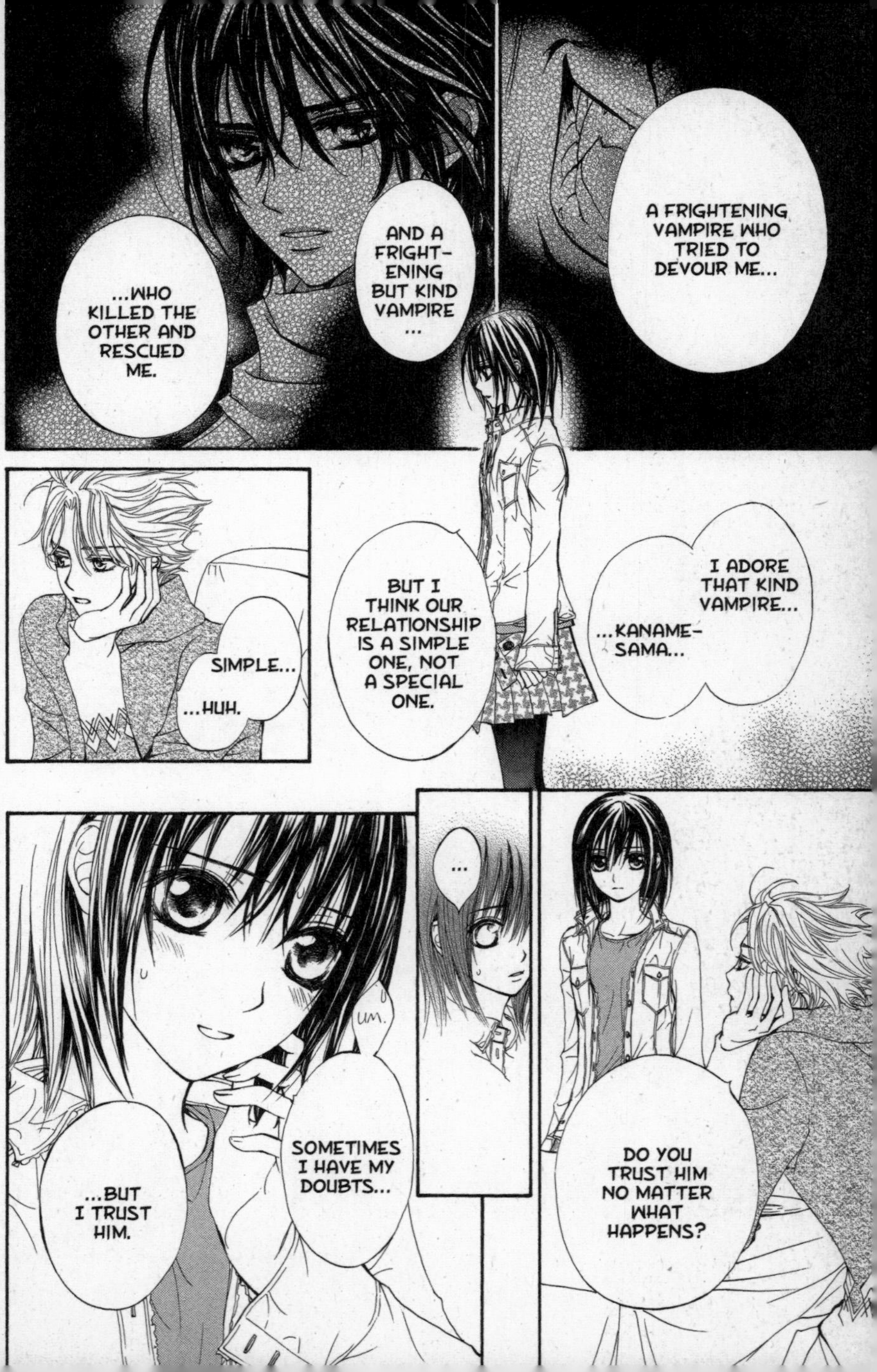
A FRIGHTENING VAMPIRE WHO TRIED TO DEVOUR ME...
AND A FRIGHTENING BUT KIND VAMPIRE ...
...WHO KILLED THE OTHER AND RESCUED ME.
I ADORE THAT KIND VAMPIRE...
...KANAME-SAMA...
BUT I THINK OUR RELATIONSHIP IS A SIMPLE ONE, NOT A SPECIAL ONE.
SIMPLE...
...HUH.
DO YOU TRUST HIM NO MATTER WHAT HAPPENS?
...
UM.
SOMETIMES I HAVE MY DOUBTS...
...BUT I TRUST HIM.

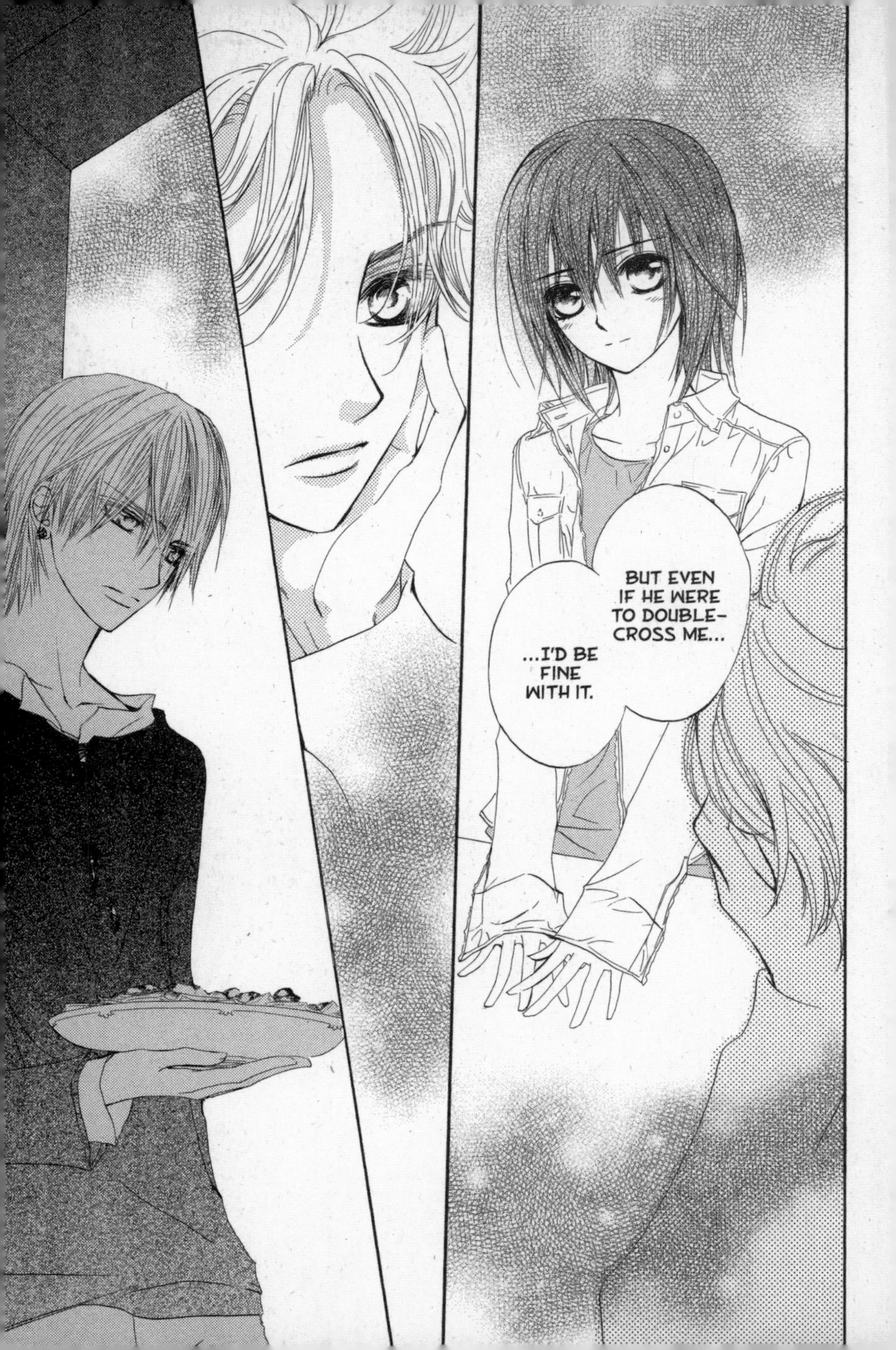
BUT EVEN IF HE WERE TO DOUBLE-CROSS ME...
...I'D BE FINE WITH IT.

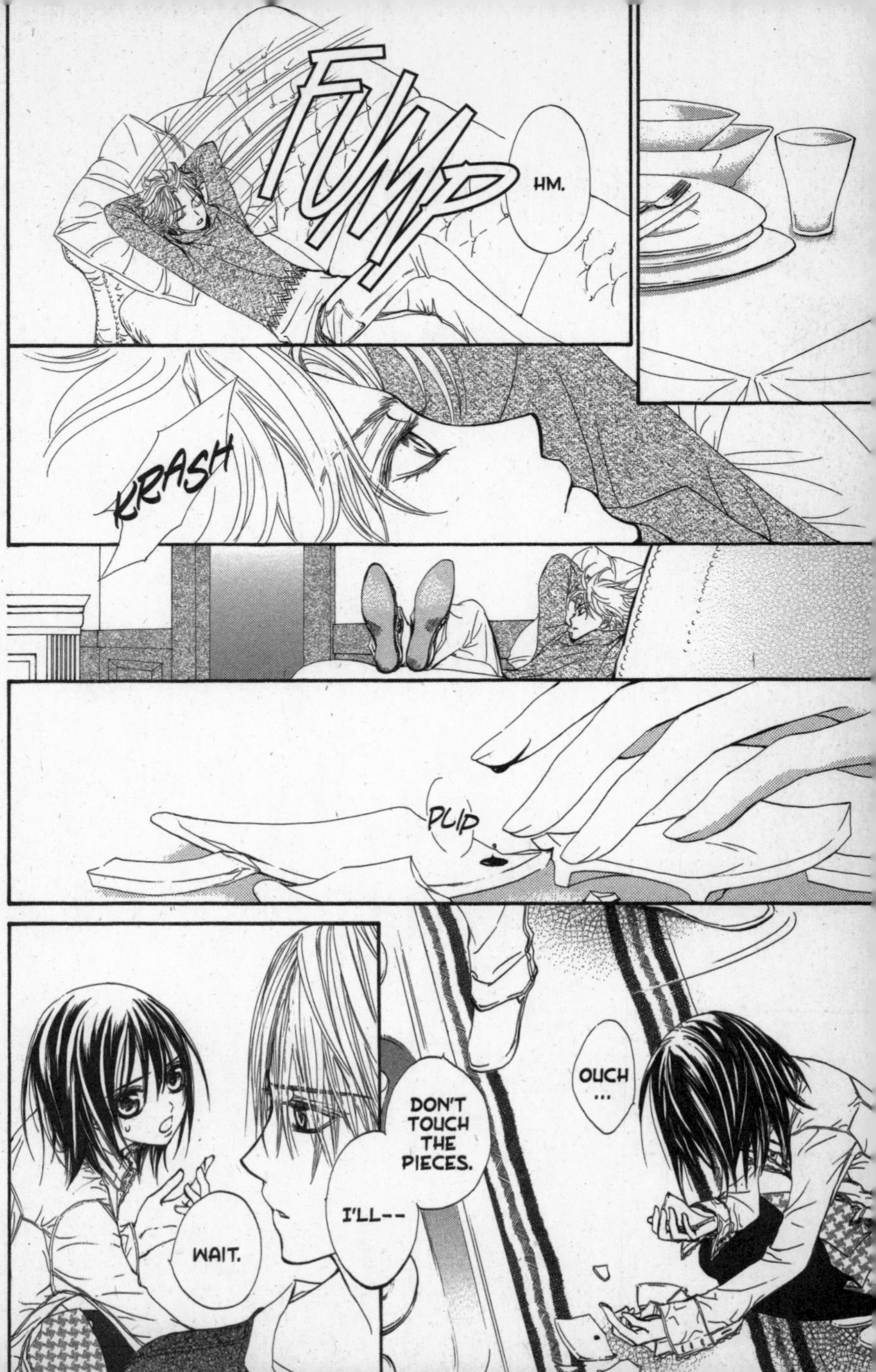
FUMP!
HM.
KRASH
PLIP
OUCH ...
DON'T TOUCH THE PIECES.
I'LL--
WAIT.

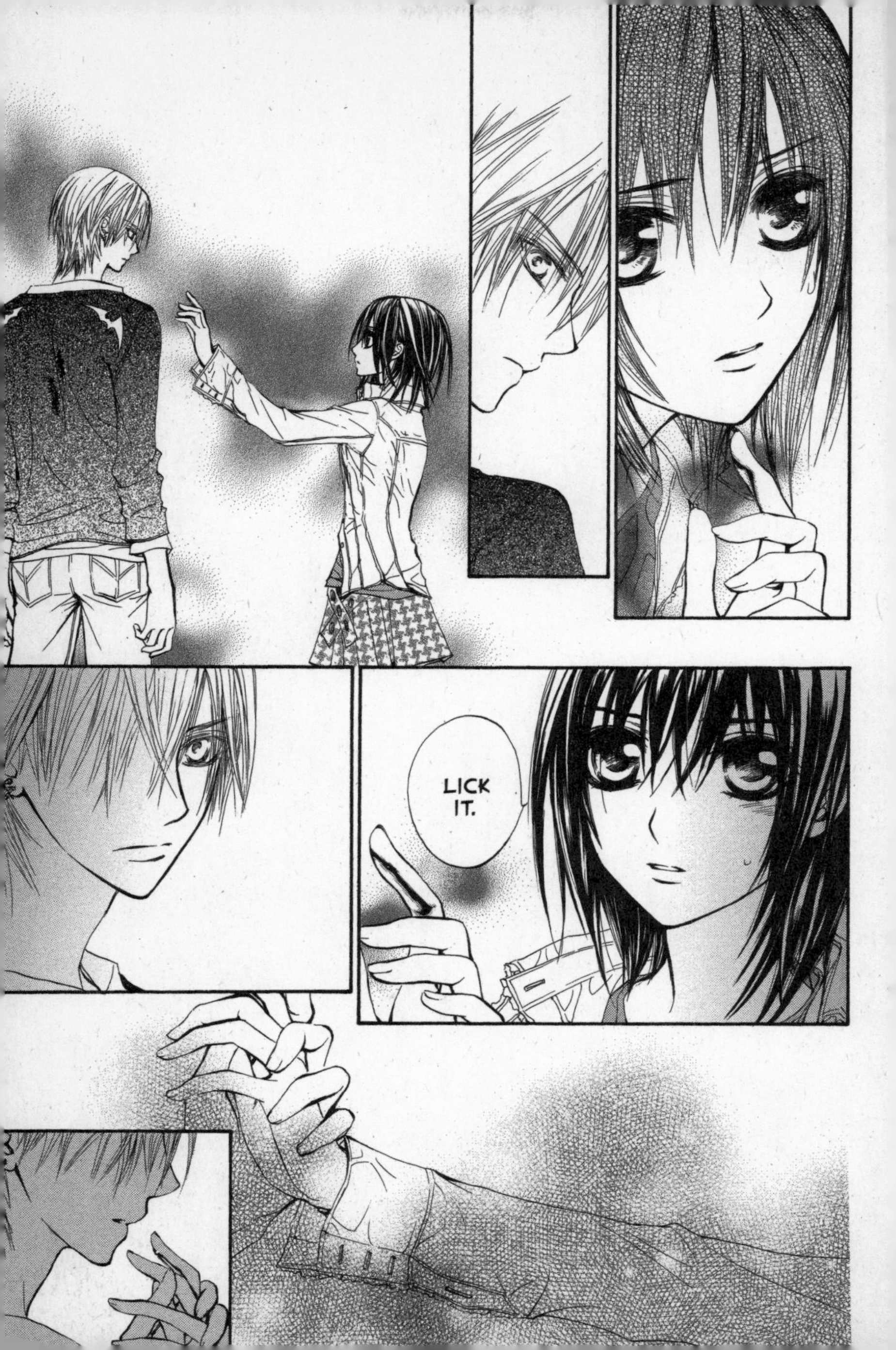
LICK IT.

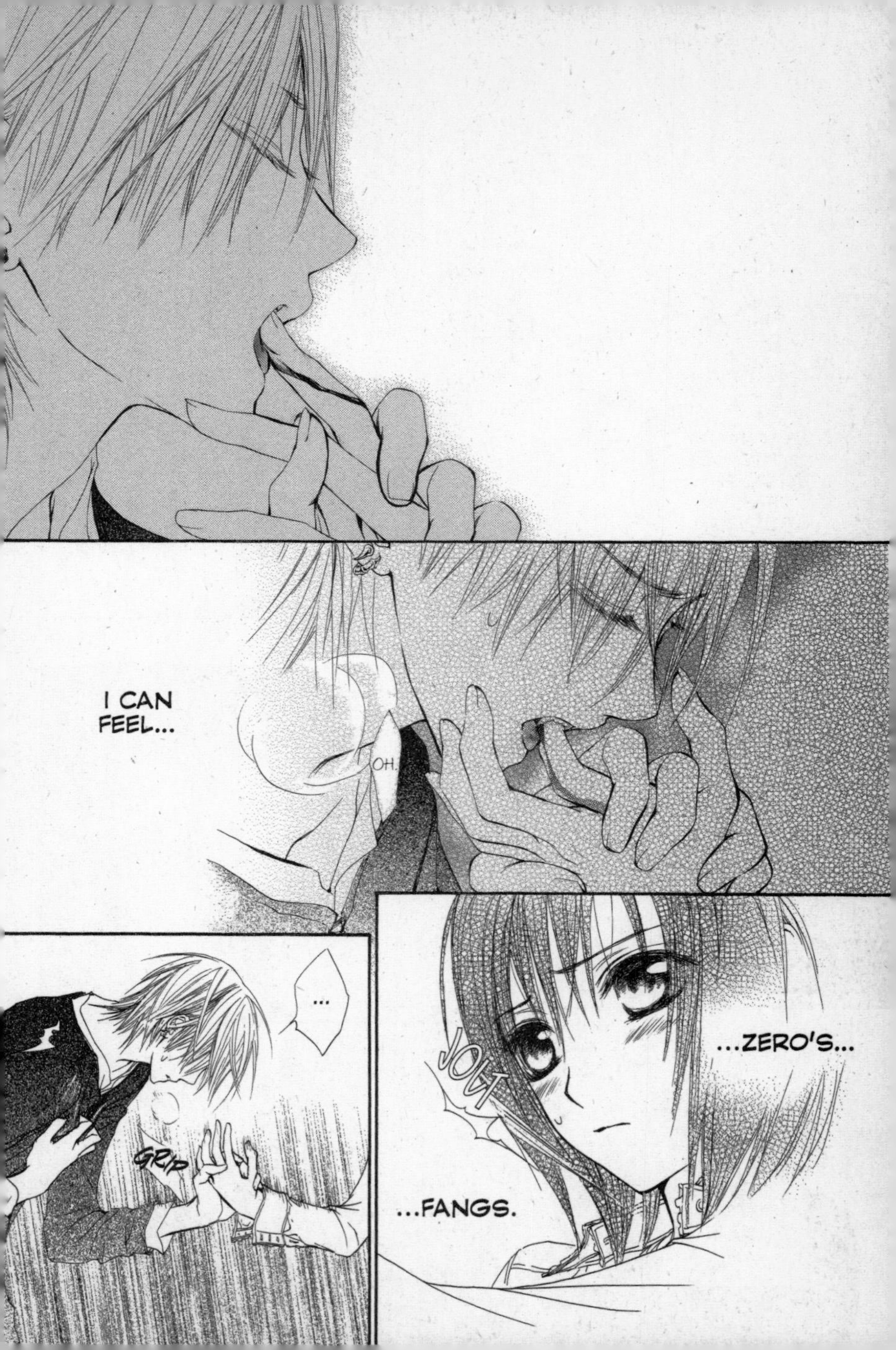
I CAN FEEL...
OH.
...ZERO'S...
JOLT
...FANGS.
...
GRIP

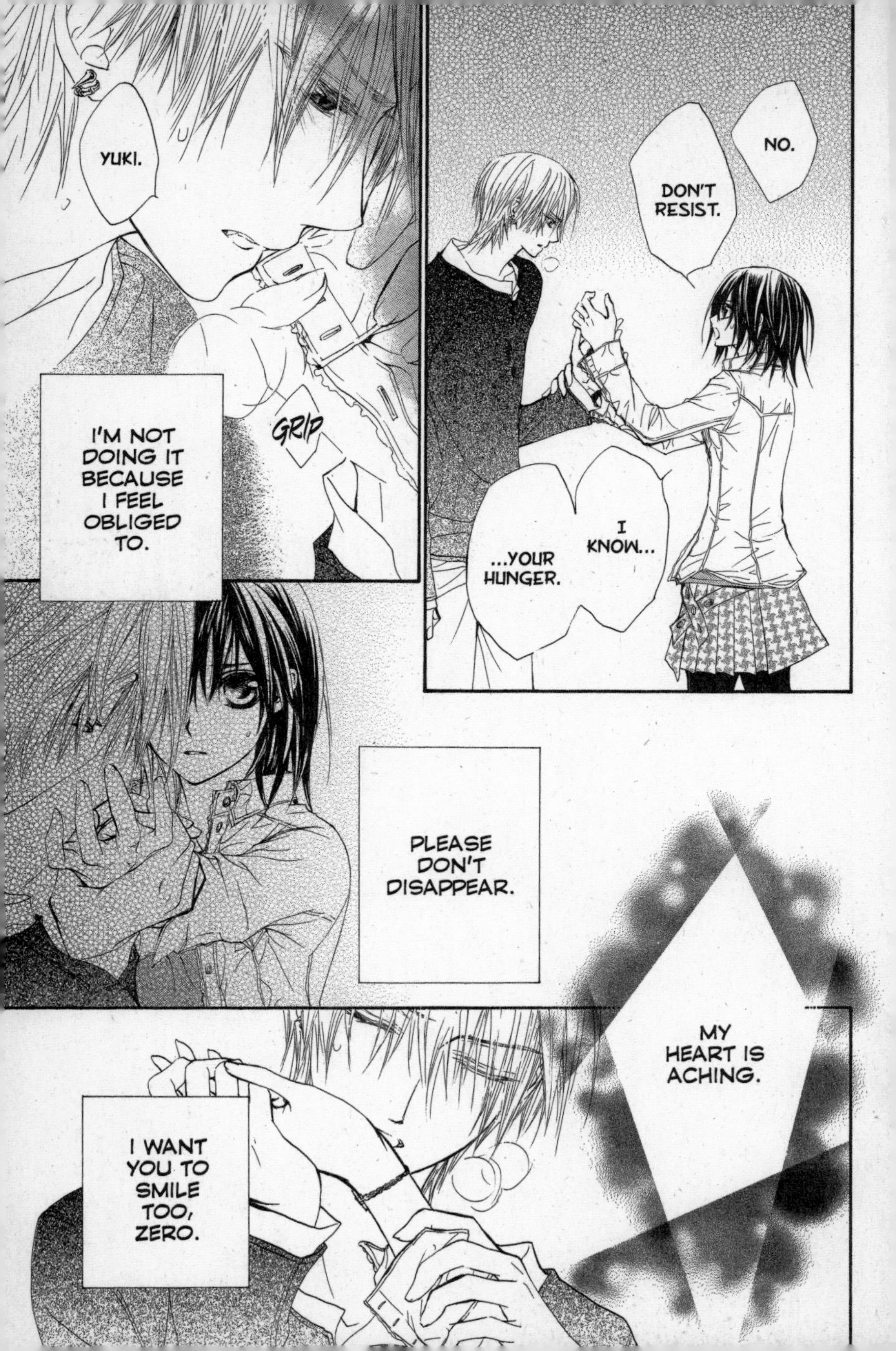
NO.
DON'T RESIST.
I KNOW...
...YOUR HUNGER.
YUKI.
GRIP
I'M NOT DOING IT BECAUSE I FEEL OBLIGED TO.
PLEASE DON'T DISAPPEAR.
MY HEART IS ACHING.
I WANT YOU TO SMILE TOO, ZERO.

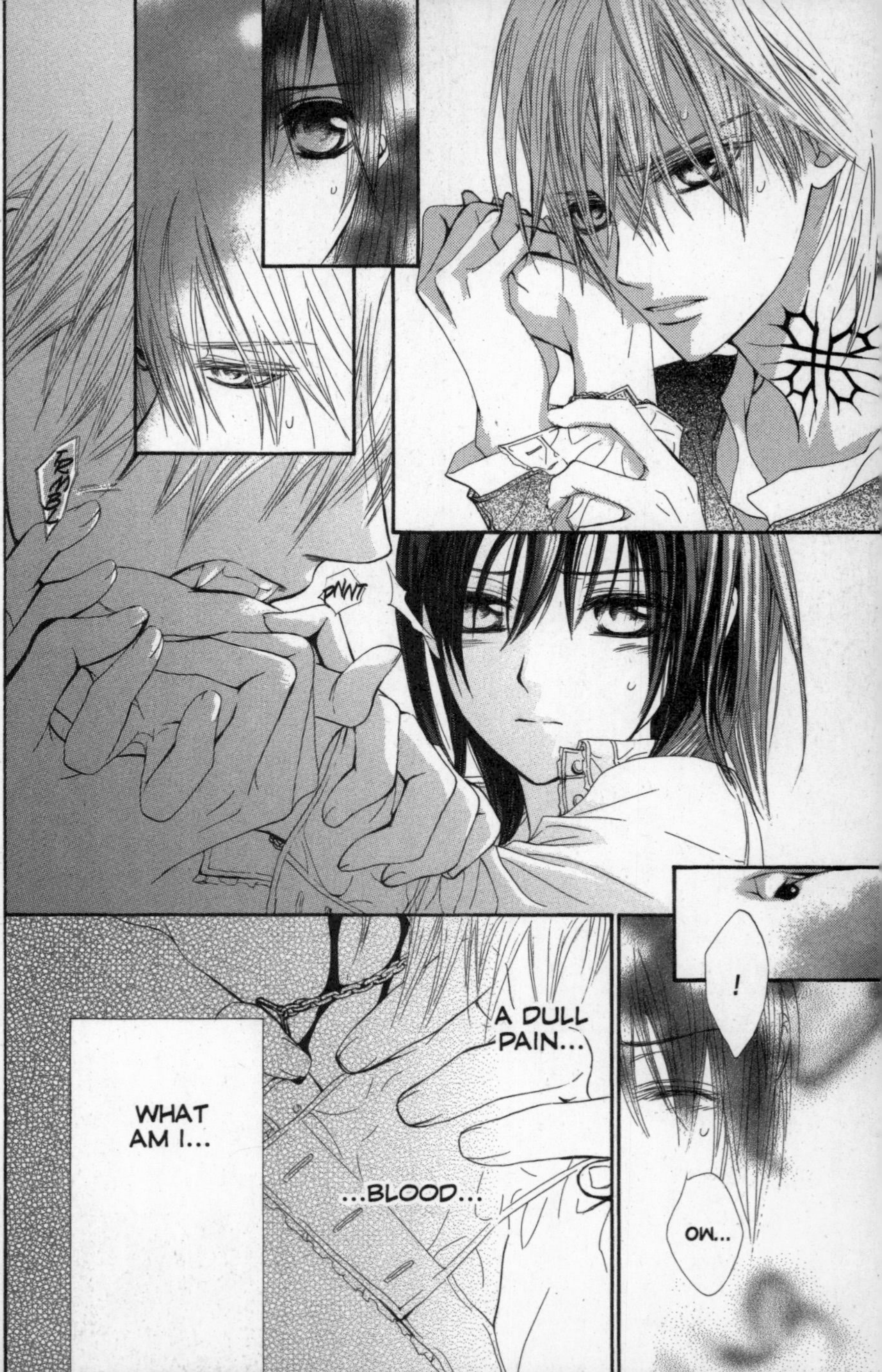
PNNT
!
OW...
A DULL PAIN...
...BLOOD...
WHAT AM I...

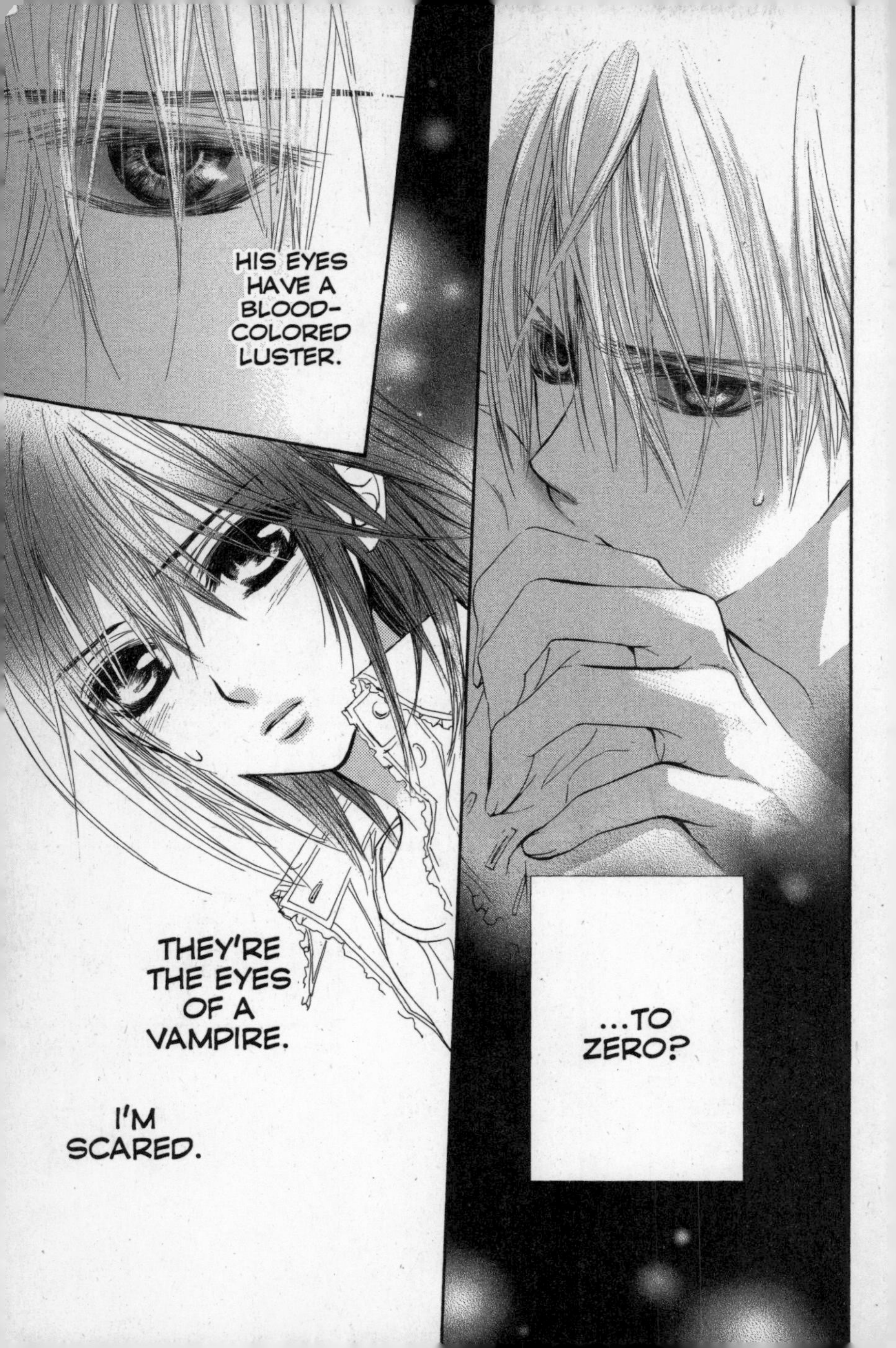
...TO ZERO?
HIS EYES HAVE A BLOOD-COLORED LUSTER.
THEY'RE THE EYES OF A VAMPIRE.
I'M SCARED.

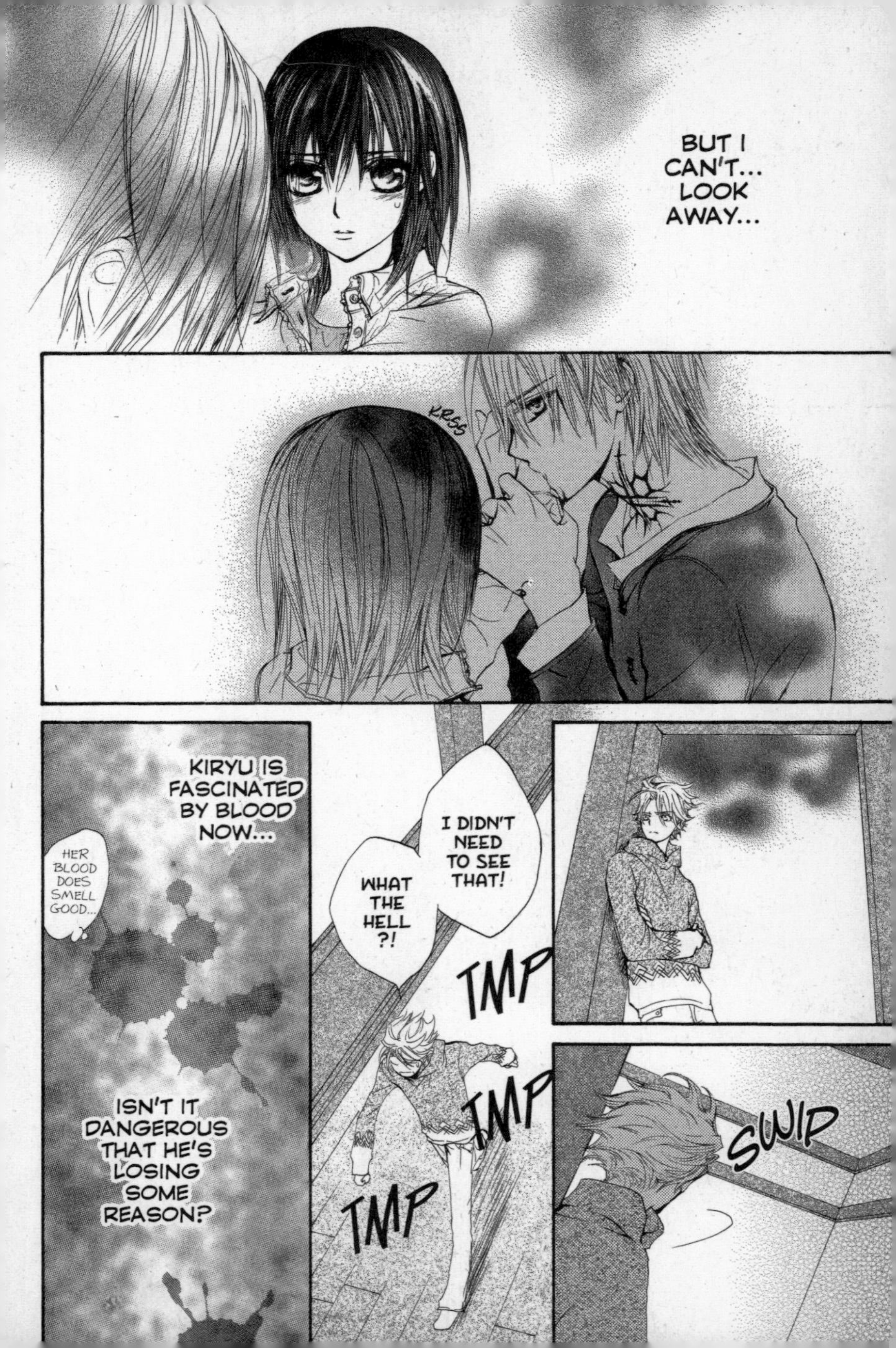
BUT I CAN'T... LOOK AWAY...
KRSS
SWIP
I DIDN'T NEED TO SEE THAT!
WHAT THE HELL ?!
TMP
TMP
TMP
KIRYU IS FASCINATED BY BLOOD NOW...
HER BLOOD DOES SMELL GOOD...
ISN'T IT DANGEROUS THAT HE'S LOSING SOME REASON?

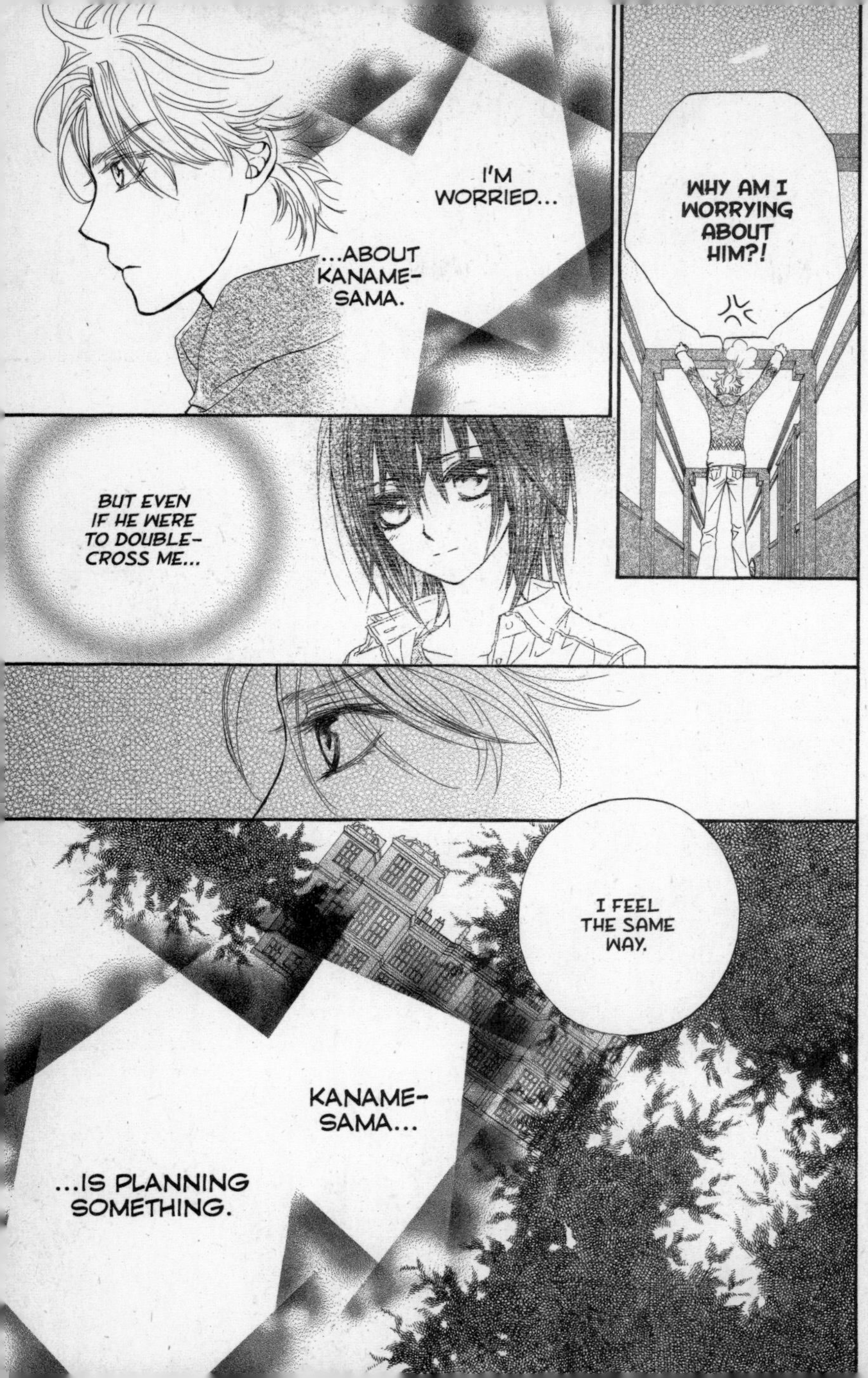
WHY AM I WORRYING ABOUT HIM?!
I'M WORRIED...
...ABOUT KANAME-SAMA.
BUT EVEN IF HE WERE TO DOUBLE-CROSS ME...
I FEEL THE SAME WAY.
KANAME-SAMA...
...IS PLANNING SOMETHING.

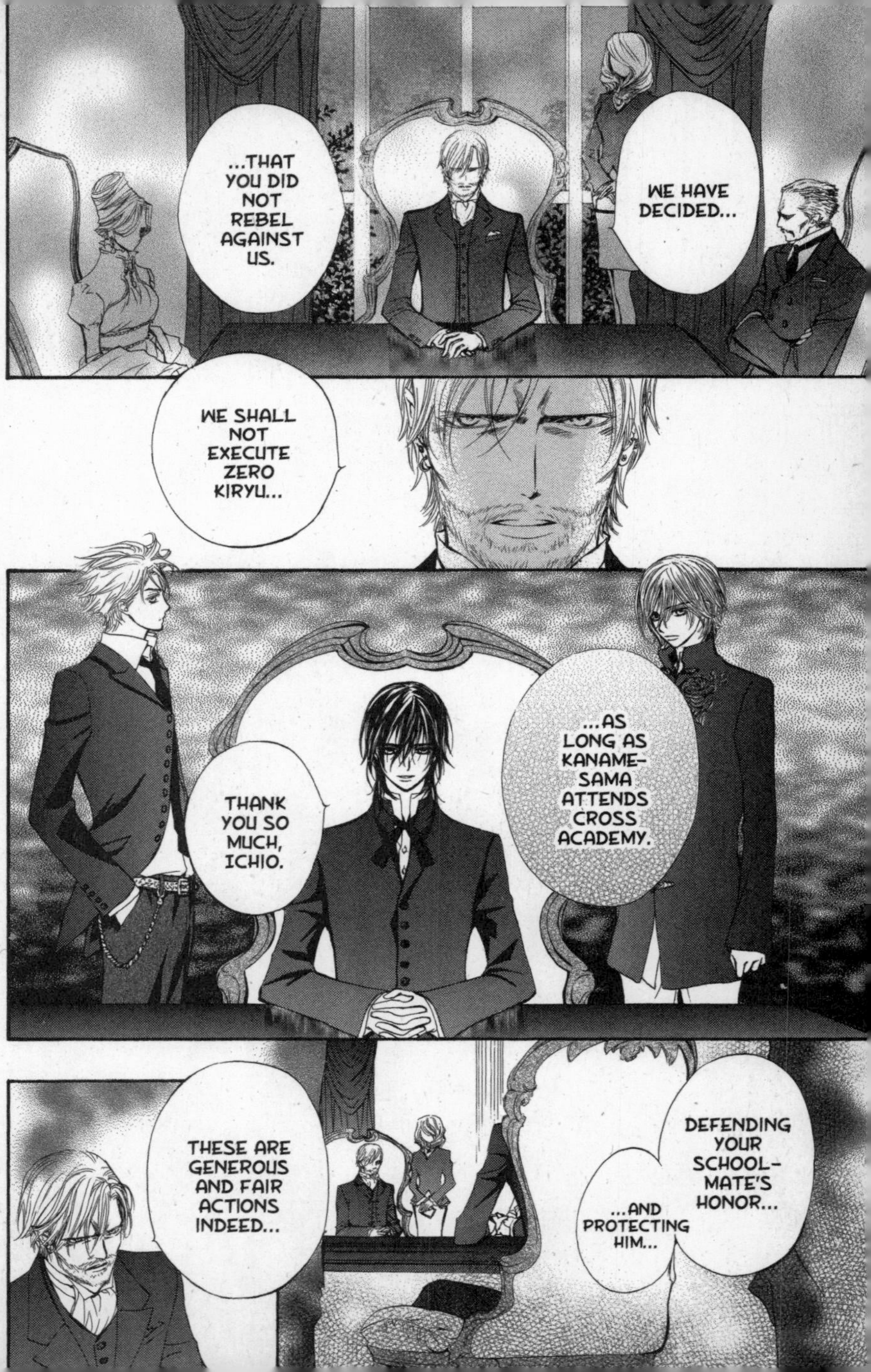
WE HAVE DECIDED...
...THAT YOU DID NOT REBEL AGAINST US.
WE SHALL NOT EXECUTE ZERO KIRYU...
...AS LONG AS KANAME-SAMA ATTENDS CROSS ACADEMY.
THANK YOU SO MUCH, ICHIO.
DEFENDING YOUR SCHOOL-MATE'S HONOR...
...AND PROTECTING HIM...
THESE ARE GENEROUS AND FAIR ACTIONS INDEED...

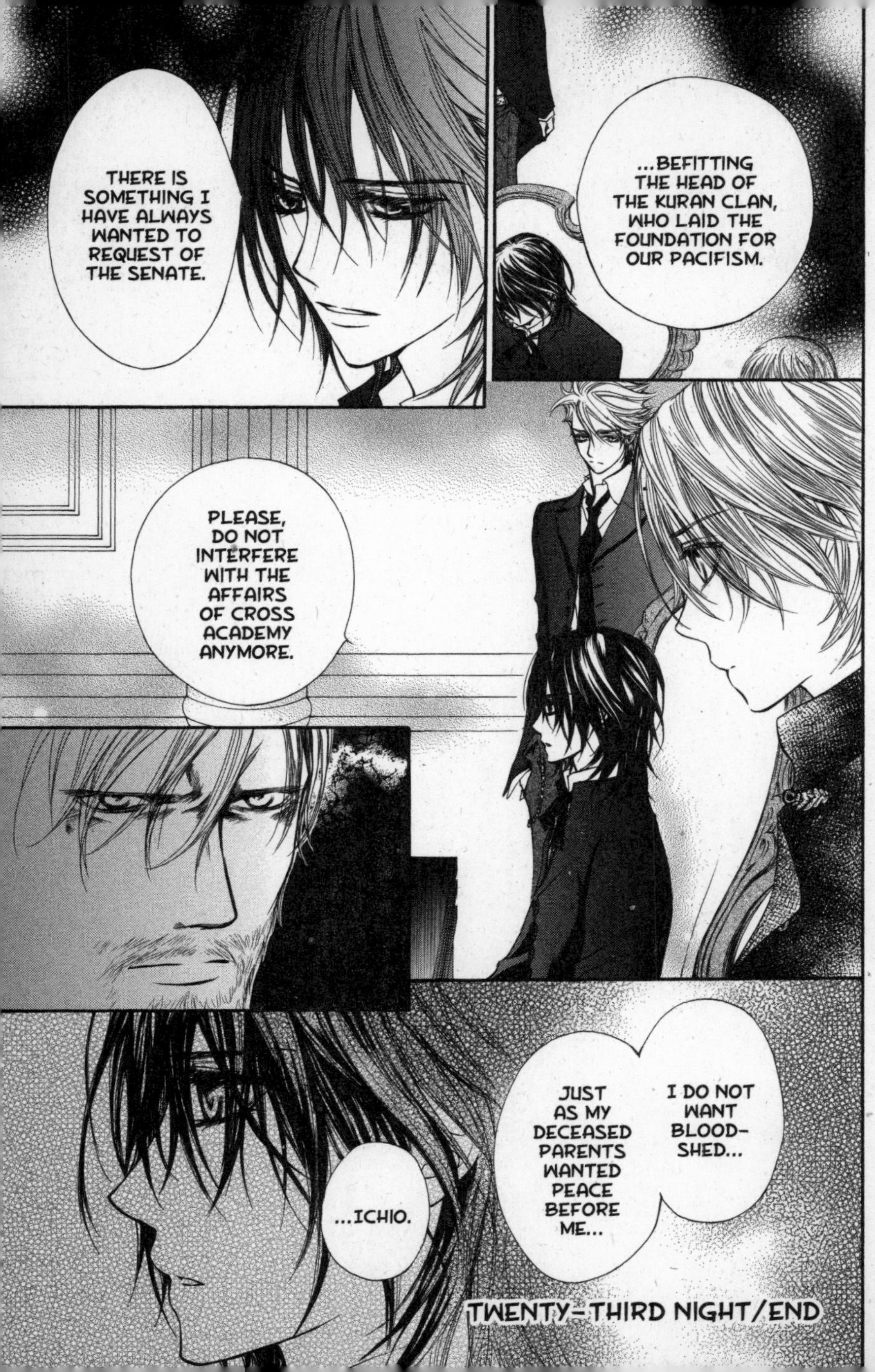
...BEFITTING THE HEAD OF THE KURAN CLAN, WHO LAID THE FOUNDATION FOR OUR PACIFISM.
THERE IS SOMETHING I HAVE ALWAYS WANTED TO REQUEST OF THE SENATE.
PLEASE, DO NOT INTERFERE WITH THE AFFAIRS OF CROSS ACADEMY ANYMORE.
I DO NOT WANT BLOOD-SHED...
JUST AS MY DECEASED PARENTS WANTED PEACE BEFORE ME...
...ICHIO.
TWENTY-THIRD NIGHT/END

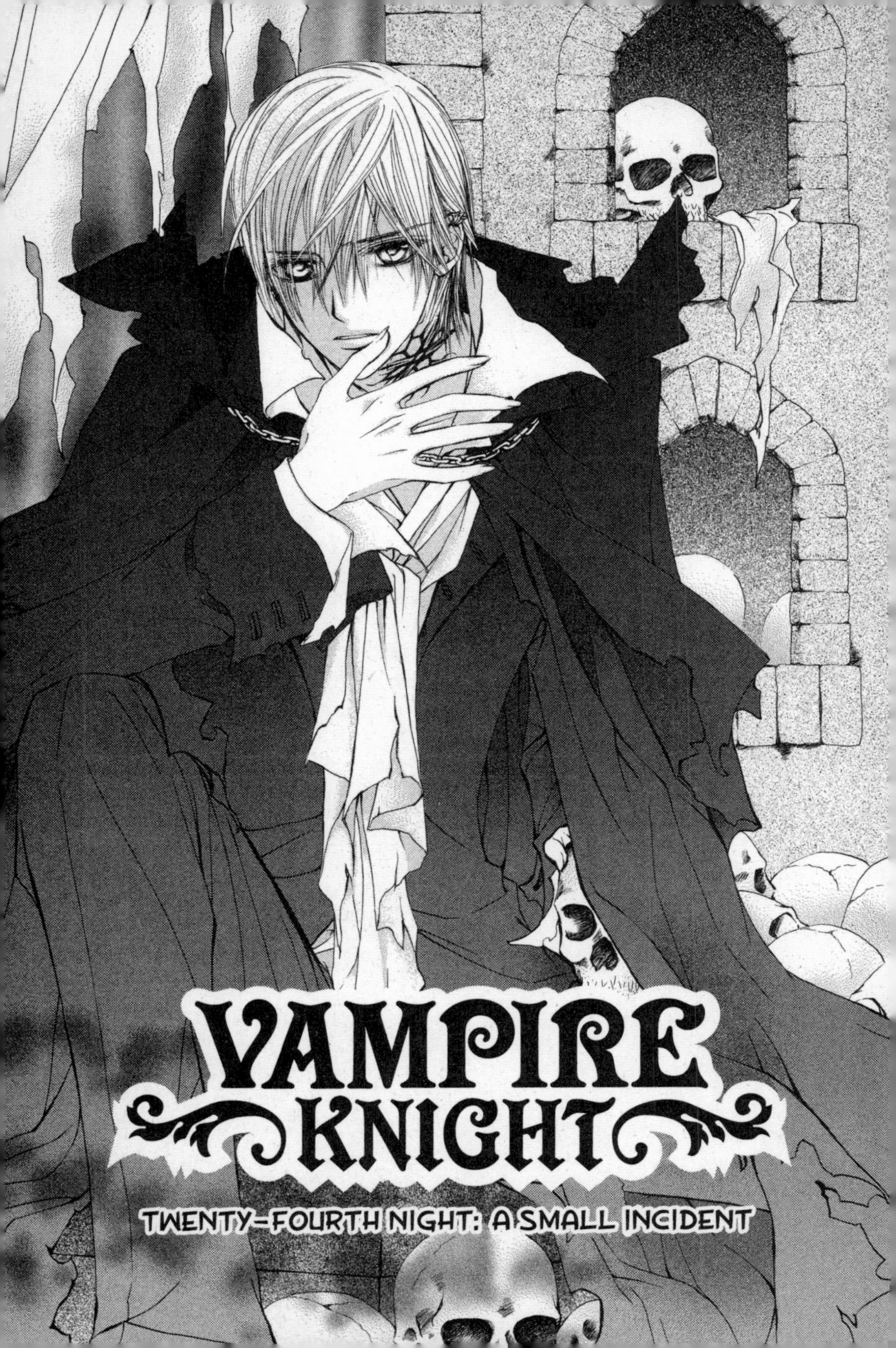
VAMPIRE KNIGHT
TWENTY-FOURTH NIGHT: A SMALL INCIDENT

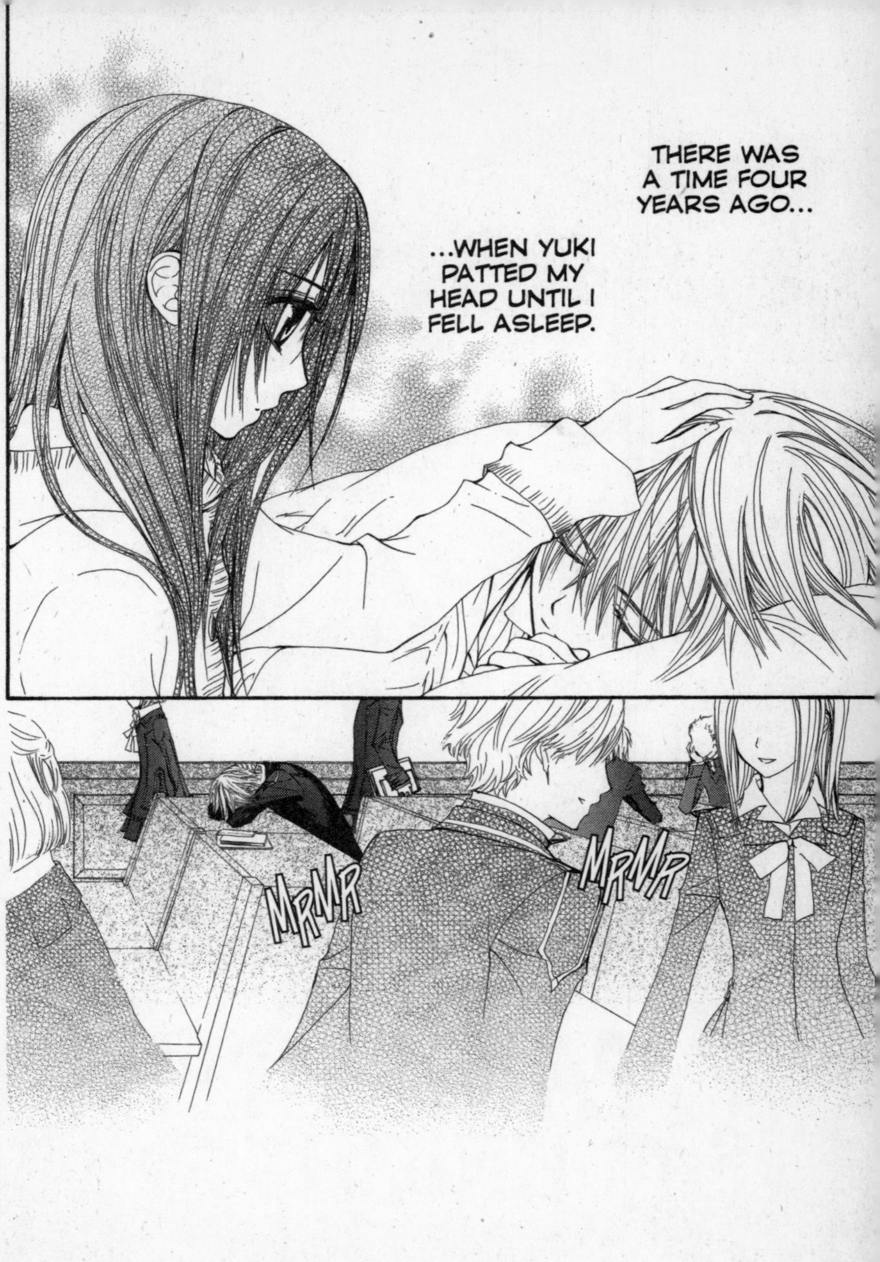
THERE WAS A TIME FOUR YEARS AGO...
...WHEN YUKI PATTED MY HEAD UNTIL I FELL ASLEEP.
MRMR
MRMR

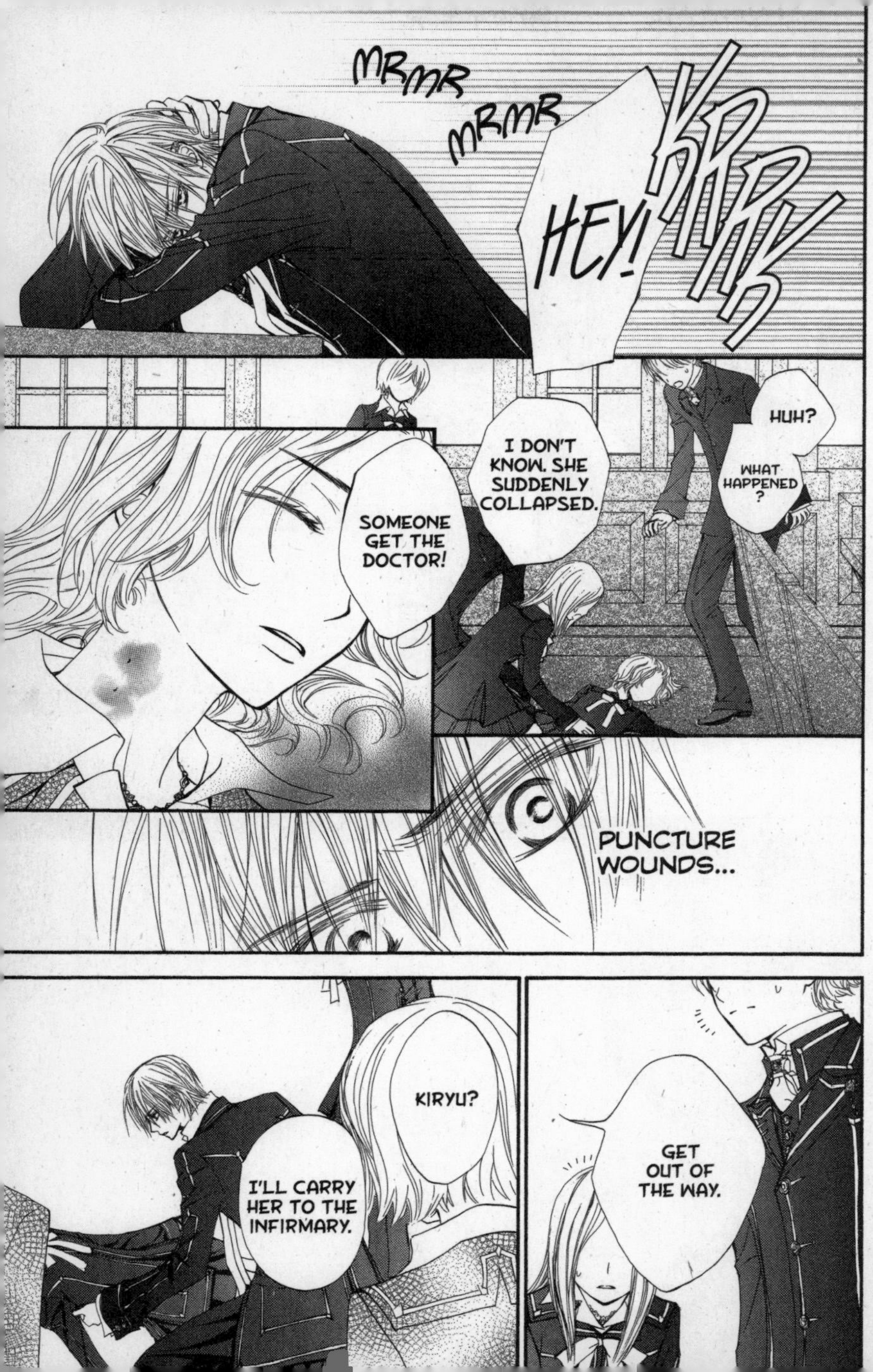
KRRRK
HEY!
MRMR
MRMR
HUH?
WHAT HAPPENED?
I DON'T KNOW. SHE SUDDENLY COLLAPSED.
SOMEONE GET THE DOCTOR!
PUNCTURE WOUNDS...
GET OUT OF THE WAY.
KIRYU?
I'LL CARRY HER TO THE INFIRMARY.

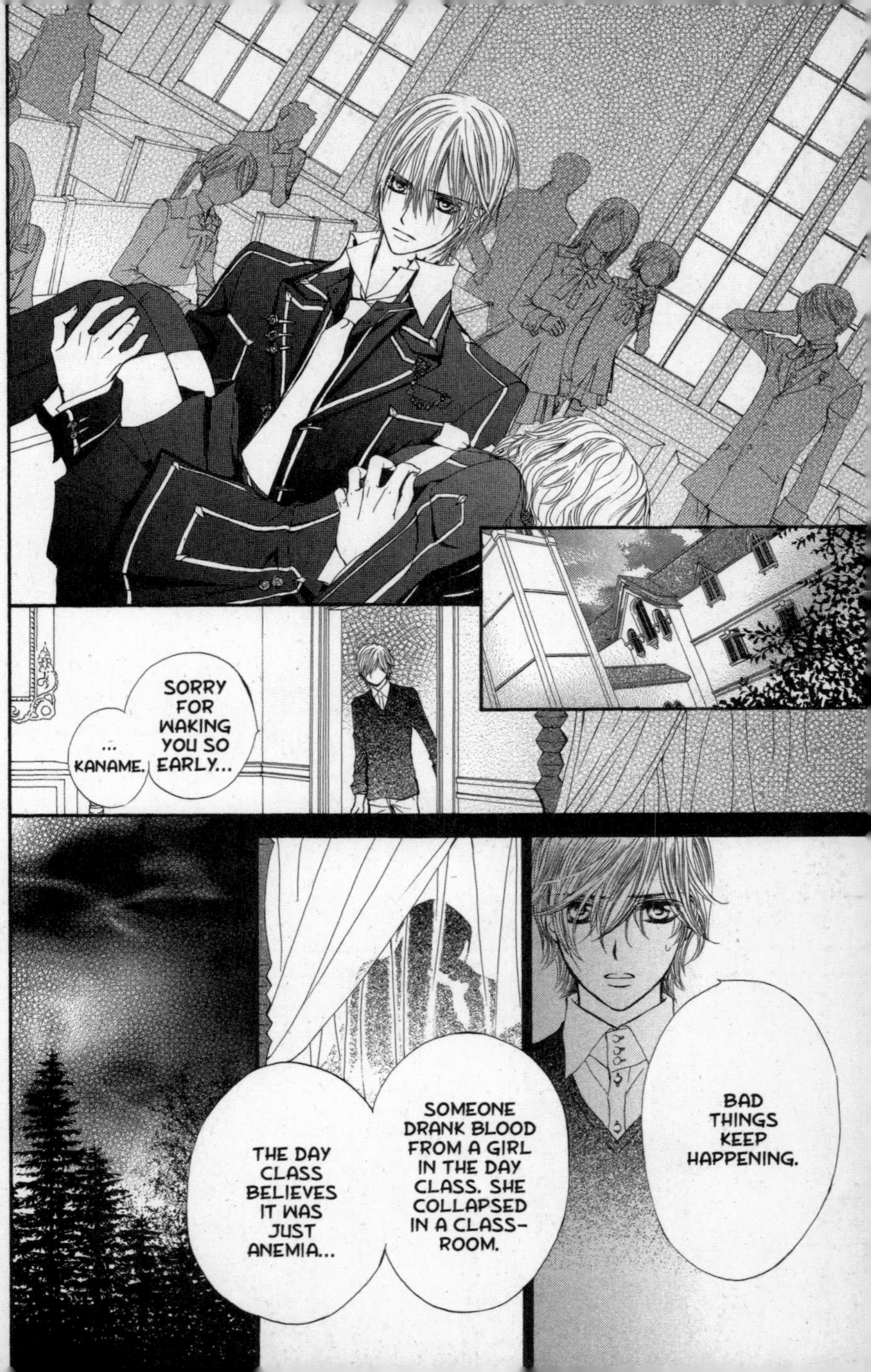
SORRY FOR WAKING YOU SO EARLY...
... KANAME.
BAD THINGS KEEP HAPPENING.
SOMEONE DRANK BLOOD FROM A GIRL IN THE DAY CLASS. SHE COLLAPSED IN A CLASS-ROOM.
THE DAY CLASS BELIEVES IT WAS JUST ANEMIA...

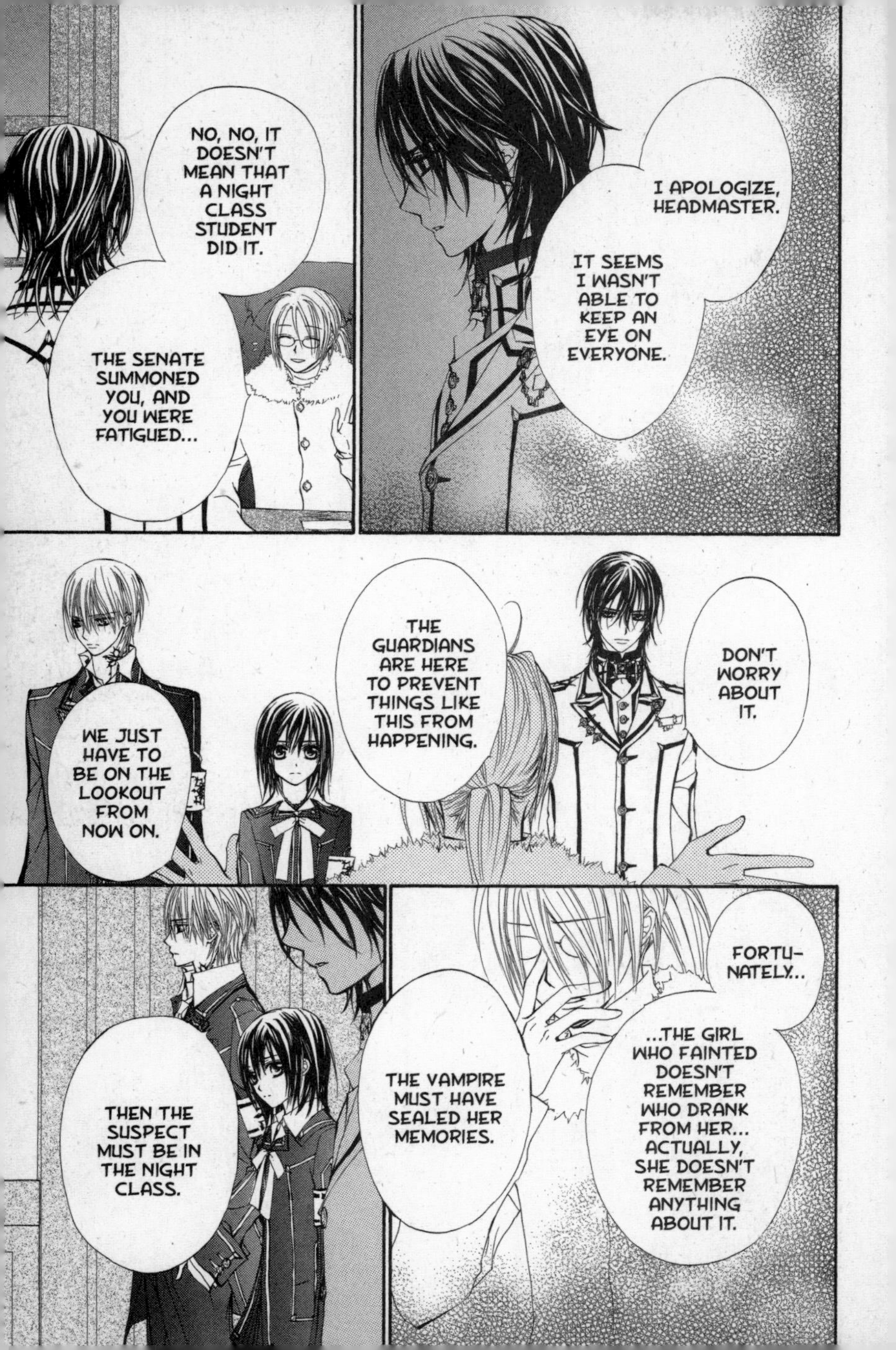
I APOLOGIZE, HEADMASTER.
IT SEEMS I WASN'T ABLE TO KEEP AN EYE ON EVERYONE.
NO, NO, IT DOESN'T MEAN THAT A NIGHT CLASS STUDENT DID IT.
THE SENATE SUMMONED YOU, AND YOU WERE FATIGUED...
DON'T WORRY ABOUT IT.
THE GUARDIANS ARE HERE TO PREVENT THINGS LIKE THIS FROM HAPPENING.
WE JUST HAVE TO BE ON THE LOOKOUT FROM NOW ON.
FORTU-NATELY...
...THE GIRL WHO FAINTED DOESN'T REMEMBER WHO DRANK FROM HER... ACTUALLY, SHE DOESN'T REMEMBER ANYTHING ABOUT IT.
THE VAMPIRE MUST HAVE SEALED HER MEMORIES.
THEN THE SUSPECT MUST BE IN THE NIGHT CLASS.

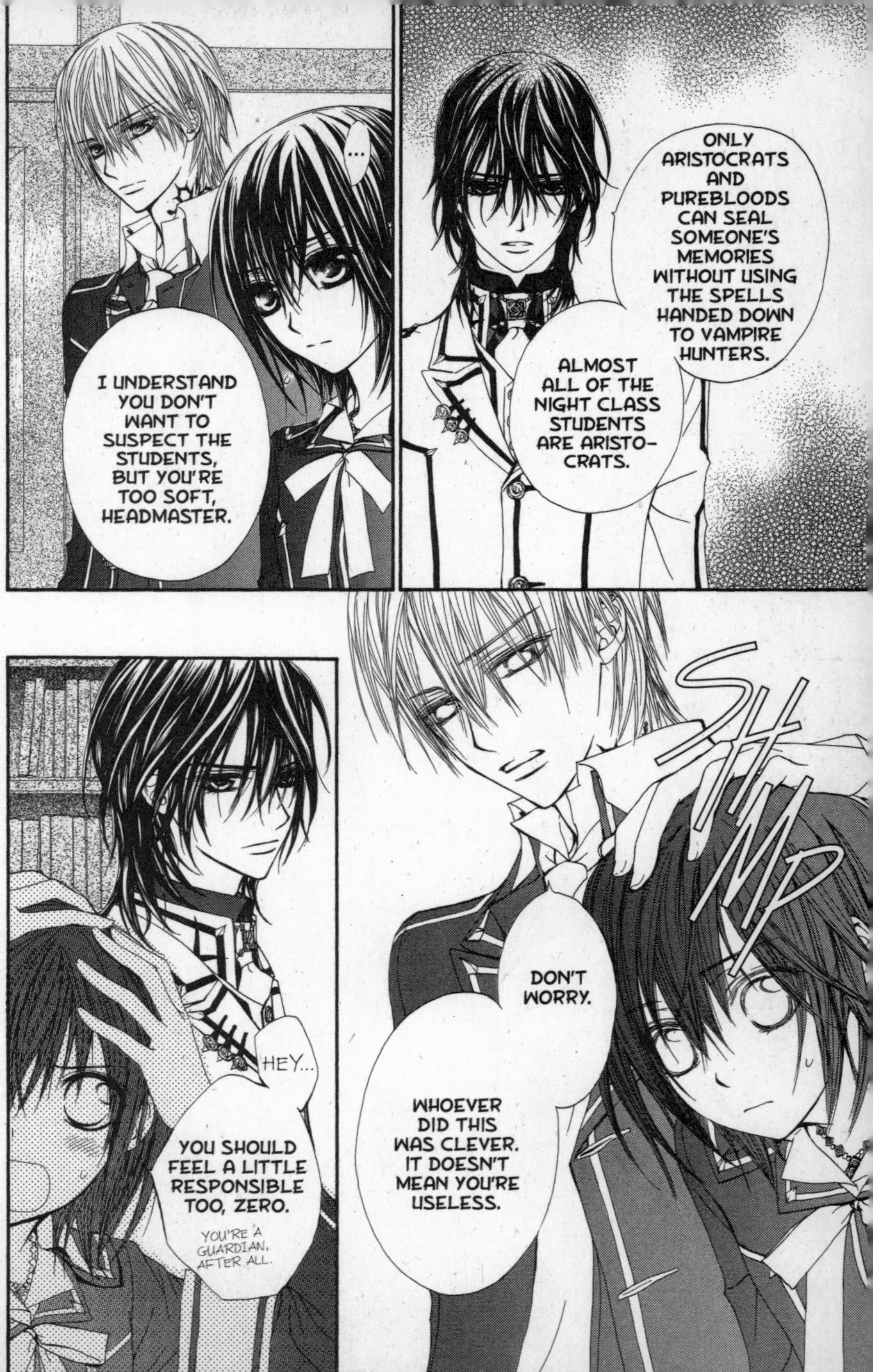

ONLY ARISTOCRATS AND PUREBLOODS CAN SEAL SOMEONE'S MEMORIES WITHOUT USING THE SPELLS HANDED DOWN TO VAMPIRE HUNTERS.
ALMOST ALL OF THE NIGHT CLASS STUDENTS ARE ARISTO-CRATS.
...
I UNDERSTAND YOU DON'T WANT TO SUSPECT THE STUDENTS, BUT YOU'RE TOO SOFT, HEADMASTER.
SHMP
DON'T WORRY.
WHOEVER DID THIS WAS CLEVER. IT DOESN'T MEAN YOU'RE USELESS.
HEY...
YOU SHOULD FEEL A LITTLE RESPONSIBLE TOO, ZERO.
YOU'RE A GUARDIAN, AFTER ALL.

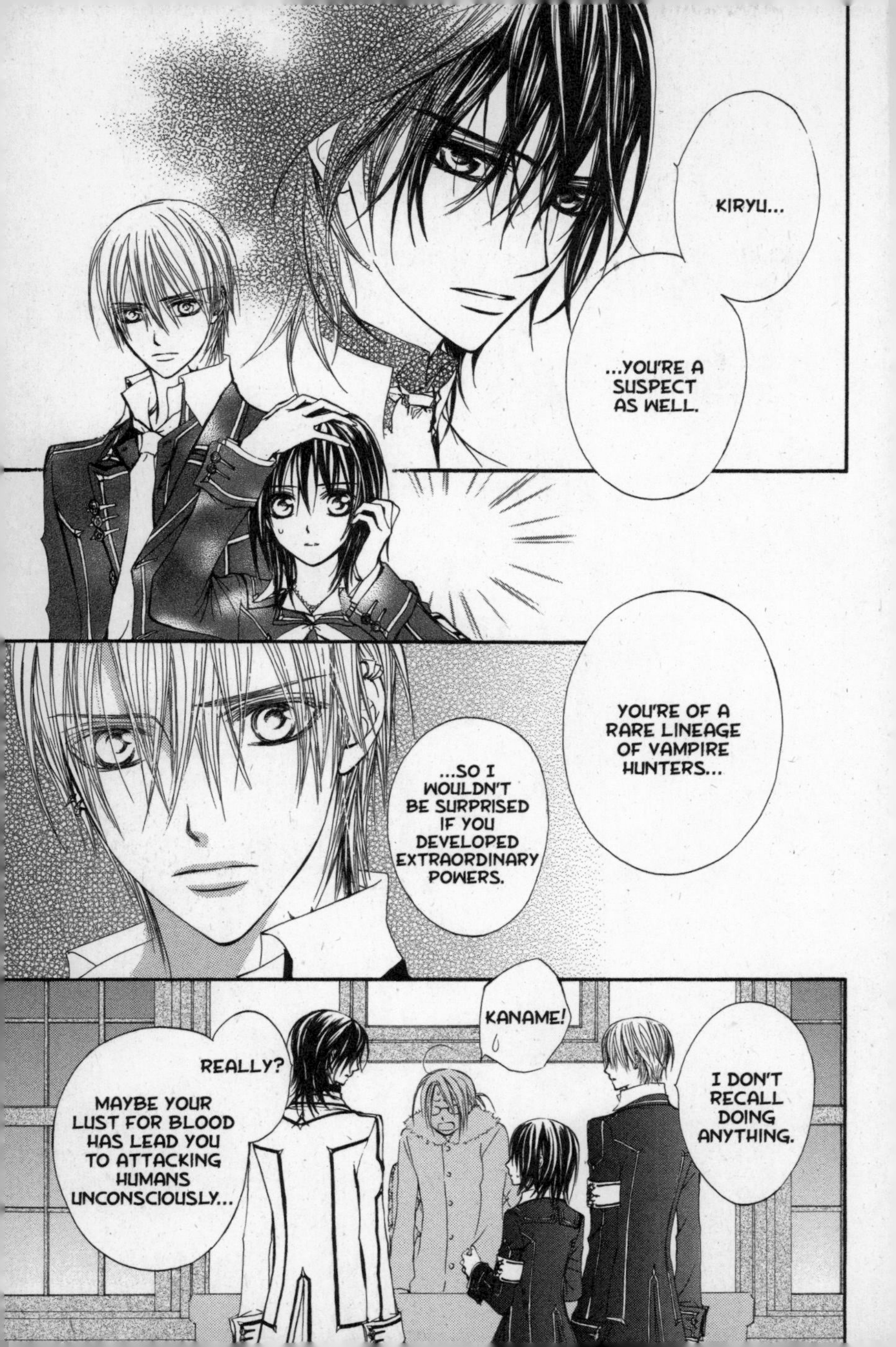
KIRYU...
...YOU'RE A SUSPECT AS WELL.
YOU'RE OF A RARE LINEAGE OF VAMPIRE HUNTERS...
...SO I WOULDN'T BE SURPRISED IF YOU DEVELOPED EXTRAORDINARY POWERS.
I DON'T RECALL DOING ANYTHING.
KANAME!
REALLY?
MAYBE YOUR LUST FOR BLOOD HAS LEAD YOU TO ATTACKING HUMANS UNCONSCIOUSLY...

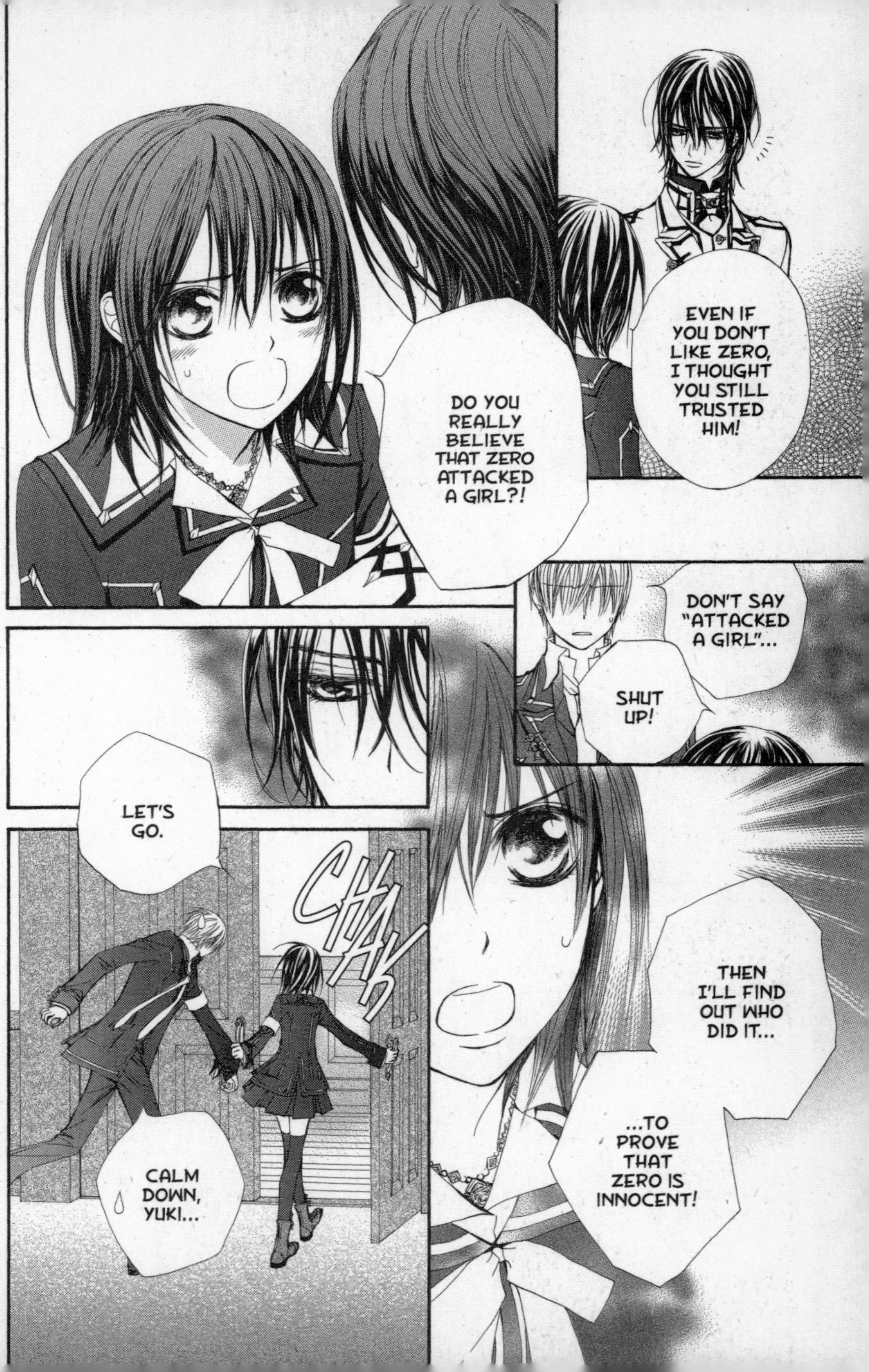
EVEN IF YOU DON'T LIKE ZERO, I THOUGHT YOU STILL TRUSTED HIM!
DO YOU REALLY BELIEVE THAT ZERO ATTACKED A GIRL?!
DON'T SAY "ATTACKED A GIRL"...
SHUT UP!
THEN I'LL FIND OUT WHO DID IT...
...TO PROVE THAT ZERO IS INNOCENT!
LET'S GO.
CHAK
CALM DOWN, YUKI...

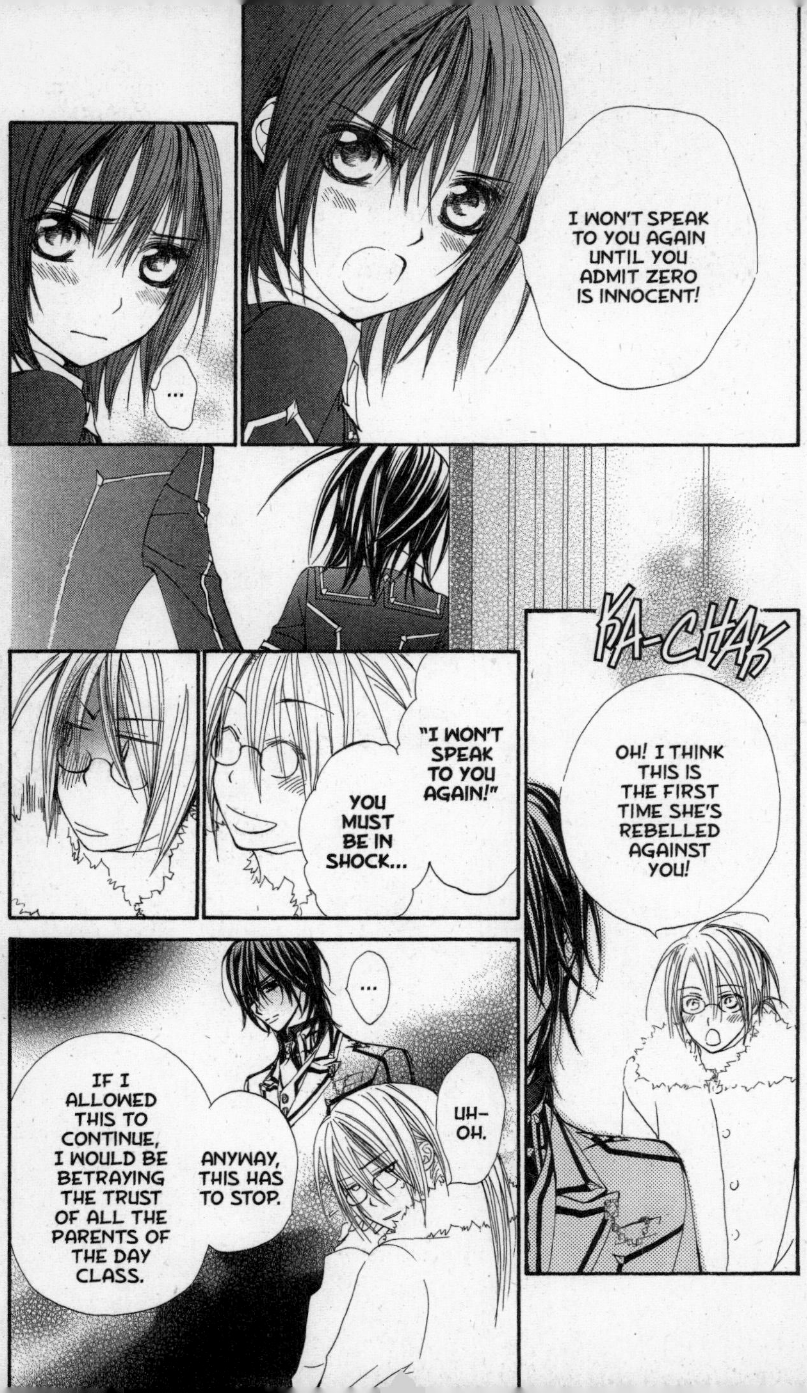

I WON'T SPEAK TO YOU AGAIN UNTIL YOU ADMIT ZERO IS INNOCENT!
...
KA-CHAK
OH! I THINK THIS IS THE FIRST TIME SHE'S REBELLED AGAINST YOU!
"I WON'T SPEAK TO YOU AGAIN!"
YOU MUST BE IN SHOCK...
...
UH-OH.
ANYWAY, THIS HAS TO STOP.
IF I ALLOWED THIS TO CONTINUE, I WOULD BE BETRAYING THE TRUST OF ALL THE PARENTS OF THE DAY CLASS.

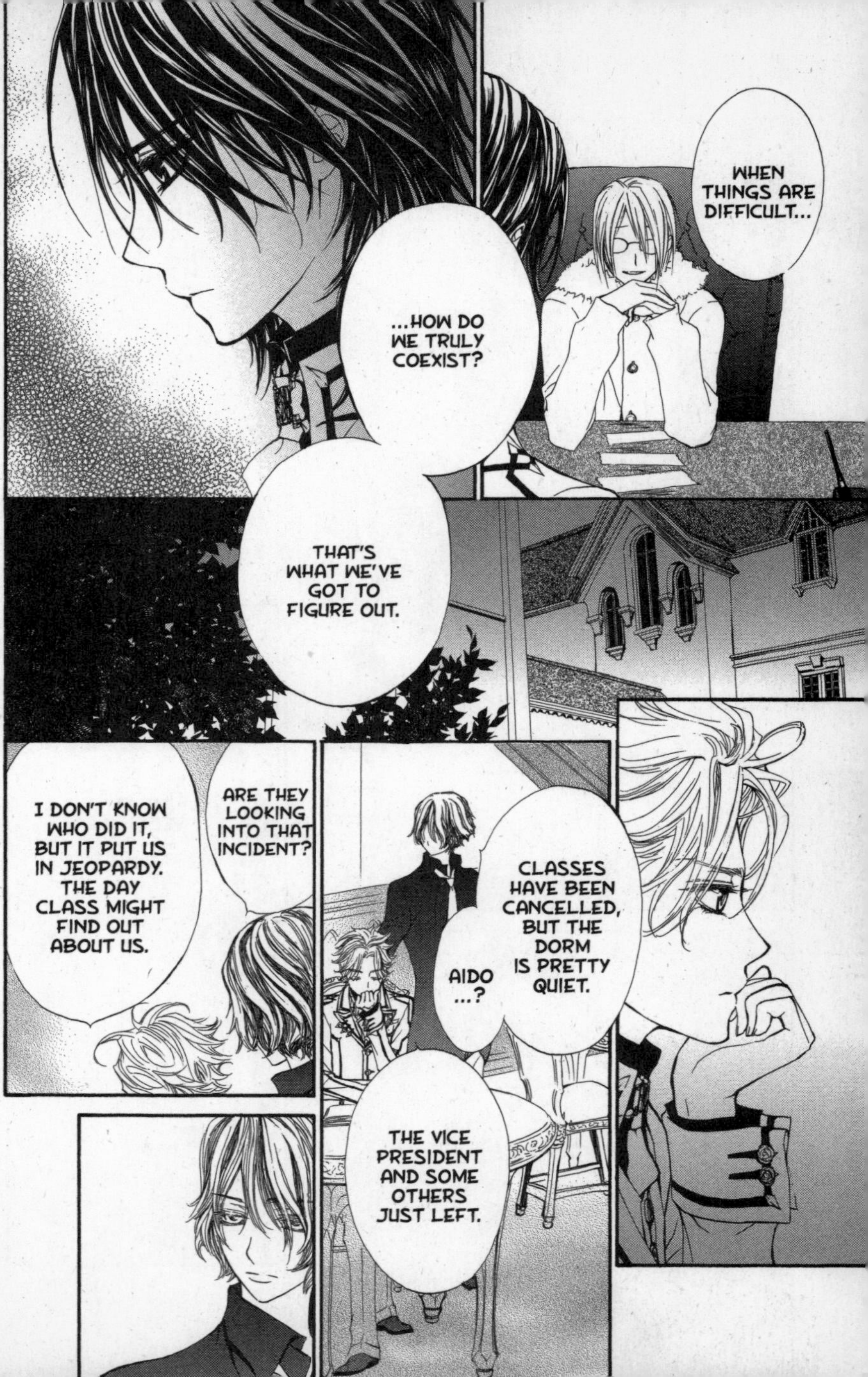
WHEN THINGS ARE DIFFICULT...
...HOW DO WE TRULY COEXIST?
THAT'S WHAT WE'VE GOT TO FIGURE OUT.
CLASSES HAVE BEEN CANCELLED, BUT THE DORM IS PRETTY QUIET.
AIDO ...?
THE VICE PRESIDENT AND SOME OTHERS JUST LEFT.
ARE THEY LOOKING INTO THAT INCIDENT?
I DON'T KNOW WHO DID IT, BUT IT PUT US IN JEOPARDY. THE DAY CLASS MIGHT FIND OUT ABOUT US.

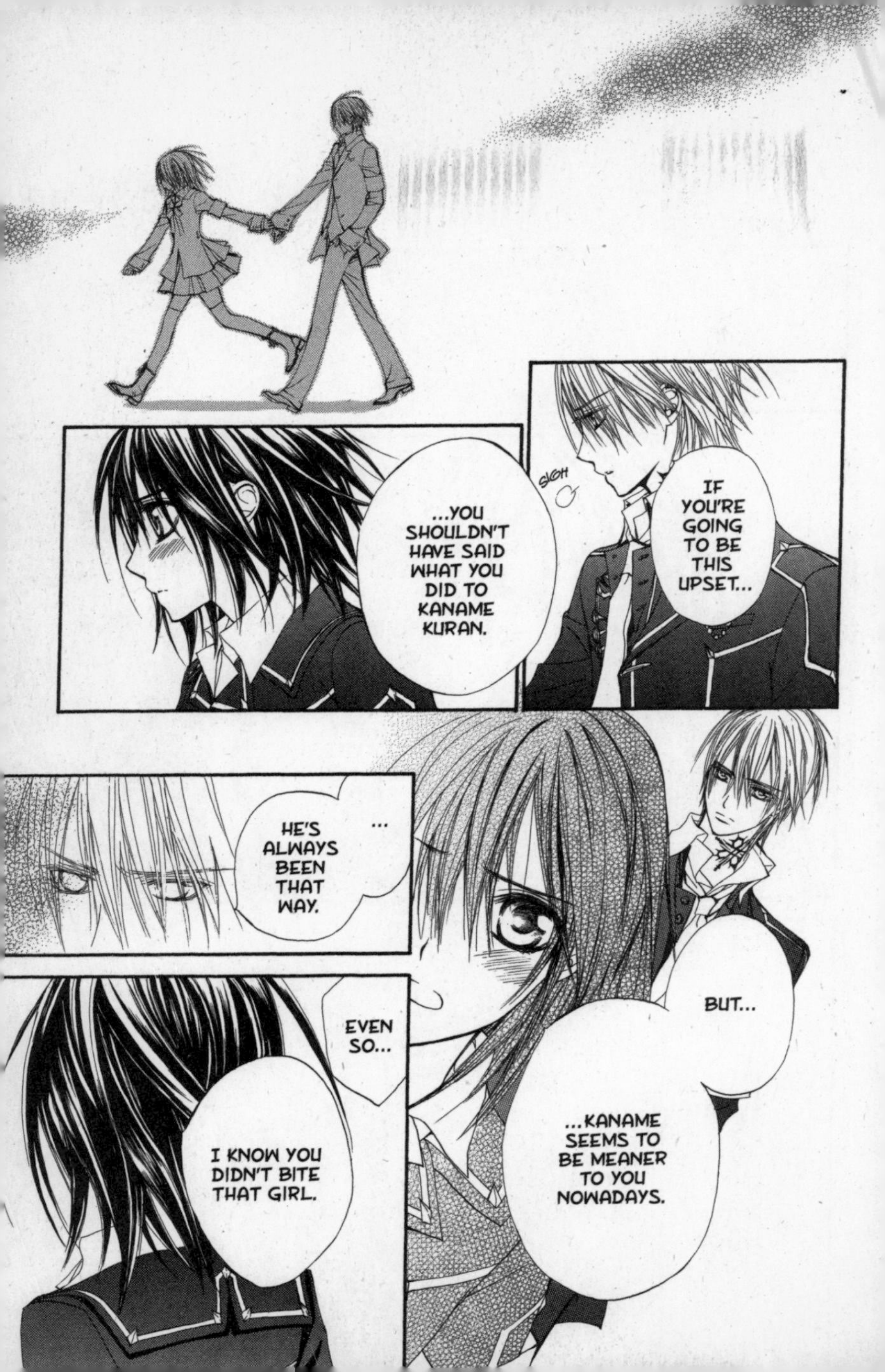
SIGH
IF YOU'RE GOING TO BE THIS UPSET...
...YOU SHOULDN'T HAVE SAID WHAT YOU DID TO KANAME KURAN.
BUT...
...KANAME SEEMS TO BE MEANER TO YOU NOWADAYS.
...
HE'S ALWAYS BEEN THAT WAY.
EVEN SO...
I KNOW YOU DIDN'T BITE THAT GIRL.

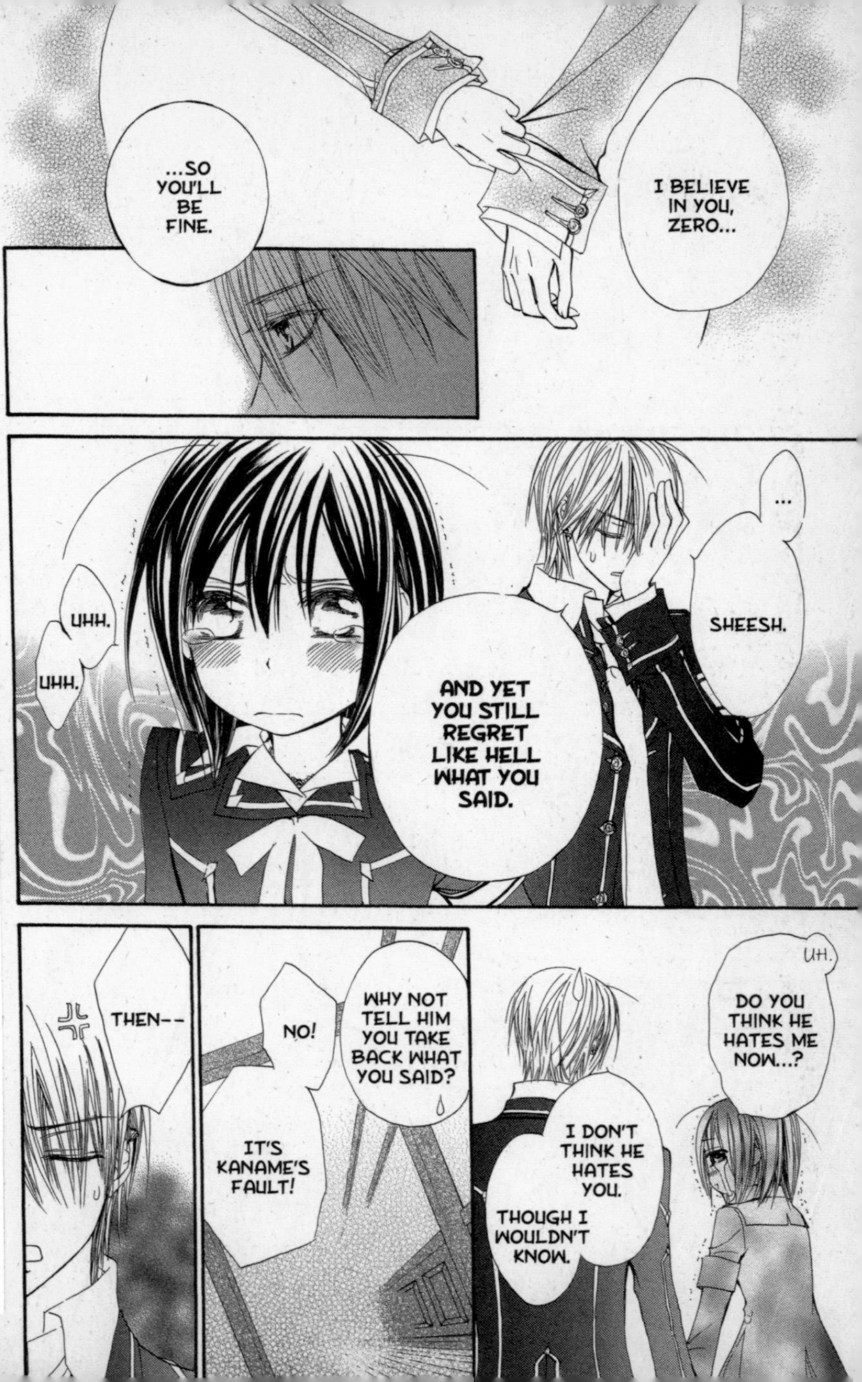
I BELIEVE IN YOU, ZERO...
...SO YOU'LL BE FINE.
...
SHEESH.
UHH.
UHH.
AND YET YOU STILL REGRET LIKE HELL WHAT YOU SAID.
UH.
DO YOU THINK HE HATES ME NOW...?
I DON'T THINK HE HATES YOU.
THOUGH I WOULDN'T KNOW.
WHY NOT TELL HIM YOU TAKE BACK WHAT YOU SAID?
NO!
IT'S KANAME'S FAULT!
THEN--

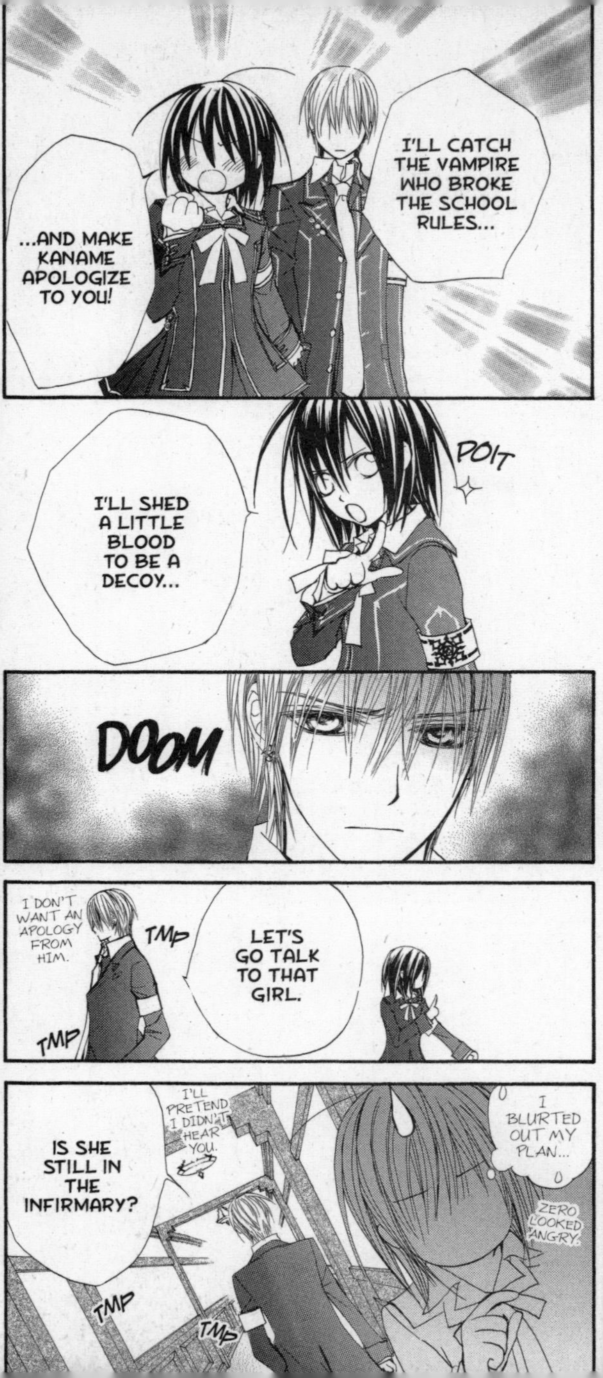
I'LL CATCH THE VAMPIRE WHO BROKE THE SCHOOL RULES...
...AND MAKE KANAME APOLOGIZE TO YOU!
POIT
I'LL SHED A LITTLE BLOOD TO BE A DECOY...
DOOM
LET'S GO TALK TO THAT GIRL.
TMP
I DON'T WANT AN APOLOGY FROM HIM.
TMP
I BLURTED OUT MY PLAN...
ZERO LOOKED ANGRY.
I'LL PRETEND I DIDN'T HEAR YOU.
IS SHE STILL IN THE INFIRMARY?
TMP
TMP

VI

Shizuka's role was to torture Zero, so I was expecting that people who love Zero would hate her. But judging from the letters I've received, quite a lot of readers like her. It sure seems that way. (I-I'm happy!)

I wanted to include the side story of Shizuka and Ichiru, but because of page count, we decided to include it in a later volume. For those of you who are anxious to read it, we'll try to get it out as soon as possible. I'd be happy if you wait for it...!!

I can't promise it, but this year I would like to reply to the letters I receive... I want to learn English and visit English gardens... My ambitions keep growing...

Please enjoy the bonus manga at the end of this volume!

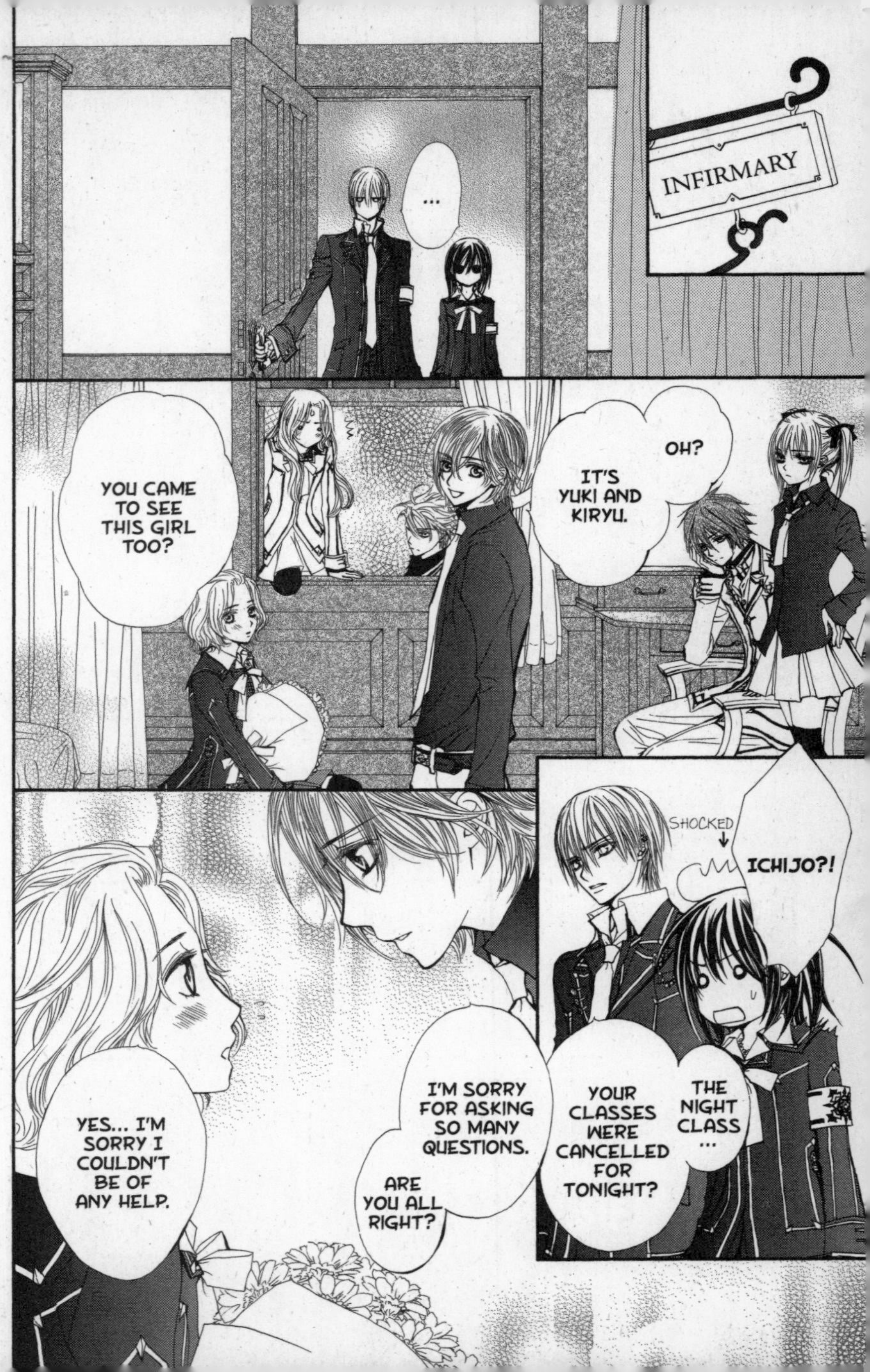
INFIRMARY
...
OH? IT'S YUKI AND KIRYU.
YOU CAME TO SEE THIS GIRL TOO?
SHOCKED
ICHIJO?!
THE NIGHT CLASS...
YOUR CLASSES WERE CANCELLED FOR TONIGHT?
I'M SORRY FOR ASKING SO MANY QUESTIONS.
ARE YOU ALL RIGHT?
YES... I'M SORRY I COULDN'T BE OF ANY HELP.

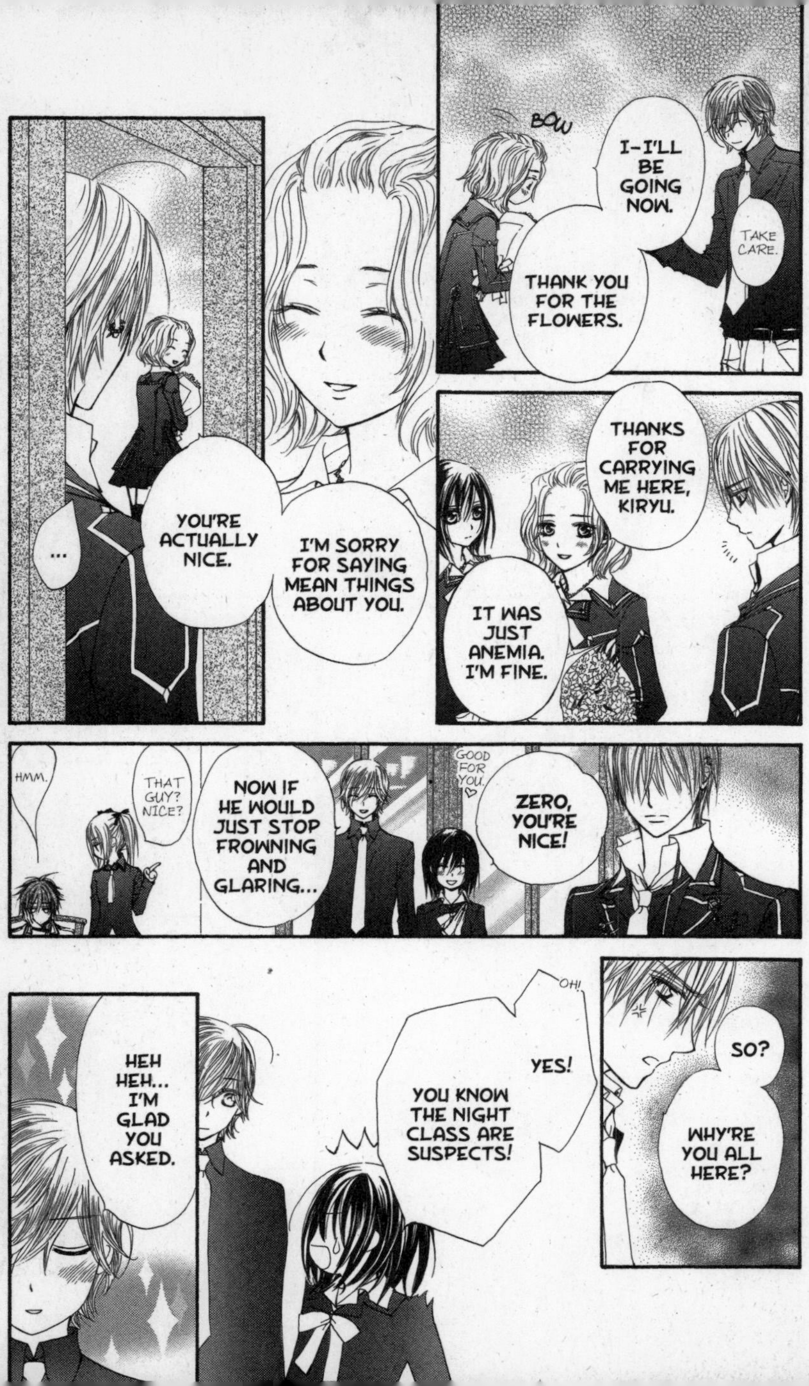
BOW
I-I'LL BE GOING NOW.
TAKE CARE.
THANK YOU FOR THE FLOWERS.
THANKS FOR CARRYING ME HERE, KIRYU.
IT WAS JUST ANEMIA. I'M FINE.
I'M SORRY FOR SAYING MEAN THINGS ABOUT YOU.
YOU'RE ACTUALLY NICE.
...
ZERO, YOU'RE NICE!
GOOD FOR YOU. ♡
NOW IF HE WOULD JUST STOP FROWNING AND GLARING...
THAT GUY? NICE?
HMM.
SO?
WHY'RE YOU ALL HERE?
OH!
YES!
YOU KNOW THE NIGHT CLASS ARE SUSPECTS!
HEH HEH... I'M GLAD YOU ASKED.

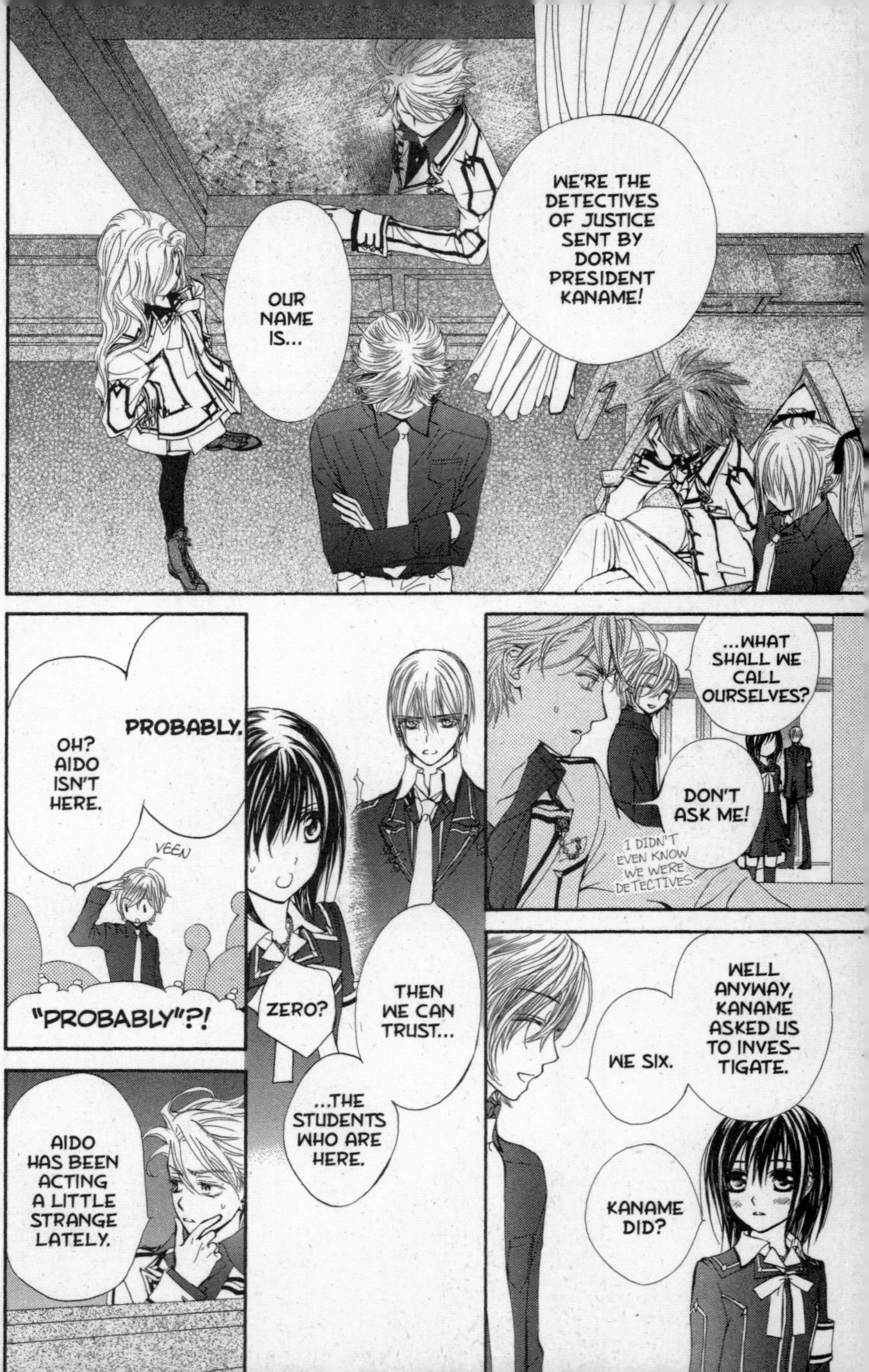
OUR NAME IS...
WE'RE THE DETECTIVES OF JUSTICE SENT BY DORM PRESIDENT KANAME!
...WHAT SHALL WE CALL OURSELVES?
DON'T ASK ME!
I DIDN'T EVEN KNOW WE WERE DETECTIVES.
WELL ANYWAY, KANAME ASKED US TO INVES-TIGATE.
WE SIX.
KANAME DID?
ZERO?
THEN WE CAN TRUST...
...THE STUDENTS WHO ARE HERE.
OH? AIDO ISN'T HERE.
PROBABLY.
VEEN
"PROBABLY"?!
AIDO HAS BEEN ACTING A LITTLE STRANGE LATELY.

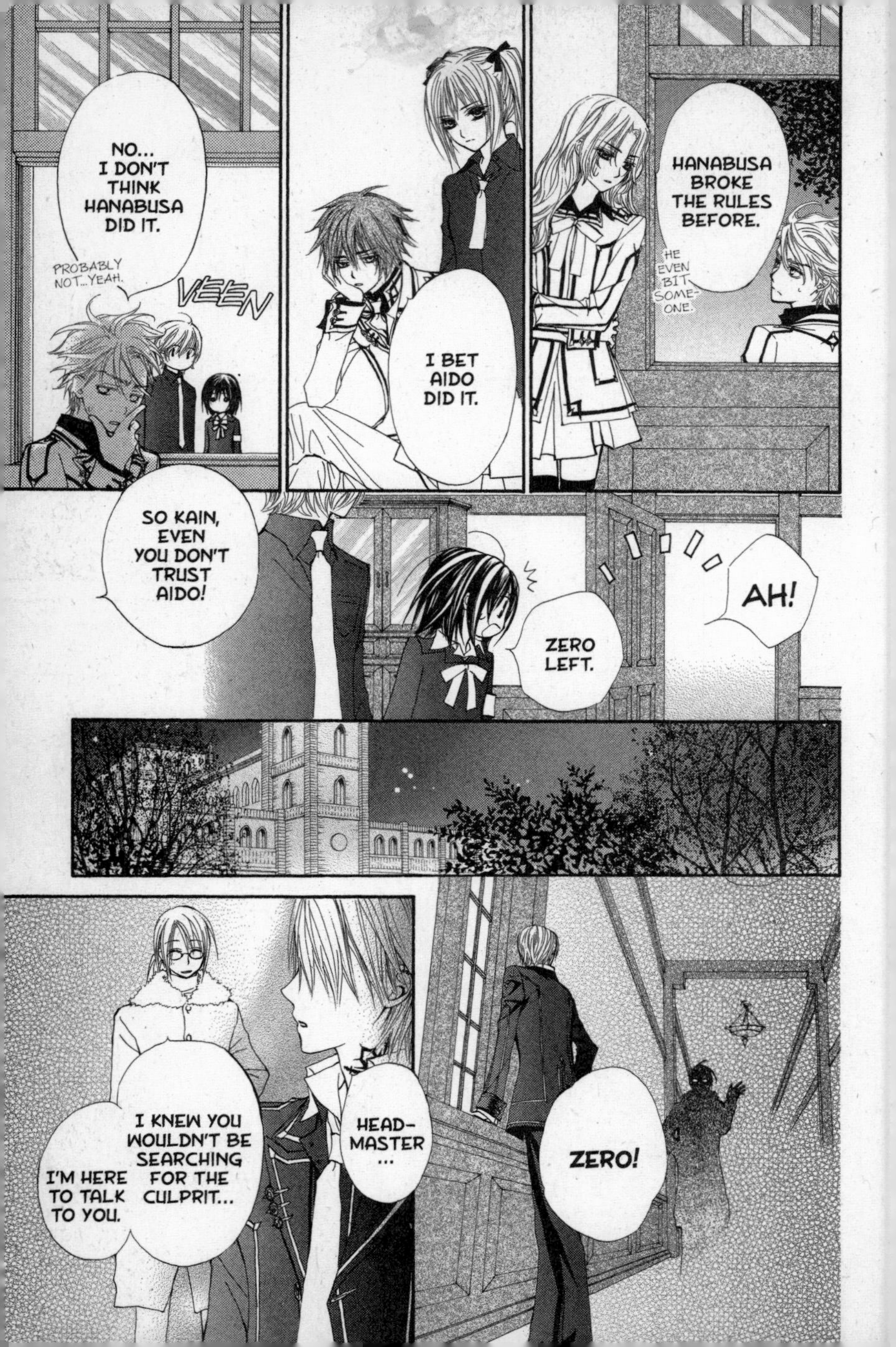
HANABUSA BROKE THE RULES BEFORE.
HE EVEN BIT SOME-ONE.
I BET AIDO DID IT.
NO... I DON'T THINK HANABUSA DID IT.
PROBABLY NOT...YEAH.
VEEN
AH!
SO KAIN, EVEN YOU DON'T TRUST AIDO!
ZERO LEFT.
ZERO!
HEAD-MASTER ...
I KNEW YOU WOULDN'T BE SEARCHING FOR THE CULPRIT...
I'M HERE TO TALK TO YOU.

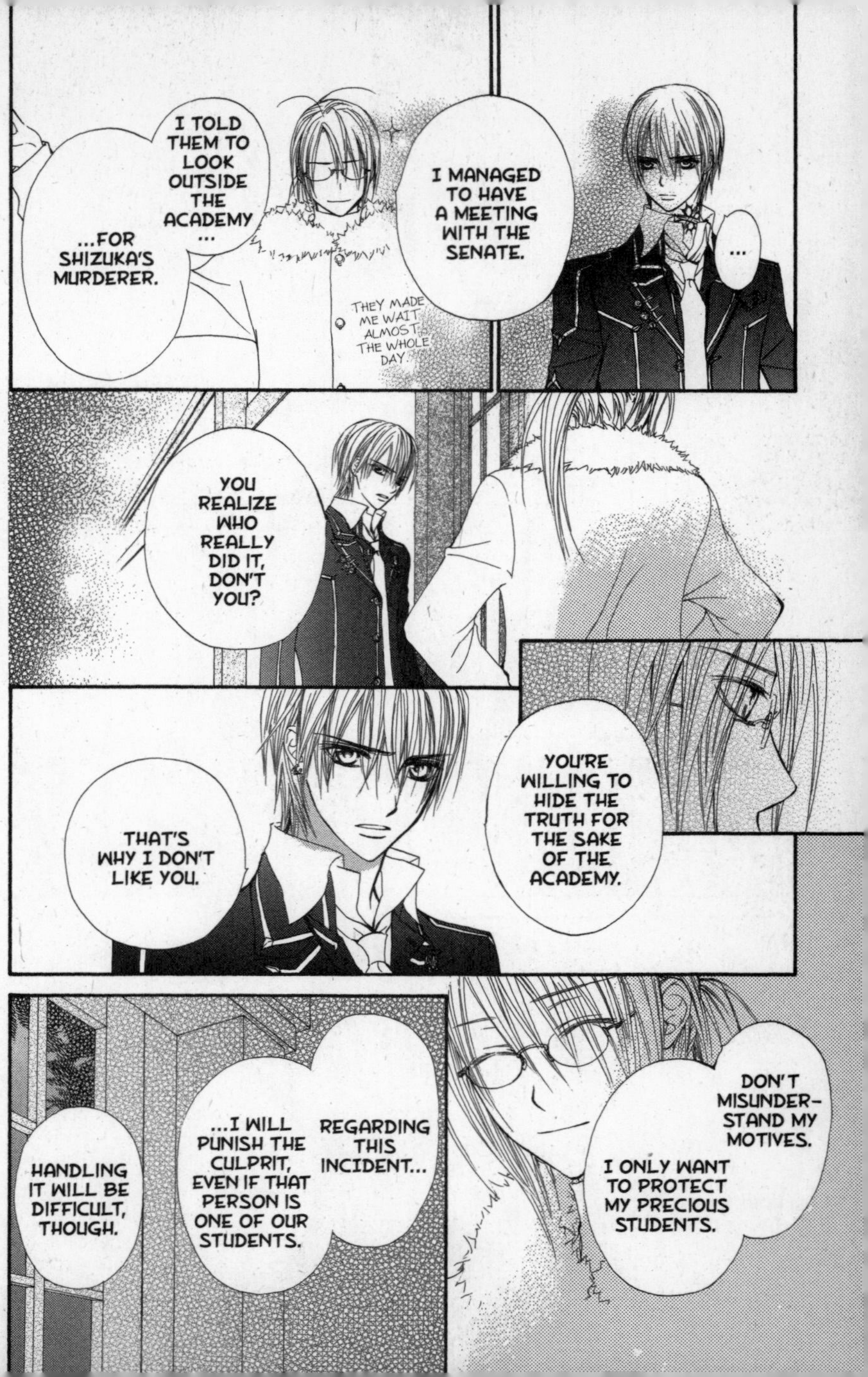
I MANAGED TO HAVE A MEETING WITH THE SENATE.
THEY MADE ME WAIT ALMOST THE WHOLE DAY.
...
I TOLD THEM TO LOOK OUTSIDE THE ACADEMY ...
...FOR SHIZUKA'S MURDERER.
YOU REALIZE WHO REALLY DID IT, DON'T YOU?
YOU'RE WILLING TO HIDE THE TRUTH FOR THE SAKE OF THE ACADEMY.
THAT'S WHY I DON'T LIKE YOU.
DON'T MISUNDER-STAND MY MOTIVES.
I ONLY WANT TO PROTECT MY PRECIOUS STUDENTS.
REGARDING THIS INCIDENT...
...I WILL PUNISH THE CULPRIT, EVEN IF THAT PERSON IS ONE OF OUR STUDENTS.
HANDLING IT WILL BE DIFFICULT, THOUGH.

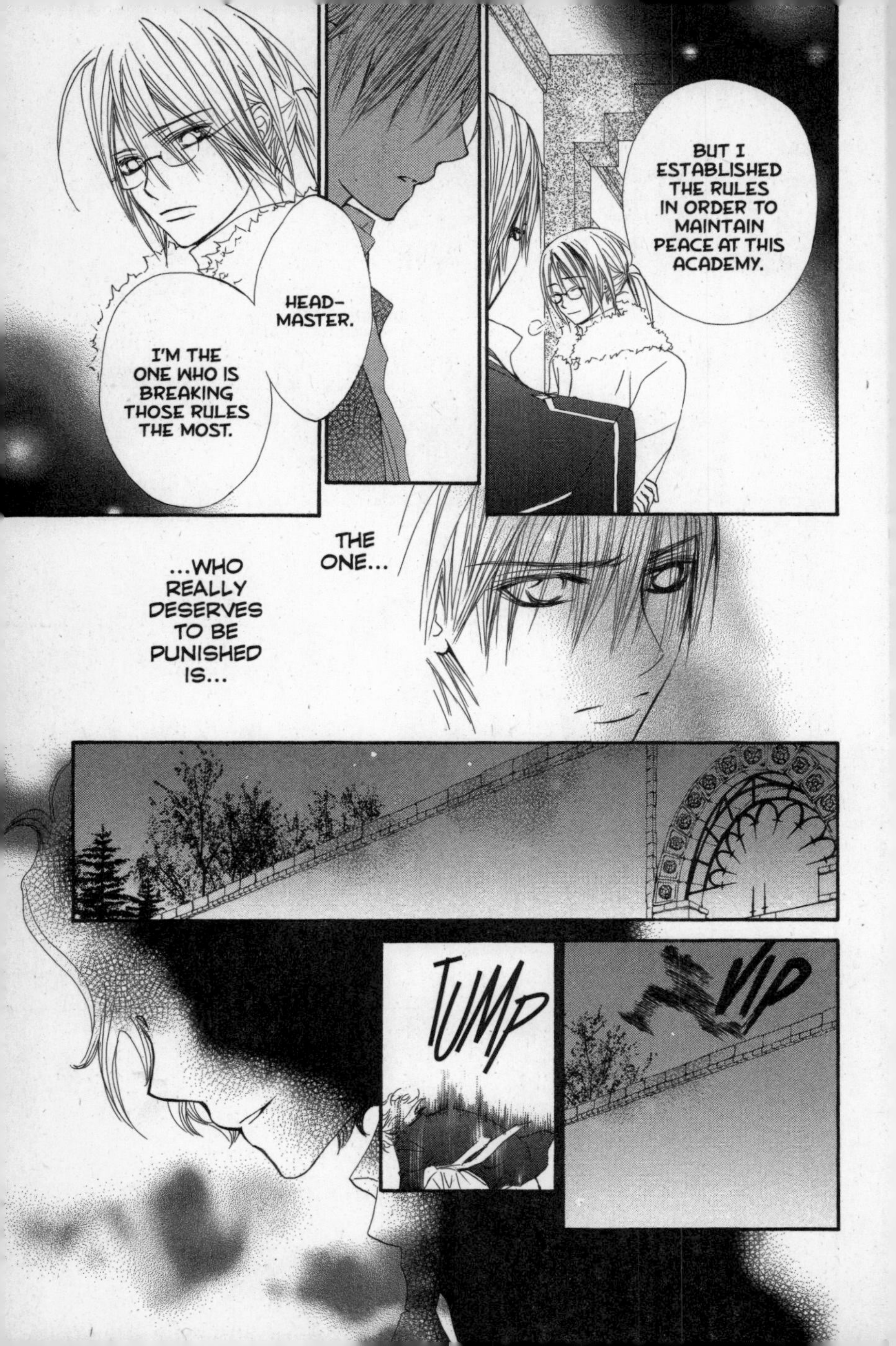
BUT I ESTABLISHED THE RULES IN ORDER TO MAINTAIN PEACE AT THIS ACADEMY.
HEAD-MASTER.
I'M THE ONE WHO IS BREAKING THOSE RULES THE MOST.
THE ONE...
...WHO REALLY DESERVES TO BE PUNISHED IS...
TUMP

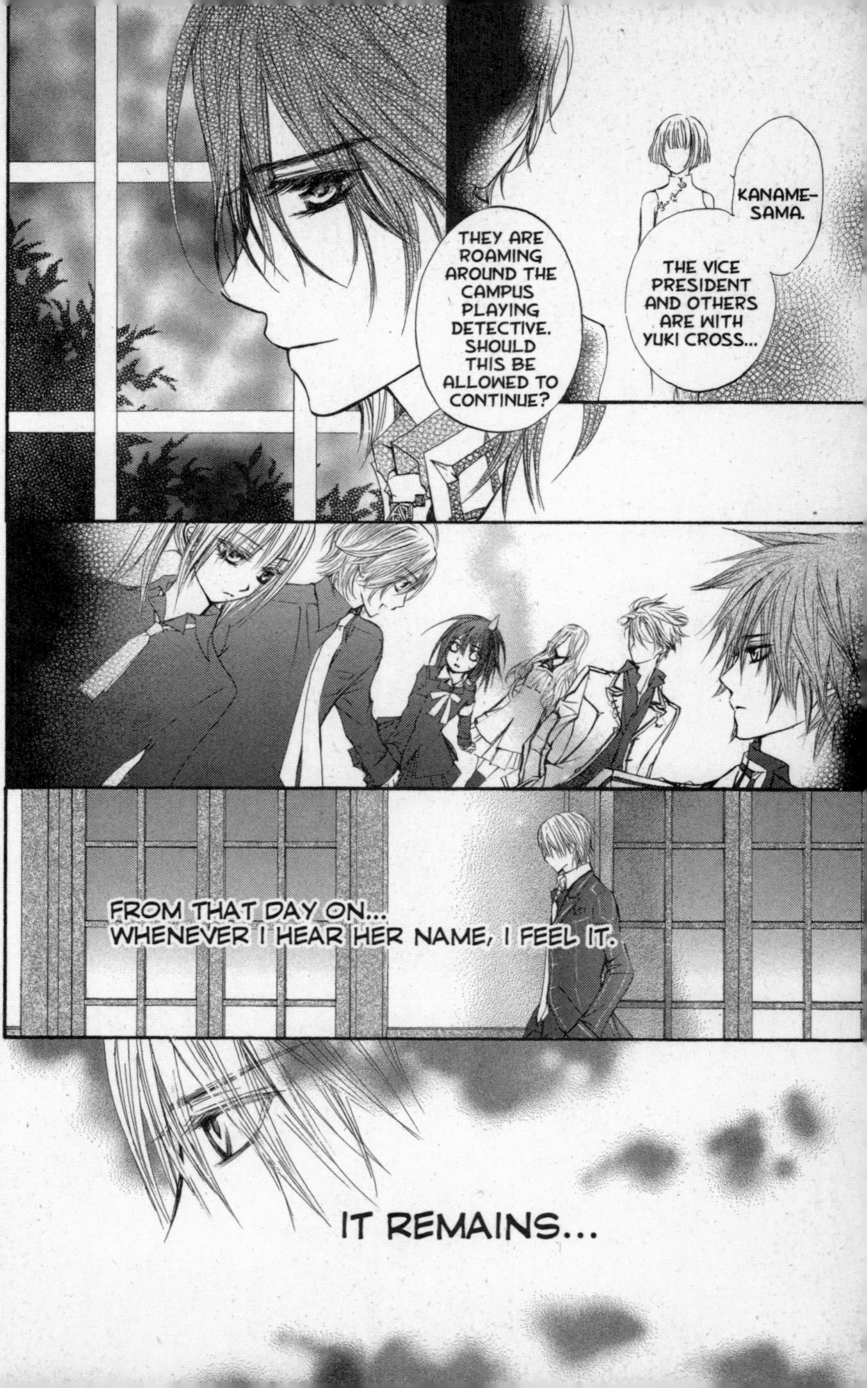
KANAME-SAMA.
THE VICE PRESIDENT AND OTHERS ARE WITH YUKI CROSS...
THEY ARE ROAMING AROUND THE CAMPUS PLAYING DETECTIVE. SHOULD THIS BE ALLOWED TO CONTINUE?
FROM THAT DAY ON... WHENEVER I HEAR HER NAME, I FEEL IT.
IT REMAINS...

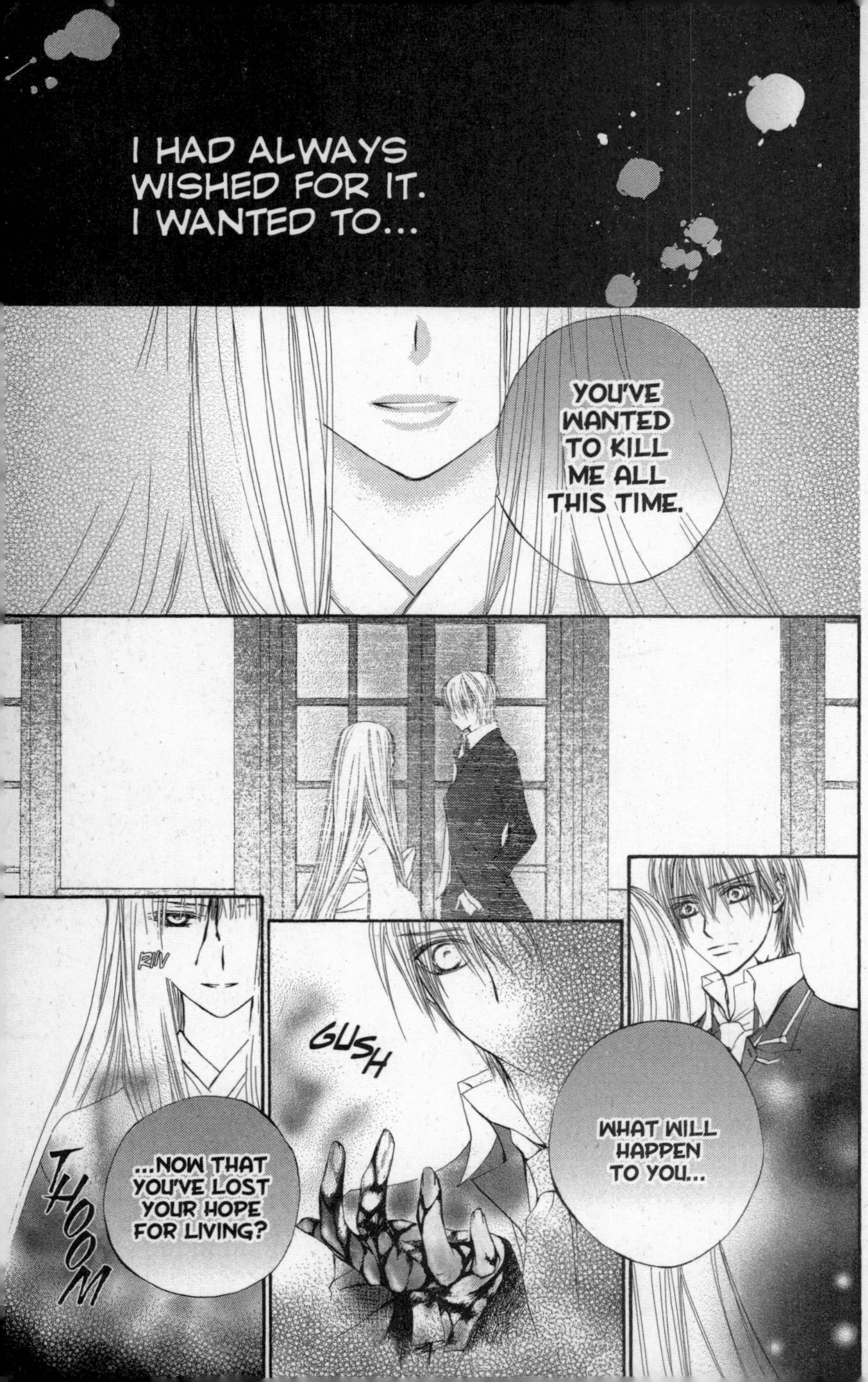
I HAD ALWAYS WISHED FOR IT. I WANTED TO...
YOU'VE WANTED TO KILL ME ALL THIS TIME.
WHAT WILL HAPPEN TO YOU...
GUSH
RIIV
...NOW THAT YOU'VE LOST YOUR HOPE FOR LIVING?
THOOM

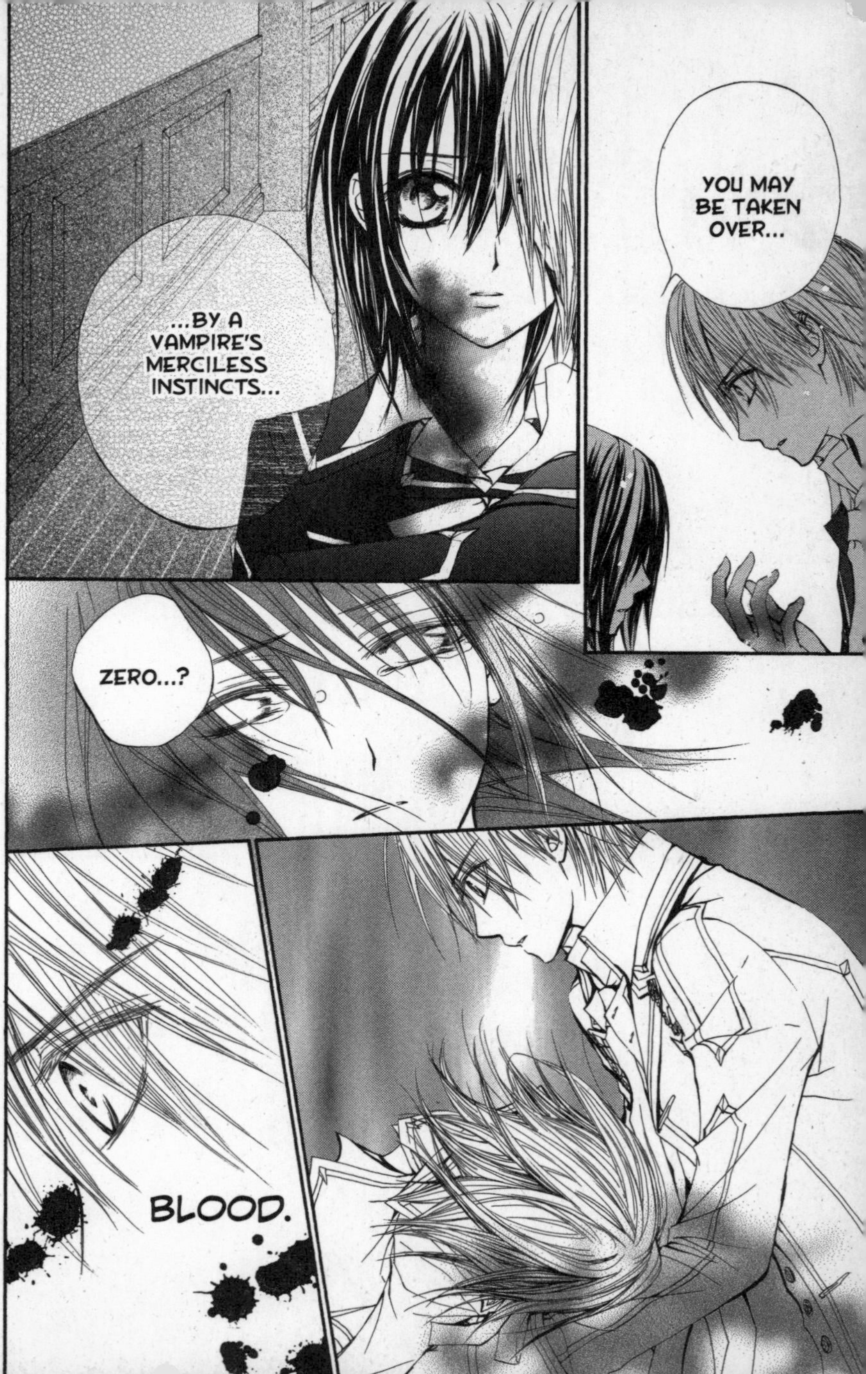
YOU MAY BE TAKEN OVER...
...BY A VAMPIRE'S MERCILESS INSTINCTS...
ZERO...?
BLOOD.

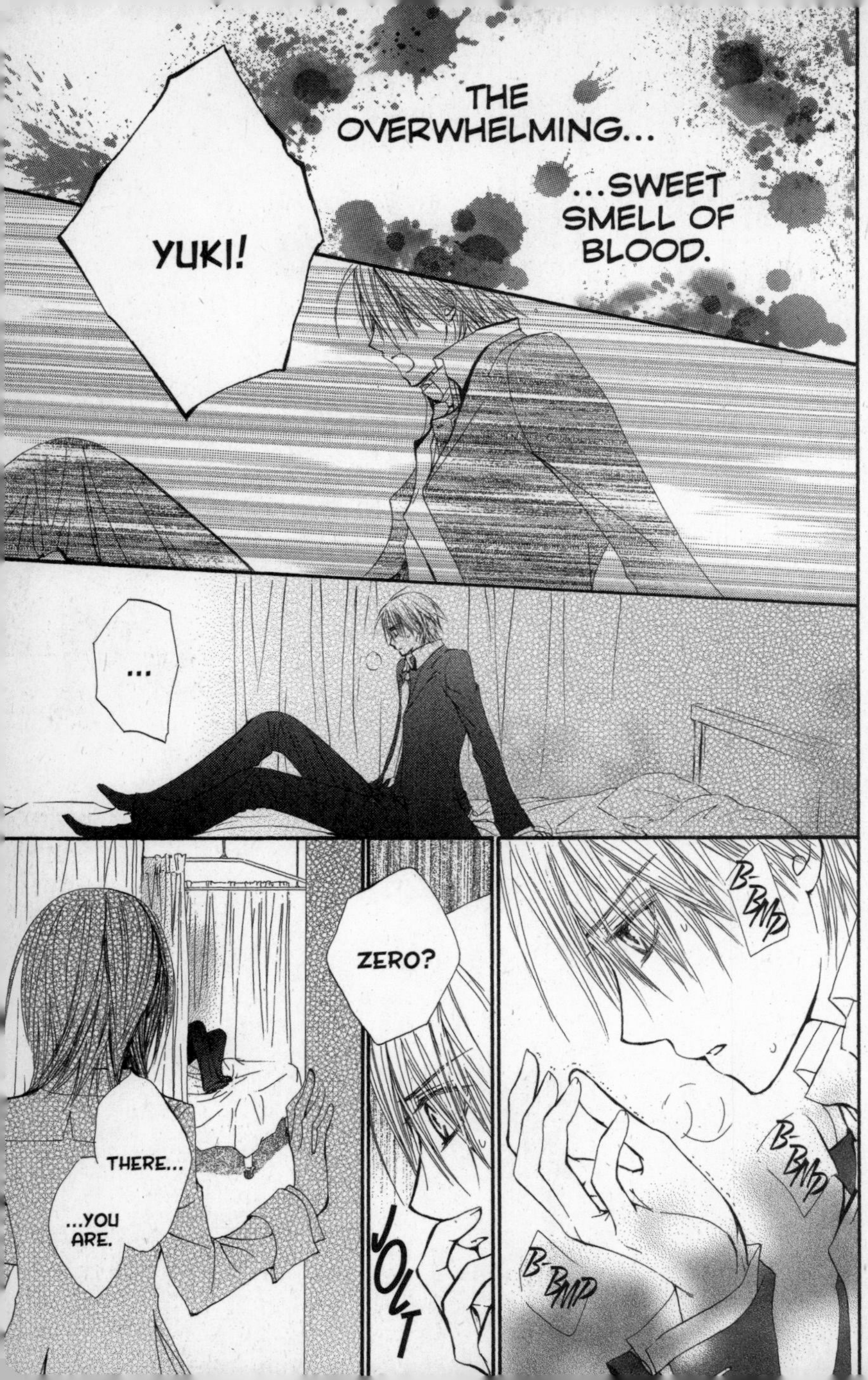
THE OVERWHELMING...
...SWEET SMELL OF BLOOD.
YUKI!
...
B-BMP
B-BMP
B-BMP
ZERO?
JOLT
THERE...
...YOU ARE.

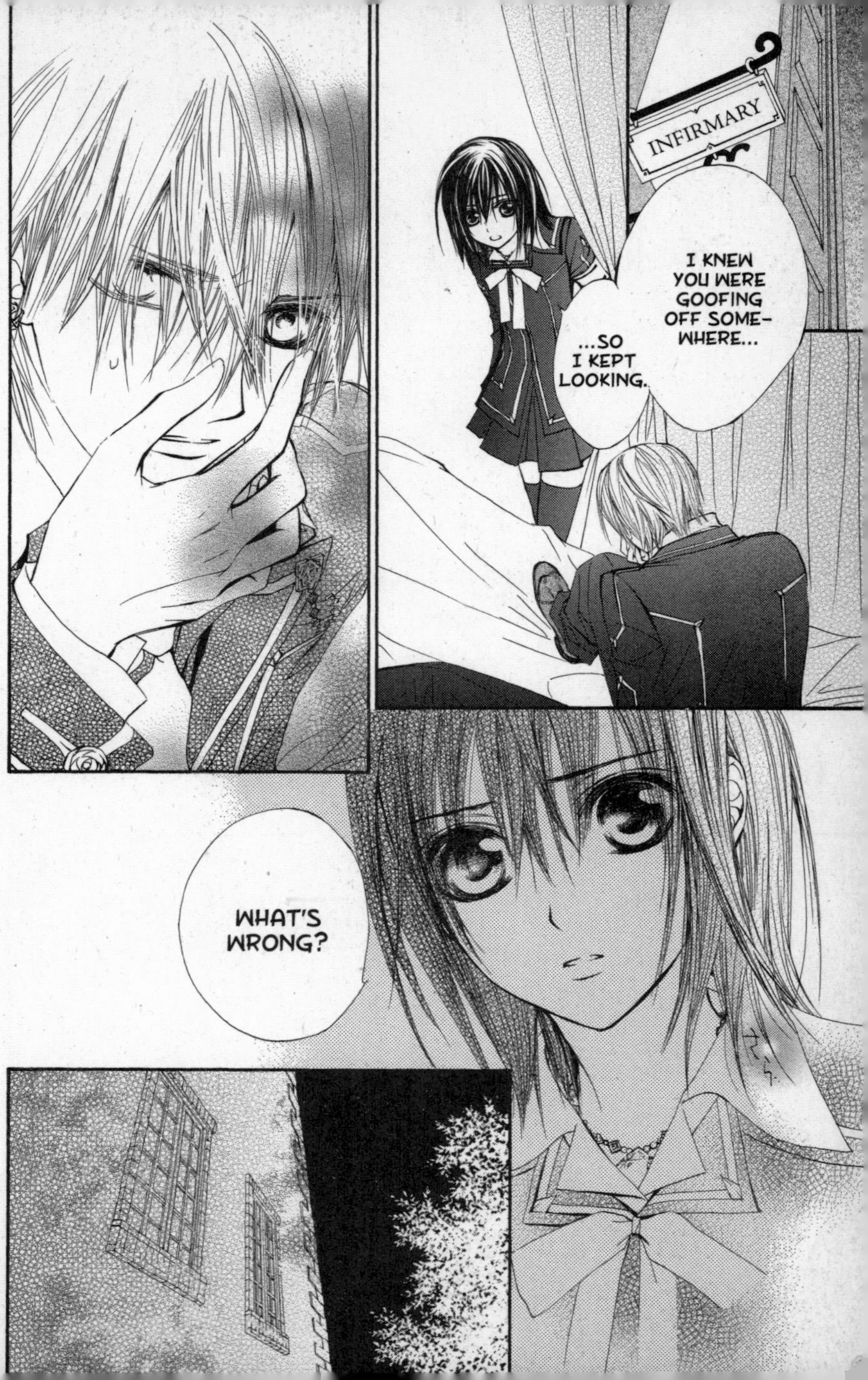
INFIRMARY
I KNEW YOU WERE GOOFING OFF SOME-WHERE...
...SO I KEPT LOOKING.
WHAT'S WRONG?

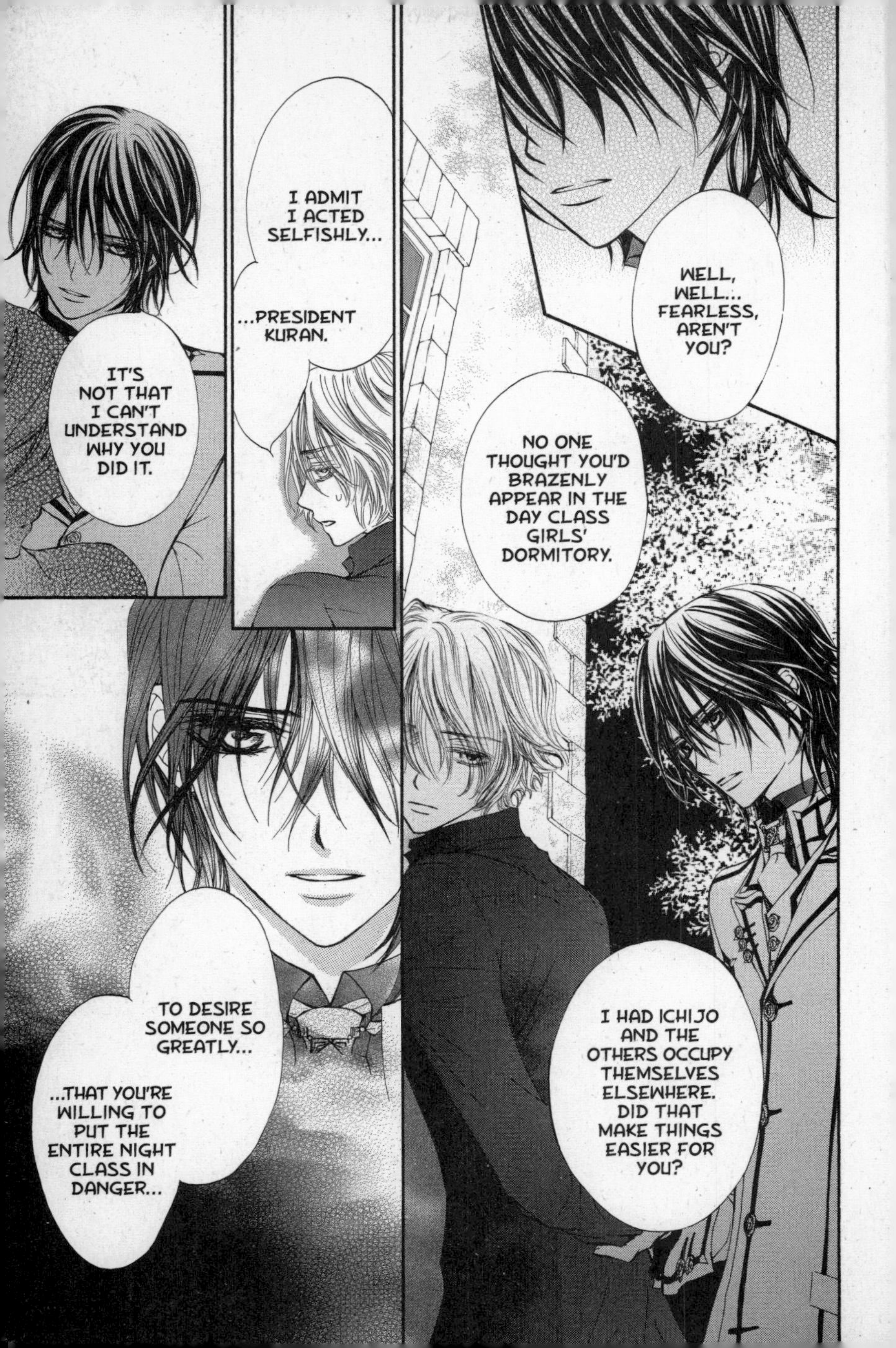
WELL, WELL... FEARLESS, AREN'T YOU?
NO ONE THOUGHT YOU'D BRAZENLY APPEAR IN THE DAY CLASS GIRLS' DORMITORY.
I HAD ICHIJO AND THE OTHERS OCCUPY THEMSELVES ELSEWHERE. DID THAT MAKE THINGS EASIER FOR YOU?
I ADMIT I ACTED SELFISHLY...
...PRESIDENT KURAN.
IT'S NOT THAT I CAN'T UNDERSTAND WHY YOU DID IT.
TO DESIRE SOMEONE SO GREATLY...
...THAT YOU'RE WILLING TO PUT THE ENTIRE NIGHT CLASS IN DANGER...

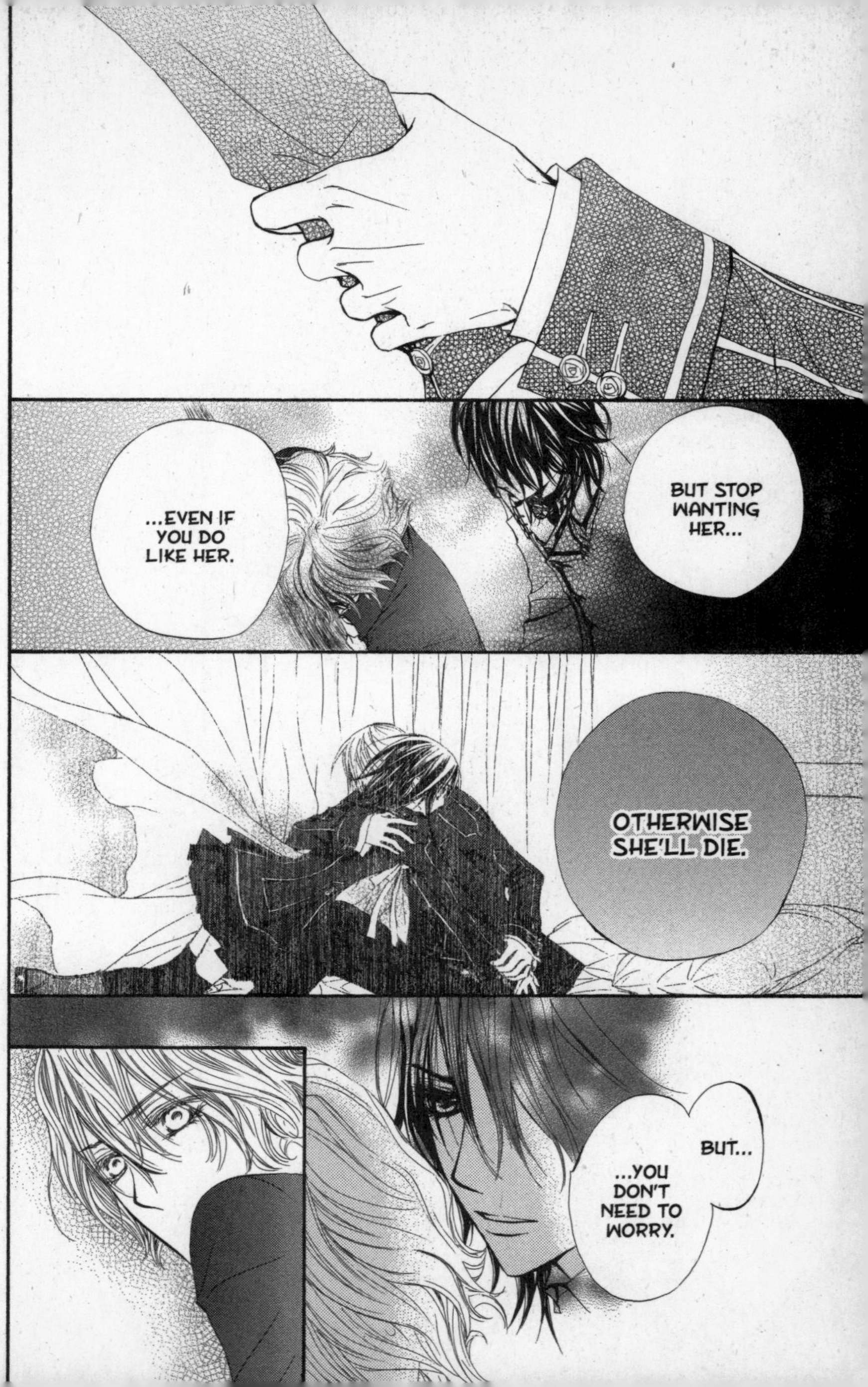
BUT STOP WANTING HER...
...EVEN IF YOU DO LIKE HER.
OTHERWISE SHE'LL DIE.
BUT...
...YOU DON'T NEED TO WORRY.

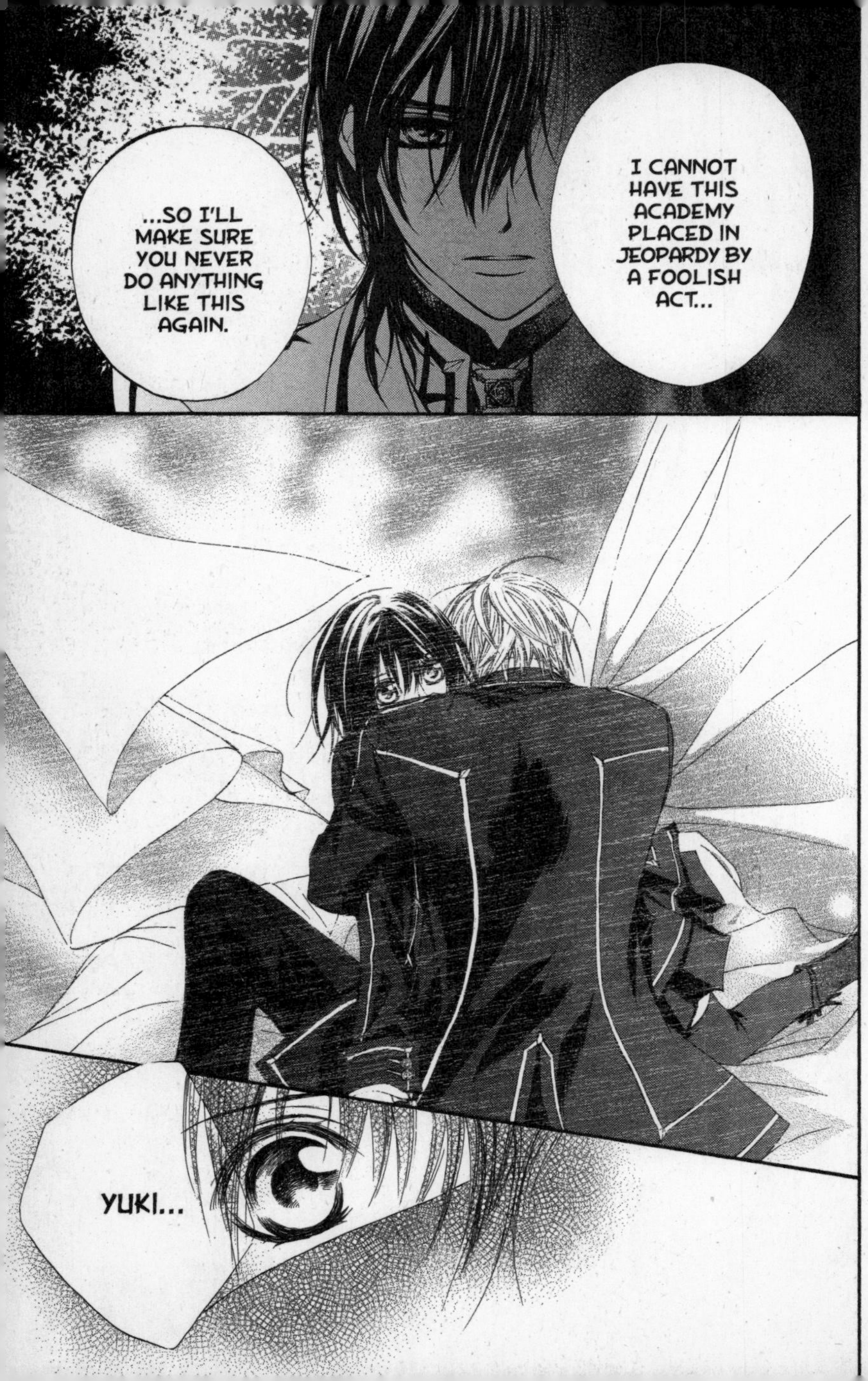
I CANNOT HAVE THIS ACADEMY PLACED IN JEOPARDY BY A FOOLISH ACT...
...SO I'LL MAKE SURE YOU NEVER DO ANYTHING LIKE THIS AGAIN.
YUKI...

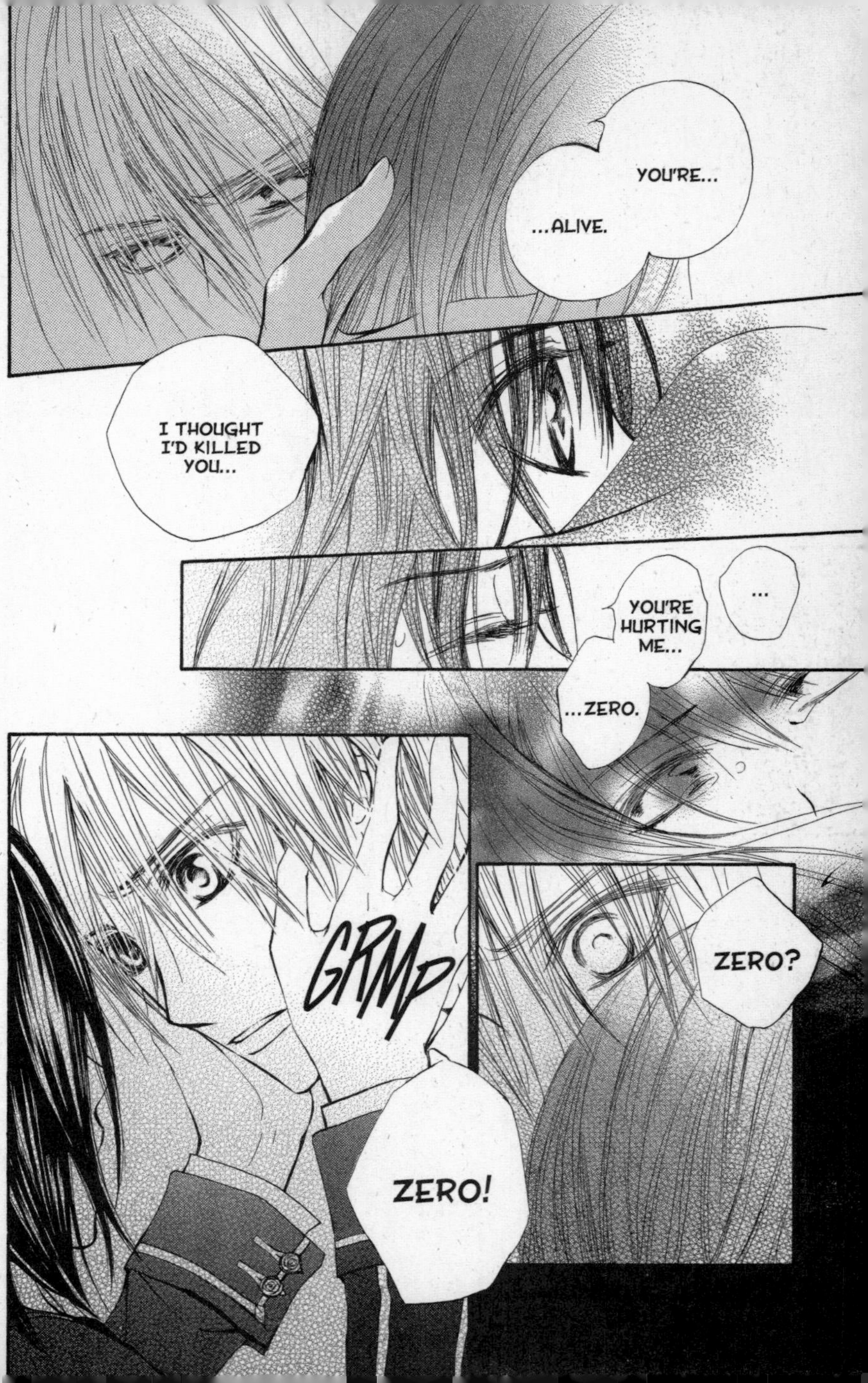
YOU'RE...
...ALIVE.
I THOUGHT I'D KILLED YOU...
...
YOU'RE HURTING ME...
...ZERO.
ZERO?
GRMP
ZERO!

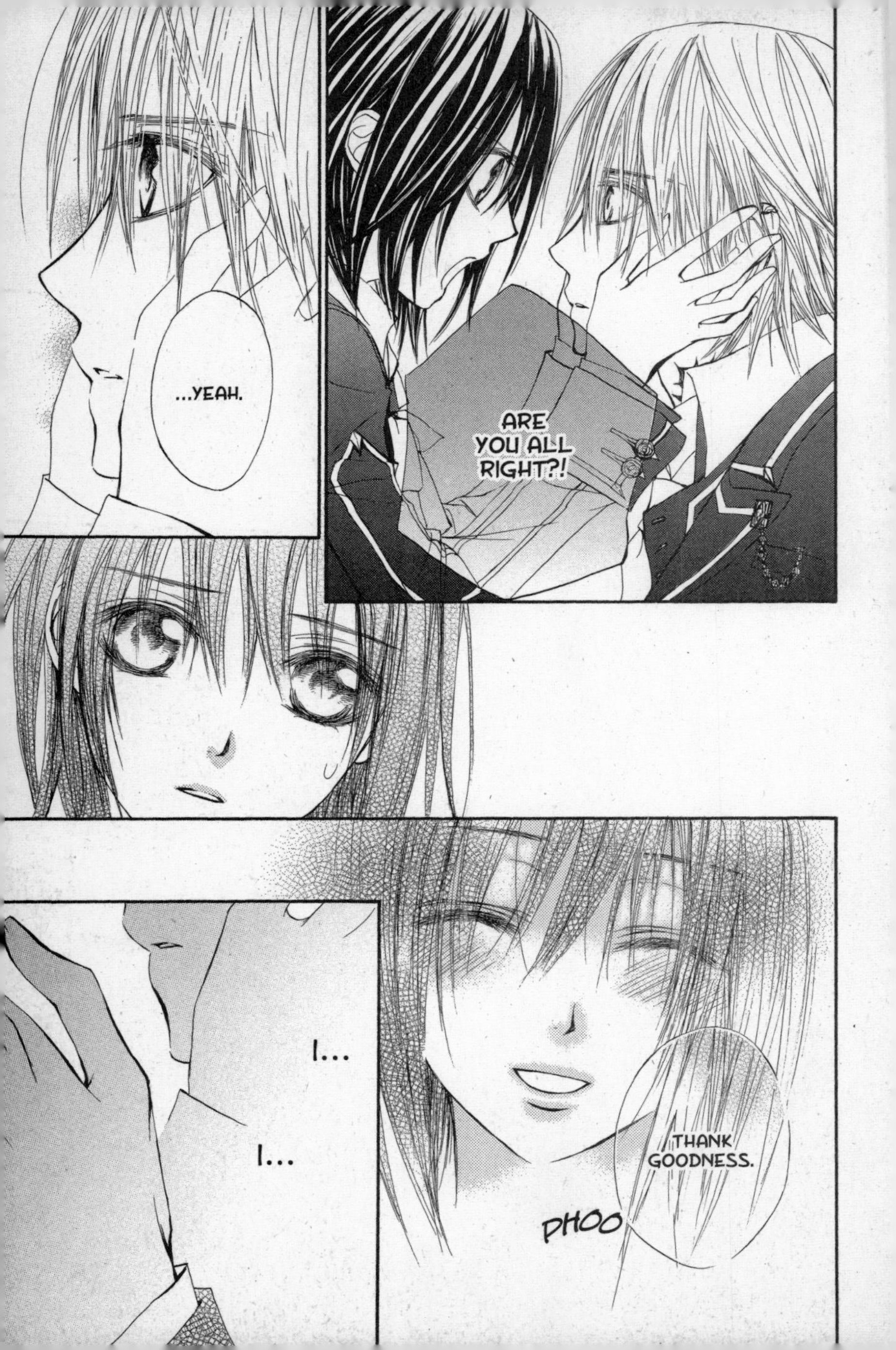
ARE YOU ALL RIGHT?!
...YEAH.
THANK GOODNESS.
PHOO
I...
I...

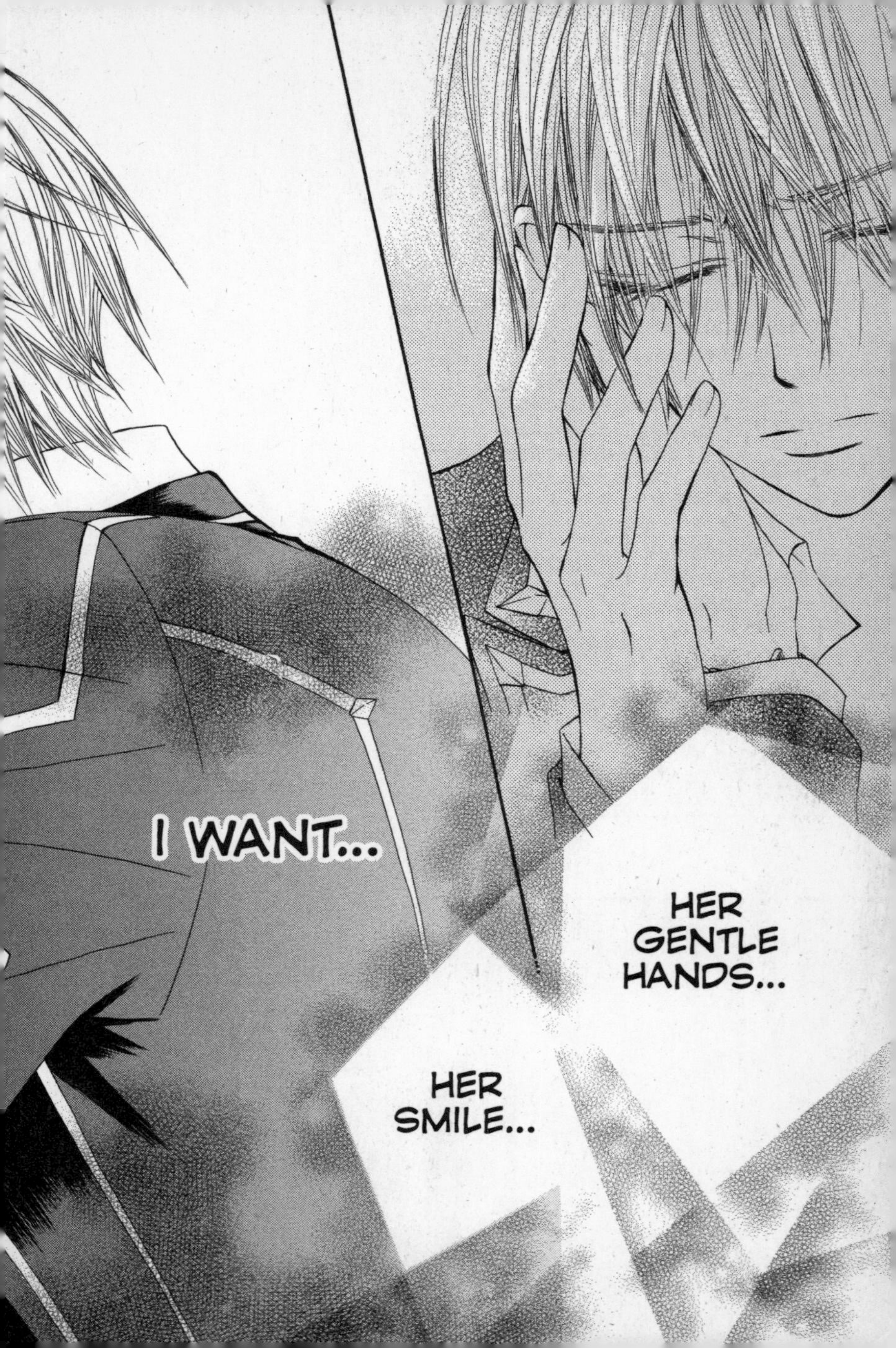
I WANT...
HER GENTLE HANDS...
HER SMILE...

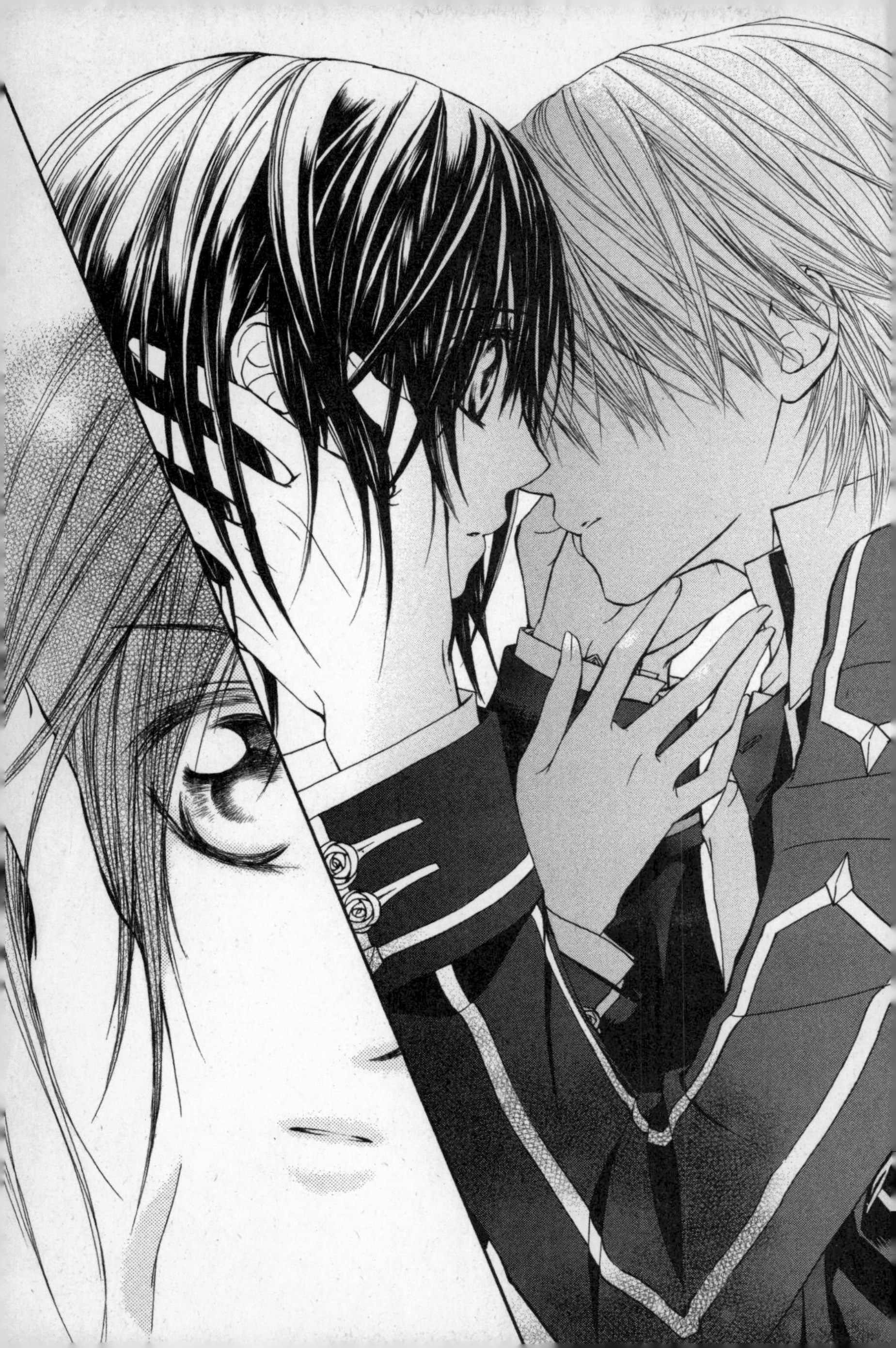

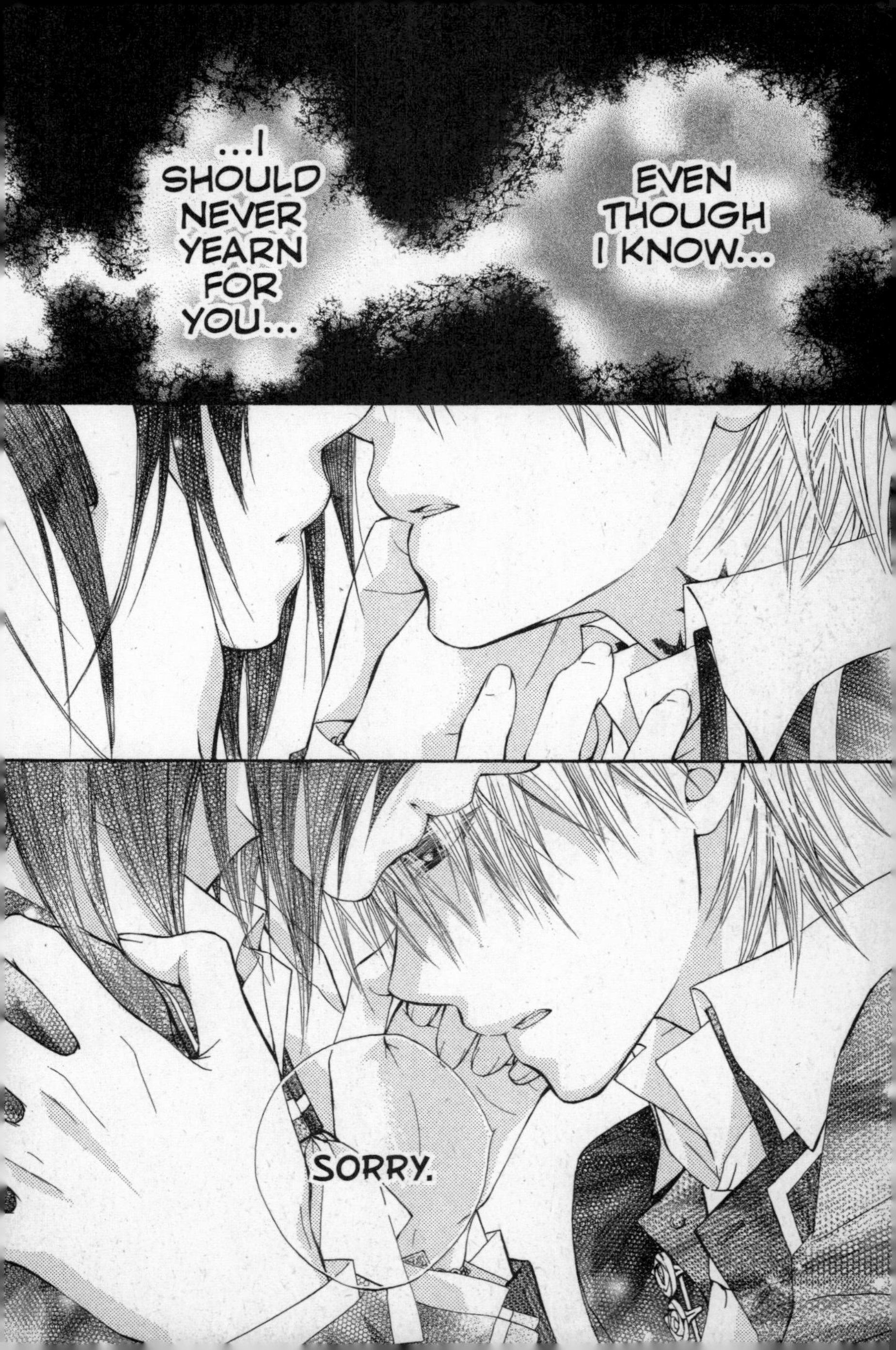
EVEN THOUGH I KNOW...
...I SHOULD NEVER YEARN FOR YOU...
SORRY.

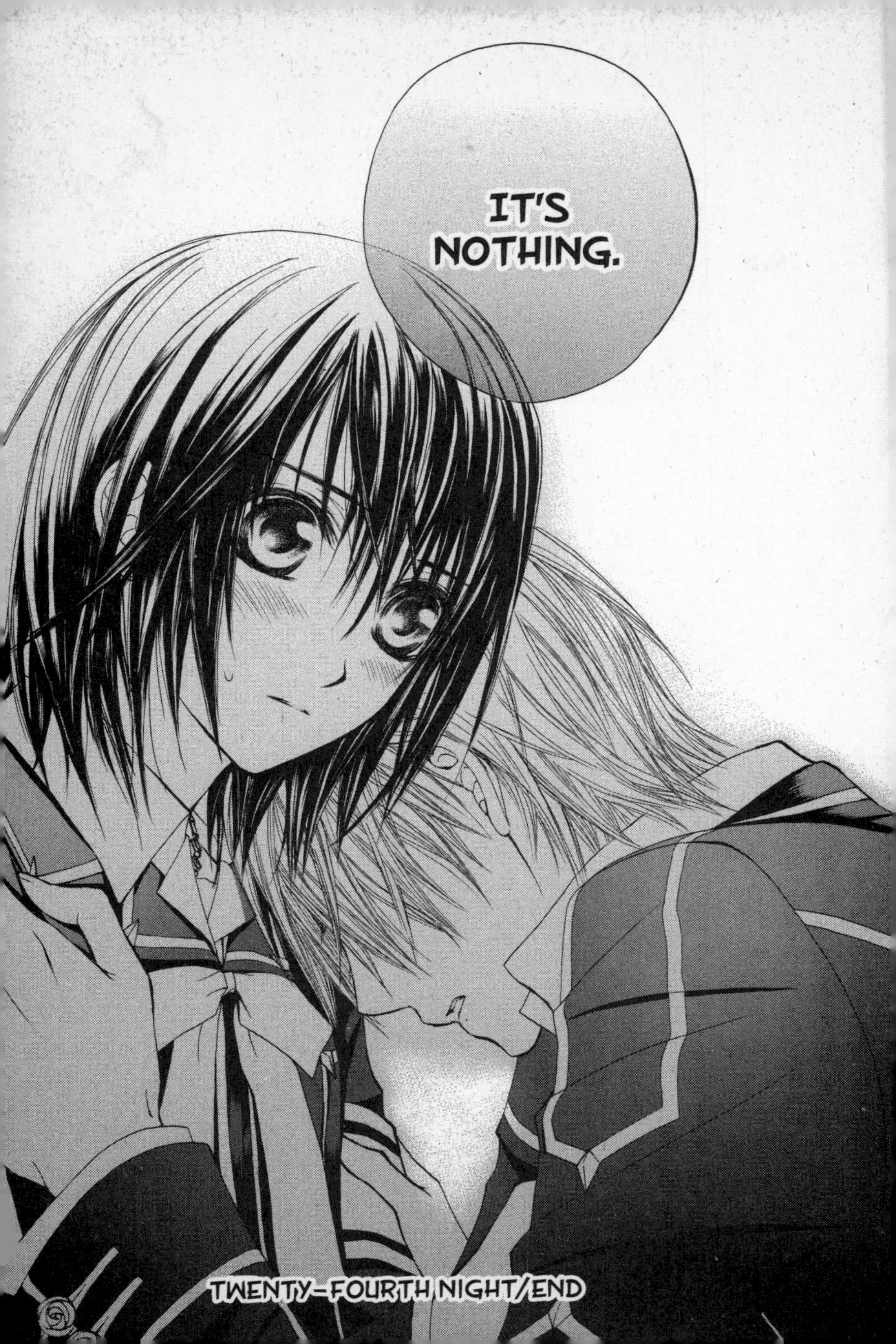
IT'S NOTHING.
TWENTY-FOURTH NIGHT/END

VAMPIRES
COVERED IN
BLOOD ARE
PROHIBITED
FROM
ENTERING
THIS PAGE!!

◇MEANWHILE, IDOL...

(TWENTY-FOURTH NIGHT)◇

IDLE

GARICH
GARICH

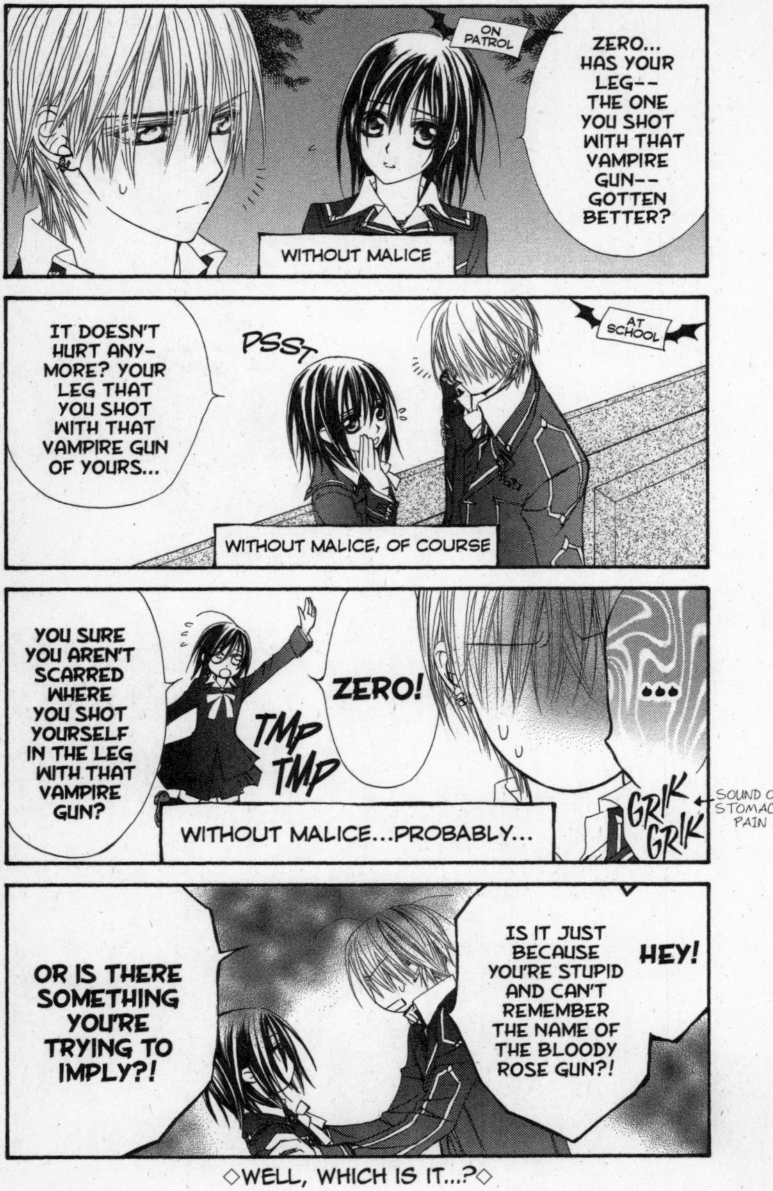
ON PATROL
ZERO... HAS YOUR LEG-- THE ONE YOU SHOT WITH THAT VAMPIRE GUN-- GOTTEN BETTER?
WITHOUT MALICE
AT SCHOOL
PSST
IT DOESN'T HURT ANY-MORE? YOUR LEG THAT YOU SHOT WITH THAT VAMPIRE GUN OF YOURS...
WITHOUT MALICE, OF COURSE
...
SOUND OF STOMACH PAIN
GRIK GRIK
ZERO!
TMP TMP
YOU SURE YOU AREN'T SCARRED WHERE YOU SHOT YOURSELF IN THE LEG WITH THAT VAMPIRE GUN?
WITHOUT MALICE...PROBABLY...
HEY!
IS IT JUST BECAUSE YOU'RE STUPID AND CAN'T REMEMBER THE NAME OF THE BLOODY ROSE GUN?!
OR IS THERE SOMETHING YOU'RE TRYING TO IMPLY?!

◇WELL, WHICH IS IT...?◇

◇STATIONARY CAMERA (KANAME'S ROOM)◇

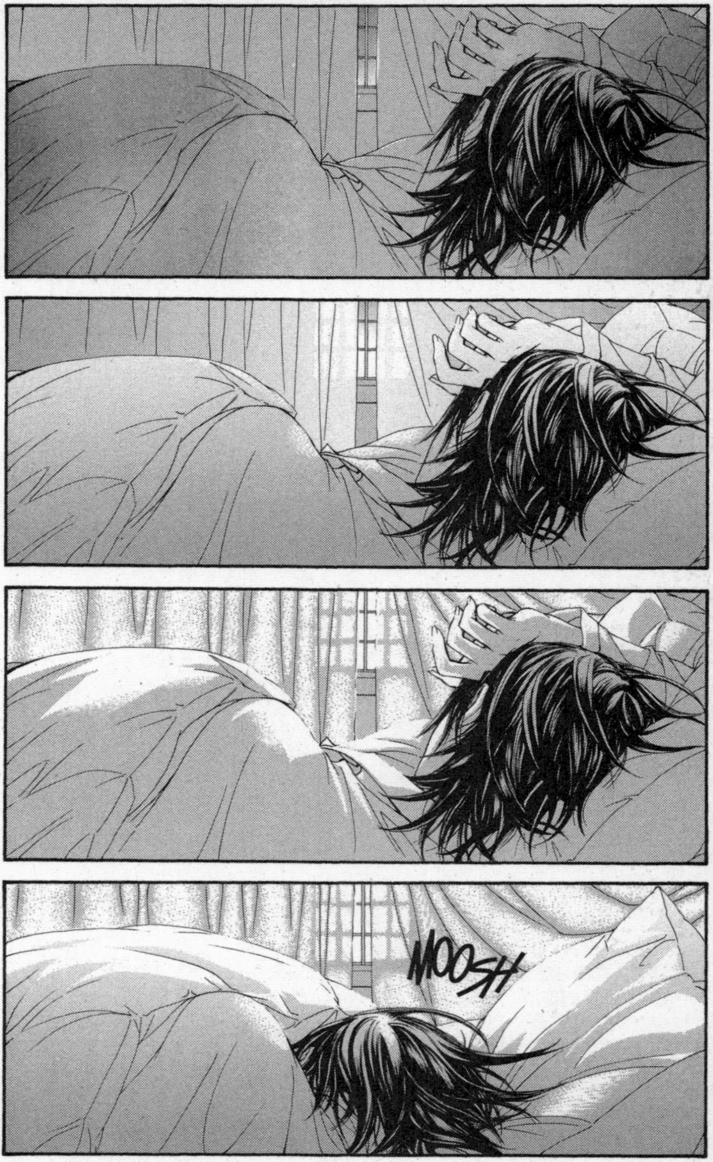
MOOSH

◇ SENATE HENCHMEN (TWENTY-SECOND NIGHT) ◇

...NO, NEVER MIND.

I WAS ABOUT TO SAY THE SAME THING.

PSST

MEGANES?

At last...

Thank you to those who really give me the willpower to work:
all my readers. To my editor, whom I truly, truly end up worrying and
inconveniencing, and the LaLa department and everyone involved in this
work O. Mio-sama and K. Midori-sama, who are steadily improving and help me
with my manuscripts. To family and friends who help me at various times.
Without everyone, this volume wouldn't have existed.
Thank you so much!!

Matsuri Hino

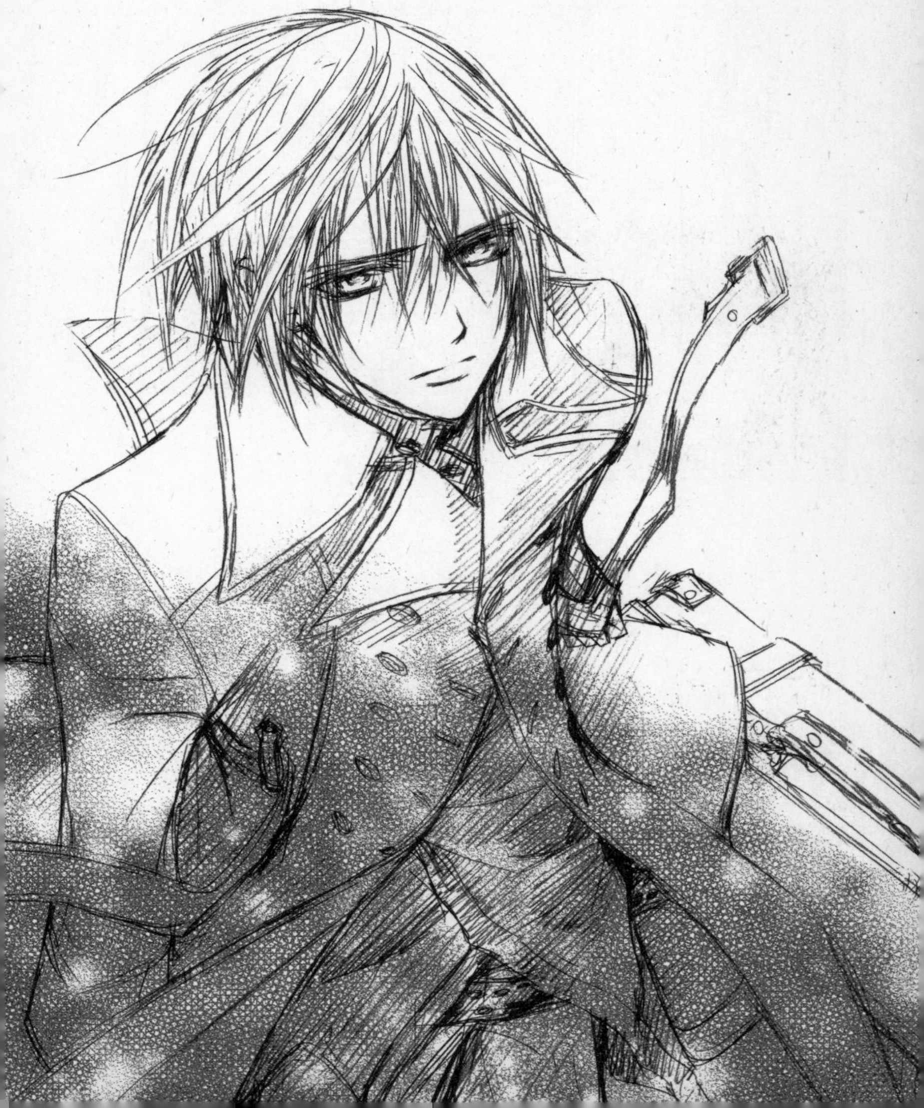

EDITOR'S NOTES

Characters

Matsuri Hino puts careful thought into the names of her characters in *Vampire Knight*. Below is the collection of characters through volume 5. Each character's name is presented family name first, per the kanji reading.

黒主優姫

Cross Yuki

Yuki's last name, *Kurosu*, is the Japanese pronunciation of the English word "cross." However, the kanji has a different meaning—*kuro* means "black" and *su* means "master." Her first name is a combination of *yuu*, meaning "tender" or "kind," and *ki*, meaning "princess."

錐生零

Kiryu Zero

Zero's first name is the kanji for *rei*, meaning "zero." In his last name, *Kiryu*, the *ki* means "auger" or "drill," and the *ryu* means "life."

玖蘭枢

Kuran Kaname

Kaname means "hinge" or "door." The kanji for his last name is a combination of the old-fashioned way of writing *ku*, meaning "nine," and *ran*, meaning "orchid": "nine orchids."

藍堂英

Aido Hanabusa

Hanabusa means "petals of a flower." *Aido* means "indigo temple." In Japanese, the pronunciation of *Aido* is very close to the pronunciation of the English word *idol*.

架院暁

Kain Akatsuki

Akatsuki means "dawn," or "day-break." In *Kain*, *ka* is a base or support, while *in* denotes a building that has high fences around it, such as a temple or school.

早園瑠佳

Souen Ruka

In *Ruka*, the *ru* means "lapis lazuli" while the *ka* means "good-looking," or "beautiful." The *sou* in Ruka's surname, *Souen*, means "early," but this kanji also has an obscure meaning of "strong fragrance." The *en* means "garden."

一条拓麻

Ichijo Takuma

Ichijo can mean a "ray" or "streak." The kanji for *Takuma* is a combination of *taku*, meaning "to cultivate" and *ma*, which is the kanji for *asa*, meaning "hemp" or "flax," a plant with blue flowers.

支葵千里

Shiki Senri

Shiki's last name is a combination of *shi*, meaning "to support" and *ki*, meaning "mallow"—a flowering plant with pink or white blossoms. The *ri* in *Senri* is a traditional Japanese unit of measure for distance, and one *ri* is about 2.44 miles. *Senri* means "1,000 *ri*."

夜刈十牙

Yagari Toga

Yagari is a combination of *ya*, meaning "night," and *gari*, meaning "to harvest." *Toga* means "ten fangs."

一条麻遠，一翁

Ichijo Asato, aka "Ichio"

Ichijo can mean a "ray" or "streak." Asato's first name is comprised of *asa*, meaning "hemp" or "flax," and *tou*, meaning "far off." His nickname is *ichi*, or "one," combined with *ou*, which can be used as an honorific when referring to an older man.

若葉沙頼

Wakaba Sayori

Yori's full name is Sayori Wakaba. *Wakaba* means "young leaves." Her given name, *Sayori*, is a combination of sa, meaning "sand," and *yori*, meaning "trust."

星煉
Seiren

Sei means "star" and *ren* means "to smelt" or "refine." *Ren* is also the same kanji used in *rengoku*, or "purgatory."

遠矢莉磨
Toya Rima

Toya means a "far-reaching arrow." Rima's given name is a combination of *ri*, or "jasmine," and *ma*, which signifies enhancement by wearing away, such as by polishing or scouring.

紅まり亜
Kurenai Maria

Kurenai means "crimson." The kanji for the last *a* in Maria's given name is the same that is used in "Asia."

錐生壱縷
Kiryu Ichiru

Ichi is the old-fashioned way of writing "one," and *ru* means "thread." He shares the same surname as his twin, Zero.

緋桜閑，狂咲姫
Hio Shizuka, Kuruizaki-hime

Shizuka means "calm and quiet." In Shizuka's family name, *hi* is "scarlet," and *ou* is "cherry blossoms." Shizuka Hio is also referred to as the "Kuruizaki-hime." *Kuruizaki* means "flowers blooming out of season," and *hime* means "princess."

Terms

megane: A person who wears glasses.

-sama: The suffix *sama* is used in formal address for someone who ranks higher in the social hierarchy. The vampires call their leader "Kaname-sama" only when they are among their own kind.

Matsuri Hino burst onto the manga scene with her series *Kono Yume ga Sametara* (When This Dream Is Over), which was published in *LaLa DX* magazine. Hino was a manga artist a mere nine months after she decided to become one.

With the success of her popular series *Captive Hearts* and *MeruPuri*, Hino has established herself as a major player in the world of shojo manga. *Vampire Knight* is currently serialized in *LaLa* and *Shojo Beat* magazines.

Hino enjoys creative activities and has commented that she would have been either an architect or an apprentice to traditional Japanese craft masters if she had not become a manga artist.

VAMPIRE KNIGHT

Vol. 5

The Shojo Beat Manga Edition

This manga contains material that was originally published in English in *Shojo Beat* magazine, February–June 2008 issues. Artwork in the magazine may have been slightly altered from that presented here.

STORY AND ART BY
MATSURI HINO

Translation & English Adaptation/Tomo Kimura
Touch-up Art & Lettering/George Caltsoudas
Graphic Design/Nozomi Akashi
Editor/Nancy Thistlethwaite

Editor in Chief, Books/Alvin Lu
Editor in Chief, Magazines/Marc Weidenbaum
VP, Publishing Licensing/Rika Inouye
VP, Sales & Product Marketing/Gonzalo Ferreyra
VP, Creative/Linda Espinosa
Publisher/Hyoe Narita

Printed in the U.S.A.

Published by VIZ Media, LLC
P.O. Box 77010
San Francisco, CA 94107

Shojo Beat Manga Edition
10 9 8 7 6 5 4 3 2
First printing, September 2008
Second printing, December 2008

PARENTAL ADVISORY
VAMPIRE KNIGHT is rated T+ for Older Teen and is recommended for ages 16 and up. This volume contains sexual themes and violence.
ratings.viz.com

store.viz.com

Shojo Beat™

MANGA from the HEART

The Shojo Manga Authority

The most **ADDICTIVE** shojo manga stories from Japan **PLUS** unique editorial coverage on the arts, music, culture, fashion, and much more!

12 GIANT issues for ONLY $34.99*

That's 51% OFF the cover price!

Subscribe **NOW** and become a member of the Sub Club!

- **SAVE** 51% OFF the cover price
- **ALWAYS** get every issue
- **ACCESS** exclusive areas of www.shojobeat.com
- **FREE** members-only gifts several times a year

Strictly VIP!

3 EASY WAYS TO SUBSCRIBE!

1) Send in the subscription order form from this book **OR**
2) Log on to: www.shojobeat.com **OR**
3) Call 1-800-541-7876